Pelican Books

The Other Half

Women in Australian Society

The Other Half

Women in Australian Society

Edited by Jan Mercer

Penguin Books

Penguin Books Ltd,
Harmondsworth, Middlesex, England
Penguin Books Australia Ltd,
Ringwood, Victoria, Australia
Penguin Books Canada Ltd,
41 Steelcase Road West, Markham, Ontario, Canada
Penguin Books (N.Z.) Ltd,
182-190 Wairau Road, Auckland 10, New Zealand

First published 1975
Reprinted 1977

Made and printed in Australia at
The Dominion Press, Blackburn, Victoria
Set in Monotype Plantin, by Dudley E. King, Melbourne

CIP

National Library of Australia
Cataloguing in Publication data

Mercer, Jan, ed.
The other half: women in Australian society/
edited by Jan Mercer.–Ringwood, Vic.:
Penguin Books Australia, 1975. – (A Pelican
original).
Index.
Bibliography.

1. Woman – Rights of women – Addresses.
essays, lectures. I. Title.

301.4120994

Contents

Part 3 The Acquisition of Sex Roles

Part 4 Women Labelled as 'Deviants'

Part 5 The Politics of Change

Foreword

Every society is in part a product of social theory and every theory is in part a social product of the society. It is therefore impossible to make a critique of one without the other, although one may have a false consciousness and may think this possible. This particular kind of false consciousness, common to many theorists, is often called 'Objectivism'.

Alvin W. Gouldner, *For Sociology**

This book is about Australia, a society bedevilled by oppression which is both blatant and subtle yet never acknowledged. It is about a society of people where men oppress women, where white oppress black. Little mention will be made of the male oppressors, for their atrocities have been recounted elsewhere, often as great deeds. Their versions of history are well known; to many they are Australia. Rather, this book is concerned with the women of Australia who, though exceeding men in numbers, are powerless.[1] We live in a society designed by men, for men and controlled by men who offer us a social organization and a set of values alien to us.

These oppressive values are reflected in and reinforced by the writings of social scientists who have written history as if women did not exist and who have theorized about the societies of man-kind as opposed to people-kind. They proceed from heavily value-laden premises which are far from the value-neutral position many of them blindly aspire to. General theoretical and descriptive works on Australia such as that edited by Davies and Encel,[2] the 'texts' of Australian sociology, are glaring examples of such biased and prejudiced standpoints. If they deign to mention us at all, we are treated as a residual category. 'Woman'

* Allen Lane, 1973, p. 84.

appears in the subject index but not so 'man'. We are ignored because we are of little importance in the object of their supposedly thorough sociological enquiries, the public sector. They describe the social order rather than question it and so tacitly defend existing social relations by a complete lack of discussion of alternatives or of existing dissent within Australian society. They treat racism, sexism (if at all), communism, and anything else that questions the social order, as irritating though not serious ailments to be treated and suffered by a basically healthy social system, not as indicators of the need for radical and fundamental social change. They defend as rational and logical that which the establishment defines as such, and so accept as natural 'a man's world' where a woman's place is in the home, discussing her as sociologically significant only in chapters on 'the family'.

What of those few 'radical' critiques of Australian society? They may be questioning of the social order but the changes they contemplate are changes in the power balance among men. For example, the 'angry young men' of Australian academia explicitly and chauvinistically exclude women from consideration. McQueen, in his preface to the second edition of *A New Britannia*,[3] acknowledges that women were excluded from his study. He paternalistically tries to justify their exclusion by saying that he was 'suitably admonished' on reading Ann Curthoys's article 'Historiography and Women's Liberation' in *Arena 22*, and is now certain of the importance of women's liberation whereas previously for him 'propaganda' had never been convincing. A 'radical' who scorns all material written by generations of women on their oppression as propaganda? Who had to be told of the oppression of women by a 'legitimate' fellow academic before he would believe it? McQueen then washes his hands of guilt by saying that he must leave the task of writing the history of the oppression of women to women; feeling cleansed of guilt by his half-page apologia, he does not bother to alter the text to include any further mention of more than half Australia's population. In the Introduction to *Australian Capitalism*,[4] which is supposed to be not only a hard-hitting critique of Australian society but something of a blueprint for change, Playford and Kirsner say that they have excluded any discussion of the oppression of women 'for practical reasons'. They obviously couldn't be bothered to go to the trouble of investigating something they knew nothing about, and which they saw as completely irrelevant to their own power struggle. By mentioning the oppression of women as a reality but still ignoring it they showed themselves even more chauvinistic than if they had been unaware of its existence.

Books written specifically about women have fallen into the same trap as the 'texts' mentioned earlier: descriptive of the social order rather than questioning of it. They acknowledge the need for some reform but never the need for fundamental change, for revolution. Stevenson and MacKenzie are particularly conservative.[5] They have done the important job of drawing attention to the fact that women exist but they imply that reform is underway and that equality is just around the corner, without really asking what 'equality' is. They assume that women want to be equal to compete within the present male-defined system. Barbara Thiering, purporting to attack the establishment of church and society for their oppression, is also very conservative, promoting the family and woman's conventional role in it as sacred, and again assuming that the system is basically good, that we should keep the present institutional structure and simply make a few internal changes. She is happy when a woman is accepted as 'one of the boys' and is very concerned that her argument is presented tastefully; that in contrast to extreme radicals like Robin Morgan, her case is presented 'somewhat more analytically and without, it is hoped, being shrill as a banshee'.[6]

The collection of readings edited by Julie Rigg is different.[7] It does not simply describe and give reams of statistical information, and it does not support the existing social system. It attempts to give some idea of how women feel in Australian society, to show that they are not happy and that things need to change. But it does not ask *why* women are not happy. The blurb on the dust jacket states that 'the tone is ironic rather than angry'. Surely the time has come to be angry and if jolting the establishment's refined sensibilities requires shrillness then that anger must be shrill.

This book is called *The Other Half: Women in Australian Society* in order to show that women are not a residual category and that so far social science has not provided 'an overall picture of Australian Society and its mores in scope and depth', as Davies and Encel claim to have done. Neither have they provided 'a challenge to all of us concerned with our own society in the most critical and creative sense'. They left unquestioned the basic assumptions through which Australia justifies a system of gross inequalities and failed to explain why we have a society based on social roles rather than people.

Our aim is to examine the subjugation of women in Australia today, and to explore some of the processes which make this possible by examining the relationship between the present position of women and the role structures and institutions which support their oppression. Inevitably this raises the question of whether equality is possible within the present economic system as many of the early feminists believed, or whether we need a different basis on which to build a society where equality in social relationships really exists and is not simply an empty political slogan.

Finally, unlike the establishment version of *Australian Society*, this book is not a 'symposium by distinguished contributors'. Few if any would wish such doubtful honour the way the present system of rewards operates. In the words of Alexandra Kollantai, 'for me "what I am" was always of less importance that "what I can", that is to say what I was in a position to accomplish'.[8]

The book is divided into five parts. Part I contains a general introduction to Australia as a sexist society and a detailed look at the relationship between biology and human behaviour. Chapter I outlines the way sexism permeates Australian society, a society in which men and women are conceptualized as different, as having different social tasks to perform and differential rights to the rewards of their labour. This notion that men and women are different results in a constant exploitation of women for the benefit of men. This vital but usually neglected perspective on Australian social behaviour has shaped this book. Are the differences in the behaviour of men and women due to biology or are they due to learning? Chapter 2 discusses the relationship between sex and gender. 'Sex' refers to the biological differences which determine whether one is male or female while 'gender' refers to the categorization of things as masculine or feminine on the basis of psychological and cultural criteria. This system of categorization results in people behaving in ways which are thought of as essentially either feminine or masculine. Sex is a result of biology, gender a result of social learning, and the question posed in this chapter is 'how does sex affect gender?'. What Part 1 establishes is that social learning is far more crucial for human behaviour than differences in biology, and it clears the way for discussion of a discrimination based on false assumptions. If it is learning which establishes and perpetuates sexual discrimination, who dictates and controls such a discriminatory learning process? The past is hazy and the book concentrates almost entirely on the present, the reasons for which are clearly explained in Chapter 3 which examines the problems involved in writing about women in Australian history and concludes that we cannot yet write women's history.[9]

Part 2 looks at the actual status of women in Australia today with regard to major institutions and to certain groups, such as Aborigines and migrants. It is concerned with establishing that Australia is a sexist society by examining the position of women in some of the main areas of Australian social life. It is a patchy section because it depends on facts – and these are scarce.[10] Chapter 5 on women and the law is the most complete because ours is a written law; the chapter on migrants, Chapter 9, is the smallest because of a dearth of information. The chapter on Aborigines, Chapter 8, is a case study because overall information is lacking, but it starkly demonstrates the way in which the combination of racism and sexism deny to Aboriginal women competence in any sphere of life, in white society and in their own. An examination of social welfare, Chapter 7, demonstrates one result of the low status of women in the institutions of Australian society, for it reveals just how many women are in such an inferior economic position that they are forced to rely on a series of paternalistic handouts from the system.

Part 3 is largely concerned with processes, with the ways in which institutions transmit their ideologies, how what is defined as 'natural' for a female is internalized. Ideologies and values are passed on from one individual to another in a variety of ways. Much of what we assume to be 'objective' or 'fact' is merely an accepted value position passed on to us by others. Socialization is the process by which we come to accept values and thus the way we learn what is acceptable behaviour for our sex. The chapters in this section deal with this socialization process within four institutions – the family, education, communications media and religion. Chapter 10 looks at the evidence available to support the mistaken belief that because women bear children they must necessarily rear them, a belief which is often given pseudo-scientific support to perpetuate the idea that biology is destiny and that the woman's rightful place is in the home. The other chapter on the family, Chapter 11, deals with the problems raised by present sociological research on the family and highlights the way in which social science research can serve to maintain the *status quo*. Chapters on school and church, Chapters 12 and 14, examine how these two organizations offer belief systems which maintain sexism, and lead on to the conclusion that in order to prevent the continuing inculcation of sexist attitudes, education and religion as we know them today must disappear. Other factors in society reinforce the role of women as incompetent, decorative, dependent and emotional. From an early age, children are bombarded by a selection of books which emphasize these stereotypical images of women. Chapter 13 looks at both picture books and school readers, examining the way in which they establish and perpetuate that behaviour which is seen as acceptable for girls compared to boys. The more general chapter on the mass media, Chapter 15, indicates the subtle and insidious way in which women are continually bombarded by television, radio and newspaper advertising with the image of what is an acceptable woman.

However, not all women accept the ridiculous prescriptions for behaviour handed out to them by society. A few have the courage to escape, to go outside the behaviour that men have dictated for them. While their numbers remain small they pose no threat to society and are seen as deviant. Part 4 therefore starts with a discussion of deviance, assuming that deviance is relative to prevailing norms rather than something in the particular individual defined as such. Then follow accounts of the difficulties experienced by certain women who do not accept the prevailing definitions of behaviour set down for them by men – the housewife who became disillusioned with motherhood, the woman who found and accepted that she related to other women rather than to men, the prostitute, and the Aboriginal woman who is abused sexually and forced into what is labelled by society as a deviant role.

The final section looks at areas where change is occurring within Australian society – situations where there are sufficient numbers of women working towards change for the label of deviance to be ignored or inapplicable. The growth of political awareness and political action is discussed generally, and two specific organizations concerned with reform are examined. Chapter 24 is a critical appraisal of the counter culture which has been suggested by some as a possible Utopian solution. In Chapter 26 we examine the problems surrounding social change – reform or revolution?

This is therefore an attempt to begin to look at some of the bases of sexism in Australian society. There are many omissions and no section aims to be comprehensive. If some areas of Australian society are ignored and much of the book in general appears rather light on information, it is sometimes because there is little or no information available, but more often because the available information is so oriented towards reinforcing existing sexist attitudes, so sexist in its choice and description of data that it is of little use in compiling a book about women in Australia.

Women have been so neglected that this book can only aspire to be a beginning. The process of editing this book has at times been very rewarding, but it has also been a revealingly frustrating experience, for time and time again the desire to provide a comprehensive coverage has been thwarted by the combination of a paucity of data and a corresponding scarcity of people capable of or interested in writing about women. But this has simply demonstrated over and over the shocking neglect that women have received at the hands of social commentators and academics. The book therefore ends with 'a beginning' not a conclusion.

Notes

1. This lack of power means that women should be regarded as a minority group despite their greater numbers than men. Political minorities are not necessarily numerical minorities.
2. A. F. Davies and S. Encel, (eds), *Australian Society*, Cheshire, Melbourne, 2nd edition, 1970.
3. H. McQueen, *A New Britannia*, Penguin Books, 1970.
4. J. Playford and D. Kirsner, (eds), *Australian Capitalism*, Penguin Books, 1972.
5. R. Stevenson, *Women in Australian Society*, Heinemann, Melbourne, 1970; N. MacKenzie, *Women in Australia*, Cheshire, Melbourne, 1962. See note 10 below on the new edition.
6. B. Thiering, *Created Second?*, Family Life Movement of Australia, Adelaide, 1973, pp. 7–8.
7. J. Rigg, (ed.), *In Her Own Right*, Nelson, Melbourne, 1969.
8. A. Kollantai, *Autobiography of a Sexually Emancipated Woman*, Orbach and Chambers, London, 1972, p. 8.
9. See also Anne Summers, *Damned Whores and God's Police*, Penguin Books, in press.
10. This paucity of facts has to some extent now been rectified by the publication of the material collected by Margaret Tebbutt for her updating with Sol Encel of Norman MacKenzie's *Women in Australia*, S. Encel, N. MacKenzie and M. Tebbutt, *Women and Society, an Australian Study*, Cheshire, 1974. This book has been published since the manuscript for *The Other Half* went to press and so we have not been able to incorporate Margaret Tebbutt's data. It should be noted however that the data collected to update MacKenzie was collected under a substantial financial grant made to a male professor whereas no grants were available to facilitate the compilation of this reader. The data in Encel, MacKenzie and Tebbutt's volume is valuable but the highly academic paternalism of Encel's commentary which constantly lays the onus on women to bring about change means that the evaluation of MacKenzie's original book made above is fully applicable to this new edition.

PART ONE

Human Behaviour and Society

Human Behaviour and Society

There is only one thing more fierce than the tiger, and that is the tigress. Women in rebellion have something of this fierceness . . . In the ordinary conception of women, this is overlooked. They are usually regarded as domesticated animals who require protection, and who never willingly come out of the shelter of the home . . .

Lily Gair Wilkinson, 'Woman's Freedom' in *Women in Rebellion–1900: Two Views on Class, Socialism and Liberation**

Women and men are different. But how different are they, and are these differences greater than the similarities between the sexes? If differences in physiology exist are there any necessary concomitant differences in behaviour? Even if sex-linked differences due to biology can be found is this sufficient justification for the males of a society to oppress the females?

In Western culture it has been assumed that males and females act and behave in very different and clearly-defined ways. Males in this context are seen as sexually aggressive, dominant, independent and having an uncontrollable sex desire which is easily aroused by a variety of stimuli and may need to be satisfied by a number of females. Females on the other hand are seen as passive, submissive, and dependent, with little sex drive. Sexual arousal too is seen as different. A woman supposedly has two types of orgasm, a clitoral one and a vaginal one, and feelings associated with both of these are said to be diffuse and romantic.[1] More importantly, a woman is taught that her whole sexuality is bound up with the notion of maternal instinct. Motherhood is seen as fulfilment.[2] 'Woman's sexuality is therefore defined by men to benefit men, has been downgraded and perverted, repressed and channelled, denied and abused until women

* Square One Publications, 1973, p. 19.

themselves (are) thoroughly convinced of their sexual inferiority to men.'[3]

Are differences in the behaviour of people which are evident today due to biology or to learning, that is to socialization, a process which starts at birth? It is doubtful whether science is at a stage where it can answer such questions but to date there has been little if any unbiased research on the subject. Most research has concentrated on trying to show that differences in social behaviour are due to biological factors, for scientists are not immune to the prevailing values around them. For example, many psychologists interpret boys' higher scores on intelligence tests as being due to biological differences rather than to social conditioning.

Chapter 1 shows that Australia is a sexist society; that in Australia there has always been differential treatment of women and men in the major institutions of society and in the home, to the constant disadvantage of women. Chapter 2 demonstrates that such differential treatment cannot be justified in terms of biology, and also emphasizes the concern of a growing number of scientists that any conclusions to questions such as the nature of the relationship between biology and human behaviour are extremely premature. The belief that differences in the behaviour of men and women can be explained in terms of physiology is one of the most pervasive ideologies in the rationalization of the oppression of women, in fact so pervasive that many women also believe it to be true. Such differences, even if shown to exist, should not be used as rationalizations for the present distribution of power and the subjugation of women.

Chapters 1 and 2 show clearly that we cannot take most of the available literature on human behaviour at its face value. Social reality is a male-defined social reality and the examinations of biologists and ethologists have been manipulated to support these biased definitions. Indeed, this whole book is oriented towards trying to reverse some of the myths which sociology in particular has fostered. Just as an extensive discussion of the relationship of biology to society is impossible in terms of current literature, so too is an extensive history. Chapter 3 raises the question of whether it is possible to write a history of women at all, and on considering the problems involved in such a task concludes that it could not be done using the theory and methodology of current historiography. History has been white, male history, written from the point of view of those in power, constantly concerned with world affairs – with wars, the economy, the polity, diplomacy – with the public sector, the world of men. Women in the home have not been of interest to the recorders and interpreters of the past.

So Part 1 concerns itself with the destruction of myths – myths of equality, myths of biological difference and myths of an unbiased, objectively recorded past. It clears the ground for a beginning to the examination of women in Australian society.

Notes

1. See for example Chapter 19, 'Life as a Lesbian', and A. Oakley, *Sex, Gender and Society*, Sun Books, Melbourne, 1972.
2. See Chapter 10, 'The Motherhood Myth'.
3. See S. Lydon, 'The Politics of Orgasm' in R. Morgan (ed.), *Sisterhood is Powerful*, Vintage Books, New York, 1970.

One

The Sexist Society: An Introduction

Australia is a sexist society. Women are exploited for their sex, their breeding power and their labour. In our homes, on the labour market, in schools, in the church, the law and in politics their needs are subjugated to those of men. They are manipulated by an increasingly subtle exploitative social system into regarding themselves as incompetent in the performance of those tasks which carry the greatest prestige and economic reward. Therefore they rarely enter the professions, they balk at coming to grips with day-to-day legal and financial matters, and in general lack confidence to perform any tasks other than those oriented towards the service of men or children. When they do enter the workforce most perform either menial repetitive tasks for a pittance, or those defined as essentially female – nursing, teaching, waitressing – all of which are extensions of home duties, caring for people, rearing the young and serving people with food.[1]

Women are not simply placed second to men. Rather, their subordination to men is so great that they have no identity in their own right. So, Donald Horne writes that 'The image of Australia is of a man . . . ',[2] and Craig McGregor says:

> Ask most people to describe an Australian . . . they will probably reply in terms of a bloke . . . who calls his wife 'the missus' . . . the typical Australian isn't a worker any longer, *he* is more likely to be a youngish clerk or businessman with nice button-down shirts, sincere tie, last year's Holden, a cheque account and wife in the suburbs. [my italics][3]

Thus the best that most Australian women can hope for is to be regarded as status images like the family car, to be dressed up, painted and displayed. They are property to be used by men to the best advantage.

None of this is new. Today, much of the exploitation is hidden behind a huge facade of created fulfilment, behind the beauty contests, the TV quizzes, the charity drives, the mothers' clubs and the endless race to be trendy. But it is there and it is firmly based on a history of overt exploitation.

From the beginning of white settlement in Australia women were 'brought out' to fulfil the needs of men. The first were convicts, brought out to be servants to the free settlers and administrators, to be exploited for their sex and for their labour. Governor Macquarie was under orders from the British Government 'to keep the female convicts separate till they can be properly distributed among the inhabitants',[4] but a Report of the Select Committee on Transportation written in 1800 had commented that female convicts 'were *received* rather as prostitutes than as servants' [my italics].[5] They thus fulfilled some male needs but they were not seen as fit wives for the free settlers and administrators who thought of themselves as the founders of a nation.

So in 1831 the British Government began to offer assisted passages to Australia to females who were 'single, young and of good health and character'. They were packed off to satisfy sexual appetites respectably, to keep house, to bear and raise children, and by doing so to provide men with contentment and a feeling of wholeness as family heads building a nation, rather than to be whole themselves. But they were grateful for the opportunity, for in England a disproportionate ratio of men and women had left many women single and unemployed. In migrating to Australia they saw the possibility not only of greater employment prospects but also of a husband, the only avenue through which they could become respectable members of society. So 'The Needlewoman's Farewell' published in *Punch* in 1850 read:

'Now speed thee, good ship, over sea, and bear us far away,
Where food to eat, and friends to greet, and work to do await us –
Where against hunger's tempting we shall not need to pray –
Where in wedlock's tie, not harlotry, we shall find men to mate us.'[6]

Many did indeed marry – one newspaper account of 1848 records that of the female immigrants who arrived on one ship eight were married within twenty-four hours[7] – but the plight of many was soon desperate. The men of Australia had decided they needed women and the men of England decided that they needed to get rid of some, but none made much effort to help the women once they arrived. In 1841 there were 600 unemployed female immigrants in Sydney, and despite the comfort provided by Caroline Chisholm, who set up reception homes for female immigrants, life for most was miserable and degrading.

Those who did not marry were expected to enter domestic service. Some did but many chose instead to work shorter hours in factories, much to the horror of the men at the top. R. E. N. Twopenny, in *Town Life in Australia*, bemoans the unwillingness of young women to labour long hours in domestic service and fails to understand their preference for the free evenings that factory work afforded them.

> In spite of constant shipments from England, servants are always at a premium ... Unfortunately, but a very small proportion of the daughters of the poorer colonial working-class will go into service. ... so great is the love of independence in the colonial girl, that she prefers hard work and low wages in order to be able to achieve freedom of an evening.[8]

The prospects for these women were few for if the hope of an almost immediate marriage was not fulfilled then they were left to choose between the long and restricting drudgery of domestic service and the shorter, less well-paid but less restricting drudgery of factory work.

Since it was, and still is, regarded as natural for women to be either wives and mothers or domestic servants, they were regarded with little sympathy when they sought factory work. They received no security of employment, no minimum wages and so-called 'protective' legislation soon banned them, along with children, from working long hours. Treated by men like children they were denied the opportunity still available to men of increasing their incomes through overtime.[9] The working conditions of women were, and are, controlled by men. Outside the home they became the system's most manipulable form of labour power. So the subcommittee appointed by the Trades Hall Council to report upon the operation of the Factories and Workshops Act in Victoria in 1884, agreed with its 'witnesses' that 'a great deal of female labour could and ought to be dispensed with'.[10] Women were brought to Australia to serve beneath the bodies of men, in the houses of men, on the farms and stations of men and in the factories of men, not for themselves.

Australia's cities were the centres of a growing capitalist economy inherited directly from England, the birthplace of capitalism, and the immigrant women were soon helpless pawns in a mad male world which willingly sought to exploit them as cheap labour but at the same time set out to paternalistically protect them from the evils of the real world; to protect them not for their own sakes but rather to ensure that in the rearing of their husbands' children these women would maintain the hypocritical double moral standards which kept their husbands in their privileged positions. Thus the women of Australia soon became part of that shifting manipulated pool of depersonalized labour power which the bourgeoisie shuffled about for its greatest possible profit. But from the beginnings of capitalism their exploitation was extreme because they were regarded as a surplus pool of labour to be fired without the slightest qualms. When performing non-domestic tasks their behaviour was defined by their male-dominated society as unnatural. By defining domestic tasks as 'natural' and non-domestic tasks as 'unnatural' for women, a society of male masters succeeded in creating both a cheap manipulable labour pool and a constant supply of unpaid domestic slaves. To digress for a moment to a piece of *Alice in Wonderland*, quoted by Stokely Carmichael:

> In the book there's a debate between Humpty Dumpty and Alice around the question of definitions. It goes like this:
> 'When I use a word,' Humpty Dumpty said, in a rather scornful tone, 'It means just what I chose it to mean. Neither more nor less.'
> 'The question is,' said Alice, 'whether you can make words mean so many different things.'

'The question is,' said Humpty Dumpty, 'who is to be master. That is all.'
Now I think that Lewis Carroll is correct. *Those who can define are masters.* [my italics] [11]

So men defined women into perpetual servitude.

The exploitation of women in their 'natural' roles was also blatant in the early days of white Australia, particularly their exploitation as breeding machines for the creation of a populous white Australia. For example, a decline in the birth-rate in NSW between 1880 and 1900 gave rise to great concern. A report on this problem and on the corresponding evils of contraception concluded that unlimited child-bearing was the duty of every married woman. Limitations on family size were viewed as extreme selfishness and as an unjustifiable intervention in the 'true' course of nature.[12] The white male settlers of Australia wanted a populous white Australia and so they defined it as the duty of the women of Australia to 'labour' towards that end.

Today women still labour in factories for little return, with virtually no security of employment. Home and family are still defined as a woman's prime responsibility. She must not compete with men but should rather subjugate herself to them, for it is only regarded as legitimate for a woman to work if such work does not interefere with the performance of her duties as a wife and mother. Thus moves for equal pay and a minimum wage for women are regarded by the male society as a threat to family life and therefore as a threat to the continued domination of women. Pay them poorly and give them no security and women will not be inclined to move away from the home – this is still the blatantly discriminatory reasoning of a male-dominated society which is happy to reap an even greater surplus from the labour of women who must work.

Even in 1966 that great spokesman for 'cultural freedom', for the 'Christian way of life' and for 'liberal' politics, B. A. Santamaria, could claim that to encourage women to work is to divert them from their natural duty to increase Australia's population and so save Australia from possible 'hostile absorption' by a populous Asia. He could claim that 'the declining birth-rate is

Australia's most serious internal problem'[13] and that women can legitimately 'find interest in outside work' only after 'having fully discharged their family responsibilities'.[14] Women in Australia are *still* defined primarily as breeding machines.

The exploitation of convict women, of early immigrants who had only Caroline Chisholm to look to for comfort, of women in nineteenth century factories and domestic service was direct and blatant, and the statements made about women needing to breed non-stop more extreme than most made today. But the apparent easing and even disappearance of exploitation of women in terms of sex is simply a change in the nature of capitalism, not a real change in the relationship between men and women. The exploitation of women has simply become more subtle and devious. In *Sexuality and Class Struggle*, Reimut Reiche discusses the shift from 'direct exploitation' to 'manipulative exploitation', and says:

> This change is indicative of a change in the structure of capitalist rule itself. Not that manipulation has replaced and cancelled out exploitation. But it becomes evident, when one observes the manipulation of needs, and of situations producing pseudo-satisfaction in the commodity market, in communications, and in sexuality, that exploitation is not now confined to its direct physical form but relies upon a gigantic apparatus of created needs which are constantly manipulated to get people to comply with meaningless social goals.[15]

So women are manipulated into a range of incompetences and a bevy of useless activities. To ensure that they do not begin to compete with men, they are kept washing, ironing and cooking and struggling to be sexually attractive and satisfying. The manipulation ranges through all the institutions of Australian society, manifesting itself in the organizations which have been formed to maintain traditional behaviour: the schools, the courts, parliament, the political parties, the family, the churches, radio, television and the press, hospitals, universities and in the labour market.

This book examines the position of women in these institutionalized activities and demonstrates beyond doubt that Australia is a sexist society. The book has been organized from a sociological perspective in that it is concerned to show how the forces which regulate the way people relate to each other, how the rules, formal and informal, which govern their behaviour and mould their attitudes, and even the language they use, are all essentially geared to the maintenance and promotion of sexual discrimination in the service of male dominance.

In their relationships with each other people are constantly faced with having to decide how to behave, both in terms of what they want to achieve from the social exchange and in terms of how they evaluate the position and expectations of the other person or persons. Sometimes such assessments must be based on personal characteristics, on the known and appreciated idiosyncracies of an individual, but much behaviour has become so habitual as to be stereotyped or 'institutionalized'. To regulate such habitual and repetitive behaviour, organizations develop and provide constraints which are external to the participants but binding on them – the school has rules not the headmistress – and which allow the personnel within such organizations to change without disturbing the continuous performance of institutionalized tasks. This is achieved through the occupation by individuals of roles – 'teacher', 'policewoman', 'housewife' – each of which is associated with a range of expected behaviour patterns. The 'travelling salesman' treats the 'housewife' in accordance with a predetermined set of expected behaviour patterns, as she does him. He is polite, comments on the decor and weather, but would not dream of bothering her with the intricacies of finance or mechanics. He leaves those details to be taken care of by the 'husband' who will be expected to be practical and competent, unlike 'the wife'. When the salesman moves on to the next house he repeats the same behaviour, greeting the next housewife with the same package of expectations. The personnel change but the roles remain constant. There is room for varying interpretations of how roles ought to be performed, even sometimes for personal creativity in the interpretation of a role, but the roles and their organizations are essentially apart from and more resilient than the personalities of their inhabitants. Though the roles change gradually as their occupants reinterpret and criticize the behaviour expected of them, the roles radically constrain the behaviour which can go on within the organizations they maintain.

We must examine the nature of the organizations which have developed in Australia to regulate institutional behaviour, for these organizations reflect the manipulative powers of those who have achieved privileged positions in Australian society, who wish to maintain as habitual patterns of behaviour those which support and promote their positions of privilege. The privileged, the 'masters', have *defined* the roles and structured the organizations. They define the nature of institutionalized behaviour to their advantage, for when behaviour is institutionalized and defined in terms of depersonalized roles it is lifted beyond the control of individual personalities. People become pawns to be manipulated by the powerful, and the organizations soon begin to mould the values and fortunes of the people in them. People are manipulated into believing in their roles. Women believe that they are incompetent outside home and family. They live through their husbands, accepting reflected glory, reflected prestige and reflected fulfilment. It is in the examination of the institutions of Australian society and of the ideologies which bolster them that we come to appreciate how men, as masters, have moulded Australian society to their ends at the expense of Australia's women.

Notes

1. In 1970 the then Minister for Labour and National Service the Hon B. M. Snedden, Q.C., M.P., stated in a press release that 'nearly two-thirds of the 1,727,000 women in the workforce are in the following eight occupations: Clerk, Saleswoman, Typist, Stenographer, Domestic, Clothing and Textile Worker.' This point is also developed in Chapter 4.
2. Donald Horne, *The Lucky Country*, Penguin Books, 1964, p. 32.
3. C. McGregor, *Profile of Australia*, Penguin Books, 1968, p. 21.
4. Report of Select Committee on Transportation, 1812, II, 341 quoted in M. Clark, *Selected Documents in Australian History, 1788–1850*, Angus and Robertson, Sydney, 1950, p. 117.

5. Ibid., p. 117.

6. Quoted in C. Rover, *The Punch Book of Women's Rights*, Hutchinson, London, 1967, p. 19.

7. Ibid., p. 20.

8. R. E. N. Twopenny, *Town Life in Australia*, London, 1883, p. 49, quoted in M. Clark, *Selected Documents in Australian History, 1851–1900*, Angus and Robertson, Sydney, 1950, p. 681.

9. See the speech on the Factories and Shop Act amendment Bill, 17 October 1895, Vic. P.D. 1895–6, Vol. 78, pp. 2633–7 quoted in Clark, op. cit. p. 613.

10. *Final Report of the Sub-Committee appointed by the Trades Hall Council to Inquire into and Report upon the operation of the Factories and Workshops Act in Victoria*, quoted in Clark, op. cit. p. 604.

11. S. Carmichael, 'Black Power' in D. Cooper (ed.), *The Dialectics of Liberation*, Penguin Books, 1968, pp. 152–3.

12. *Report of the Royal Commission on the Decline of the Birth-rate and on the Mortality of Infants*, NSW pp. 1904, Vol. 4, quoted in Clark, op. cit. p. 670.

13. B. A. Santamaria, *Point of View*, Hawthorn Press, Melbourne, 1969, p. 219.

14. Ibid., p.218.

15. R. Reiche, *Sexuality and Class Struggle*, NLB, London, 1970, p.20.

Two
Biology and Human Behaviour

The psychological profession has provided us with extensive lists of behavioural tasks on which men and women score differently.[1] To mention but a few, there are differences in sensory thresholds, verbal and spatial ability, and in tasks *claiming* to measure creativity, aggression, memory and IQ. In most cases the range of values overlaps, but the means are significantly different. Occasionally, as in the case of IQ, the means coincide but the distribution or range around the mean varies[2]; the IQ spread is broader for males. Psychologists have traditionally explained these differences in terms of sexually different cultural conditioning, which begins virtually at the moment of birth, when the child is assigned to its appropriate gender.[3]*

Many recent writers have sought to replace culturally based theories of sex differences in behaviour by explanations more firmly rooted in physiology[4]. This naturally has social and political significance. If sexually dimorphic behaviour results purely from learning, it should be possible to replace one type of conditioning by another with relative ease, thus liberating women from their second place in society. If, on the other hand, the differences are firmly fixed in our physiology and genes and that the sex roles existing in our society today have been moulded through natural selection pressures acting on the genome†, then this could be taken as providing strong support for the maintenance of traditional sex roles; that is, as evidence against Women's Liberation. In my opinion, biology at the level of the genome has not yet reached a stage where it is possible to use it to explain human behaviour.

* 'Gender' refers to an individual's identification as being masculine or feminine regardless of physical sex.

† Each species has its own characteristic set of genes, or *genome*.

In her book *Males and Females* Corinne Hutt argues that sex differences are caused by innate hormonal factors.[5] She sees sex roles as fixed and biologically determined. I strongly disapprove of the way in which she has abused existing scientific data to develop this argument. She extrapolates from animals to man with gay abandon, often quoting studies without even a reference to the species on which they were done. For example, work by R. J. Andrew and myself on chickens was quoted in a context which made it appear like data for humans (page 118 of ref. 5)*. The presence of testosterone in male chickens alters their attention so that they became more persistent.[6] Once they begin to respond to a given stimulus, they will persist in responding to it for longer than will a chicken without testosterone (e.g. a hen or capon). In the scientific paper reporting this Andrew and I raised the possibility that a similar effect *may* occur in man, and also that such an effect on attention *may* influence rate of learning in different situations. We simply used our animal data to ask testable questions about the human species, and did not extrapolate our findings to humans. The study of animals in controlled experiments is useful in drawing guidelines for the study of humans, and for assisting in the design of experiments on humans, which are invariably more difficult to perform. One must recognize the fact that behaviour varies considerably from species to species. My work on chickens is just a beginning, and I am enraged by writers who quote it dishonestly. Since this is a frequent fault in popular literature, I can only suggest that readers turn their critical eyes to the original sources of all the data quoted.

Pop science is on the increase. It appears in extravagant extrapolations from animals to man made by people like Ardrey, Desmond Morris and even Konrad Lorenz.[7] These writers parade under the guise of science to issue sweeping statements about human sexual behaviour and aggression. Newspapers and popular magazines regurgitate their views in

* In a more recent publication by Arianna Stassinopoulos (*The Female Woman*, Fontana, London, 1974), this same research is also misquoted as if it applies to humans.

even more superficial nonsense. Indeed, as witnessed by the astounding popularity of these books, humankind seems all too ready to grasp on to glossy generalizations. They do make entertaining reading, but people *believe* them because they reinforce the *status quo*, and that, in my opinion is why they are dangerous.

Ardrey and Lorenz preach 'innate aggression' in both animals and Man*, which means that wars can never be completely avoided. What explains the popular craze for such prophets of doom? Perhaps it results from Man's recognition of the fact that his behaviour towards his own species is often quite monstrous, and a resignation to this as being 'human nature'. In this way 'human nature' becomes an excuse for thinking. Similarly, belief that sex differences are innately determined leads not only to acceptance of the present status of women in modern society, but also to active opposition to any changes.

Biology is being increasingly used in discussions about human social structure, particularly now that fewer people are inclined to use religion as a strong support for our social customs. Such simplistic, biological theories should be kept out of Women's Liberation.

It must also be recognized that most science is performed by men and that its so called 'objectivity' is biased towards those values which are designed to reinforce male superiority.† The doubting reader need only glance at some crutch-heavy papers written by Broverman's group in the States.[8] One of their papers sets out to muster up all the evidence that can be found to support a preconceived male-chauvinistic idea, ignoring all contrary evidence and making wildly incorrect statements about brain biochemistry and physiology. It is not surprising to find that they can 'prove' that females are best at 'simple, over-learned, perceptual-motor tasks' and males surpass them on 'complex, perceptual-restructuring tasks'. Good reasons for

* 'Man' is used here to refer to men and women collectively.

† Successful women scientists frequently take on and support these male-dominated views. Dissenting women tend to be eliminated by the system.

keeping women in the factories and out of the professions! Women should aim to expose such researchers.

The course of science is not independent of society's attitudes. Science interacts with society; society shapes the questions explored by science and, in its turn, science influences society. If society is sexist, then frequently so will be that area of science which studies behaviour of the sexes. Why do we always look for sex differences and race into publication when we find them? Why are we not more ecstatic about similarities between the sexes? Is it simply this terrible need for mankind to see things in terms of dichotomies, or is there more to it? Might it not be derived from the fact that a large amount of our social activity is organized around sex differences rather than similarities. Small sex differences in mental abilities may therefore be emphasized as subjects important for scientific research, and the results will not fail to justify the *status quo* of sex roles and division of labour on the basis of sex. Society acts at two levels, in biasing researchers to the male sex and in framing questions around differences and not similarities. The popular media can be no more, or indeed no less, biased than many of the scientific papers which it quotes. It is in this manner that myths develop and persist.

Theories for a Biological Basis to Sex Differences in Human Behaviour

Hormones circulating in the blood stream

Several biological theories have been proposed to account for differences in behaviour between the sexes. Broverman et al. developed a theory which based sex differences in behaviour on differences in the levels of sex hormones circulating in the blood streams of adult males and females. Females have higher levels of oestrogen and males have higher levels of androgens and each of these is supposed to produce different behaviours by interacting with a different transmitter system within the brain. The physiological evidence that they used to support this theory was rather gross and dubious*, and possible cultural influences were completely ignored. How the influence of learning on the sorts of sex differences in behaviour which they discussed could be ignored is beyond my comprehension. Women were asserted to perform better than men on so called simple, over-learned, repetitive tasks (such as speed of naming colours, reading speed, verbal ability, and clerical abilities like typing, coding speed and simple calculations), while men were superior on so called complex, restructuring tasks (such as finding a simple figure hidden in a larger pattern, and habit reversal – counting backwards). This classification obviously involves a preconceived value judgement. As Parlee points out, verbal ability can hardly be regarded as a simple, over-learned ability.[10] The theory falls down both on physiological and behavioural grounds.

Part of Broverman's evidence for the importance of circulating levels of androgens rests on the finding that males with high levels of androgens perform differently on these tasks than do males with lower levels of androgens. However, high androgen males differ physically from men with lower androgen levels. They have broader shoulders, shorter necks, narrower hips and more hair on their chests. That is, physically they tend to fit more closely the classical picture of the muscly hero image and for this reason their social conditioning may be quite different.

Hormones affecting brain development

Other theories have postulated an influence of the sex hormones on the developing brain rather than on differences in circulating levels of hormones in the adult. The presence or absence of different sex hormones during different stages of brain development is said to make some forms of learning easier than others, so that learning can play a role but it is channelled by the genes and hormones. For example, Dawson suggested that action of androgens on the young brain in males facilitates learning that will later lead to a superior ability in spatial and numerical tasks,

* A full discussion of this aspect would be too involved to develop here, but interested readers are referred to the original paper plus critiques by Singer and Montgomery and Parlee.[9]

while the action of oestrogen on the young female brain promotes superiority in verbal fluency.[11] Most of his evidence for humans was drawn from studies on West African males suffering from Kwashiorkor disease, caused by protein deficiency in early life. These males have above average levels of oestrogen and have female cognitive style in spatial and verbal ability. However, Dawson conveniently ignores that these males also have physical feminization, such as breast development, and, therefore, may be socialized in a feminine direction rather than a male direction simply because they look more like females.

Buffery and Gray similarly concentrated on early brain development to explain sex differences in verbal and spatial ability.[12] The language centre is localized in the left hemisphere of the brain, and they suggest that this lateralization occurs earlier and more completely in females thus determining their superiority in verbal tasks while masculine supremacy on spatial tasks results as an indirect consequence of this. With less lateralization of language, spatial ability in males can be located more bilaterally, thus giving better three-dimensional representation. So little is known about brain processing of spatial and verbal material that such an hypothesis is at best premature if not completely simplistic. However, even if it were correct, location of the information processing centre could not be used as evidence for innate, biologically determined sex differences, as Buffery and Gray have suggested, because it is quite possible that learning itself could cause differential and speeded lateralization. For example, mothers may talk more to their daughters than to their sons and this may direct their brain growth and speed lateralization of the language centre.

It is clear than none of these theories for cognitive development in men and women has successfully differentiated between biological and cultural components.

The developing brain and sex-role conditioning

Let me now consider some of the data available in sex-role conditioning, or gender identity, in humans. Most of this research has been carried out in the United States by Money and Ehrhardt, and basically it has shown that cultural learning plays the major role in sex-role typing.[13] Sex hormones may determine physical sex and so set the scene for conditioning into either a male or female gender identity, but in cases where genetic sex has been at variance with initial assignment of a child into the male or female category learning seems to out-weigh the biological factors. For example, in some rare cases of hermaphrodism, a child may be assigned to one sex at birth but undergo a complete reversal in output of sex hormones when puberty is reached, so that he or she now secretes sex hormones completely opposite to that of the gender in which he or she has been reared. In almost every case like this, Money and Ehrhardt have found that the individual chooses to retain the gender identity of rearing and not to change to conform to his or her biological condition.

Last year at a conference[14] I heard Money report data for a pair of identical, male twins. During circumcision of one of them the doctor's knife slipped and tragically excised the penis. The parents decided to raise this one as a girl and the other as a boy. At ten years old Money reports that the girl is 'every bit a girl' and completely different from her genetically and sexually identical twin. Their performance on sexually dimorphic tasks would be extremely enlightening, for differences could only have resulted from sex-role conditioning.*

Ehrhardt and Money have also studied females exposed to excess levels of androgens while in the uterus, either because they suffered from adrenal hyperplasia† or because their mothers took progestin to prevent miscarriage.[15] This study stemmed from earlier findings on differentiation of the rat hypothalamus from a cyclic to an acyclic control of hormonal output from the pituitary gland by the action of androgen in the first five days after birth.[16] Absence of androgen during this critical period leads to a cyclic hypothalamus characteristic of females. Female

* It should be noted that the parents felt it necessary to *choose* between raising this child as either a male or a female and that it was not possible for them to simply raise it as 'a person'.

† Adrenal hyperplasia is increased production of adrenal gland hormones, which include androgens.

rats treated with androgen during the critical period do not ovulate in adulthood, and they do not copulate with males even when they are adequately supplied with female sex hormones. In rats, then, early androgen exposure seems to organize the central nervous system both for control of hormonal output from the pituitary and for sexual behaviour. In androgen exposed human females, Money has claimed to show the same organization of behaviour (i.e. here he claims to have shown some biological determinant of gender identity). Some of these females had masculinized genitalia, but behavioural 'masculinization' was apparent even in those with normal genitalia. On the last report they were aged between ten and fourteen years, and in comparison to the control group they were reported to prefer 'masculine' clothes and 'boys' toys, to indulge in more aggressive play, and to score above average on IQ tests. While these findings are interesting, the explanation for them is not as clear-cut as it may first appear.

It is known that miscarriage can be caused by psychological factors, and it is therefore quite possible that mothers who needed to take progestin to prevent miscarriage may have been different from mothers who did not. Merely taking this drug could also have made them different. Alternatively, mothers worried about possible abnormalities in their daughters who have been exposed to androgen may have given extra care to their up-bringing in order to compensate for this. It is also possible that mothers who had access to progestin treatment came from a limited social stratum. Indeed, three-quarters of these children were found to have at least one parent who was a college graduate, and half had a parent working at a professional or business executive level.[17] Class differences like these could well influence all of the behaviours scored. At least one child exposed to progestin had a sister who was not exposed to it, and she too had an above average IQ and other behavioural characteristics similar to those exposed to androgen. Money has not controlled for these familial factors. Premature inductions based on 'rat evidence' about the organizing effect of androgens on human behaviour obviously need further critical examination.

The maternal role

Common belief in an innate maternal or mothering role in humans is another area of extrapolation from rats to man. Maternal behaviour can be triggered in rats by administering female hormones (oestrogen and progesterone) normally present in high concentrations in pregnancy. It is believed that these same hormones circulating in women during pregnancy prepare them for the maternal role, which is therefore not present in males because they do not have these hormones. However, there is absolutely no evidence for this in the human species. Studies on primates by Harlow's group show that learning plays a profound role in maternal behaviour.[18] Rhesus monkeys reared in isolation with substitute mothers made of cloth are found to make very poor mothers. They have little interest in their offspring. In fact, this effect carried over even to their grandchildren; the offspring of these motherless-mothers are also 'bad' parents. It has been a common finding in zoo management that hand-reared animals are difficult to mate and, when they do mate, they make bad parents. Rearing conditions are more important than hormones in determining the mothering role.

Homosexuality

People who do not fit the traditional norms of role behaviour in our society are considered to be deviant, and a cause for this is often sought to lie in some abnormality of hormone condition. For this reason, 'treatment' often takes the form of sex hormone administration. Homosexuality is a typical example of this.

Society often holds the mistaken belief that homosexuals are people who have adopted a gender role opposite to their physical sex. Some have, but these are a conspicuous minority. Perhaps it is this belief that has stimulated the search for a hormonal difference between homosexuals and heterosexuals, which has been continuing for some years now.

Until recently everyone has looked for a difference in circulating levels of sex hormones between homosexuals and heterosexuals. Varying reports can be found in the literature, but the sum total of all work done on large enough samples of males and females and with reasonable controls, which are always difficult to achieve, is that there are no hormonal differences.[19] Homosexuals are simply people who prefer to relate sexually to their own sex, and misconceptions arise because society associates this choice of a sexual partner with a reversal in sex-role playing.

More recently there has been a rush to jump on to the bandwagon of the rat cyclic-acyclic hypothalamus and to attempt to link homosexuality to an effect of sex hormone action on the developing brain. However, Money and Ehrhardt found no increase in homosexual behaviour or interests in their women exposed to androgen in early life. Similarly a Russian study of older women (eighteen subjects ranging in age from thirteen to forty-three years) exposed to excess levels of androgen in early life found no increased incidence of homosexual experience or interests.[20]

Many medical practitioners seem unaware of the fact that there is no evidence connecting hormones to homosexuality, because they attempt to 'cure' the 'disease' by hormone therapy.

Evolutionary theories

So far I have discussed theories of causation of sex differences in cognitive style and role playing. A separate, but related, area of discussion is concerned with the evolutionary origins of these differences.

Evolutionary theories trace the differentiation of sex roles in our society to division of the sexes in reproduction, and thereby either imply, or state, that these roles are genetically determined. Female animals, including humans, are said to have evolved to play the role of child-bearing and nurturing, while males aggressively defend the mating territory and gather food. The adaptive significance of this division of labour is said to have conferred a selective advantage, which has led to genetic selection of these characteristics still persisting in modern man. Mead suggests that women are fulfilled and occupied by having babies, while men must seek fulfilment elsewhere in other achievements.[21]

Wynne Edwards and Hutt accept that the basic division between the sexes began with reproduction, and throughout evolutionary history this has become even further specialized in more general characteristics of behaviour which extend even into the realm of cognitive style.[22] Conformity and consistency in women are seen to have been evolved as an adaptive consequence of their mothering role, which required stability and reliability in nurturing dependent infants.

Tiger also saw sex roles as an elaboration of differences in reproduction.[23] He suggested that males needed to band together to hunt for food and this led to genetic selection for male-bond formation but not for bonds between females. He even goes so far as to say that this explains male superiority in the political systems of today!

While the female members of many animal species may be primarily concerned with rearing the young and the males with defending territory or gathering food, this is certainly not true of all species. In many species of birds (e.g. emus) and rodents (e.g. gerbils) care for the young is shared by the sexes or performed entirely by the male. In marmosets, a primate species, the male rears the offspring. Anthropological evidence also shows that some societies in New Guinea have sex role reversals with respect to practices of child-rearing and food-gathering.[24] Such exceptions strongly contest generalized theories based on evolution because, if such behaviour is so deeply rooted genetically, it should be consistent across all cultures.

A survey in 1959 by Barry et al. covered many human societies and found that division towards nurturance, obedience and responsibility in females and towards self-reliance and achievement in males was more pronounced in societies which hunted large animals.[25] Sex-role differentiation would therefore seem to be based on cultural differences related to the economy of the society.

Evolutionary arguments like those discussed before also have a static quality which cannot be a characteristic of evolution. Evolutionary processes are dynamic. If sex differences have arisen by genetic selection, this could have only been possible under the action of a dynamic process. Why then is it not also possible to argue that the same dynamic process is now selecting *against* sex differences in our modern culture? In present day society child-bearing and rearing is not the time-consuming occupation that it was in the past, and specialization of women purely for this role would seem to be a definite waste of ability, a non-adaptive trait being selected against by the pressures of evolution. It seems to me that those who adhere to evolutionary theories in order to explain and support sexual differentiation of roles in our present culture merely display an inability to adapt to a changing world.

Genes in the cell and behaviour

But, finally, the most cogent argument against people who would attribute sex differences to genes comes from a consideration of how genes work within the cell and how they interact with the environment. The nature-nurture dichotomy becomes a non-question when we consider the process of development and genetic expression.

Development is an unfolding of the organism's genetic potential in continuous interaction with the environment at each step of differentiation. An organism begins at conception, and so too does its environment. Except for monozygotic*, identical twins, each organism has its own unique complement of genes and each gene makes a single protein, which has a specific task to perform within the cell. The first cell makes protein and then divides. Its growth is influenced by the surrounding environment (e.g. the uterus for mammals or sea-water for starfish). This process of growth and division repeats itself over and over, always in continuous register with environmental controls. Both the internal and the external environments of a cell affect its genes, determining which ones will be translated into protein. In this way cells differentiate into tissues and organs. Each cell, each tissue, each organ, has its own environment in addition to the environment of the whole organism. What then is the relationship between a gene and a character at the level of the whole organism? For some characters, such as eye colour or

* Monozygotic twins form from one fertilized egg and, therefore, each has the same genes. Dizygotic twins each form from separate fertilized eggs and have different genes.

blood group, the relationship is quite simple, since these characters are determined by only one or a few proteins. But behavioural characteristics such as sex differences, intelligence and personality must be determined by the interaction of millions of cells and by countless proteins. It is impossible to tie them to genetic development because of the intertwining, interacting, recursive and branching chains of cause and effect which interconnect the various organizational levels of a complicated organism like man. Behavioural characters are measurements of the whole organism made at a completely different level of organization to that of the gene and its protein. While we may find correlations between certain genetic constitutions and certain behavioural traits, we can never infer that one causes the other. Behaviour is scored at one hierarchical level of analysis, the gene at another. There is no communication between these levels, since each level speaks a different language.[26] This is why the nature-nurture dichotomy becomes naive, or even ridiculous, when applied to behaviour. It fails to take into account that it is the whole organism interacting with its environment, not just a gene. In this context, nature means genes, nurture means environmental influence or behaviour; this does not constitute a dichotomy. Each level is valid on its own terms, and only on its own terms.

Summary

Since biology is not yet ready to explain behaviour at the genetic level, it would be most unwise for Women's Liberation to base any ideology on such biological explanations. It is, of course, essential for women to criticize old notions of biological confinement to sex roles, and to expose bad science. Even if a genetic or hormonal basis for sex differences is definitely proven, this of course, cannot be used as an argument to subjugate women in a changing world. To adopt a purely critical position is not only politically sensible, but it is also biologically sound. The time has not yet come for us to accept a biological basis for sex differences in behaviour, and indeed it may never arrive. In the meantime, let us cease using biology to explain human society, lest, instead of being part of the solution, we become part of the problem.

Notes

1. E. E. Maccoby, *The Development of Sex Differences*, Tavistock, London, 1967.

2. L. Tyler, *The Psychology of Human Differences*, Appleton-Century-Crofts, New York, 3rd edition, 1965.

3. J. Kagan and H. A. Moss, *Birth to Maturity*, Wiley, New York, 1962.
D. A. Hamburge and D. T. Lunde, in Maccoby, op. cit.

4. C. Hutt, *Males and Females*, Penguin Books, 1972.
J. L. M. Dawson, 'Effects of sex hormones on cognitive style in rats and men', *Behavior Genetics*, 2, 21–42, 1972.
A. W. H. Buffery and J. A. Gray, in C. Ounsted and D. C. Taylor (eds) *Gender Differences: Their Ontogeny and Significance*, Churchill Livingstone, Edinburgh, 1972.

5. Hutt, op. cit.

6. R. J. Andrew and L. J. Rogers, 'Testosterone, search behaviour and persistence', *Nature*, 237, 343–346, 1972.
L. J. Rogers, 'Persistence and search influenced by natural levels of androgens in young and adult chickens'. *Physiology and Behaviour 12*, 197–204, 1974.

7. R. Ardrey, *African Genesis*, Collins, London, 1961.
R. Ardrey, *The Territorial Imperative*, Collins, London, 1969.
R. Ardrey, *The Social Contract*, Collins, London, 1972.
D. Morris, *The Naked Ape*, Corgi, London, 1967.
D. Morris, *The Human Zoo*, Jonathan Cape, London, 1969.
K. Lorenz, *On Aggression*, Bantam Books, New York, 1967.

8. D. M. Broverman, E. W. Klaiber, Y. Kobayashi and W. Vogel, 'Roles of activation and inhibition in sex differences in cognitive abilities', *Psychology Review 75*, 23–50, 1968.

9. G. Singer and R. B. Montgomery, 'Comment on roles of activation and inhibition in sex differences in cognitive abilities', *Psychology Review, 76*, 325–327, 1969.
M. B. Parlee, Comments on 'Roles of activation and inhibition in cognitive

abilities by D. M. Broverman, E. L. Klaiber, Y. Kobayashi and W. Vogel', *Psychology Review* 79, 180–184, 1972.

10. Parlee, ibid.

11. Dawson, op. cit.

12. Buffery and Gray, op. cit.

13. J. Money and A. A. Ehrhardt, *Man and Woman: Boy and Girl*, Johns Hopkins University Press, Baltimore, 1972.

14. Thirteenth International Ethological Conference in Washington, D.C., 1973.

15. J. Money in R. P. Michael (ed.) *Endocrinology and Human Behaviour*, Oxford Medical Publications, Oxford, 1968.

16. G. W. Harris, 'Sex hormones, brain development and brain function', *Endocrinology* 75, 627–648, 1969.

17. A. A. Ehrhardt and J. Money, 'Progestin-induced hermaphrodism: IQ and psychosexual identity in a study of ten girls', *Journal of Sex Research* 3, 83–100, 1967.

18. H. F. Harlow, 'Love in infant monkeys', *Scientific American*, June, 1959.

19. A. H. Buss, *Psychopathology*, John Wiley, 1966.

20. A. Lev-Ran, 'Sexuality and educational levels of women with the late-treated adrenogenital syndrome', *Archives of Sexual Behavior* 3, 27–32, 1974.

21. M. Mead, *Male and Female*, Penguin Books, 1950.

22. V. C. Wynne-Edwards, *Animal dispersion in relation to social behaviour*, Oliver & Boyd, Edinburgh, 1962; Hutt, op. cit.

23. L. Tiger, 'The possible biological origins of sexual discrimination', *Impact of Science on Society* 20, 29–45, 1970; and L. Tiger, *Men in Groups*, Panther, London, 1971.

24. M. Mead, op. cit.

25. H. Barry, M. K. Bacon and I. L. Child, 'A cross-cultural survey of some sex differences in socialization', *Journal of Abnormal and Social Psychology* 55, 327–33, 1959.

26. S. Rose, *The Conscious Brain*, Weidenfeld and Nicholson, London, 1973.

Three
An Object Lesson in Women's History

While academic historians cling preciously to the idea that there are many kinds of history – labour history, religious history, economic history, political history and social history – it is becoming increasingly clear to many women that the similarities between these various 'types' of history are more remarkable than their differences. During the past few years, as the forces of the new feminism have begun to gather strength and confidence, some of us have begun to ask questions about ourselves. Not just to explore the intricacies of our own oppression and the frontiers of our own rebelliousness, but to wonder about our uniqueness. Could we really, we wondered, be the first women in the two hundred years of white settlement of this country, to have risen in anger against the strictures of our sex? Were there not, lurking somewhere in the recesses of our recorded past, other groups or movements of women who had challenged and resisted the prescriptions they felt impinged on *their* freedom? We knew very little about the Australian suffrage movement but those gleanings we had collected seemed to suggest that the radicalism of these women was rather circumscribed, and that their puritanical stance made identification with them difficult.

We felt slightly uneasy about the possibility of our historical isolation; if we were the first then we assumed the precarious but exciting expectation that we might be able to alter the future course of women's lives, but we felt as well the deprivation of having no links with the past. Those of us who had been involved in socialist groups knew how having solid historical roots provided consoling nostalgic evocations of past struggles to ward off momentary disillusion, while the very continuity of the movement reinforced and validated our convictions. If we were the first radical feminists in this country we were denied access to this kind of refurbishment. On the other hand, if we could not trace a genealogy of women's rebellion we were not burdened with the failures of the past. We inherited neither the cumbersome and often ossifying myths and dogmas which have often stultified the Left, nor did we have the millstone of years of frustration of our movement's aims to carry. But especially because of the hostility which our rebelliousness generated it was still important to know, one way or the other, how unique our expressions of revolt were.

It did not take very long to find that virtually none of the works of Australian historians could in any way help us answer this question. Although each branch of study claimed to have carved out a special and separate area of investigation, all were pre-eminently concerned with chronicling and analysing the history of *men*. That word 'history' is unnervingly accurate. In none of the books of recognized historians could we find even a mention of what women in the past were doing. The most authoritative, and most widely acclaimed works of Australian history – such as those of C. M. H. Clark, or Brian Fitzpatrick or R. A. Gollan,[1] to name just a few – all fail to include in their interpretative frameworks any consideration of what women were doing. If by chance there was the odd line or paragraph devoted to discussing women it was generally because it illuminated the general point. For instance, Jauncey's book on conscription does discuss in more detail than is usual the activities of some women anti-conscriptionists, but it does not occur to him to ask how these women came to be involved in a public, political campaign.[2] Such a question might seem irrelevant to the historian who merely examines the activities of those actors who force themselves before his focus, but for those who write about women or who are interested in discovering what women have done in the past, it is a vital one. If most history books ignore or suppress the activities of women, then the occasional author who does pay them some attention ought to consider why it is that the elements of his analysis differ from those of his fellow practitioners.[3] What was it about *this* campaign, or *these* women, which made it different from other historic Australian political events? Why were some women involved in this particular campaign whereas the number of women active in, say, the federation movement was so tiny?

To have got to the point where such questions can be even considered is to have made a considerable advance. Most Australian history works are so closed, so suffocating, so self-assured in their preoccupation with the activities of men that such questions could not even occur to the reader. To read them is to be lulled into the false assumption that women did not even exist. It is true that many books which consider colonial history do single out two groups of women for cursory attention. The works of Robson, Cannon, Shaw and Madgwick concede the existence of female convicts and/or female emigrants but almost always in separate chapters, underlying their inability to relate those women specifically to their particular schemas. But virtually every general political or economic history engages in blanket omission. Even a radical reinterpreting of much past historiography, such as Humphrey McQueen's *A New Britannia*, despite its introductory *mea culpa*, is unable to see how women might fit into such a reappraisal.[5]

Thus the question for contemporary feminists to pursue becomes, not just were there any radical feminist groups squeezed in somewhere in our past, but what were other women, all women, doing? What was expected of them, what did they actually do and, very importantly, what did they think of what they did? To even begin to answer these questions has launched us into a much longer and more encompassing project than we could ever have envisaged because we have to start from scratch. Much of the information we seek – if it exists – remains hidden in dusty archives, tucked away in the evidence of Royal Commissions and Select Committees, still awaiting tabulation in ancient census returns. But before we can really begin the massive job of bringing it all to the surface, of making it available to those who are curious about women's past, we need to consider just how to go about writing such a history – the kinds of frameworks to adopt, the direction of the questions to be pursued – for this will determine the way in which we conduct the research.

We have to ask the basic question, is a history of 'women'

possible and if so, is it desirable? One of the main points of the radical feminist critique of contemporary society is the way in which women have been objectified, how one distinguishing category – their sex – has been thought more significant than the heterogeneity of individuals. This arbitrary categorization of individuals on the basis of their genital sex has been identified as 'sexism', an ideology and a social practice which attempts to unite, and denigrate, a large and varied group as an economically, socially and culturally convenient means of organizing society. Women have been lumped together, just as blacks, or migrants, have been grouped together, and individual differences are subsumed under this one sexist, undifferentiated category. This criticism has been made mainly about sex-role prescriptions, but it could apply equally to the way women are written about historically, sociologically or within any other discipline. A book about Australian men would be considered absurd; it is of course unnecessary since Australian history to date has been the history of Australian men, but what is important is that there has been no assumption that men of differing classes, regions or religions, for instance, could be lumped together. The very diversity of conventional history, recognizes that men are different from each other. The sexist category is not applied to men – should we apply it to women?

Certainly it is the case that virtually all women share a number of common experiences, and the expectations which society makes clear it has of them are less mitigated by class, regional and religious differences. All women learn that motherhood is the most desirable vocation for them and that such an ambition must displace or take priority over any other aims they may entertain. While men are taught that their major role in life is to be bread-winners they are allowed some choice as to the exact way in which they will fulfil this role, what kind of job they will take. Whatever their social class, all women are expected to adopt a supportive and subservient role in relation to the men with whom they are associated. A feminine stereotype, the product of sex-role socialization, can be identified even though women vary in the extent of their conformity to it. Similarly, there are standardized views about women, prejudices, jokes or insulting homilies such as those about women drivers or mothers-in-law, which suggest that many men not only agree with but actively perpetuate this sexist way of classifying women. While a male stereotype also exists, women lack the political, economic and social power to enforce male conformity to it: its perpetuation depends largely on men themselves.

Women's liberation groups have given much time to exploring female conditioning and to confirming that what unites women is greater than that which separates them, giving rise to the notion of 'sisterhood'. However this idea (and ideal) has lately been criticized from within the movement as a means of denying those important differences between women which do exist.[6] While some unifying solidarity against an initially hostile world was necessary, increasingly radical feminists are beginning to recognize that even within the movement women do have differing aims and aspirations and that one of the movement's goals must be to force society to accommodate these. Some women want children, others don't. Some want to relate to men, others don't. Some want equality of job opportunity, others want a radical restructuring of the capitalist economy. Once this pluralism is conceded, to what extent does it still make sense to speak of women as a universal category? Are we not in danger of reproducing that very form of sexism which we so vehemently reject?

It is probably the case that the perception of the possibility of revolt has made this pluralism possible or has at least increased its scope. But can we assert, without some evidence, that it has not always existed – even if only in a covert and largely unacknowledged way? In the past, those women who have been singled out by historians have either been exemplary conformers to the female stereotype in that they were good wives and mothers, e.g. Elizabeth Macarthur, or they worked in fields which were considered compatible with or contributing to this prescription, e.g. Caroline Chisholm. Or they have been notorious for their *failure* to conform to it. Hence much attention has been lavished on famous prostitutes, criminals, e.g. Tilly Devine, or eccentrics like Bea Miles. These latter women have been singled out because of their refusal to conform to the great

Australian imperative of motherhood and dutiful domesticity but the very fact that they were able to buck the sex-role system at the times and in the ways that they did, implies that it was perhaps less embracing than we have been led to imagine.

Thus we have a problem if we are to write a history of women in Australia. Which women are we going to select? Will it be possible to devise some methodology which encompasses *all* women: can Tilly Devine and Caroline Chisholm be considered within the one framework? Certainly few historians have been bold enough to try and cram all men into a single theme, and those who have tried have usually been criticized for their selectivity, for the glaring omissions they have made. For instance, Russel Ward's postulating that the Australian male character was formed by the experiences of the men of the bush has been criticized by McQueen and others, most of them pointing out that his thesis was based on the experiences of only one group of men and that generalizations based on their experiences were simply unfounded.[7] Not only did Ward's thesis exclude women, blacks and other identifiable minority groups, it also failed to consider whether or not the working and social lives of large segments of the men he selected could be accommodated by it.

It would be easy enough to draw up a thesis about Australian women's role as mothers, to show how this has developed and changed over time and to trace its implications for other societal institutions, e.g. the family, schools, the church, and for male/female relationships. We could perhaps have then a theory which would explain much about women's exclusion from the concerns of historians – for mothering has been largely a private labour and historians concentrate on public enterprises – and which would provide a lot of information about how some women have lived their lives. But such a theory would have the same limitations as Ward's. It would single out one activity – mothering – which applies potentially to all women by virtue of their reproductive organs (and in this sense it has wider application than Ward's categories) but which in fact has never been either the sole activity of all women, or even adopted at all by substantial proportions of women.[8] This is only one example.

Other categories could be used which describe work usually undertaken by women, but the point remains the same. In selecting one or even several of these parts of the female stereotype, and trying to generalize about all women in terms of them, we are falling into the trap of *monofeminism*, of assuming that women are all the same. This is the kind of sexist categorization which the women's movement has rejected from men and from other kinds of social theory (psychology, sociology, etc.). Can radical feminists themselves perpetuate this? I do not think that we can, and this means that we must reconsider what women's history might be.

Initially we were led to ask how all women in the past had lived because of their complete neglect by conventional historians: this totalist repudiation seemed to require a totalist restoration. But perhaps the first approach is the more valid one, for the time being at least. That is, individuals and groups of women write their own history, searching the past for instances of other women in similar positions to those in which they now find themselves. Thus radical feminists can try to discover whether or not the suffrage movement contained pockets of radical revolt against sex-role prescriptions and the extent to which the protest of fifty years ago has affinities with what is happening now. It would also be possible to embark on specific projects, to try and find out for instance the extent to which women have fought against compulsory motherhood. This would entail looking at the extent of women's use of contraception, abortion, infanticide or chastity as methods of controlling their fertility. There are countless areas of study into which we could delve: co-operative and trade or craft union activity by women, sexual libertarianism, women's participation in paid employment, various kinds of political activities. Sometimes the study of a particular woman, if embarked upon with both a critical and sympathetic stance, could illuminate the dilemmas, conflicts and attainments of a wider group – this would apply especially to women who were involved in some form of public activity such as politics. The results of many such studies would be to unearth a vast amount of information about the activities and attainments of groups and individual women in the past, and would hopefully include some indication of what these women thought about their activities or about the constraints which curbed them from realizing their ambitions. But they would also provide historical validation for our current contention that women are a diverse and heterogenous sex who cannot be reduced to a single standard based on reproductive capability.

Once this pluralism was recognized it might then be possible to construct meaningful generalizations. Certainly, a legitimate field of study would be to look at how women have been objectified in the past, at the way in which sexist imperatives have both disguised this pluralism and forced a degree of conformity to what was considered to be 'women's sphere'. But such a study would have a critical ambit; it would not be simply duplicating the objectification it identified but would be pointing it out in order to prevent its perpetuation. And such small studies might also point the way to other kinds of generalizations which would permit a meaningful examination of, if not *all* women, at least large groups. For instance, it would be possible to conduct a large-scale theoretical and empirical study of female productivity and its relation to male (what is at present called national) productivity. This would include consideration of at least three kinds of productivity: (i) the social labour of housework – a form of productivity which now goes unrecognized and is not included in calculations of the GNP, (ii) the productivity of women employed in the paid workforce and (iii) the reproduction of the labour force, including the housework force, which, as Mariarosa Dalla Costa argues, is a form of productivity to which previous theoretical frameworks have given scant if any recognition.[9] If such a study proceeded without the material generated by the smaller sectional studies, it would be in danger of substituting sexist objectification for empirical data. Without detailed information about the extent of women's contribution to each of these three areas of productivity in the past, it would be very easy to simply assume that the vast majority of women were mostly engaged in (i) and (iii). The contribution of women who engaged only in (ii) could be neglected.

Such a study of productivity would most likely be conducted

within a Marxist framework* and would incorporate the assumptions about exploitation (surplus value) and alienation contained within that scheme. But even an exegesis of this scope could neglect important areas of alienation and oppression. In recent years contemporary Marxists have recognized the critical importance of superstructural factors such as ideology and culture to the maintenance of the capitalist system; this recognition has to be extended to the position of women and the multifarious ways in which sexism is perpetuated by these factors. It would be important to ask how the alienation of women is different from that of men, what precise role men play in exploiting women, and then to inquire into exactly how this complex network of oppression reinforces the traditional division of labour and the capitalist and bureaucratic mode of production. These questions have been considered in a generalized way by other feminists such as Millett, Firestone, Greer, Figes and Mitchell but it is now time to consider their insights in relation to particular facets of Australian historical development. But for those who wish to study the history of women in Australia, some caution is required. Many of us have been blithely ploughing into this field without realizing that in our eagerness to correct the complete neglect by historians we were unwittingly setting up a new model of oppression. It is not enough to try and fit women into the categories devised for the study of men's history: new questions have to be formulated and these will require the evolution of new concepts or at least the extensive revision of some of the old ones. Just as it can be rightly pointed out that many labour historians or those writing the history of the genocide of the Aboriginal race have objectified their subject matter and, in order to make their important points about

* That is a framework which sees the system of relations within the system of economic production as the crux of the whole socio-cultural system, exerting an over-riding influence on the way religious, political and family life are conducted and on the values which influence them. See also Shulamith Firestone, *The Dialectic of Sex*, Paladin, 1970, and Chapter 26 'Liberation – Reform or Revolution' for a critical development of this perspective. (*Editorial note*)

exploitation and oppression, have ignored the diversities and complexities of the groups they were writing about, we have to be careful not to perpetuate our own complaints by turning women into historical objects.

Notes

1. C. M. H. Clark, *A History of Australia*, Melbourne University Press, Melbourne, vol. 1, 1962, vol. 2, 1968.
Brian Fitzpatrick, *The British Empire in Australia*, Macmillan, London, 1939.
R. A. Gollan, *Radical and Working Class Politics*, Cheshire, Melbourne, 1960.
2. Leslie C. Jauncey, *The Story of Conscription in Australia*, Allen & Unwin, London, 1935.
3. Linguistic convention, forcing the use of 'he' and 'his', leads to the assumption that all historians are male. In fact women have been prominent in the writing of Australian history and two of the first works in the field were the work of women, Marion Phillips and Myra Willard. Women historians have however generally failed to defect from the trend of writing men's history.
4. L. L. Robson, *The Convict Settlers of Australia*, Melbourne University Press, Melbourne, 1965.
Michael Cannon, *Who's Master, Who's Man?* Nelson, Melbourne, 1971.
A. G. L. Shaw, *Convicts and the Colonies*, Faber, London, 1966.
R. B. Madgwick, *Immigrants into Eastern Australia, 1788–1851*, Longmans, London, 1937.
5. Penguin, Melbourne, 1970.
6. Hobart Women's Action Group, 'Sexism and Women's Liberation, or why do straight sisters sometimes cry when they are called lesbians?' *Refractory Girl*, no. 5, Spring 1974.
7. Russel Ward, *The Australian Legend*, Oxford University Press, Melbourne, 1958.
8. Larger numbers of women are marrying and having children now than at any time in our past and the illegitimacy rate has also increased, thus it can be deduced that in the past fewer women were mothers than is the case today. See W. D. Borrie, 'Recent trends and patterns of fertility in Australia', *Journal of Biosocial Science*, vol. 1 no. 1 (January 1969), pp. 57–70.
9. Mariarosa Dalla Costa, *Women and the Subversion of the Community*, Falling Wall Press, London, 1972.

PART TWO

The Status of Women in Australia Today

The Status of Women in Australia Today

This book owes its existence to the presence throughout Australia of discrimination against women on the basis of sex. But it is not enough to simply state that such a state of affairs exists. It must be demonstrated to be so, for society abounds with so many ideologies designed to preserve male privilege and to convince women that they are equal but different, that the majority of people believe the ideologies expounded by the establishment and dismiss accusations about sexual discrimination as nonsense. This section aims to look at the actual position of women in Australia. Do they have equal legal rights with males? Are employment opportunities the same? Will they be refused a job, not given permanency of occupation, or paid less simply because they are female? What happens to girls in the education system? Why do so few girls, compared to boys, go on to higher education? Why do so many more women than men come under the paternalistic care of social welfare departments? Can a society which is truly egalitarian have, for example, one law for women and another for men?

The first four chapters in Part 2 demonstrate clearly the secondary status of women in the major institutions of society: the economy, the law, education and social welfare. The position of women within the church is examined as part of a broader discussion of 'Religion, Socialization and the Role of Women' in Part 3. No single chapter attempts to provide an overall picture of the position of women in the family, but Chapters 10 and 11 examine particular aspects of the role of women in the family. The family is such an all-pervading institution that it comes up for discussion in most chapters. It is, after all, the institution in which men have defined it as natural for women to spend their lives and therefore much discrimination outside the family is based on the rationale that women outside the home are unnatural and unworthy of fair treatment. The last two chapters look at two groups which, while being subject to all the injustices described in the other chapters, are doubly discriminated against because they possess additional characteristics which are also targets for discrimination. Scarcity of information about these two groups has resulted in the discussion on Aborigines being limited to a case study and in the chapter on migrant women being a collection of notes and suggestions for research.

Four

Women and the Australian Labour Market: Problems and Policies

The Current Situation

Inequality of pay

At the time of writing there still remain in Australia situations where the legal minimum award rate of pay established by an industrial tribunal differs between males and females employed in identical circumstances performing *identical* work. For example, a determination of the Victorian Law Clerks Wages Board, which was operative from August 1974, specified that an adult male law clerk in his fifth year should receive a minimum salary of $122.75 per week, while an equivalent female should receive a minimum of only $115.35. The Hairdressers' Wages Board, in November 1974, specified identical minimum rates for the dressing of male hair, but where female hair was involved the minimum male rate was set at $10 per week above the female rate. Equal award rates are to be introduced for Victorian law clerks as from January 1975, and it can be expected that equal minimum rates will be introduced into other determinations of the Victorian Wages Boards following the recent ratification by the Australian Government of Convention 100 of the International Labour Office.

Such differences in *minimum* rates in no way oblige an employer to pay different *actual* rates, but their existence has certainly operated to the disadvantage of females. The 1972 Joint Orientation Committee of Monash University was to discover this when it recommended that female students employed as casual labour during orientation week activities be paid a special 'over-award' payment to bring their actual rate up to that minimum rate, which was of legal necessity being paid to male students who were performing *identical* duties. The Professorial Board endorsed the principle of 'equal pay for identical work' in July 1972 and referred it to the University Council for further action. There then followed a protracted debate, both within the Council and between its Staff and Finance committees. The Finance Committee agreed in November 1972 that it

> could see no financial grounds on which to support the proposal that overaward payments be made to female staff of some categories to lift their remuneration to be on a level with male staff similarly employed. Further it felt that the long term effect of such a move could be extremely damaging to the University's relations with the State Treasury. It resolved therefore, not to support the recommendation of the Staff Committee on overaward payments for this purpose.[1]

In the face of this opposition Staff Committee withdrew, with subsequent Council approval, its previous recommendation for such over-award payments. In April 1973 however Staff Committee resurrected this recommendation, only to find Finance Committee reaffirming its previous position and warning 'that the long term effect of such an action could be extremely damaging to the University's relations with governments'.[2]

In view of the Whitlam Government's proposed intention to assume the complete funding of Australian universities and its ratification of Convention 111 of the International Labour Office (ILO), the position which Finance Committee took would seem to be a more than somewhat pessimistic one. Under Article 2 of Convention 111, 'Each Member for which this Convention is in force undertakes to declare and pursue a national policy designed to promote, by methods appropriate to national conditions and practice, *equality of opportunity* and *treatment in respect of employment* and occupation, with a view to eliminating any discrimination in respect thereof' [emphasis added]. While Article 1(3) specifies that, 'For the purpose of this Convention the terms "employment" and "occupation" include access to vocational training, access to employment and to particular occupations and *terms and conditions of employment*' [emphasis added]. An Australian Government committed to the promotion of equality of treatment in respect of terms and conditions of employment could hardly penalize a university which had moved to implement such. Nevertheless Council accepted Finance Committee's advice and at its May meeting rejected the recommendation of Staff Committee for over-award payments, where necessary to equate the pay of males and females similarly employed. The matter was raised in Council yet again at its July 1973 meeting and referred, yet again, to Staff Committee. In October 1973 Staff Committee was informed that Pro-Vice-Chancellor Swan had been advised by the Acting Vice-Chancellors of La Trobe and Melbourne Universities and by the Vice-President of the Victorian Institute of Colleges that their institution would, in each case, be 'very concerned indeed if Monash were to make any unilateral move to institute equal pay ahead of determinations of appropriate arbitral authorities'. Staff Committee then reported back to the November 1973 meeting of Council that it saw the recently completed agreements between unions, employers and arbitral authorities, which involved the phasing in of equal pay by July 1975, as a satisfactory resolution of equal pay in the areas covered.

When we turn to consider those areas of employment where the workforce is entirely (or almost entirely) female, such as in secretarial work, so that no males are available for immediate and obvious comparison, we are faced with the difficulty of establishing what is in fact 'equal pay'. What all-male job is it that contains the same total job content, by way of skill, effort and responsibility, as a stenographer or typist, which can be used as a yardstick in determining what constitutes 'equal pay' for secretarial work? Convention 100 of the ILO, which was ratified by the Australian Government in December 1974, is framed to encompass such all-female areas of employment. It specifies that females should receive 'equal pay for work of equal value' – that pay should be determined by job content and conditions, and that sex *per se* should not be a reason for wage inequality. But assessing relative job content, whether it be by a formal process of job evaluation or the Australian variant of a 'work value' review, inevitably involves subjective judgement. Consequently there is scope for ingrained attitudes towards sexual role distinctions and sheer prejudice to manifest themselves in the assessment process. So, while the sexual duality of our labour market remains, we can inevitably expect disputation in the process of assessing what constitutes 'equal pay for work of equal value'.

The Melbourne Building Industry agreement of October 1974 established a rate of $155.50 a week for a carpenter and $166.07 for a plumber. At that time a trained nursing sister with a single certificate employed in a large Melbourne hospital was receiving $107.60 per week in her first year – rising to $126.90 in fifth and subsequent years. Such occupations are quite disparate and difficult to compare. Nevertheless, as an illustration of the potential for disputation in assessing what constitutes equal pay in all-female areas of employment, the reader might like to discuss with acquaintances of both sexes whether this could be construed as a situation of 'equal pay for work of equal value' – given the relative degrees of skill, effort, responsibility and working conditions involved.

In December 1972 the Australian Conciliation and Arbitration Commission (ACAC) adopted the principle of 'equal pay for work of equal value' and stated that 'adoption of the new principle requires that female rates be determined by work value comparisons without regard to the sex of the employees concerned'.[3] It went on to admit that, 'implementation of the new principle by arbitration will call for the exercise of the broad judgement which has characterized work value inquiries'.[4] It is important to realize however that, apart from the difficulties involved in assessing relative 'work value' as a basis for implementing the principle of equal pay for work of equal value, the current procedures of the ACAC are such that it cannot ensure full equality of remuneration between the sexes. This is because it merely lays down the minimum rate payable for a standard working week, which leaves the employer free to discriminate between the sexes with respect to 'over-award payments' and other conditions of service. Such a situation has been noted in Norway where most collective agreements negotiated between representatives of labour and management specify only minimum rates, with additional payments ('wage drift') being determined within individual enterprises. Investigations made by Norway's Equal Pay Council have found that wage drift has been much more substantial for males, thereby partially frustrating the implementation of the equal pay remuneration principle.[5]

Convention 100 of the ILO lays down, in Article 1(a), that

> For the purpose of this Convention the term 'remuneration' includes the ordinary, basic or minimum wage or salary and any additional emoluments whatsoever payable directly or indirectly, whether in cash or in kind, by the employer to the worker and arising out of the worker's employment.

Consequently if the Whitlam Government, which has very recently ratified this convention, is to ensure its full and faithful implementation it will need to modify the procedures of the ACAC. Alternatively it could seek the cooperation of the states in the enactment of direct legislation which specified that, where work of equal value had been assessed, an individual employer must not differentiate between the sexes with respect to the total emolument and benefits paid. It is worth noting that the United Kingdom Equal Pay Act of 1970 provides that a woman entitled to equal treatment under the legislation is able to claim any contractual right enjoyed by men, including the right of 'day release' for further education.

Inequality of employment opportunity

In the 1971 census 21 per cent of the female workforce was shown to be concentrated in a group of occupations where they represented in excess of 80 per cent of total employment. In contrast, less than 1 per cent of the male workforce was employed in this same group of occupations. Whereas, at that time, females represented 32 per cent of the total Australian workforce, not one female plumber, electrician, carpenter, cabinet maker, plasterer, or radio-television mechanic was recorded – although there *were* 2 axewomen-cum-timbergetters and 23 femalê panel-beaters. In the professional group women amounted to less than 7 per cent of the workforce in architecture, engineering, physics, geology, law and accountancy. The areas of heaviest female concentration were nursing, routine office work, catering and domestic work and machining in textiles and leather.

This phenomenon, whereby the labour market is divided in such a way that distinguishable groups of individuals (blacks and whites: males and females) are largely compartmentalized into separate job sets, is sometimes referred to as a 'dual labour market'. Just as a highly disproportionate number of the black population in the USA has traditionally been concentrated in the low wage, poor security jobs which provide little opportunity for advancement, the 'sexual duality' in the Australian labour market involves a disproportionate representation of females in unskilled, low-paid jobs.

As a very limited illustration of the penetration into the professional labour market which Australian women have made, compared with their sisters overseas, the Australian census of 1966 showed that 11 per cent of medical practitioners were female; elsewhere the figure was: England and Wales, 18 per cent; France, 13 per cent; Germany, 20 per cent; Israel, 24 per cent; USA, 7 per cent. In 1966 5 per cent of Australian dentists were female, which equalled the figure for England and Wales, and exceeded the USA figure of 2 per cent, but was well behind France and the Scandinavian countries where the figure ranged between 23 and 30 per cent.[6] By 1971 the Australian figure had crept up to 13 per cent for medical practitioners and 6 per cent for dentists.

However this unequal occupational distribution of the sexes does not *necessarily* demonstrate that females face inequality of employment opportunity, by being precluded from entry to skilled trades and professions. The sexual duality in the Australian labour market may instead be self-imposed – women may deliberately opt for those jobs which are unskilled, semi-skilled and/or which represent an extension into the market place of tasks which they traditionally perform within the household – nursing, cooking, sewing and cleaning.

An important reason for the preference which many females exhibit for this latter group of jobs lies in the conditioning process which takes place within many of the institutions of contemporary society, particularly the family, the school and the church. These institutions are discussed elsewhere in this volume and all we need to note here is that the traditional docile, submissive role for which most females are prepared, and which carries with it the domestic and child-care responsibilities, conflicts with a career in business or the professions. So a consequence of the conditioning process, as it operates to 'bestow' such home-based family responsibilities on females, is that many of them are devoid of any desire to choose a role within the workforce which involves long-term career commitments – or, indeed, any such role at all.

A related reason why the unequal occupational distribution of the sexes may reflect the preferences of female workers rather than employers, lies in the period of workforce absence which is virtually mandatory even for those women who have been less than totally subjugated by the conditioning process. Those females who do choose to combine marriage and domestic involvement with a career may, nevertheless, express a more confined range of job preferences than males, who are traditionally free of major domestic responsibility. This occurs because the lengthy withdrawal from the workforce which is still virtually inevitable for married females during the period of 'family formation' deters many of them from training for skilled trades and professions. The shorter and more interrupted nature of their working careers, as compared with men, provides women with less incentive to undertake the costly and lengthy preparation for such occupations and diverts them instead into jobs lower down the skill spectrum.

Part of the responsibility for the sexual duality of the Australian labour market, however, rests with *employers* – in many cases a clear, sometimes exclusive, preference in employment is exhibited for one or other sex. The obvious overt demonstration of this preference is to be found in the employment columns of almost every Australian newspaper, and even where the sexual qualification of the desired employee is not specified in advertisements the employer frequently has a firm conviction about the sex of the person he (or she) will accept to fill a vacancy. The various bases from which these preferences derive, and the way they act to limit the labour market access of females, is the subject of the following section.

The Sources of Sexual Discrimination in the Labour Market

The profit motive

One sexual characteristic, from which a preference for male labour derives, is the alleged higher turnover and absentee rates of female employees. On this basis it is argued that the disinclination of businessmen to employ females in a wide range of jobs is the outcome of rational, cost-minimizing behaviour rather than sheer prejudice. To the extent that on-the-job training and experience are an important element in worker education, so that familiarity with the specific procedures of a particular work-place are significantly correlated with worker performance, businessmen can be expected to prefer applicants who possess the superficial characteristics of more stable employment groups. The profit motive acts as a deterrent to the employment of workers who might be expected to resign after a period of fully efficient performance, which is insufficient for the employer to recoup the training costs which he has borne. There is also an element of 'worker subsidy' involved during the period when full rates might be paid to a worker who is in the process of acquiring maximum efficiency through the process of on-the-job experience. If a group of workers which is readily identifiable by some superficial characteristic, such as race, sex, accent or educational background, exhibits *on average* a higher job-turnover rate, then individual members of that group will be disadvantaged in seeking employment which involves a significant quantity of knowledge specific to that work-place. Similarly, in jobs where regularity in attendance is important to the efficiency of an enterprise, the individual members of any readily recognizable group, which records *on average* higher absentee rates, will face barriers which reflect the application of cost-minimization principles rather than sheer prejudice.

So much for assertions and theoretical analysis – what of the facts? The Australian Bureau of Census and Statistics conducts, each March, a sample survey of labour turnover and publishes the results for broad classes of industry. These surveys do show that the overall 'voluntary separation rate' (the ratio of employees leaving employment at their own initiative to total employment) of females is higher than that of males in almost all cases.

Table 1

Voluntary Separation Rates of Manual Workers – Sample Survey for the Month of March

	1971		1972		1973	
Industry Group	Female	Male	Female	Male	Female	Male
Engineering & Vehicles	5.4	5.7	3.9	3.6	6.4	5.8
Textile	7.2	4.9 (Textile and Clothing combined)	5.5	4.1 (Textile and Clothing combined)	8.4	6.2 (Textile and Clothing combined)
Clothing	5.1		4.7		5.8	
Paper and Printing	5.5	3.2	5.1	1.7	5.3	3.4
Chemicals and Oil Refining	5.5	4.0	4.8	2.5	5.2	5.7

Source: Australian Bureau of Census and Statistics, *Labour Turnover*, March 1972 and March 1973.

Only in Engineering and Vehicles for 1971, and in Chemicals and Oil Refining for 1973 was the female rate lower than the male rate. But such crude overall data, which lump together all manual workers regardless of age, occupation, or skill level, conceal those very factors which overseas research has shown to bear a closer relationship to turnover than sex does. This point was demonstrated in research undertaken at the request of the United States Presidential Commission on the Status of Women. Turnover patterns of Federal employees were investigated in detail by the Civil Service Commission and it was reported that

In the Civil Service Commission study, women's quit rates, overall, were found to be between two-and-a-half and three times those of men. This is because women predominate in younger age groups and low-paid occupations, where turnover is higher for both men and women. When comparisons were made by age groups, salary levels, and occupations, it appeared that women's rates, while still higher, are much closer to men's: the loss of employees by turnover decreases significantly with increasing grade level. Women in the middle-age ranges are a more stable group than either men or women under twenty-five; women who enter the labour market in their forties show very low turnover rates compared with other women.[7]

When the United States Civil Service Commission investigated absentee rates for Federal employees a similar story emerged – the difference between the male and female rates diminished when the crude overall data were broken down and comparisons made between men and women of similar age or salary level.[8]

Research by government agencies in Britain has produced similar findings – first, that the real difference between the sexes in turnover and absentee rates has been much exaggerated in popular mythology, and second, that much of the difference in the overall rates is the outcome of the disproportionate representation of females in jobs which are low in skill, status and responsibility, and high in monotony.[9]

A full-scale investigation of absenteeism and voluntary separation, in Australia, which classified the rates by skill, age, occupation etc., as well as by sex, would be extremely valuable to the feminist cause. It is reasonable to expect that the results would mirror those obtained overseas. If so, it would provide a valuable basis for challenging those employers who argue that their reluctance, or refusal, to hire females is the outcome of an employment policy which is motivated by nothing other than the rational quest for cost-minimization. A detailed examination of absentee and turnover rates to establish the actual, as opposed to the *alleged*, intersexual difference in these rates, and therefore in employment costs, should be an important priority if a full-scale inquiry into sexism ever does eventuate in Australia.

It is certainly an area of inquiry which should be seriously considered either by the current Royal Commission into Human Relations and/or by the proposed Victorian inquiry into the factors preventing equal opportunity for women.

Even in those circumstances where a significant difference in *average* turnover and/or absentee rates, of males and females within some specific workforce group, does exist to provide a cost-based rationale for preferring males, the implementation of a crude sexual preference does involve discrimination against that category of women whose career pattern is comparable to men's. The difficulty which employers face in establishing which of their female job applicants come within this 'career-oriented' category induces them to make their employment decisions on the basis of the *average* performance of these two workforce groups readily distinguishable by their sexual characteristics. In applying such a stereotyped view to all members of a group, who are identifiable by common superficial characteristics, employers are engaged in a form of discriminatory action which economists have termed 'statistical discrimination'.[10]

Prejudice

An additional source of sexual discrimination in the labour market is sheer prejudice. Females experience difficulty in entering some fields of employment for reasons which are unrelated to any objective difference in their own overall workforce performance. Just as a black skin is, in itself, sufficient to preclude a person from certain areas of employment in South Africa, physical characteristics which have nothing to do with an individual's own productive contribution preclude females from parts of the Australian labour market. The total absence of females in crafts such as carpentry, plumbing, and electrical fitting, along with their minimal representation in professions such as architecture, law, and accountancy, *may* be the outcome solely of female employment preferences. Alternatively, if this is not so, it *may* be that any responsibility which employers bear for the male-dominance of these crafts and professions derives solely from their rational cost-minimizing pursuits in the face of disadvantageous workforce performance by female employees. But it might also be the consequence, at least in part, of prejudice – females encountering barriers to employment because of their sex *per se*. It would require an extremely elastic imagination to accept that no Australian female wishes to enter the crafts listed above, or to drive a Melbourne tram, for that matter. Likewise it is difficult to believe that the potential workforce performance of females appears so universally inferior relative to males in the craft area, that any responsibility which employers have for the total absence of females could be rationalized away completely in cost-minimizing terms. In the professional and senior managerial area it would be equally difficult to credit that female preference patterns, allied with cost-minimizing reactions by businessmen to female workforce performance, could between them provide a complete explanation for the failure of females to make any significant inroads elsewhere than in nursing, teaching, librarianship, social work, professional medical work (such as pharmacy and physiotherapy) and the arts.

An indication of the way in which general community prejudices can operate to bar females from various employments is contained in a volume published by the National Manpower Council in the United States of America. As part of its study of 'Womanpower' the Council organized several conferences of employers to obtain first-hand information on their employment problems and policies. The findings are of an impressionistic rather than a definitive nature, but nevertheless they illustrate the difficulties females can face in the labour market:

Many employers reported that the hiring of women is frequently governed by traditional attitudes which establish what jobs are suitable for them. These traditional attitudes, it was emphasized, are operative among workers, as well as at the management level. The distinction between 'men's' and 'women's' jobs appears to be particularly sharp in certain manufacturing fields, and in professional, service, and sales work, jobs are often closed to women because it is taken for granted that they should be held by men. It is believed that, if women are placed in such jobs, they are likely to produce negative reactions not only among male supervisors, fellow employees, and customers, but also in the public at large.[11]

A detailed investigation of the nature, extent, and operation of sexual prejudice in the Australian labour market would be an essential component of any wide-ranging Australian inquiry into sexism. When an employer exhibits reluctance or outright refusal to hire females, for reasons other than inferiority in their own overall workforce performance, it may be his own prejudice to which he is giving vent, or he may be acting as an agent for prejudiced male employees, trade unions and/or customers. Where the individual who is implementing his own prejudice in the employment decision is an owner of the business and a recipient of residual profit, such behaviour implies that he is prepared to forego the objective of profit-maximization in order to avoid female employees – in other words, he is personally prepared to pay a price in return for the satisfaction which the application of his prejudice provides. In many situations, however, the person making the employment decision is a salaried employee, in which case the application of his prejudice is costless to him personally.

In those cases where the employer's avoidance of female labour is solely in response to the prejudice of male employees and/or trade unions, such behaviour is quite compatible with the application of profit-maximizing principles. For even where the overall workforce performance of individual males and females is identical, a businessman who is devoid of prejudice himself, but who seeks maximum profits, will avoid or minimize female employment if he feels that male reaction and antagonism at having to work with them would be such that the productivity of the enterprise as a whole could be impaired. Likewise if consumers react unfavourably to the presence of female labour in situations where direct contact between customers and employees is involved, the profit maximizer, who is inevitably concerned to protect his sales volume, will discriminate against females regardless of any lack of prejudice on his own part.

Thus, that discrimination in employment against females which occurs as a result of pure prejudice can in some cases arise as a direct outcome of the application of profit-maximizing principles, whilst in other cases it operates in direct contravention to that objective; although any profit sacrifice involved may not necessarily be borne by the individual who is implementing his own personal prejudice in the employment decision.

A consequence of discrimination

This variety of forces, which creates barriers to females in wide areas of the labour market, has important implications for their relative scarcity in those areas where they are acceptable. While females are limited to a relatively narrow range of jobs, males are not similarly affected, with few, if any, jobs being closed to them. Men *can* become nurses if they so choose, and also air-hostesses for that matter, in which case they are relabelled as 'stewards'. This differential restriction on workforce access means that females are 'overcrowded' in those limited areas where they are acceptable, that is, they are in *relatively* abundant supply. This weakens their 'market' or 'economic' power, and in turn their bargaining power as individuals or as collective groups in trade unions, with the outcome being depressed levels of earnings. The limited alternative employment prospects of females enable their retention in many traditional female jobs at rates of pay which would be inadequate to attract male workers, who have access to virtually the whole spectrum of employment. Thus it is in these discriminatory employment practices that the fundamental source of sexual wage inequality lies.

Policies to Facilitate Sexual Equality in the Labour Market

Because discrimination in employment derives from a variety of sources it is necessary to apply a range of policies if the sexual duality in the Australian labour market is to be successfully eliminated. In fact it would be desirable to implement such policies simultaneously on an integrated basis, as they could be expected to have a reinforcing effect. In terms of policy impact it is a situation where it is likely that the whole would be greater than the sum of the parts.

Equality within the household

The consequences of the traditional home-based, wife-cum-mother responsibilities which are 'bestowed' on females have been discussed above. To the extent that the imposition of this role does produce differential job turnover and absentee rates between the sexes, employers will express a cost-based preference for male labour. In addition, the virtual inevitable identification of this domestic role with the female sex leaves many women devoid of any desire for long term workforce commitment; whilst others are discouraged from entering those occupations which require lengthy training and experience, because of the shorter and more interrupted nature of their career as compared with men. It follows therefore that full sexual equality in the labour market can only be achieved if this differential role within the domestic/family arena is eliminated. Only when males as a group adopt a completely equal role in the household, including initial child care during the period of 'family formation', can females as a group attain full equality in the labour market. In such an eventuality, with the likelihood of either sex interrupting their work career to perform the child-care function, the employer would be equally at risk in investing in on-the-job training and experience for either females or males. In which case one source of sexual discrimination in employment would be removed. Also, with the removal of the current asymmetrical career pattern of the sexes, by this re-allocation of household duties, females would no longer face a relative disincentive in preparing for a professional, craft, or managerial career.

The work which is undertaken within society can be divided into a simple dichotomy: both categories involve effort, physical and mental; both categories provide goods and services which are of benefit to the consumer. But one category is performed primarily within the household, and the goods and services so produced are consumed within that same unit. As a consequence it does not involve any exchange in the market-place, is not 'priced' in the customary fashion through the interaction of supply and demand, and is not included in the calculation of the 'almighty' Gross National Product. This category of work can be designated as 'non-market' work. The other category of work is that which is performed on a specialized basis in factories, offices, mines, laboratories, building sites, etc. This work is priced in the market-place and, in return for their efforts, the participants receive a monetary reward which they can exchange for a variety of goods and services produced in such workplaces. This half of the dichotomy can be designated as 'market' work. In Australian society it is females who predominate in the 'non-market' work and males who predominate in the 'market' work: it is the abolition of this distinction which is being advocated here.

What is implied in the foregoing proposal is that, of any group which did opt for a lifetime entirely of 'non-market' work, half might be males rather than close to zero as at present. So that, in those households where the market/non-market activities remained specialized between the partners, the conventional work roles would be reversed in 50 per cent of households. This would naturally necessitate some sorting process in the marriage market (legalized and solemnized or 'de facto') to achieve the appropriate pairing (permanent or temporary), but this would add but one dimension to an already multi-dimensional selection process. On the other hand, in those households in which both partners engage in market activity to an approximately equal extent (dual-career families), the implication is that each partner should assume a fully equal role in the various 'non-market' functions involved in domestic and child-care responsibilities.

The achievement of such a change in attitudes and work role distinctions is one which is central and fundamental to the feminist movement, and its labour market implications have been well captured by Sandell –

> Perhaps the greatest step women can take toward achieving equal opportunity in the labour market is to achieve real equality in the household ... to ignore the labour market implications of the differences in household behaviour that society has forced upon men and women would be ... naive. Only when expected labour market behaviour is the same for both sexes could we expect occupational and wage differences between males and females to disappear.[12]

If equality within the household is a necessary prerequisite to equality in the labour market, what policy measures might be applied to achieve such an end? What measures might help first to *encourage*, and second to *enable* males as a group to accept equal involvement in domestic work? Obviously the objective involved here is essentially a long-term one with its fundamental basis in the educational/conditioning process as it takes place in the family, the school, and other social institutions. There are, however, some measures which could appropriately set the process in motion. To *encourage* males to assume their full share of household work, compulsory childcraft and domestic science courses for both sexes could be introduced into the curriculum of all schools at the appropriate age levels. Such courses have been obligatory in Swedish comprehensive schools for several years.[13] The obvious counterpart to such action would be the removal of any barriers and relative discouragement which female students encounter in the selection of traditionally 'male' subjects. To aid in the development of symmetrical work roles between the sexes, the taxation and social security system should be restructured so that the same benefits, credits, deductions, etc., are available to any individual, regardless of sex, who opts for a full-time 'non-market' function. For policies which will *enable* males to play a full and equal role in the non-market activity of dual career families it is possible again to turn to Swedish experience. In the Swedish civil service all employees, whether male or female, have the right to fifteen days absentee leave per annum to care for sick children.[14] Also there has been discussion of the proposition that males should be entitled to leave of absence to perform the initial child-care function after birth.[15] A statutory entitlement to male post-pregnancy leave would facilitate the separation of the child-*rearing* function from the child-*bearing* function. While the latter is inevitably a female function, the former can quite properly be performed by either sex. Therefore, for those dual-career families who decide that one partner interrupt their workforce participation to perform the child-care function during the period of 'family formation', the existence of this provision would facilitate males opting to undertake such a responsibility.

An additional range of policies could be applied to aid the functioning of dual-career families. These policies would facilitate the sharing of 'market' and 'non-market' work by the partners, and would enable those dual-career families who so chose to minimize the workforce interruption of both partners – especially during the period of 'family formation'. In the first place, there are possible re-arrangements at the work-place which minimize the time period when husband and wife were simultaneously absent from the household. This includes the provision for a four-day week, and for more flexibility in working hours – both with respect to timing and amount. Such flexibility is currently offered to both sexes in some West European work-places. There may be many families who would prefer a total 'market work week' of something like sixty hours, shared equally between the partners, rather than one of forty or more, performed entirely by one partner. It is most desirable that such families have the opportunity to exercise such a preference. There should also be provision to ensure that husband and wife can take their annual and long service leave simultaneously. Secondly, there are various institutional arrangements which could be introduced to enable dual-career families to purchase more readily services which are usually performed as 'non-market' work in the household. The most obvious facility in this category is an adequate range of child-care services to meet the variety of needs which working parents have. A more wide-ranging and innovatory measure, however, would be the provision of Swedish-type 'service houses'. These are housing complexes which contain individual living units for each family, along with a built-in child-minding centre which may operate on an around-the-clock basis seven days per week. Also provided, within the complex, are cleaning and laundry facilities, restaurants, shops, and a reception desk to cope with messages and deliveries. There are several such centres in Stockholm and Gothenburg.[16]

Besides such institutional changes, there needs to be a change in social attitudes and a greater tolerance of alternative life styles. Political and Economic Planning (PEP), in its study of British dual-career families, found that such tolerance was often lacking:

It is important that society, while being reasonably critical of patterns that are new and untried, should accept that breakaways can be constructive and should be given their chance. The histories of PEP's dual-career families suggest that too often this has not been the case. Families operating a new pattern which has in fact turned out to be highly successful for people in their particular circumstances, and applicable to many others besides themselves, have found themselves subject to criticism and social pressures based, as the case histories show, on failure by the critics to take the trouble to enquire into and understand the new pattern before criticizing it. No one should be expected to accept his (or her) neighbour's pattern of family living as ideal, or as applicable to himself, simply on his neighbour's word. But neither is it helpful to the future development of family life, in a world where variety and adaptation to individual circumstances are likely to be the rule, if new and perhaps creative variations are shot down before their nature and real implications are understood.[17]

Transferring the costs of job turnover

The policies outlined in the foregoing section could only be expected to effect a gradual change in society, and not even the most optimistic feminist would anticipate a dramatic overnight reallocation of 'non-market' work to males. Consequently, in the short run at least, the basis for 'statistical discrimination' will still exist, and this calls for an additional policy initiative to ensure that those females, who are *currently* committed to a full-time career with no greater incidence of interruption than the average male, are not disadvantaged by a higher *average* job turnover rate for females in general.

In effect, what is needed are measures which would transfer any costs of job turnover from the employer to the employee, or to society at large. If this could be achieved the profit motive would no longer discourage employers from selecting from distinguishable workforce groups which display, on average, higher job turnover rates.

The most viable solution would be for the Australian Government to accept responsibility for the cost of on-the-job training, and reimburse employers for the expenditure involved, including any wage payments made with government agreement during the period when employees are training rather than producing. In recent years the Australian Government has been assuming an increasing financial responsibility for that category of education which takes place in institutions such as Universities and Colleges of Advanced Education. With the growing concern about redundancy and adaptability in the workforce it has, even more recently, begun to display interest in this alternative category of education which takes place at the workplace. Two schemes have been introduced in which the Australian Government does accept *some* responsibility for the costs of on-the-job training. Firstly, there is the National Apprenticeship Assistance Scheme which provides employers with reimbursement for a proportion of the payroll costs of apprentices, where they equal 25 per cent or more of tradesmen. Secondly, there is the National Employment and Training System (NEAT). Under this system employers, who are providing approved on-the-job training, receive a subsidy equal to 50 per cent of the average adult male award wage for the first half of each employee's training period and 25 per cent thereafter. For persons under twenty-one the percentage is somewhat reduced. A scheme of the NEAT type on even more extensive and generous lines, which made the reimbursement conditional upon some minimum proportion of female employees and/or trainees, would do much to remove the basis for statistical discrimination in the Australian labour market.

An attack on prejudice

To the extent that prejudice on the part of consumers, entrepreneurs, male employees, and/or trade unions creates barriers to female employment, which are unrelated to any objective difference in their own overall workforce performance, the foregoing 'cost-oriented' policies will be insufficient to eliminate the sexual duality in the Australian labour market. Therefore there is need for an additional policy initiative to persuade male employees that they should accept females as complete equals in the workplace, who would frequently occupy supervisory roles over them; to persuade consumers that they should accept a service without regard to the sex of the person performing it; to persuade some trade unions that the job security of their male members can be safeguarded by more positive and equitable methods than the exclusion of females; and to persuade employers that, in the context of the foregoing policies to minimize any cost differential in the employment of the sexes, females should be denied neither appointment nor promotion because of their sex *per se*.

To achieve such a change in social attitudes would be a difficult and lengthy task, which would have to be based fundamentally in the educational process. It is necessary that the community at large recognize the injustice involved where females are denied access to various jobs solely because of physical characteristics which have nothing to do with work performance. The various measures aimed at achieving greater sexual equality in domestic or 'non-market' work, which were outlined above, should help to pave the way for such a change in attitudes. But additional publicity would be necessary to bring to the awareness of those, who have been long conditioned by the mores of our sexist society, that the expression of such preferences, whether it be in the role of employee, unionist, consumer or employer, demonstrates a form of prejudice which is no more desirable than racial or religious prejudice. A wide-ranging government-sponsored, nation-wide inquiry into sexism, such as those held in Canada and the United States of America in the 1960s, could help to expose such discrimination for what it is, and stimulate people to rethink the work role dichotomy which is foisted on the sexes from the crib. Hopefully, both the Royal Commission into Human Relations and the proposed Victorian inquiry into sexual inequality will make some contribution in this direction. An alternative approach would be the type of semi-official study which was undertaken in Britain in recent years by Political and Economic Planning in collaboration with the Tavistock Institute. This work was sponsored by the Leverhulme Trust and resulted in several valuable volumes.[18]

At the very least, an intensive government educational campaign, directed at this variety of discriminatory groups, is needed as part of an overall policy package aimed at the creation of full sexual equality of opportunity in employment and occupation. This latter procedure is of special relevance in view of the Whitlam Government's ratification of Convention 111 of the ILO in mid-1973. Article 2 of this Convention, which specifies the basic obligation of ratifying governments, was quoted earlier in this chapter. In their pursuit of equality of employment opportunity, such governments are required, under Article 3(b) 'to enact such legislation and to *promote such educational programmes* as may be calculated to secure the acceptance and observance of the policy'. In his Ministerial Statement in May 1973, when he announced the Government's decision to ratify Convention 111, Mr Cameron stressed this educational aspect and gave notice of the Government's intention to undertake a wide-ranging educational programme.[19] It is to be hoped that this programme is executed with diligence and persistence – going, in appropriate format, to all educational institutions and the whole range of the media. The aim should be to provoke people of all ages to re-examine their preconceptions about the appropriate role of males and females – to consider why they take it as self evident that females should dominate in child-care and domestic work – to consider why they do not, and should not encounter females as plumbers, engineers, directors, or first secretaries in government departments. Mr Cameron reported that all the state Ministers of Labour had agreed to co-operate in the ratification of this Convention and to the proposed programme of action. Such agreement is important because, in our federal system, the state governments have an important complementary role to play in any concerted attack on prejudice.

Whilst such educational measures are a fundamental requirement in getting at the root cause of prejudice their impact can only be gradual; therefore an additional set of policies is desirable to provide some modicum of relief in the short term. We must look to the interests of the current generation of female workers as well as those of future generations. Britain and the United States of America are two countries which have recognized that measures of a more direct nature, and with a more immediate impact, can be a useful complement to educational action. Such measures include legislative action to make it an unlawful practice to specify a required or preferred sex in advertisements offering employment, or to discriminate between the sexes in appointment and promotion. Title Seven of the United States Civil Rights Act of 1964 outlawed such practices, amongst others, and established an Equal Employment Opportunity Commission (EEOC) to administer the new law and pursue the elimination of the specified discriminatory employment practices. Upon receipt of a written complaint that an unlawful employment practice has been perpetrated the EEOC is required to investigate the circumstances, and if there is reasonable cause to believe an infringement has occurred, it endeavours to eliminate the practice by conciliation and persuasion. If this attempt to achieve voluntary compliance is unsuccessful the complainant may subsequently take the matter before a civil court, which has power to enjoin the unlawful employment practice and to order reinstatement or hiring of employees, with or without backpay.

In September 1973 the British Government published a 'Consultative Document' titled *Equal Opportunity for Men and Women* which outlined the legislation which that Government proposed to introduce to deal with sexual discrimination and the prejudiced attitudes which give rise to it. The measures cited therein bear a close resemblance to those contained in Title Seven of the 1964 Civil Rights Act. The legislation which is proposed would make it an unlawful act to specify a single sex in advertisements, or to discriminate in employment on the grounds of sex; with non-discrimination defined to include equality of treatment with respect to recruitment, training, promotion, lay-offs, and access to overtime and shift work. An Equal Opportunities Commission is proposed with the power and responsibility to conduct wide-ranging inquiries into the current state of sex discrimination, to publish reports providing policy advice for the Government, and to conduct educational programmes aimed at encouraging those changes in public attitudes which are necessary if women are to have full equality of opportunity with men. Individuals who consider they have been discriminated against within the terms of the legislation will be able to seek redress via the existing British network of industrial tribunals. It is suggested that a complaint would be first considered by the Conciliation Officers (Tribunal) of the Department of Employment, which would attempt to promote a voluntary settlement through the medium of conciliation. Where this technique failed the complainant would have access to a local industrial tribunal which had the power to make an order determining the rights of the parties and to recommend a course of action and/or to award compensation.

In September 1974 the Wilson Government, which had replaced the preceding Heath Government in February 1974, published a White Paper titled *Equality for Women* (CMND. 5724). It also recognized that legislation is a necessary but insufficient precondition for an efficient equal opportunity policy. In this White Paper various modifications to the proposals contained in the preceding Consultative Document are mooted, with the objective of widening the scope and strengthening the enforcement of anti-discrimination legislation. In particular it is proposed that the Equal Opportunities Commission would play a major role in the enforcement of equal opportunities legislation, and that it would have the power to serve a non-discrimination notice requiring the recipient to modify his behaviour.

Such action and proposed action by two countries with which we have a reasonably close cultural affinity carries clear implications for Australian policy towards sexism in the labour market. It suggests that, at the very least, we should give serious consideration to the implementation of such direct measures as complementary action to an educational programme. Mr Cameron did make reference to legislative action and penal sanctions in his Ministerial Statement in May 1973, but he noted that these alone would be inadequate, and that legislation would involve delay because of the need for complementary Commonwealth and State action. Therefore he laid his emphasis on the educational programme noted above, and on a conciliatory approach to those practising discriminatory activities: 'There will be no attempt to prosecute or bludgeon the persons who commit the offences into submission; they will simply have pointed out to them the enormity of the thing ...'[20] The procedure is that complaints about discriminatory employment practices will first be investigated by a secretariat located within the Department of Labour, and officers of that secretariat will attempt to resolve any breach of the Convention by conciliation and persuasion. If their efforts prove unsuccessful the matter is passed to a tripartite State committee, with reference on to a tripartite National Committee on Discrimination in Employment in the event of a further failure. But, where all three stages of conciliation fail, there is currently no provision for an ultimate reference to a civil court or industrial tribunal with the power to enjoin a discriminatory employment practice – as exists in the United States of America and as is proposed in Britain. However when Mr Cameron placed his emphasis on education and conciliation he did warn that '... this does not preclude legislation either on a particular matter or generally at a later stage should the need for such action become evident. Should that need arise, my Government will not hesitate to legislate to prevent the discrimination'.[21] In the light of this latter statement it is to be hoped that officers of the Department of Labour and the National Committee on Discrimination in Employment will keep a close watch on the relative degree of success which Britain and Australia experience in breaking down discriminatory employment practices in the coming months and years. The almost simultaneous introduction of anti-discriminatory employment policies in these two countries – one with, and one without legislative action – will provide an opportunity to assess the impact which an ultimate threat of legal sanctions may have.

Whilst the specification of various unlawful employment practices, with enforcement via the courts and penal sanctions, is certainly not a policy in itself, it does have a useful place as part of an overall and integrated policy package of the type being proposed in this paper. At the very least, legislation outlawing various long-standing discriminatory practices would jolt community attitudes and force people to reconsider the 'conventional unwisdom' about the appropriate work roles of the sexes. It is, in fact, the firmly expressed view of both major British political parties that legislative action can *contribute* to the ending of sexual discrimination in the labour market. Commenting upon the reports of two Select Committees which had been set up in the House of Lords and the House of Commons, the 1973 Heath Government concluded

All this finally convinced the Government that legislation was necessary and likely to be effective in remedying certain kinds of sex discrimination.

Both Select Committees were of the opinion that legislation was now necessary to secure reform. But while proposing legislation as 'at least a partial remedy for discrimination on the grounds of sex' the House of Lords Select Committee reported: 'Nobody believes that legislation by itself can eradicate over-night a whole range of attitudes which are rooted in custom and are, for that very reason, often unchallenged because unrecognized. But if the law cannot change attitudes over-night it can, and does, effect change slowly.[22]

This accords with the view expressed by the ILO Committee of Experts on the Application of Conventions and Recommendations, in its report to the fifty-sixth session of the International Labour Conference in 1971:

Discrimination based on sex is another form of discrimination whose elimination also calls for constant attention and the development of a series of positive measures in various fields. One view which is often implicit in governments' reports is that such discrimination as may exist in this respect may be ascribed to sociological factors which must be left to evolve. Nevertheless, the efforts that have been made in some countries show that it is possible in the end to secure acceptance of the fact that many of the distinctions between the sexes which it has become customary to accept as 'normal' are really discriminatory; and there is a risk that sociological practices and circumstances may not evolve in the desired direction unless specific efforts are made with this end in view.[23]

Whilst neither sole nor principal reliance should be placed on legislative action, it is one of those specific, positive measures which will help to provoke the more rapid evolution of sociological practices.

An alternative and somewhat less Draconian form of sanction to stimulate the removal of discriminatory employment practices is contained in the Recommendation which accompanies ILO Convention 111, and has been introduced by Executive Order in the United States of America. This is to deny government contracts to firms which are in breech of any of the specified non-discriminatory provisions. Mr Cameron indicated in his Ministerial Statement that the possibility of this procedure being introduced in Australia was under examination, and certainly it would not pose the difficulties which court procedures and penal sanctions would. This is because it is a policy which can be introduced by administrative decree rather than legislation, and because action by the Australian Government alone would have a substantial impact. This is not to say that complementary action by State Governments would not be desirable – rather that action by the Australian Government alone would not be an empty gesture.

In Conclusion

A concerted and persistent government initiative, involving action on a broad front, is needed if the sexual duality in the Australian labour market is to be eliminated, so that both sexes can have full and equal access to all areas of 'market' and 'non-market' work. A co-ordinated approach involving a package of educational, economic, personnel, industrial, social, and legislative policy is needed if such an end is to be achieved. Only when there is full equality within the household, and only when customers, employers, trade unions, and employees (of both sexes in each case) view the participants in the labour market as a single group of human beings, rather than as representatives of separate sex groups to which some preference attaches, will females cease being 'overcrowded' into a relatively narrow range of occupations. Only then will they cease being at the relative market and bargaining disadvantage which is the fundamental source of sexual wage inequality.

The object of breaking down both prejudice in the labour market, and the unequal distribution of market and non-market work between the sexes, is to provide greater freedom of choice than exists currently – to enable those females who wish a full-time, uninterrupted career in the labour market to exercise such a preference with the same ease that a male does. The object is *not* to coerce those females who are content with a full-time 'non-market' role into entering the labour market. But just as they should have the right to exercise their preference, the alternative category of 'career-oriented' females should be perfectly free to opt for a full-time uninterrupted market role. If we can achieve such a freedom we will have created a better society for men and women – and for their children.

Editor's Note

This chapter has clearly outlined changes within the economic system which hopefully would bring about greater equality for women. However, these changes are envisaged within the present capitalist mode of production. It is questionable whether this is at all feasible, for as Sheila Rowbotham argues:

> The inequality of women at work is built into the structure of capitalist production and the division of labour in industry and in the family. The equality of women to men, even the equal *exploitation* of women in capitalism, would require such fundamental changes in work and at home that it is very hard to imagine how they could be effected while capitalism survives.
>
> Sheila Rowbotham, *Woman's Consciousness, Man's World**

This problem is also taken up in Chapter 26.

Notes

1. Minutes of Meeting, Finance Committee, Monash University Council, 3/11/1972.
2. Ibid. 4/5/1973.

* Penguin Books, 1973, p.121.

3. 'National Wage and Equal Pay Cases 1972: Reasons for Decision', *Industrial Information Bulletin*, vol.27, no.12, December 1972, p.2453.
4. Ibid.
5. Kari Vangsnes, 'Equal Pay in Norway', *International Labour Review*, vol.103, no.4, April 1971, p.385.
6. Janice N. Hedges, 'Women Workers and Manpower Demands in the 1970s', *Monthly Labor Review*, June 1970.
7. Margaret Mead and Frances B. Kaplan, *American Women: The Report of the President's Commission on the Status of Women*, Scribner, New York, 1965, p.52.
8. Nona Glazer-Malbin and Helen Youngelson Walhrir, (eds) *Woman in a Man-Made World*, Rand McNally, Chicago, 1972, p.270.
9. C. A. Larsen, 'Equal Pay for Women in the United Kingdom', *International Labour Review*, vol. 103, no.1, January 1971, pp.10–11.
10. Michael Piore, 'The Dual Labor Market: Theory and Implications', in David M. Gordon, (ed.) *Problems in Political Economy: An Urban Perspective*, D. C. Heath, Lexington, 1971.
11. National Manpower Council, *Womanpower*, Columbia University Press, New York, 1957, pp.88–9.
12. Steven H. Sandell, 'What Economic Equality for Women Requires: Discussion', *American Economic Review*, vol.62, no.2, May 1972, p.176.
13. *Sweden Today*, 'The Status of Women in Sweden: Report to the United Nations 1968', The Swedish Institute, Stockholm, p.34.
14. Anna-Greta Leijon, *Swedish Women – Swedish Men*, The Swedish Institute, Stockholm, 1968, p.55. A similar provision exists in the *Family Code* of the German Democratic Republic – M. Fogarty, with Rhonda and Robert Rapoport, *Women and Top Jobs: The Next Move*, P.E.P., London, 1972, p.54.
15. 'The Status of Women in Sweden . . .', p.6.
16. Ibid., p.63.
17. *Women and Top Jobs*, pp.41–2.
18. M. P. Fogarty (ed.), *Women in Top Jobs*, Allen and Unwin, London, 1971. M. P. Fogarty, Rhonda and Robert Rapoport, *Sex, Career and Family*, Allen and Unwin, London, 1971.

Rhonda and Robert Rapoport, *Dual Career Families*, Penguin Books, 1971. M. P. Fogarty with Rhonda and Robert Rapoport, *Women and Top Jobs: The Next Move*, P.E.P. London, 1972.

19. Clyde Cameron, 'Ministerial Statement', *Australia Parliamentary*

Debates (*Hansard*), Twenty-Eighth Parliament, First Session 1973 (First Period), House of Representatives, Tuesday 22 May, p.2374.

20. Ibid. p.2378.

21. Ibid. p.2374.

22. *Equal Opportunities for Men and Women*, H.M.S.O. London, September 1973, p.8.

23. *Report of the Committee of Experts on the Application of Conventions and Recommendations*, Report III (Part 4B), International Labour Conference, 56th Session, Geneva, 1971 (Geneva, ILO, 1971), p.53.

Bibliography

O. Ashenfelter and A. Rees (eds), *Discrimination in Labor Markets*, (forthcoming).

B. Bergmann and I. Adelman, 'The Economic Role of Women', *American Economic Review*, vol. 63, no. 4, September 1973.

K. M. Davidson, R. B. Ginsburg and H. H. Kay, *Sex-Based Discrimination and the Law*, (forthcoming).

Equal Opportunities for Men and Women, H.M.S.O. London, September 1973.

M. P. Fogarty (ed.) *Women in Top Jobs*, Allen and Unwin, London, 1971.

M. P. Fogarty and Rhonda and Robert Rapoport, *Sex Career and Family*, Allen and Unwin, London, 1971.

M. P. Fogarty with Rhonda and Robert Rapoport, *Women and Top Jobs: The Next Move*, P.E.P., London, March, 1972.

Nona Glazer-Malbin and Helen Youngelson Walhrir (eds) *Woman in a Man-Made World*, Rand McNally, Chicago, 1972.

M. P. Goldberg, 'The Economic Exploitation of Women', in D. M. Gordon (ed.) *Problems in Political Economy: An Urban Perspective*, D. C. Heath, Lexington, 1971.

Janice N. Hedges, 'Women Workers and Manpower Demands in the 1970s', *Monthly Labor Review*, June 1970.

Joan Jordan, 'The Place of American Women', in D. Mermelstein (ed.) *Economics: Mainstream Readings and Radical Critiques*, Random House, New York, 1970.

Juanita Kreps, *Sex in the Marketplace: American Women at Work*, John Hopkins, Baltimore, 1971.

C. A. Larsen, 'Equal Pay for Women in the United Kingdom', *International Labour Review*, vol. 103, no. 1, January 1971.

Anna-Greta Leijon, *Swedish Women—Swedish Men*, The Swedish Institute, Stockholm, 1968.

R. B. Mancke, 'Lower Pay for Women: A Case of Economic Discrimination', *Industrial Relations*, vol. 10, no. 3, October 1971.

G. B. McNally, 'Patterns of Female Labor Force Activity', *Industrial Relations*, vol. 7, 1968.

Margaret Mead and Frances B. Kaplan, *American Women: The Report of the President's Commission on the Status of Women*, Scribner, New York, 1965.

National Manpower Council, *Womanpower*, Columbia University Press, New York, 1957.

U. K. Oppenheimer, 'The Sex-Labelling of Jobs', *Industrial Relations*, vol. 7, 1968.

M. Piore, 'The Dual Labor Market: Theory and Implications', in D. M. Gordon (ed.) *Problems in Political Economy: An Urban Perspective*, D. C. Heath, Lexington, 1971.

P. A. Riach, 'Equal Pay and Equal Opportunity', *Journal of Industrial Relations*, vol. 11, no. 2, July 1969.

S. H. Sandell, 'Economic Equality for Women: Discussion', *American Economic Review*, vol. 62, no. 2, May 1972.

I. V. Sawhill, 'The Economics of Discrimination Against Women: Some New Findings', *Journal of Human Resources*, (forthcoming).

N. Seear, 'The Position of Women in Industry', *Royal Commission on Trade Unions and Employers Associations, Research Papers 11* H.M.S.O., London, 1968.

F. A. Seidenberg, 'The Submissive Majority: Modern Trends in the Law Concerning Women's Rights', *Cornell Law Review*, vol. 55, 1970.

M. McL. Semchak, 'Equal Pay in the United States', *International Labour Review*, vol. 103, no. 6, June 1971.

Sweden Today, 'The Status of Women in Sweden: Report to the United Nations 1968', The Swedish Institute, Stockholm, 1968.

K. Vangsnes, 'Equal Pay in Norway', *International Labour Review*, vol. 103, no. 4, April 1971.

F. B. Weiskoff, 'Women's Place in the Labor Market', *American Economic Review*, vol. 62, no. 2, May 1972.

H. A. Zellner, 'Discrimination Against Women, Occupational Segregation, and the Relative Wage', *American Economic Review*, vol. 62, no. 2, May 1972.

Five
Women and the Law

The aim of this chapter is to examine briefly the way in which women are treated by the law. The law is by its nature an instrument of oppression within the community. Although in many instances no overt distinction is made on sexist lines the overall attitude of the law is aptly summed up by the old Portuguese proverb, 'Do not trust a good woman and keep away from a bad one'. We have chosen to look at four areas of particular discrimination: marriage, crime, care and custody of children, and employment. It should be noted that the precise legal rules applicable will vary to some degree from state to state and we have used Victorian references as a basis for the chapter. Furthermore, legislation may effect reform at any time and this chapter depicts the situation only at the time of writing, August 1974.

Marriage

Marriage in our society involves a change in the legal and social status of both the male and female parties, but in many ways it is of more legal significance for women than for men. Although the British Royal Commission on Marriage and Divorce has stated 'marriage should be regarded as a partnership in which the husband and wife work together as equals, and the wife's contribution to the joint undertaking in running the home and looking after children is just as valuable as that of the husband in providing the home and supporting the family',[1] in fact the various legal provisions relating to the rights and duties of parties to a marriage do not always reflect this theory of equality. In some cases this is because the wife is legally regarded as being in special need of protection and consequently the law discriminates in her favour. In others the law still reflects the nineteenth century attitude which regarded married women as having a status and capacity inferior to that of their husbands, or even of single women. In still other cases, the legal situation merely reflects the community's conditioned conception of the different social roles played by men and women. It should also be noted that some apparent discriminations are not based on any legal rule but rather on social custom. An example of this is the habit, still almost uniform throughout Australia, whereby a married woman adopts her husband's surname. This custom is tacitly recognized in legislation and administrative procedures throughout the community, for instance in relation to the issuing of passports or transfer of land documents. On the other hand a woman has a continuing right to use her husband's name even after his death or their divorce, unless she uses it to mislead the public into a belief that she is still married to him. Similarly the procedure of some firms of requiring male guarantors for female credit is not based on any law but on commercial practice.[2]

Marriageable age

The provisions of the Commonwealth Marriage Act relating to minimum age of the parties to a marriage distinguish between males and females. A girl may marry if she has attained the age of sixteen, but a boy must reach eighteen to do so.[3] The provisions relating to lowering the minimum age limit in exceptional cases maintain the two year distinction to fourteen and sixteen for girls and boys respectively. The rationale behind the distinction is not clear; it may be a recognition of the supposed earlier maturity of girls, or it may merely be based on an assumption that boys should undergo a longer period of training before marriage in view of their accepted roles as breadwinners, while girls whose duties will be in the home should not.

Domicile

Upon marriage a woman acquires the 'domicile' of her husband. This is the legal concept of a person's 'permanent home'. It may or may not coincide with actual present residence, but it is by the law of the place where domicile is deemed to be, that many questions of legal rights and duties are determined. Because of the rule of a wife's dependent domicile, a married woman's domicile may change against her will – for instance where her husband takes up domicile elsewhere – or even without her knowledge. Although the basic principle has been modified to some extent to take care of some problems of deserted wives the continued existence of such a rule is inconsistent with a concept of equality.[4]

Real property

Although the legislation in the late nineteenth century which reinvested married women with the power to hold and acquire property themselves largely removed the major disabilities imposed on women in this area, there is still some difficulty in showing exactly what property a married woman holds in, for instance, the matrimonial home. The situation varies somewhat between the states.

In Victoria, the Marriage Act s.161 provides that husband and wife shall be presumed to hold the matrimonial home jointly. This presumption can be rebutted by evidence of a contrary intention and regrettably in some cases the courts have found that evidence that the husband had unilaterally decided at the time of acquiring the home that his aim was to benefit himself alone was sufficient to rebut the presumption.[5] Under the Marriage Act, at least, the registration of the house in the husband's name alone will not be decisive in determining whether or not the wife has any legal property in it. The Victorian court has wide powers to make settlements of property between the parties to a dispute as it thinks just in all the circumstances.

In the other states, the position is less satisfactory. If the names of both husband and wife are on the certificate of title effect will normally be given to this. If the name of the husband appears alone, the wife will have to show that she has made some direct contribution to the purchase price, or that her husband has clearly arranged to vary the title. Indirect contributions such as housekeeping so that the husband can work are unlikely to be taken into account. When the house is in the wife's name, and the purchase price has been paid by the husband, there is a presumption that he intended it to be an absolute gift to her. This presumption can be rebutted by sufficient evidence to the contrary. Of course if the wife paid the purchase price and the title is in the husband's name there is no such presumption at work, an example of a discriminatory rule in favour of women. The Commonwealth Matrimonial Causes Act s.86 permits a flexible distribution of matrimonial property where there is a dispute ancillary to a petition for matrimonial relief.

Savings from housekeeping

In the absence of a clear intent to make a gift to the wife, any savings she may make from housekeeping money provided by her husband remain his property.

Joint bank accounts

This depends largely on the intention of the parties when the account was opened. If a court takes the view that a wife has the mere authority to withdraw from the account then she will have no right to part of the balance if there is a dispute. On the other hand if the court takes the view that both parties are intended to have rights of ownership in the fund, it will be divided evenly between them. The view taken depends on the facts and circumstances surrounding each case. Although the Probate Duty Act 1962 Victoria provides[6] that a deceased's interest in property held jointly with another is dutiable on his death, the practice is to assume that only half the property in a joint account is dutiable. Of course evidence may show that such an assumption is unfounded. In any case all dealings in joint accounts are liable to be temporarily frozen by the Probate Commissioner on the death of a spouse and there is much to be said for spouses having separate accounts to avoid possible hardship.

Maintenance and consortium

Marriage gives a wife a right to be maintained at the standard of living appropriate to her husband's status, although a reciprocal right is not vested in the husband. The law protects her right indirectly by providing her with the possibility of legal action if her husband's maintenance is lost through his death caused by the negligence of another, or under Workers' Compensation legislation if caused by an industrial accident. It is interesting to note that even *de facto* wives may recover under Workers' Compensation legislation in the appropriate circumstances. However, the law does not go so far as to provide her with protection if his capacity to provide her with maintenance and the ordinary incidents of conjugal life is only impaired by another's negligence.[7] This inability in a woman to obtain recompense for loss of consortium[8] must be contrasted with the enforceable right to damages for loss of consortium vested in the husband. This discrimination is an anomalous hangover from the now obsolete view of a husband having quasi-proprietory rights over his spouse, an attitude inappropriate to modern community ethics. However, in the cases cited in note (7) above, the courts refused to compound the folly of the continued existence of such an action by extending its availability to a wife.

Although the right to maintenance is usually regarded as being vested only in the female partner to a marriage, it is now possible for a husband who has been left by his wife without adequate means of support and is unable to support himself because of illness or some other reasonable cause to bring an action for maintenance against her. The need to show that he is unable to support himself places a burden on a man which a woman in similar circumstances does not face.[9] A deserted wife[10] need only show that she is without adequate means of support; she is not regarded as being under a duty to maintain herself if possible. However, in fixing the sum to be paid as maintenance, some states[11] provide that the financial position and earning capacity of the recipient is to be taken into account.

Contract

The common law rules which removed almost all contractual capacity from a woman on her marriage have been virtually abrogated throughout Australia. There do remain certain anomalous advantages and restrictions which are rarely invoked and need not concern us here.[12] There are however, .several points relevant to a married woman's contractual capacity which do deserve attention. First the courts have been reluctant to infer an intention to create legal relations in arrangements between husbands and wives. This is not based on any policy of discrimination between sexes, but applies equally. It is based on an assumption that in such an intimate relationship the parties do not usually intend to invite the interference of the law into their arrangements. It is by no means impossible for a husband and wife to enter a contract but if they intend to do so they should take steps to make their intentions quite clear.

The other significant effect of marriage on contractual capacity arises out of the protective doctrine referred to in the discussion above, that a wife has a right to the support of her husband. While a wife is living with her husband a presumption is made that she can pledge his credit for the supply of necessaries for herself and her children. This means that a tradesman who supplies her with such necessary services, food or clothing has an enforceable contract with the husband for payment even though he did not deal directly with him. Similarly a deserted wife who has not herself committed any matrimonial offence may obtain necessaries in this way if no other course is available to her. These presumptions of agency can be rebutted by the husband notifying those concerned of his intention to refuse to be bound by his wife as agent.

Criminal Law

Although criminal responsibility may differ according to sex and age generally men and women are held equally responsible for a breach of the criminal law.

However, there are certain presumptions based on the special relationship created by marriage. These deny or limit the criminal responsibility of those concerned; for instance a married couple cannot be convicted of conspiring with each other to commit a crime or of stealing each others property during marriage.

The area of the criminal law which discriminates greatly between women and men relates to sexual offences. Women involved in sexual activity are seen either as sexual exploiters of men for material gain, or victims of men's sexuality. Such widely divergent thinking apparently owes its origin to the view that women are either devoid of a sex drive, or alternatively that they are a band of rapacious houris. Thus, as exploiters of men, prostitutes are charged with soliciting while the men who accept the solicitations of a prostitute are rarely prosecuted.

On the other hand, women seen at law as the victims of men's sexuality, can be the authors of few other sexual offences. For example, the crime of rape consists in having carnal knowledge of a woman without her consent. Although violence is usually a component of the offence, it is possible for the crime to be committed without any violence. The essential point is that a woman's free and conscious permission is not obtained. Therefore, men have been guilty of rape when they have impersonated a woman's husband, had intercourse as the result of threats or by representation that they were performing a surgical operation. Clearly in similar circumstances a woman is also capable of having carnal knowledge of a man without his real consent. However, the offence remains defined as one which men only can commit. Nevertheless, a woman who aids and abets the commission of a rape on another woman may be convicted as a principal offender.[13] The ridiculous point has been reached that a woman may be convicted of the rape of a woman as a principal offender when she acts as an accessory, but cannot be convicted as a principal in the rape of a man when she actually is one.

Other areas when the criminal law discriminates between women and men may be noted.

It is an offence for a man to have carnal knowledge of a woman who is an idiot, imbecile, lunatic or mental defective. However, there does not appear to be any offence prohibiting a woman from intercourse with men in these categories.

Abduction of females (it is unnecessary for this to be for an immoral or improper purpose) but not of males, procuration of a female but not of a male, and homosexual acts performed between consenting adult males but not those between consenting females, as offences, are all examples of this type of legal discrimination.[14]

If the death of a child under twelve months of age occurs and is due to an act or omission on the mother's part which is caused by the balance of the mother's mind being disturbed due to the affect of giving birth or of lactation, this crime – infanticide – will carry the penalty of manslaughter and not of murder. As this statutory crime was introduced in 1922 it is possible that the medical knowledge upon which it rested no longer has validity. Research should be undertaken to determine whether in fact those women who are charged with the lesser offence of infanticide are in fact motivated by physical post-natal factors, or if they commit the offence due to the stresses placed on anyone having the constant care of a baby. If the latter proposition is true the plea of infanticide should be extended to anyone who, having the constant care of a child, kills it within the first twelve months of its life or even so long as the stresses of child care remain. An alternative or complementary solution would be to relieve such people of the pressures which might lead to such an act occurring.[15]

A further discrimination arises not through the law but in practice. Women – at least in Victoria – are far less likely to be sentenced to jail for any crime than men.

Care and Custody of Children

Legitimate children

The common law recognized the father of a legitimate child as having a 'sacred' right to its custody and control.[16] It was not until the late nineteenth century that a mother's right to custody was supported to any extent. Today, however, legislation has placed both parents on equal footing and in fact requires a court which is determining a question of custody to place the interests and welfare of the child concerned above the wishes or welfare of the parents. It may take into account their behaviour, not so as to amount to an automatic disqualification from the battle for custody but rather the better to determine the interests and happiness of the child.[17] A mother now has technically equal rights to custody, to appoint a guardian and, more qualifiedly, to determine the religious education of her children. However, as a matter of practice, it might be that the mother of small children has a slightly greater chance of being awarded custody than their father. This would seem to stem from the arguable belief that it is likely to be better for a small child to be with its mother than with anyone else.

There is still one area of patent discrimination against mothers in their relationship with their children. A legitimate child automatically takes its father's surname, and while an adult can change his or her own surname by deed poll a child cannot. However, although a father can change his child's name in this way, it appears that a mother cannot.[18]

Illegitimate children

The father of an illegitimate child has no automatic rights to its custody, and those rights once sacred to the father of a legitimate child are in the case of an illegitimate child vested in the mother.[19] Although the father (or anyone else) may apply for custody, he must show that it is to the positive advantage of the child for him to have custody before his claim can be upheld. The mother has a concomitant duty to maintain her illegitimate child, although she can proceed under the maintenance legislation of the various states for some contributions from its putative father. As a matter of fact this legislation is far from being completely successful in achieving its end, and a good argument could be put for its abandonment and replacement with a better system of state support. The provision of adequate state-run child-care centres, which would enable such mothers to support themselves if they chose to do so during the infancy of their children, is fundamental.

Employment

Many factors operate to restrict the employment of women on equal terms with men. Variations in socialization and education (referred to elsewhere) help to establish the terms on which women enter the workforce. The law also acts as a medium through which people are employed on a sexist basis.

Preconceptions as to women's role in society appear to be the basis of discriminatory laws. For example, the assumption that women should be the people primarily responsible for child nurturing may lead to restrictions on overtime.

A woman's wage tends to be seen either as supporting an individual only, or as supplementary to that of a breadwinner. This may lead to a lower rate of pay and has led to anomalies in workers' compensation payments. The image of women as frail creatures requiring protection may lead to restrictions of entry to certain trades, and working conditions different from those of men in the same occupations.

All workers are affected by legislation, regulations and by decisions and awards of industrial tribunals. As Australia has a federal system of government each state has its own legislation and awards or determinations which operate only in that state. To settle industrial disputes extending beyond the limits of one state the Federal Tribunal makes awards which are legally binding upon the parties concerned. Where there is a conflict between federal and state laws the former prevail to the extent of the inconsistency. Where a Commonwealth award is silent a state law may be invoked.

Because of the number of sources from which laws governing employment emanate it is impossible to discuss all the sexually discriminatory laws that exist throughout the Commonwealth. Therefore, some important aspects of employment have been chosen with examples of laws which lead to different terms of work for women and men.

Remuneration

The concept of equal pay for equal work was accepted by the Australian Conciliation and Arbitration Commission in 1969. As a consequence equal pay is being implemented in certain industries and there has been flow-on into other areas. However, where the work in question is essentially or usually performed by females 'equal' pay is not required. Due to the nature of the female workforce, this precludes a vast number of women from receiving pay on a scale concomitant with that of the male workforce. The Canadian, English and United States experiences indicate that even where equal pay is mandatory, some employers go out of their way to find or mark a difference in the duties of women and men so that different rates can be paid within the letter of the law.

Discrimination against entry to a trade

Women are prevented from entering certain areas of the footwear, butchering, printing and engineering trades. In Victoria, females are not permitted to work certain hours in factories until they are eighteen, but the same restrictions cease for males when they are sixteen. This has the effect of precluding girls from earning their living in some occupations for a longer period than males. An eighteen-year-old boy with two years experience on the job will then probably be preferred by employers to an eighteen-year-old girl who is a beginner. A useful comparison might be made here with the age requirements for entry to marriage referred to above.

Health and safety

Legislation in all states, and many industrial awards both state and federal, embody safeguards to protect the health and safety of workers. Some of these relate only to women. They include the Graphic Arts Award 1957, under which women are not permitted to use certain types of machinery, and the Tasmanian Mines Inspection Act 1968 and similar legislation in other states which prohibit the employment of women in underground mines, apart from professional women who are permitted to enter the mines for inspection in special circumstances.

The International Labour Organization has found that work regarded as dangerous or unhealthy for women is equally so for men.[20] Therefore, attention should be focused upon the nature of the work, and the conditions under which it is performed; and appropriate improvements should be made where possible, with benefit to men and women alike. Measures protecting health and safety should be extended to all members of the workforce based on the nature of the work and the requirements of individuals. Women workers require special treatment in relation to pregnancy, but this is more adequately provided where provisions relating specifically to pregnancy are introduced. General protective measures for women based on their potential child-bearing capacity can only militate against women entering the workforce on equal terms.

Limitation on night work

The Federal Textile Industry Awards do not permit women to work later than 11 p.m. The Graphic Arts Award 1957 does not permit women to be employed in night work, nor does it allow women to work overtime between 9 p.m. and 7.30 a.m.

It is difficult to discover a rationale upon which this discrimination is based. If it is on the assumption that women are responsible for minding children and therefore should be at home at night, in fact research has indicated that many women prefer night work because their husbands are then available for child care. In such cases if night work is not available women may be precluded from working at all. If the underlying assumption for such restrictions is that it may be dangerous for women to travel at night, it must be acknowledged that men too are liable to assault. Under the Victorian Liquor Industry Award women employees working at night must be provided with transport. Such a condition could be extended to other industries and to men, rather than banning women from working at night entirely.

Maternity leave

Maternity leave provisions are in effect in most of the Public Services and Education Departments throughout Australia. Commonwealth Public Service employees have a maximum of fifty-two weeks leave of absence, six weeks of which must be taken before and after confinement. New South Wales is the only state where maternity leave is paid. In the other states employees may use recreational or sick leave that has accrued to them.

Under legislation introduced in 1973 women employees of the

Australian Government are entitled to at least twelve weeks maternity leave on full pay and to a total period of absence of up to 52 weeks in respect of each confinement. Provision is also made for one week's paternity leave.

There is specific provision that an actual or possible pregnancy shall not be a ground for discrimination to refuse to employ, for dismissal, or for action disadvantageous to woman's employment. However, it appears possible that as the maternity leave provisions differ from that of paternity leave they may be used to discriminate against women in employment, although this may often be difficult to detect as other, acceptable reasons may be given, for example, a woman may not be employed initially because of the potential loss of work time likely to arise from maternity leave. It is suggested that if the same provisions were equally applicable to both men and women all people would be employed on equal terms. It is also suggested that legislation should be introduced to make these provisions applicable to all employees throughout Australia.

Economically, if not ideologically, society accepts wives and mothers as members of the labour force and it therefore has an obligation to ensure that the dual role of a working woman who becomes pregnant does not affect her health or that of her child. To do this adequate maternity leave provisions must exist and it is essential that this leave is paid. At a time of increased financial pressure a woman's source of income should not be removed.

Where maternity leave provisions exist, without paternity leave being on the same basis, they may be used as a basis of discrimination in the terms under which women are employed.

Apart from the many social and emotional advantages gained by making paternity leave available on the same terms as maternity leave it would mean that all married people would be employed on the same terms.

Workers' compensation

Although women are automatically compensated for the death of their husbands at work, men are recompensed for the death of their wives only upon proof of dependency on their wife's earnings. This distinction is based on the view that a man is primarily responsible for the financial resources of a family. However, there are situations in which a woman is the breadwinner of the family and it should be realized that any married woman who works will normally assume part of a family's financial responsibilities.

Retirement

Where compulsory retiring ages exist they are usually sixty for women and sixty-five for men. This places a financial hardship on women who live longer than men, because earlier retirement means a shorter number of years in which to acquire adequate savings and superannuation and a longer period in which these resources will be required.

It might also be regarded as unfair to men, who have to work five years longer in order to gain optimal superannuation rights.

Superannuation

At present variations exist under the many superannuation schemes in Australia on a sexist basis, but many of these including that of the Australian Public Service are under review. It is therefore thought unproductive to deal with them more fully here.

Taxation

Women as taxpayers face problems peculiar to their situation. The present tax system unfairly discriminates against married women, or women with children who work for pay, and acts as a disincentive to their entering the labour market.

The married women who enter the labour force indirectly raise the effective tax rates paid by their husbands. The personal exemption of $364 allowed to a husband because of his dependent wife is reduced dollar for dollar by the amount the wife earns in annual income over $130; it is, therefore, eliminated entirely if she earns $494. Since the net addition to the family's income may not be worthwhile, this tax 'penalty' may deter married women from joining the labour force.

Money spent on child care by a working mother cannot be legitimately deducted from her gross salary or wages as an expense necessarily incurred in earning her income. Therefore, a woman who works outside the home and has one or more children who require care pays a tax on her earnings out of which she also has to pay for child care. Therefore, a working mother has to earn a substantial salary if working outside the home is to be more profitable than the value of her services in the home. This discrimination is particularly hard on single mothers or deserted wives who have only social service benefits to rely on for their income.

The tax system should reflect a just balance between the legitimate aspirations of married women and mothers and the interests of other taxpayers. Women must have a free choice as to whether they join the labour market or remain at home. The present system acts as a disincentive that deters some women from working outside. Existing disincentives to work should be removed without necessarily creating a positive incentive for all married women or mothers to seek paid employment.

Other areas of legal discrimination between the sexes exist. The Juries Act 1967 (Vic.) classifies women as being a class of persons entitled as of right to be excused from serving as jurors, an attitude adopted by most states with only procedural variations. There is no provision for the payment of pensions to deserted husbands or widowers in situations where their female counterparts would be eligible to receive them. Although there are no compulsory National Service requirements presently in force, it has never been the practice to extend such legislation to include women even in time of open and declared war. These, and there are doubtless other similar examples, embody a fundamental assumption about the role and capabilities of women in the community which may not truly reflect current standards and are in any case clearly sexist discriminations.

Thus it appears that in many instances the law as the authoritative arm of the community still forces women into the roles either of rapacious succubi or virginal and dependent waifs, rather than treating them as sensate individuals. Of course, legislation to remove the protective devices developed over the centuries would not remedy the situation, but would leave many members of the community in measurably worse conditions than before with little to comfort themselves other than empty cries of equality before the law. In order to truly produce an equality in the community it is necessary first to re-order the various sources of sexist conditioning which are merely reflected in the law.

The Family Law Bill: *An Editorial Postscript*

It should be noted that at time of writing the re-elected Labor Government will again try to pass through both Houses of Parliament their Family Law Bill, a Bill designed 'to replace the Matrimonial Causes Act 1959–1966, and to deal with additional areas of family law presently dealt with by state legislation'. It is by no means certain that the Bill will be made law but a few comments on the Bill need to be made because of the extent of the proposed changes. It should be stressed however that this chapter has been concerned with the law as it stands, not as it might be; with legal realities rather than political promises.

If made law, the Family Law Bill will in fact legislate for greater theoretical legal equality between men and women. It will for example no longer be possible to obtain decrees for restitution of conjugal rights. Also, husband and wife will be regarded as joint guardians of their children and custody orders will take full account of the wishes of the child where this is possible. However, unlike many situations where the law grows out of acceptable social norms, the Family Law Bill aims to legislate *as if* equal opportunities for men and women already exist in society. It is framed in relation to an ideology of equality not in relation to existing social realities. For example, Clause 51, by stating that 'a party to a marriage is liable to maintain the other party to the marriage so far as the first-mentioned party is reasonably able to do so and to the extent that the other party is unable to support himself or herself adequately', does not mention specifically that the wife should be compensated for years spent out of public life, for forgoing training to keep house and have children.

The Bill has certain important disadvantages. Under the Matrimonial Causes Act if cruelty exists within a marriage, and it is possible for a spouse to remain within the matrimonial home[21] for a period of twelve months, provided that appropriate evidence can be adduced, a divorce can be obtained. However, it appears possible that under the concept of irretrievable breakdown of marriage that in some cases of cruelty no matrimonial relief will be available for the economically weaker party, almost invariably the woman. This will be due to the difficulty that will be found in living 'separately and apart' for the twelve months prescribed period.

Because most women have been reared for marriage and are totally dependent financially on their husbands they are unlikely to be able to support themselves if they leave the matrimonial home. Such women can usually only obtain unskilled work which is very poorly paid,[22] and the problems of obtaining child care[23] may be so great that it may be more economically worthwhile for a woman to obtain social service benefits. Although a woman living separately from her husband is entitled to a widow's pension from the Commonwealth this will not be obtainable for six months. Before this becomes effective an application may be made for state assistance. The maximum amount payable to a woman with one child is $27.75 from which is deducted any other income including maintenance from the husband. The state requires that a woman should seek maintenance, but if this is awarded for the children only this is taken as indication that there was no justification for leaving the matrimonial home, and the wife's pension is withdrawn. State pensions are generally paid within two to three weeks of an application to the Social Welfare Department. On occasions a small emergency grant of $5 to $10 may be made immediately.

A woman may also apply for maintenance for herself and her children from her husband. But there will be a lapse of time between when she leaves the matrimonial home and when this becomes available. Also, even if a maintenance order is made in her favour she may have great difficulty in enforcing it.[24]

Therefore, it is apparent that to bridge the gap between separating from her husband and receiving social service benefits or maintenance, a woman will require a capital sum to pay for rent, possibly key money, food and other necessities. The amount that will be necessary has been estimated as being at least $100.[25] For women who earn no income the only possibility of accumulating sufficient resources is by saving from their housekeeping allowance. This will in many cases be an insurmountable task. Therefore, because of economic pressures many women will be forced to remain within the matrimonial home.

The possibility then remains that a wife may establish the ground of irretrievable breakdown by remaining within the matrimonial home and living 'separately and apart'. Parties may be held to be living 'separately and apart'

> In cases where they are living under the same roof, that point is reached when they cease to be one household and become two households; or in other words, when they are not residing with one another or co-habiting with one another.[26]

The body of law applicable to desertion, as was the ground in the case referred to, is the same as for separation. In *Crabtree v. Crabtree*[27] it was held that the common law principles applied to the ground of separation under the Matrimonial Causes Act, and it was therefore possible to live 'separately and apart' under the same roof. Recognition of this concept is specifically provided at Cl. 27 (2) of the Family Law Bill.

However, if the husband does not want the consortium to be broken it may be very difficult for a woman to comply with this requirement.

It therefore appears probable that a large number of women in Australia, those most obviously requiring matrimonial relief, may be precluded from obtaining it because of the difficulty of establishing the evidentiary requirements to prove the ground of irretrievable breakdown.

Also a wife's domicile will continue to be that of her husband under the Family Law Bill, although the position is somewhat ameliorated. The Family Law Bill allows a party who is an Australian citizen[28] or domiciled in Australia[29] or is ordinarily resident in Australia and has been so resident for one year immediately preceding that date[30] to initiate proceedings for dissolution of marriage. Matrimonial causes other than dissolution proceedings may be instituted if either party to the marriage is an Australian citizen[31] or is present in Australia.[32] These provisions are an advance upon those of the Matrimonial Causes Act but may still cause some hardship where a wife not domiciled within the jurisdiction establishes the divorce grounds outside Australia, as she will have to complete twelve months residence in this country before being able to bring an action. It would have been more logical and more in keeping with contemporary thinking[33] to introduce legislation similar to that of New Zealand,[34] under which 'the domicile of a married woman wherever she was married, shall be determined as if she were unmarried, and (if she is a minor) as if she were adult'.

Thus, in brief, the Bill is discriminatory in that it removes some of the protection but not all the discrimination afforded under the present law and leaves enormous areas open to interpretation by an almost entirely male judiciary. Given the present sexist values operating in Australia it is extremely doubtful whether any attempt will be made to take into account the effects of socialization on women when assessing maintenance and property rights; socialization which results in lower educational achievement, lower status and less well paid jobs, and often a belief in marriage and the family as essential to a woman's status (see Section 3). The Bill thus legislates for a hollow equality.*

Notes

1. Cmd. 9678 para. 644.
2. See e.g. *Choice* (Journal of Australian Consumers Association) vol. 14, no. 10, October 1973.
3. *Marriage Act* 1961 (Cth.) ss. 11 and 12.

* The detailed information on the Family Law Bill contained in this postscript was provided by the authors of the chapter as the book went to press.

4. *Matrimonial Causes Act* 1959 (Cth.) ss. 23 and 24.
5. *Moore* v. *Moore* [1965] V.R. 61. See also generally R. Sackville, 'The Emerging Australian Law of Matrimonial Property', *Melbourne University Law Review*, no. 7, p.353.
6. S.7 (1) (e).
7. *Best* v. *Samuel Fox* [1951] 2 All E.R. 116.
Wright v. *Cedzich* [1930] 36 A.L.R. 105.
8. Consortium: This is a term used to cover the variety of mutual rights and duties of a married couple. Over the years the emphasis has changed from the husband having all the rights and the wife the duties to a current view which sees consortium more in terms of a partnership with reciprocity of support. More specifically, it includes the duty of husband and wife to cohabit, to share sexual relations and perhaps to have children.
9. *Uniform Maintenance Acts.* Note also that the provision relating to imprisonment on proof of disobedience of a maintenance order refers only to men. *Maintenance Act* 1965 (Vic.) 543.
10. Only Tasmania extends this right to *de facto* wives provided they have cohabited with the man for at least twelve months.
11. Victoria, South Australia and Tasmania.
12. For a discussion of these provisions see H. A. Finlay and A. Bissett-Johnson, *Family Law in Australia*, Butterworths, pp. 138 ff.
13. *R.* v. *Ram* (1893) 17 Cox 609.
14. *Crimes Act* 1958 (Vic.) ss. 59, 60, 61 and 62; ss. 56, 57; s. 68.
15. D. Bialestock, 'Neglected Babies: A study of 289 babies admitted consecutively to a Reception Centre', The *Medical Journal of Australia* 1966 no.2, p.1129.
B. F. Steele and C. B. Pollock, 'A Psychiatric Study of Parents who abuse Infants and Small Children', in R. Helfer and C. H. Kempe, *The Battered Child*, University of Chicago Press, 1968, pp.103, 107.
16. Re *Agar-Ellis* (1878) 10 Ch.D. 49, 71. This recognition of a 'proprietary' right vested in the father alone gave rise to the availability to him of actions for damages for the loss of his child's services through negligence or seduction which were not available to their mother; cf. above note.
17. Much legislation affects custody and care of children. A few examples are: *Marriage Act* 1958 (Vic.) ss. 132 ff; *Matrimonial Causes Act* 1959–1966 (Cth.) ss. 83 ff; *Uniform Adoption Acts.*
18. Re *T.* (*an infant*) [1962] 3 All E.R. 970 followed in Australia by *K.* v. *D* [1969] A.L.R. 311.

19. See for example *Marriage Act* 1958 (Vic.) s. 14 which restates the common law.

20. 'Women Workers in a Changing World', 48th session of International Labour Conference, 1964.

21. Cl. 26 (2).

22. M. Power, 'The Wages of Sex', 46, *Australian Quarterly*, 1974.

23. Department of Labour and National Service Women's Bureau 'Child Care Centres'.

24. Krupenski 'The deserted mother in Victoria' in David Hambly and J. Neville Turner, *Cases and Materials on Australian Family Law*, Law Book Company, Sydney, 1971.

25. *The Age*, 31 August, 1973.

26. Lord Denning, *Hopes v. Hopes* (1949) p.227.

27. (1963) 5 Fed. L.R. 307.

28. Cl. 18 (3) (a)

29. Cl. 18 (3) (b)

30. Cl. 18 (3) (c)

31. Cl. 18 (4) (b)

32. Ss. 23–24.

33. United Nation's Economic and Social Council 1958, recommended, '. . . that governments take all necessary measures to ensure the right of married women to an independent domicile.' Adopted by 890th Plenary meeting.

34. Matrimonial Proceedings Act (1963) S. 3. (1).

Six (Part one)

Inequalities in the Australian Education System An Overview

During the last decade a mass of evidence has destroyed Australia's comfortable myths about an egalitarian educational system. A multitude of disadvantaged groups – the poor, the migrant, the Aboriginal, the country dweller, the handicapped – have been recognized as requiring special consideration.

One group has been singularly neglected, namely, women and girls. The paucity of research data and information becomes more understandable when it is realized that the overwhelming majority of educational researchers are males. Although educational services are increasingly dominated by women this is a matter of numbers only; senior positions at school and tertiary levels are almost completely male territory.

Second-rate opportunities for women are far from recent, and indeed until the first years of this century were ensured by legal barriers. Ailsa Zainu 'Uddin has written an excellent paper on the struggle for female access to the University of Melbourne, a battle which lasted thirty years.[1] Most Australian universities experienced similar late nineteenth century disputes, and fought long and hard before capitulation. Remnants of this attitude were removed only at the end of 1974 from the Melbourne University Act where Section 43 concluded: 'But the Council may if it thinks fit exclude females from attendance at any lectures, but not from any examination in the University'.[2]

Nineteenth century arguments that women were inferior were discussed at the Victorian Era Exhibition held in London during 1897. Sir William Windeyer, ex-Chancellor of Sydney University, speaking at the education section referred to women having 'the right to win any position in our social system . . . one of the most remarkable advances in our conception of a complete social system'.[3] On another occasion Windeyer is quoted as saying:

The threadbare phrase that women should keep their place, as some are pleased to call the position of registered inferiority, to which so many men, with assumed superiority, relegate women often superior to themselves in all that gives dignity to character, we are thankful to say finds no voice amongst us as an argument against the educational enfranchisement of women, and has entirely disappeared before the nobler view that woman is entitled to the place which her God-given talents enable her to win.[4]

Thirty years before, an anonymous Adelaide pamphlet 'Education and the Rights of Women' had claimed: 'Whether a girl marries or remains single, it is of the highest importance that she be well educated and grounded in whatever knowledge she may have a taste for.'[5]

While a man may by physical force push his way through life, C.S.A. the pamphleteer believed that if parents didn't have a fortune for their daughter it was essential that she learn a profession or a trade.

In the 1870s an attempt was made in Melbourne to publish a regular *Women's Advocate* 'to stimulate the press, and keep the subject alive before the public, until our legislators are aroused to action'.[6] This failed, but not before a second issue appeared with a concentration on education and a proposal for the foundation of a women's college. Ms Webb, the writer, was however unable to break away from the strong attitudes of her day: 'the domestic character should never be severed from females, however high or however low their position in life'.[7]

The battle for legal equality, in education at least, has been won with the minor exception of a couple of agricultural colleges. What has persisted is the domestic emphasis of Ms Webb and, though more subtly than before, the suggestion of intellectual inferiority which was attacked by Windeyer.

Since the beginning of the century overseas researchers have interested themselves in wide-ranging examinations of psychological and learning differences based on sex. Attitudes, habits, interests, personality characteristics, scholastic attainment and intelligence have been investigated. To take just one key factor, overall intelligence measures (variously defined) fail to reveal significant sex differences. It appears that girls do better on verbally-weighted tests, while boys do better when tests are loaded towards scientific, mathematical and spatial content. Whether these minor differences are genetic or environmental is open to dispute. The basic conclusion remains that, on balance, the two sexes are intellectually equal.

If intelligence is evenly distributed across the sexes what is the Australian situation in actual performance? I have already referred to the paucity of data; many detailed studies fail to give sex differences. Much of the material which follows is Victorian-based, simply because even less research has been done elsewhere. However it would be surprising if the situation in Victoria were distinctly worse than in the other states. Even then, most data has been of a pragmatic counting nature, as noted by Professor Jean Martin: 'No serious work has been done in Australia to develop the fruitful lines of inquiry relating sex differences in educational achievement to socialization, adolescent orientations and ambitions or peer group experience.'[8]

Norman MacKenzie's almost forgotten book* *Women in Australia*[9] presented detailed state by state figures showing lower female retention rates in secondary school and the tendency of so-called more intelligent girls to enter the workforce rather than continue on to university.

In 1957 an official bulletin issued by the Queensland Department of Public Instruction contained the following table.[10]

See Table 1 on Page 120

Educational Levels in the Community as a Whole

Statistics are now available under five headings: census data; secondary retention rates; tertiary participation; scholarship winning; subjects taken and actual performance. All indicate the disadvantaged position of women in education in Australia.

* As this book went to press MacKenzie's book was issued in an updated version, S. Encel, N. MacKenzie and M. Tebbutt, *Women and Society: An Australian Study*, Cheshire, Melbourne 1974. However most of the statistics end at 1970.

Table 1

Retention of pupils reaching 85 per cent in the Queensland Scholarship Examination 1951

Level	*Boys*	*Girls*
Scholarship	339–100	340–100
Junior	93	80
Senior	58	43
University	37	11

Another table showed that of the 165 'gifted' who went to university only 40 were female.

The first census which provides information on education is that of 1966.[11] Males had higher qualifications than women – 11.3 per cent of males had reached matriculation or higher compared with a female figure of 8.2 per cent.

Far more detailed information is contained in the 1971 census. If all normally accepted post-secondary qualifications are counted, males have 75.1 per cent as opposed to a female figure of 24.9 per cent.

Table 2

Level of Qualifications of Population 15 years and Over*[12]

	All		Still Studying† (Victoria only)	
	Male	*Female*	*Male*	*Female*
Trade	92	8	93	7
Technician (all)	49	51	78	29
(excl. Nursing)	83	17		
Non-degree Tertiary (all)	52	48	67	33
(excl. Education)	77	23		
Bachelor Degree	72	28	67	33
Postgraduate Diploma Higher Degree	82	18	80	20

* Each category is treated as self contained, the male and female percentage being the percentage of the total group with such qualifications.

† Calculated from printouts provided by the Bureau of Census and Statistics.

In addition another category 'qualifications not classified by level' revealed a male proportion of 24 per cent and female 76 per cent. This category was defined in the introductory notes as follows: 'Some qualifications could not be classified to any of the above levels. Most of these related to short specialized courses in such fields as typewriting and shorthand, farm book-keeping, dressmaking, automotive maintenance.' Even with these skills classified as qualifications the female percentage of all qualifications is only 30 per cent.

Writers, including myself, often fall into the trap of emphasizing university access; yet the above table reveals the major difference lies in the trade area where, in numerical terms, 812,629 males had qualifications compared with 69,668 females.

Analysis of those figures which I could obtain showed that differences for capital city and country areas were not significant in any category, although inside cities, for instance Melbourne, variations were frequent. In Brunswick, an inner-city largely working-class and migrant suburb, fewer females were undertaking trade courses (4 per cent compared with 7.5 per cent overall), or technical (21 per cent compared with 29 per cent).

Fortunately the census table used for Table 2 also includes information on subject areas and a selection of these included in Table 3 affirms the existence of 'male' and 'female' educational and employment categories.

See Table 3 on Page 122

If higher degrees are examined, further differences develop. For instance, while 60 per cent of degree holders in the humanities are females, only 33 per cent of higher degree holders are women. Similar percentages for education and Diploma of Education are 51 per cent and 32 per cent respectively.

Another census question yields a table on level of schooling. Of those currently attending school at level ten (fifth form or above), 54.9 per cent were males and 45.1 per cent females. Of those who had finished school, the percentages at level ten were male 56.1 per cent, female 43.9 per cent.

Although Melbourne/country differences were insignificant, there were large variations within the city. To use Brunswick

Table 3

Qualifications held – selected categories

Trade	*Male*	*Female*
Metal	99.6	0.43
Electrical	99.7	0.26
Motor	99.8	0.15
Printing	91.6	8.4
Clothing, Footwear and Textiles	49	51
Technical	*Male*	*Female*
Engineering	96.6	3.4
Mining and Metallurgy	98.1	1.9
Agriculture	96.5	3.5
Business and Administration	74	26
Nursing	3.5	96.5
Para-medical	21	79
Tertiary – excl. Degree	*Male*	*Female*
Natural Sciences	90	10
Engineering	98.8	1.2
Architecture	92.4	7.6
Business Administration and Commerce	93.1	6.9
Social and Behavioural Sciences	25	75
Education	27	73
Bachelor Degree or Equivalent	*Male*	*Female*
Natural Sciences	74	26
Engineering	99	0.76
Architecture	89	11
Economics, Commerce, Government	88	12
Social and Behavioural Sciences and Humanities with Teachers Certificate	46	54
Social, Behavioural Sciences and Humanities	40	60
Other fields with Teachers Certificate	66	34
Law	90	10
Medicine and Dentistry	79	21

again, 59 per cent of the level ten and above group were male.

Interesting migrant/non-migrant sex differences were explored in a 1971 article by J. E. Bourke, Director of the Federal Catholic Education Office.[13]

Table 4

Proportion of the Australian population 20 years and over in selected higher categories of educational attainment by birthplace – 1966 Census.[14]

		University degrees	*Other Tertiary*	*Completed Secondary*
Australian born	*Males*	2.43	3.79	7.75
	Females	0.77	2.61	6.12
Overseas born (all)	*Males*	2.83	2.80	16.52
	Females	1.02	1.78	14.09
UK	*Males*	2.47	3.82	15.66
	Females	0.84	2.15	12.73
Germany	*Males*	2.37	2.26	21.11
	Females	0.77	1.67	18.08
Greece	*Males*	0.19	0.22	9.73
	Females	0.04	0.10	7.45
Italy	*Males*	0.26	0.39	6.85
	Females	0.07	0.19	5.21
Netherlands	*Males*	1.65	3.19	22.23
	Females	0.32	1.68	15.86

Overseas-born females in general had a higher percentage with university education than Australian-born males. However, all migrant groups showed significant bias in terms of males at all higher levels. Other figures mentioned by Bourke show that females, both migrant and Australian-born, had higher percentages of primary education only or of no schooling at all.

Secondary Retention Rates

Radford's massive counting exercise, *School Leavers in Australia 1959–60*,[15] contained two relevant conclusions: girls left school at younger ages than boys, but fewer girls than boys were leaving from matriculation level. Little in the last fifteen years disturbs either of these statements. Girls are staying on longer, but boys longer still; the gap remains, if slightly reduced.

Details of retention rates shown in Table 5 indicate a slight narrowing of the sex gap. However it must be emphasized that for the 17- and 18-year-olds the gap is diminishing slowest.

Table 5

Students in each age group as a percentage of the population in the same age group 1968–1973[16]

Age (years)		*1968*	*1969*	*1970*	*1971*	*1972*	*1973*
15	*male*	80.0	81.4	83.1	83.0	83.5	83.4
	female	76.2	77.0	78.8	79.6	80.8	81.1
16	*male*	52.9	54.6	55.4	57.5	57.7	56.5
	female	43.7	46.4	47.6	49.4	50.8	52.2
17	*male*	29.1	30.9	32.1	33.3	33.9	32.3
	female	20.8	22.6	23.8	24.7	26.4	27.6
18	*male*	11.1	11.9	12.1	11.9	12.4	11.4
	female	5.0	5.6	5.8	5.8	6.3	6.4

Note: Table 3 of *Schools 1973*, from which the above table is taken shows a masculinity ratio (males per 100 females) in government schools significantly higher than in private schools.

Indeed, figures gleaned from the Martin Report show a contrary trend over time.[17] Admittedly the figures are given only up to 1961, but in 1921 more females than males in the 15–19 age group continued their education, whereas in 1961 the position was reversed. Retention rates are available for three States. The Committee of Enquiry into Education in South

Australia reported during the period 1954 to 1968, a closing of the gap at 15 but an increase at 17 and 18.

Table 6

Students in each age group as a percentage of the population in the same age group for selected years (South Australia)[18]

Age		*1954*	*1961*	*1964*	*1968*
15	*Male*	45.6	69.6	78.1	86.7
	Female	38.8	58.4	71.3	81.0
16	*Male*	24.4	40.5	51.6	61.7
	Female	18.5	26.7	38.2	48.6
17	*Male*	7.9	15.8	21.4	29.6
	Female	6.4	7.2	11.4	16.8
18	*Male*	5.1	5.8	7.1	9.7
	Female	1.7	1.2	2.2	3.1

A Queensland study of the Commonwealth Secondary Scholarship Scheme[19] revealed that more 'able' girls than boys did not undertake senior studies (matriculation level). Those who won scholarships stayed on with only a slight difference between the sexes. However, the Junior Examination Order of Merit lists show that 21 of 686 males left school whereas 163 of 844 females did so.

Victorian retention rates shown below again reveal the magnitude of the difference.[20] To use a quaint phrase, girls in the urban areas were not getting a 'fair go'.

Table 7

Victorian Retention Profiles: 1968 enrolments as percentage of 1963 Form 1 Enrolments

	Male	*Female*
Melbourne	48	23
Country	25	20
Ballarat, Bendigo and Geelong	37	18

Statistics quoted thus far have been on a simple male/female basis. If socio-economic class is added a significant pattern emerges. Retention rates vary between areas of high and low social status; so do female disadvantages. In Table 8, which is drawn from the Karmel South Australian Report for 1969–70 girls from the highest social status areas actually enter Form 5 (equivalent then to matriculation) in slightly greater percentages than boys.[21] Minor differences exist at the bottom end of the status scale but in the middle status, one might say the middle class areas, the sex gap is substantial.

Table 8

Grade 12 enrolments in 1969 as a proportion of Grade 8 enrolments in 1965 by socio-economic level, Adelaide Metropolitan Area

	Males	*Females*
Lowest	18.07	16.39
Fourth	22.06	21.06
Third	28.66	20.81
Second	33.75	21.54
Highest	42.79	45.26

Tertiary Participation*

Selection for entry to tertiary education, particularly universities, further widens the gap. Females as a percentage of all university enrolments have altered in a minor fashion from just less than 30 per cent in 1939 to 34 per cent in 1973.[22] Individual universities have higher percentages. Sydney for instance has 37.5 per cent, but this is compensated for (in a statistical sense) by the University of New South Wales with a female percentage of 24 per cent. Most others have between 32 and 35 per cent.

Other forms of tertiary education have different male/female comparisons. The table below shows the greater male dominance

* For more detailed discussion, see Chapter 6, Part 2, '*Women in the Professions*'.

in colleges of advanced education, particularly for part-time courses although as Education and Arts type courses penetrate, the balance is changing.

Table 9

Enrolments in Colleges of Advanced Education 1971–73[23]

	Year	*Male*	*Female*
Full Time	1971	70	30
	1972	66	34
	1973	63	37
Part Time Internal	1971	89	11
	1972	87	13
	1973	86	14
All	1971	80	20
	1972	77	23
	1973	74	26

Again subject differences are major. For instance, 12 per cent of the enrolment in economics and business studies is female; engineering and technology 0.71 per cent, and teacher education 65 per cent.

Victorian figures show that females make up only 16.1 per cent of the college population.[24] (However, this figure ignores nursing which, probably because it is a female-dominated occupation, is treated as sub-tertiary.) Teachers colleges are more 'female' institutions. Between 1959 and 1969 the percentage of female students enrolled in Victorian Education Department primary colleges rose from 72 to 81 per cent. In addition 54.6 per cent of secondary college students were female.[25]

National figures, now available for all teacher education,[26] including teachers colleges, colleges of advanced education and universities, show similar trends. Females comprise 63.45 per cent of all enrolments with 76 per cent of all full-time primary teacher trainees and 54 per cent of full-time secondary trainees. Interesting differences exist between the percentages of females enrolled at government teachers colleges (the lowest in the academic pecking order) – 68 per cent, and those enrolled in teachers colleges but also attending a university – 56 per cent.

One of the hoary myths is that women tertiary students do less well (I can well remember jibes about Matrimony 1). Like most arguments based on the wasted effort involved in the education of girls, it is totally inaccurate. Indeed a major study of the progress of the 1961 university intake carried out by the then Commonwealth Department of Education and Science found that 66 per cent of female full-time students passed, compared with a male figure of 63.5 per cent.[27] Furthermore those females who successfully passed first year did considerably better at the end of the second year, with a female pass rate of 84 per cent and a male rate of 77 per cent.[28] Women undertaking part-time subjects in arts and economics did have a higher tendency to drop out, but those continuing had a higher pass rate both for subjects commenced and exams sat for.[29] The overall graduation rate of women was slightly higher than that for men, but few took honours degrees and even fewer won firsts.[30]

Scholarships Won

The smaller percentage of females remaining in the qualifications race is one indicator of disadvantage; the award of scholarships is another. The Commonwealth Secondary Scholarship Scheme has now been abandoned but prior to its phasing out girls had moved towards equality, taking 41 per cent of awards in 1965 but 49 per cent in 1971. Males however dominated the equivalent technical scholarships, reopening the gap.

With the scheme's replacement by a needs-oriented selection mechanism a new sex imbalance is likely to arise. Grants will be obtained by students whose families are at the lower end of the socio-economic scale. The evidence presented so far in this chapter suggests a slightly lower participation rate for girls coming from such backgrounds. It is therefore reasonable to expect a higher percentage of these new grants going to boys than to girls. What will occur is an entirely unintentional piece of sex discrimination automatically stemming from the lack of thought given to the problem of educating girls.

Tertiary scholarships are also being phased out, and the new scheme is open to the same criticism of discrimination. How-

Table 10

Distribution of Commonwealth Tertiary Scholarships in Victoria 1964–8

		1964		
Group of Schools	*Sex*	*No. of Schols.*	*No. of Pupils*	*Index*
Government Metropolitan	Boys	411	2673	0.155
Government Metropolitan	Girls	205	1616	0.125
Government Country	Boys	100	889	0.115
Government Country	Girls	71	853	0.085
Independent Catholic	Boys	246	1296	0.190
Independent Catholic	Girls	86	802	0.105
Independent non-Catholic	Boys	329	1598	0.205
Independent non-Catholic	Girls	203	1338	0.150
		1968		
Group of Schools	*Sex*	*No. of Schols.*	*No. of Pupils*	*Index*
Government Metropolitan	Boys	519	3426	0.152
Government Metropolitan	Girls	259	2366	0.109
Government Country	Boys	159	1289	0.123
Government Country	Girls	103	1296	0.079
Independent Catholic	Boys	264	1466	0.180
Independent Catholic	Girls	143	1152	0.124
Independent non-Catholic	Boys	477	1868	0.256
Independent non-Catholic	Girls	305	1590	0.192

ever, the old scheme contained in practice a significant sex differential. Research carried out by Monash University's Professor Fensham though aimed at showing differences between school types unintentionally revealed that differences in gaining scholarships were as much a matter of sex as school type.[31]

Subjects Taken and Achievement

Females tend to take different subjects from males at both secondary and tertiary levels. An Australian College of Education report aptly noted that 'the education pattern of girls is role-oriented towards traditionally female occupations.'[32] 'Possibly the most notable evidence of the strength of female role orientation is girls' lack of participation in scientific-technical studies.'[33]

Professor Martin argues that to the older pattern of home-making subjects such as cooking and sewing, are added advanced courses oriented to the expectation that girls will enter typically female occupations such as secretarial work, food services and dressmaking.[34] At one of the schools to which Martin refers 39 per cent of the males in fourth form were enrolled in the 'academic' course, with no 'practical' subjects, compared with 17 per cent of the girls; and 68 per cent of girls were taking typing. Cooper mentions a comparison of pairs of NSW sex segregated schools.[35] Twenty per cent of boys but only 10 per cent of girls were doing pre-tertiary level science; maths was also male dominated.

Over the last twenty years the Victorian figures have moved in an unexpected direction. While more girls undertake HSC they mainly sit for the humanities; but in the sciences, they take biology and zoology, not chemistry (35 per cent of girls sat in 1946, and 18 per cent in 1970), or physics, which shows a smaller drop.[36]

Victorian VUSEB figures for 1973 show the sex breakdown for particular subjects taken as part of the matriculation examination.[37]

Table 11

Subjects taken in Victorian Matriculation 1973

	Boys	*Girls*
Pure Maths	3469	1292
Calculus and Applied Maths	3308	1082
Physics	4550	1256
English Literature	1859	4908

VUSEB examination results, however, do not show females performing less well in science exams. It is more that by long tradition boys had to do maths, after all they were boys, but girls if they had difficulty were not discouraged from dropping the subject altogether or moving to a more general and cursory arithmetic-based course. Further, girls-only schools have had less access to maths and science teachers and to science facilities. An overall national picture is presented in Table 12, from Radford and Keeves.[38]

Table 12

Indices of selectivity by sex of students in maths

Ratio male: female for all students in the pre-tertiary year	1.39: 1.00
Ratio male: female of mathematics students in the pre-tertiary year	2.32: 1.00

Keeves, the Australian co-ordinator of an international study into science and maths, has reported vastly different science and maths participation rates for males and females in the last year of secondary education and even more so at first year university level. In addition the study found significant sex differences in achievement and interest in maths and science.[39] Girls, even in the mid 1970s, rarely undertake science, engineering or medical courses.

It may be argued semi-humorously that it is the boys who are thus disadvantaged. However, what occurs is that girls from an early age are locked out of particular areas of study, the sciences and maths, and consequently from a wide range of employment possibilities.

National studies of achievement do not exist. Nevertheless a couple of studies suggest that those girls who remain at school do at least as well and in many cases better than their male counterparts. I have already referred to higher university pass rates. A 1961 publication by Drinkwater, following a survey in NSW and Queensland concluded that boys performed consistently better in science and social studies while girls were superior in art, music, literature and reading activity.[40] The previously cited enquiry into education in South Australia analysed marks for the five best subjects of each candidate at the 1968 Leaving Examination: 'The performance of the girls remained consistently superior, no matter how the total candidates were divided into sub-groups. The results of the sub-groups, metropolitan, country, high school, technical high school and non-government . . . illustrate this observation.'[41] Space precludes showing here the highly detailed table; it suffices to say that 58.1 per cent of all girls and 44.8 per cent of all boys obtained marks better than or equal to the median mark for all candidates.

The Overseas Situation

Australia is far from unique in any of these examples of covert discrimination: studies of access in Europe and North America have produced similar patterns. Any reader interested in detailed comparative tables can find then in *Access to Education from the Point of View of the School, Economic and Cultural Origins of Students* (UNESCO, Paris, 1967). Sex differences, one notes, have been omitted from the title, though not from the tables.

A recent report on opportunities for women in higher education in the USA gave chapter and verse on disadvantages in admission to college and to graduate school and in their appointment and pay as staff members.[42] Although we like to view Sweden as the mecca of educational liberation, their situation is the same as ours. It is the countries of Eastern Europe – Bulgaria, Poland, USSR and Hungary – plus Finland, where female participation rates in the final secondary, and tertiary years have moved nearest to those of males.

Keeves in his articles on maths and science puts the international picture clearly and I reproduce one of his tables.[43]

Table 13

Ratio of Male to Female Students at School and University 1964 and 1970

	Secondary School Level	*Technical Secondary School Level*		*First Year University Level*	
	14 yr old level	*Enrolled at School*	*Maths Specialist*	*Enrolled in all subjects*	*Studying Science*
Country	*1970*	*1970*	*1964*	*1964*	*1970*
Australia	1.0	1.4	2.3	2.6	3.2
Belgium	1.0	1.5	7.1	3.4	4.2
England	1.0	1.4	5.5	3.2	2.8
F. R. Germany	1.1	1.6	3.9	3.1	3.5
Finland	1.0	0.8	1.7	1.0	1.2
Japan	1.0	1.1	2.1	2.3	6.7
Netherlands	1.1	1.8	5.4	4.9	6.7
Scotland	1.0	1.3	2.0	1.9	3.0
Sweden	1.0	1.1	2.8	1.5	2.0
USA	1.0	1.1	2.4	1.4	3.8

Source: Data supplied by I.E.A. National Centres in 1964 and 1970 for this and all other tables; from Keeves, p.49.

Conclusions

This chapter has concentrated on qualifications and on the level of education which girls achieve in relationship to boys. However it does have two major and serious bases. Firstly, whether we like it or not we live in a qualifications-oriented society. Employers, tertiary institutions and the like do not ask whether a person is well educated, but for the evidence that the person is well *schooled*, and possesses an appropriate document to prove it. Those without qualifications suffer; employment and further education possibilities are restricted. The simple and unpalatable fact is that women as a group do not possess qualifications equal to those of men. Secondly, formal education as we know it does provide opportunities for intellectual, cultural and social development. The fact that so many girls are deprived of these opportunities cannot be dismissed easily.

In all this, however, it must be recognized that not all girls and women are equally affected. The South Australian material strongly suggests that socio-economic status has a major impact on the level a girl will reach. Daughters of the upper middle classes have the same retention rate as do their brothers.

To reiterate, legal barriers have to all intents and purposes disappeared. But other barriers do exist, and must be identified: amongst the inputs – the quantity and quality of educational resources – socio-psychological factors, attitudes of society, and their effect on the aspirations of women.

While the majority of schools are co-educational a substantial number are single-sex. Keeves's figures are that 36 per cent of 14-year-olds were attending single-sex schools (and 6 per cent co-ed, but taught separately) with a terminal secondary percentage of 46 per cent.[44] Firstly, on the whole, girls schools have been underprivileged in matters of staffing, in terms of qualifications, degrees, and permanency of staffing in general and in science and maths in particular. This holds true whether public or private systems are examined.[45] A recent survey by Harper and Heath matched co-educational and girls high schools in Victoria,[46] and found that 49 per cent of staff in the co-ed schools had degrees compared with 31 per cent in the girls schools. Discrepancies were even greater in maths and science where Harper reports 72 per cent of fourth form maths pupils at the co-educational schools taught by teachers with degrees, contrasted with a girls school figure of 18 per cent.

Secondly, less finance may be available; for instance, Nance Cooper in *It's People That Matter* mentions average total parental contributions to 240 New South Wales high schools of $2,131 for girls and $3,034 for boys.[47] It isn't accidental that fees at girls private non-Catholic schools are an average 25 per cent less than at schools for boys. Reference has already been made to differential scholarship-winning rates and parallel early leaving.

Thirdly, while girls may get superb domestic arts facilities, they get fewer science laboratories, libraries and other 'luxuries' for mothers-to-be.

Any conclusion from inputs must of necessity be impressionistic, but the trends are there. More crucial are the actions of the schools themselves, their expectations of girls, their male-oriented curricula. Secondary schools tend not to offer girls the same facilities and encouragement to prepare for tertiary education.

Just as a content analysis of curricula and text books is required to expose racial bias, so in the same way a study of sex-role typing in schools is essential. As an indication, a cursory glance through primary school libraries shows males as the dominant participant in adventure stories – girls in general are the admiring helpers. (For a detailed discussion see Chapter 13.) In these matters the school merely reinforces society's own view. It is parent and peer group attitudes and expectations and the girl's own self image which go furthest in explaining unequal opportunity.

If women are to 'end up' in the home why educate them or why encourage them in useless non-domestic subjects, so runs the popular argument. A 1969 Victorian Education Department study of parental and student attitudes found no parents agreeing that girls should stay at school longer than boys, but 37 per cent responding that boys should remain longer. When asked for attitudes towards particular subjects most parents saw art as female, and maths as male. A clear majority favoured economic life goals for boys and social life goals for girls.

Not only parents have such views. A survey of 86 fifth form students at six Sydney high schools[48] found boys with a clearer view of what they wanted to do, far more committed to tertiary education (male 45 per cent, female 23 per cent). To quote Bierman '78 per cent of boys agreed that they needed more education than girls while only 35 per cent of girls agreed. The boys tended to explain their agreement in terms of being the head of the future family and the girls rested their disagreement on their desire for sexual equality.'

Recent research by Dr Don Edgar of La Trobe University confirms the strength of role conditioning at home and school. 'Girls are significantly lower than boys on measures of self esteem and self confidence.'[49] While at higher educational levels girls and boys hope for similarly lofty occupations, at the lower levels boys aspire higher. When asked what level they (girls) realistically expect to achieve, girls drop their ambitions drastically. With equal pay and promotion still a myth, Edgar's sample was in fact being realistic.

Schools can improve the hopes and achievements of girls to a minor extent; radical reform must await societal change. There is however no excuse for the formal education system positively reinforcing society's attitudes and practices. Wherever change is possible it should be pursued. Undoubtedly the educational level of girls and women will continue to rise, but that of men and boys will do likewise. Without massive reform women, faced by dramatic social and technological change, will remain locked into a dependent secondary role.

Notes

1. A. Zainu 'Uddin, 'Admission of Women to the University of Melbourne', *Melbourne Studies in Education 1973*, Melbourne University Press, Melbourne, 1973, pp.50–106.
2. Melbourne University Act, Victoria, no.6405, p.29.
3. Sir William Windeyer, 'The Higher Education of Women in New South Wales', in Countess of Warwick (ed.) *Progress in Women's Education in the British Empire*, Longmans, London, 1898, p.295.
4. *Ibid.*, p.300.
5. Anonymous, signed C.S.A., 'Education and the Rights of Women', David Gall, Adelaide, 1969, p.12.
6. M. Webb, *The Women's Advocate*, First edition, no.2, T. N. Wade, Melbourne, 1873, p.2.
7. *Ibid.*, p.15.

8. J. I. Martin, 'Sex Differences in Educational Qualifications', *Melbourne Studies in Education 1972*, Melbourne University Press, Melbourne, 1972, p.97.

9. Norman MacKenzie, *Women in Australia*, Cheshire, Melbourne, 1962.

10. Department of Public Instruction, 'Reducing Wastage Among the Gifted', Bulletin no.13, Brisbane, 1957.

11. Commonwealth of Australia, 1966 Census Bulletin no. 9, 1, Canberra, Table 25.

12. Commonwealth of Australia, Australian Census 1971. p.4 table 12.

13. J. E. Bourke, 'Educational Attainment and Migration', *Australian Journal of Education*, vol.15, no.1, pp.1–15.

14. Ibid.

15. W. C. Radford, *School Leavers in Australia*, A.C.E.R., Melbourne, 1962.

16. Commonwealth Bureau of Census and Statistics, *Schools 1972*, Table 2, p.5, and *Schools 1973*, Table 2, p.5.

17. *The Martin Report on Tertiary Education in Australia*, Report of the Committee on the Future of Tertiary Education in Australia to the Australian Universities Commission 1964.

18. *Committee of Inquiry into Education 1969–70*, Government Printer, Adelaide, 1971, p.62.

19. Queensland Department of Education, Bulletin 37, 'Research findings related to some aspects of the Commonwealth Secondary Scholarship Scheme in Queensland', Department of Education, Brisbane, 1970, p.68.

20. T. W. Roper, *The Myth of Equality*, Heinemann Educational Books, Melbourne, 1970, p.43.

21. South Australia Committee of Enquiry, p.363.

22. Commonwealth of Australia, Bureau of Census and Statistics, University Statistics, 1973 (Preliminary).

23. Commonwealth of Australia, Bureau of Census and Statistics, Colleges of Advanced Education, 1973 (Preliminary).

24. Australian College of Education, Victorian Chapter, *The Education of Girls and the Employment of Women*, A.C.E.R., Melbourne, 1971, p.17.

25. Australian College of Education report, p.38.

26. Commonwealth of Australia, Bureau of Census and Statistics Teacher Education, 1973. Table 1, p.5; Table 5, p.9; and Table 7, p.11.

27. Department of Education and Science, *The 1961 Study*, Australian Government Publishing Service, Canberra, 1971, pp.204–6. See part 2 of this chapter for recent statistics.

28. Ibid., pp.214–16.

29. Ibid., p.273.

30. Ibid., p.163–4.

31. P. Fensham, *Rights and Inequality in Australian Education*, Cheshire, Melbourne, 1970, p.153.

32. Australian College of Education report, p.13.

33. Ibid., p.17.

34. Martin, op.cit.

35. N. Cooper, 'The Education of Women', in D. McLean (ed.) *It's People That Matter*, Angus and Robertson, Sydney, 1969, pp.76–7.

36. S. Encel, N. MacKenzie, M. Tebbutt, *Women and Society: An Australian Study*, Cheshire, Melbourne, 1974, p.181–2.

37. *Handbook* for 1973, VUSEB, Melbourne, 1973, pp.63–4.

38. W. Radford & J. Keeves, *Some Aspects of Performance in Mathematics in Australian Schools*, A.C.E.R., Melbourne, 1969, p.49.

39. J. Keeves, 'Differences between the Sexes in Mathematics and Science Courses', *International Review of Education*, vol.19(1), 1973, pp.47–62.

J. Keeves, 'Sex Differences in Science and Mathematics Courses', 1972, unpublished paper.

40. D. J. Drinkwater, *Development in Early Adolescence and the Structure of Secondary Education in Brisbane*, 1961, p.33.

41. South Australian Committee of Enquiry, p.74.

42. Carnegie Commission, Higher Education, *Opportunities for Women in Higher Education*, McGraw Hill, Berkeley, 1973.

43. Keeves, op.cit. p.49.

44. Keeves, op.cit. p.52.

45. For further details see Martin, pp.107–113.

46. J. Harper and D. Heath, 'Separate and Unequal', *Dissent*, no.28, 1972, p.9.

47. Cooper, op.cit. p.77.

48. D. Bierman, 'Social Forces Affecting Fifth Students in NSW, etc.' Research Notes, *Refractory Girl*, Summer 1974, p.48.

49. D. Edgar, 'Role Conditioning in Education', *Dissent*, no.30. Spring, 1973, pp.9–11.

Six (Part two)

Inequalities in the Australian Education System Women in the Professions

Included in the 1973 Monash University Report to Council was a table detailing the number of degrees and diplomas conferred, according to sex, during the year. The fact that women should have received only one-third of the total number of degrees awarded was perhaps predictable (though no more acceptable) in terms of the bias that has been noted in family, school and media towards encouraging higher education for boys, in preference to girls.[1] What is also depressingly evident however, is that, in this select sample of students of proven academic ability, only males see the full range of professional careers open to them. A disproportionate number of females (half the female enrolment) have apparently succumbed to the pressures of their socialization and perceive their career potential as limited to the social sciences (see Table 1 on Page 140). That Monash enrolments are representative of all Australian universities is evident in Table 2 on Page 141.[2]

It is apparent that university training is perceived differently by males and females. For the majority of males a first degree is an entree to the profession of their choice, or a prerequisite to postgraduate study.

For the majority of females – 65.3 per cent as Table 3 shows – the degree leads in one direction – to a teaching career, though even here most fail to rise to the top. In 1971, for example, though women comprised 65 per cent of permanent staff in Victorian state primary schools, there were no female head teachers.[3] In any event, primary and secondary teaching, despite teachers' claims to the contrary, has not yet achieved the status of 'profession' in terms of Moore's criteria since its members lack autonomy and control of entry. Moore sees a profession as a full-time occupation, identified by some form of organization to protect and enhance its interests. It must possess a body of

Table 1

Academic Developments

The following degrees and diplomas were conferred by the University at graduation ceremonies in 1973, the final column indicating the total number of degrees and diplomas awarded since the foundation of the University.

	Male	*Female*	*1973 Total*	*1961–73 Total*
Bachelor of Arts	171	345	516	3389
B.A. (Honours)	43	50	93	509
Master of Arts	17	5	22	95
Bachelor of Economics	238	64	302	1716
B.Ec. (Honours)	37	9	46	228
Master of Administration	15	1	16	22
Master of Economics	7	—	7	45
Bachelor of Education	102	34	136	335
Master of Education	12	3	15	18
Bachelor of Engineering	62	1	63	305
B.Eng. (Honours)	65	2	67	391
Master of Engineering Science	9	—	9	60
Bachelor of Jurisprudence	73	19	92	508
Bachelor of Laws	89	17	106	398
LL.B. (Honours)	10	2	12	44
Master of Laws	1	—	—	7
Bachelor of Medical Science	—	—	—	11
B. Med. Sc. (Honours)	12	4	16	76
M.B., B.S.	74	13	87	654
M.B., B.S. (Honours)	32	6	38	173
Bachelor of Science	162	89	251	1047
B.Sc. (Honours)	83	29	112	664
Master of Science	10	3	13	120
Doctor of Philosophy	83	10	93	437
Doctor of Medicine	1	—	1	8
Doctor of Science	—	—	—	2
TOTAL DEGREES	1408	706	2114	11 262
Diploma in Education	237	305	542	2523

Source: *Report of the Council of Monash University 1973*, Monash University, Melbourne, 1974.

Table 2

Full-Time First-Degree Courses, Men and Women

Course	*Men*	*Women*
Humanities	16.5%	42.2%
Behavioural Sciences	5.3%	12.1%
Economics and Commerce	17.2%	6.7%
Law	5.7%	1.8%
Education	3.8%	5.7%
Physical Sciences	6.6%	2.5%
Biological Sciences	5.8%	9.8%
Mathematics	6.8%	5.5%
Agricultural Science and Forestry	2.9%	1.1%
Earth and Environmental Sciences	6.5%	4.9%
Veterinary Science	1.4%	0.4%
Engineering and Applied Science	11.5%	0.4%
Architecture etc.	2.4%	0.5%
Medicine	5.6%	2.6%
Dentistry	1.2%	0.2%
Pharmacy	0.6%	1.4%
Para-medical Therapies	0.0%	1.1%
Music	0.2%	1.1%
	100.0%	100.0%

Comparisons, Men and Women

There are marked differences in employment between men and women. A woman is twice as likely to become a teacher, less likely to go on to higher studies and only one-third as likely to work in the private sector. She is also less likely to work in government service and slightly more likely to be unemployed. She is considerably more likely (5.0 per cent as against 1.5 per cent) to be unavailable for full-time employment. There are also significant differences between men and women in the distribution of courses undertaken (see Table 2). There is a clear interaction between employment and studies: on the one hand the choice of course affects employment while, on the other hand, perceived employment prospects for women will affect the choice of course. There is a strong tendency for men, compared with women, to take 'professional' and 'vocational' courses (see Table 2). In general women are more likely to undertake full-time study (84 per cent compared with 77.5 per cent of men).

Source: K. Gravell, and S. J. Rawling, *Destinations of 1972 Australian University Graduates*, The Graduate Careers Council, Melbourne, 1974.

esoteric knowledge based on specialized training which bestows a high degree of autonomy on its members, who in turn possess a commitment to their calling involving loyalty to peers, and a service orientation implying a relationship of trust and confidentiality with those using their services.[4]

In the professions that women do enter, significant differences exist between the proportion of males and females achieving the highest ranking positions. For example, a disproportionate number of women lawyers in America specialize in the low-ranking specialty of matrimonial law and a disproportionate percentage of women doctors practise psychiatry, a relatively low-ranking medical specialty.[5] Similarly, a disproportionately large number of professional women are likely to be found in government service (of low prestige) and few in private practice (high prestige). (Table 3 from Gravell and Rawling gives the Australian figures.) In tertiary teaching academic women tend to be associated with low-status or low-prestige institutions and/or to cluster at the lower end of the teaching hierarchy.[6] The University of Melbourne, for example, has 71 females at tutor/demonstrator level in the Faculty of Arts but no female professor; it has 45 male tutors and 17 male professors – see Table 4 on Page 144.

The overall picture of women in professions is a depressing one for feminists: women tend to gravitate to the service-oriented professions, to cluster in institutions and positions of low prestige.

Table 5 which looks at employment figures for Australian universities clearly shows how the majority of women employed in these institutions are not to be found amongst the academic staff but in the clerical, librarian and junior administrative positions.

Many women lack career commitment and see tertiary education as of secondary importance to their major goal of marriage. Increased access to higher education has been subverted, as Firestone points out, so that often the only difference between a university-educated housewife and her traditional prototype is 'the jargon she [uses] in describing her marital hell'.[7]

Part of the explanation for this strange phenomenon lies in the desire of women themselves to relegate their professional careers to a secondary position in their lives. Because some women regard marriage and family as of prime importance, they deliberately choose to pursue careers in institutions which allow them maximum freedom for family commitments, with the possibility of return to work after child-rearing. They are, in effect, looking for reasonably interesting stop-gaps to occupy them before marriage and after children enter school. These are women who have internalized the traditional female role embodied in the women's magazines: they accept as right and proper that their place is 'in the home', by their husband's side or preferably, a few paces behind. The magazine heroine of a million ads, entertaining to further her husband's career, or encouraging her children in suitable (sex-typed) activities, cannot commit herself to a career which requires that she lead a life of her own. Hence the popularity of teaching, an occupation eminently suited to 'fitting in' to family schedules. The fact that a very sharp drop occurs in the proportion of females

Table 3

Distribution of Graduates in Employment*

How Employed	*All First Degree*	*Male First Degree*	*Female First Degree*	*Higher Degree*	*P/G Diploma*
Australian Government	15.2%	16.1%	8.3%	14.4%	3.0%
States	21.8%	22.5%	13.1%	15.3%	7.4%
Private Industry and Commerce	17.3%	20.3%	5.8%	14.4%	2.6%
Professional Practice	13.2%	14.9%	5.5%	5.3%	1.0%
Education	30.3%	24.2%	65.3%	48.1%	84.7%
Other	2.2%	2.0%	2.0%	2.5%	1.3%
Total	100.0%	100.0%	100.0%	100.0%	100.0%

* Excluding those undertaking further studies and training, unemployed or unavailable for employment and overseas.

Source: K. Gravell, and S. J. Rawling, *Destinations of 1972 Australian University Graduates*, The Graduate Careers Council, Melbourne, 1974.

Table 4
Full-Time Staff at University of Melbourne 1974

	Females	Males
Professors		
Engineering	0	9
Medicine	0	34
Science	0	22
Arts	0	17
Psychology	0	3
Sr. Lecturers and Readers		
Engineering	0	53
Medicine	14	116
Science	4	96
Arts	13	80
Psychology	1	9
Lecturers		
Engineering	0	38
Medicine	10	63
Science	12	63
Arts	23	44
Psychology	4	4
Tutors and Demonstrators		
Engineering	4	14
Medicine	15	27
Science	21	35
Arts	71	45
Psychology	8	6
All Staff		
Engineering	4	114
Medicine	39	240
Science	38	216
Arts	107	186
Psychology	13	22
Permanent Staff		
Engineering	0	100
Medicine	24	213
Science	17	181
Arts	36	141
Psychology	5	16

Source: *National U*, vol.10, no.10, June 3, 1974.

taking out higher degrees in education (see Table 1) is evidence that the majority of females entering teaching are not seriously committed to reaching the top of this profession.

I will argue later that there are processes within the professions which discriminate against the women who enter them. Before doing that, however, I would like to refer briefly to the sex-stereotyping influences a female encounters which reinforce the perception that women are different and unequal and cause her voluntarily to exempt herself from the full range of human potential. Exposure to sex-role stereotyping begins at an early age with imposed preferences for clothes and toys, reinforced by sexist storybooks[8] (see also Chapter 13). Parental practice has been shown to be linked significantly with a tendency towards aggression in boys and dependency in girls[9] and this is repeated in the classroom where Davidson and Lang found teachers likely to reward girls for dependence, friendliness and conformity, and some boys at least, for autonomy, independence and creativity.[10] Coleman has drawn attention to the strength of the norms of the adolescent sub-culture in shaping girls in the traditional female stereotype, while the blatantly sexist nature of career counselling has been documented by Healy.[11] Finally, the 'models' a girl is likely to encounter – whether in the classroom teaching situation, in school texts, or magazine fiction – almost invariably reinforce the notion that a woman's true function lies in service. Social worker, teacher, librarian, housewife, are seen as pinnacles for girls' aspirations.[12]

The result of all this conditioning is, for females, a narrowly circumscribed view of their potential, which is mirrored in the university enrolment figures referred to above. Fewer girls than boys undertake tertiary training, and of those who do, most settle for an Arts degree and a career in teaching. In the sciences this service-orientation is more likely to lead to careers of laboratory assistant, engineering aide, or medical technician rather than responsible careers as scientist, engineer or doctor.[13] This is essentially an accommodation made by women to resolve the conflict aroused by different expectations of career role and traditional female role. Simone de Beauvoir puts it most succinctly when she says:

Table 5

Males and Females on the Staffs of Australian Universities – A selected table

Designation	*Males*	*Females*	*Persons*
Full-time Staff – (Teaching)			
Permanent positions –			
Professors	834	14	848
Associate professors	359	7	366
Readers	456	16	472
Senior lecturers	2110	123	2233
Lecturers	1987	306	2293
Assistant lecturers	436	198	633
Demonstrators, tutors, teaching fellows	845	473	1318
Research (other than Technical)			
Permanent positions –			
Professors	62	..	62
Associate professors, readers	124	4	128
Senior lecturers, lecturers	321	42	363
Junior positions	209	247	456
Temporary positions –			
Professors	6	..	6
Associate professors, readers	2	1	3
Senior lecturers, lecturers	189	16	205
Junior positions	170	158	328
Total research (other than technical)	1083	467	1550
Library –			
Professional	101	327	428
Other	360	810	1169
Total library	460	1137	1597

Table 5—*continued*

Designation	*Males*	*Females*	*Persons*
Central administration –			
Chief administrative officers	65	1	66
Senior administrative officers	118	4	122
Administrative officers	184	10	194
Administrative assistants	206	24	230
Clerks, typists, etc.	780	1385	2165
Total central administration	1353	1424	2777
Departmental administration –			
Chief administrative officers	1	..	1
Senior administrative officers	11	..	11
Administrative officers	30	3	33
Administrative assistants	57	16	73
Clerks, typists, etc.	127	1933	2060
Total departmental administration	226	1952	2178
Developmental work and construction			
Professional	67	2	69
Tradesmen	5	1	6
Other	34	23	57
Total developmental work and construction	106	26	132
Maintenance	2239	792	3031
Sundry	604	656	1259
Total other	8783	7205	15 988
Total full-time staff	16 935	8819	25 754

Source: *University Statistics, 1972, Part 2*, Australian Bureau of Census and Statistics.

With man there is no break between public or private life: the more he confirms his grasp on the world in action and in work, the more virile he seems to be; human and vital values are combined in him. Whereas woman's independent successes are in contradiction with her femininity, since the 'true woman' is required to make herself object, to be the Other.[14]

It is worth noting that marriage for the male professional generally means the acquisition of a help-mate – source of material comforts and sexual satisfaction, a hostess, often a typist, certainly a general factotum (even a source of income while he studies full-time for higher degrees). For his female colleague, however, marriage often involves merely a doubling of her work load and juggling of competing demands accompanied often, where children are involved, by feelings of anxiety and guilt.[15]

Ironically, this idealization of the service-oriented, homemaker role has been shown to undergo modification as women experience marriage and parenthood. In a study of 8,000 female college graduates, Rossi reported that, while only 16 per cent of single 'homemakers'* felt a mother should take on part-time employment with a child less than five years old, 35 per cent of married homemakers approved maternal employment while a child was still a pre-schooler. Similarly, Rossi found single homemakers far more strongly 'traditional'† than married homemakers. She interpreted these findings, I think rightly, as

* Women graduates who reported that they had no career goal other than being 'housewives'. The study contrasted their attitudes with those of 'traditionals', whose career goals were in fields predominated by women, and 'pioneers' whose career goals were in predominantly masculine fields.

† The *traditional* viewpoint of Rossi's questionnaire stressed the differences between the roles of men and women, in which women's lives centre on home and family and their job participation is in such fields as teaching, social work, nursing and secretarial service. The *feminist* viewpoint, in contrast, stressed greater equality and similarity in the roles of men and women than now exist, with greater participation of women in leadership positions in politics, the professions and business.

an indication that the reality of marriage and parenthood fails to provide the complete fulfilment for women that their socialization has led them to expect. Of course by the time women discover they have been 'conned' it is often too late to restructure career patterns.[16]

Apart from successful socialization into the traditional female role, a further barrier to women realizing their full potential is a stereotyped view of the professions themselves, resulting in some being perceived (illogically) as inappropriate for women. A massive sampling of women college graduates in 1961 revealed, for example, that 80 per cent perceived the reason for low representation of women in medicine as the fact that it was 'too demanding for a woman to combine with family responsibilities'.[17] As pointed out by Rossi the popular stereotype of the twenty-four-hour family physician probably has its roots in the distant past and has little relation to the reality of contemporary partnerships, group practices, increased specialization, staff appointments, restricted house calls, and so on.[18] In many instances a medically-qualified woman will have more flexibility of routine and shorter hours of work than she would as a paramedical technician. Similarly, engineering was perceived as a profession requiring 'skills and characteristics women do not have'. One is at a loss to imagine what peculiarly 'masculine' traits are involved for the majority of engineers working behind desks, unless a stereotype is involved of a rugged individual battling the elements to produce roads and bridges single-handed. Something of the sort must apply because a staggering 61 per cent of respondents considered that women were afraid of being thought unfeminine by entering this field. Plainly, as long as such occupations are defined as 'male', women who seek entry to them will be defined as deviant and subjected to social sanctions.

The typing of certain occupations as male or female has consequences for entry to them and performance within them by persons possessing the 'wrong sex'. Epstein has pointed out processes in male-dominated professions which actively inhibit women's participation in them. One of these is what she calls the 'protege system', or master-apprentice relationship.[19]

Advancement in a profession is often achieved through junior members being helped, encouraged, 'promoted' in many ways by more senior members – this is particularly evident in university departments where senior staff become involved in and identified with research of junior members. It occurs also, however, in any professional situation where young staff members are groomed to step into the shoes of retiring colleagues. Women in these circumstances can be at a disadvantage when the senior member is male, partly through reservations on his part about her total commitment (he hesitates to name as successor someone who might desert her career for marriage) and partly through pressure exerted by his wife and colleagues against establishing a too-close relationship with a female. (Note again the salience of the sex-role – in this situation she is female first and researcher, budding executive or whatever a poor second, regardless of whether her qualifications outrank those of male competitors.)

Her sex is again likely to count against her in the informal network which underpins male-dominated professions.* In order to establish a reputation in any field it is necessary to acquire not only technical competence, but a grasp of what and who make things tick. Martha White refers to a post-training period analogous to the medical internship during which the individual learns the roles, the informal values, attitudes and expectations which are an important part of real professional life.[20] Much of this professional socialization occurs in interaction with colleagues outside the work situation, but women are likely to meet opposition from colleagues and the wives of colleagues if they attempt to 'join the club', or will voluntarily give up such attempts in the face of the discomfort experienced through over-reaction to their sex.

* The situation can, of course, work in reverse – against males in a female-dominated profession. Interestingly, though, women rarely reach the top, even in their 'own' lines – how many females are school principals or chief librarians? A possible exception is the nursing matron (usually female) but even she is responsible to the hospital's chief of staff who is usually male.

If any doubt should exist that women face discrimination in professions it is worth examining those studies which have compared the relative salary and standing of equally qualified women and men. A very detailed study of income differentials between men and career women in America in 1966 was made by Suter and Miller.[21] In the most restricted analysis (i.e. using only salaries of women who had worked every year since entering the workforce) it was found that women earned 75 per cent as much as men; for those who had worked in only half the years since leaving school the figure was 23 per cent. The authors point out, however, that the ratio of the median wages between men and women actually understates the difference in earnings between the sexes because men are much more likely than women to have salaries that fall toward the upper end of the income distribution. Margaret Power's review of incomes in Australia in 1968–9 showed similar findings.[22] Power showed that the more education and training women acquire, the greater is their disadvantage relative to men. Because the equal-step increases a woman receives for educational level, age and occupational status are so much smaller than a man's, at the high-prestige end of the scale the female/male income ratio declines still further – she is relatively worse off at the top than she is at the bottom. In American universities evidence of discriminatory differences in rank and pay of equally qualified men and women was reported by Loeb and Ferber while Simon, Clark and Galway also noted that though married and single women are about as productive as men, both lag behind men in salary and rank.[23]

Conclusion

Women tend to gravitate to the service-oriented professions, to cluster in institutions and in positions of low prestige. This is the result partly of women's own desire to relegate career to a place of secondary importance behind marriage. They accept the traditional female role and voluntarily exempt themselves from many professions which they see either as too demanding in terms of commitment, or too 'masculine' in character and hence wrong for their feminine image. I have indicated some of the sources of this sex-role stereotyping.

However, in addition to this voluntary exclusion, there are informal processes at work within professions which cause special difficulties for women. I discussed reasons why women are less likely to gain professional sponsors and to enjoy the opportunities for professional socialization provided in the 'club' context of personal interaction. Finally, I drew attention to the unequal distribution of financial reward and prestige for women whose qualifications and experience are equal to those of their male colleagues – the most practical illustration of their 'wrong sex' in a male-dominated society.

Notes

1. H. H. Davidson and G. Lang, 'Children's perception of their teachers' feelings toward them related to self-perception, school achievement, and behavior', *Journal of Experimental Education*, 29, 1960, pp.107–18.
F. A. Ricks and S. W. Pike, 'Teacher perceptions and attitudes that foster or maintain sex role differences', *Interchange*, vol.4, no.1, 1973.
R. R. Sears, E. E. Maccoby and H. Levin, *Patterns of Child Rearing*, Harper and Row, New York, 1957.
D. E. Edgar, 'Competence for girls?' *The Secondary Teacher*, July 1972.
P. Healy, 'Sexism in career counselling', *Refractory Girl*, Autumn 1973, pp.14–18.

2. K. Gravell and S. J. Rawling, *Destinations of 1972 Australian University Graduates*, The Graduate Careers Council of Australia, Melbourne, 1974.

3. S. Sampson, 'Influences on the educational aspirations of girls: an Australian women's magazine'. Paper presented to the 45th Congress of ANZAAS in Perth, August 1973.

4. W. E. Moore, *The Professions: Roles and Rules*, Russell Sage Foundation, New York, 1970.

5. Cynthia F. Epstein, *Woman's Place: Options and Limits in Professional Careers*, University of California Press, Berkeley, 1970; 'Encountering the male establishment: sex-status limits on women's careers in the professions', *American Journal of Sociology*, vol.75, 1970, pp.965–82.

6. Jessie Bernard, *Academic Women*, World Publishing Company, New York, 1966.

7. Shulamith Firestone, *The Dialectic of Sex: The case for feminist revolution*, Jonathan Cape, London, 1970.

8. L. J. Weitzman et al, 'Sex-role socialization in picture books for preschool children', *American Journal of Sociology*, vol.77, no.6, 1972.

D. Bradley and M. Mortimer, 'Sex role stereotyping in children's picture books', *Refractory Girl*, Summer 1972/3, pp.8–14.

9. Sears, op.cit.

10. Davidson and Lang, op.cit.

11. Healy, op.cit.

J. S. Coleman, 'The adolescent subculture and academic achievement', *American Journal of Sociology*, 65, 1960, pp.337–347.

12. J. Hardin and C. J. Dede, 'Discrimination against women in science education', *The Science Teacher*, vol.40, no.9, December 1973.

J. L. Trecker, 'Women in U.S. history textbooks', *Social Education*, vol.35, no.3, 1971.

Betty Friedan, *The Feminine Mystique*, Chapter 2, 'The Happy Housewife Heroine', Norton, New York, 1963.

13. Bernard, op.cit.

14. Simone de Beauvoir, *The Second Sex*, Penguin Books, 1972 (first published 1949), p.291.

15. J. A. Davis, *Stipends and Spouses: The Finances of American Arts and Science Graduate Students*, University of Chicago Press, Chicago, 1962.

Helen S. Astin, *The Woman Doctorate in America: Origins, career, and family*, Russell Sage Foundation, New York, 1969.

16. Alice S. Rossi, 'Barriers to the career choice of Engineering, Medicine or Science among American women', in J. A. Mattfeld and C. G. Van Aken (eds), *Women and the Scientific Professions*, M.I.T. Press, Massachusetts, 1965.

17. NORC, 'College Graduate Study' at the National Opinion Research Center (MH-05615), 1961.

18. Rossi, op.cit.

19. Epstein, op.cit.

20. Martha S. White, 'Psychological and social barriers to women in science', *Science*, 170, 413, 23 October 1970.

21. Larry E. Suter and H. P. Miller, 'Income differentials between men and career women', *American Journal of Sociology*, 78, July 1972–May 1973.

22. Margaret Power, 'The wages of sex', *The Australian Quarterly*, vol.46, no.1, March 1974.

23. Jane W. Loeb and M. A. Ferber, 'Sex as predictive of salary and status on a university faculty', *Journal of Educational Measurement*, 8, Winter 1971, pp.235–44.

Rita J. Simon, S. M. Clark and K. Galway, 'The woman Ph.D.: a recent profile' *Social Problems*, 15, Fall 1967, pp.221–36.

Seven
Women and Welfare

Capitalism is not based on the organization of production for people but simply on the need to secure maximum profit. It is naive to expect that it will make exceptions of women.

Sheila Rowbotham, *Woman's Consciousness, Man's World**

The Australian welfare system to date has directed its energies towards remedial services to cope with the crisis situation, family or social breakdown. The system provides services which are consciously and unconsciously directed towards maintaining the *status quo*. In their most successful operations, social services attempt to provide, through remedial action, equality of opportunity for the socially disadvantaged. For persons who fail to make it in a competitive world, the welfare network may provide an alternative lifestyle, a lifestyle which emphasizes community responsibility, rather than individual achievement, a 'safety valve' which prevents the development of dangerous levels of alienation.

The position of women in this paternalistic protective system is but a reflection of their role in the wider society. The large numbers of women dependent on the state for income and social services are the inevitable result of woman's inferior position in the economic system.

Women and Income Security

Responsibility for income maintenance rests with the Commonwealth Government, apart from limited emergency financial relief provided through the State welfare departments and some

* Penguin Books, 1973, p.123.

voluntary agencies. Pensions and benefits paid by the Department of Social Security are means-tested, and the majority of recipients are entitled to the full payment, having means assessed at less than $20 per week (for a single person). A large proportion of pensioners are wholly dependent on social security payments, particularly women eligible for the widow's pension. In common with most countries, Australian pension levels are not generous, and income maintenance policies seem directed at the right to exist rather than the right to live a full life.

Table 1

Pensions Paid by Commonwealth Social Security on 30 June 1974 by Sex (Number and percentage distribution)

Pension Type	*Male*		*Female*		*Total*
	number	*percentage*	*number*	*percentage*	*number*
Age Pension	322,433	31.38	705,149	68.62	1,027,582
Invalid Pension	92,140	58.77	64,643	41.23	156,783
Wives' Pension	—	—	47,399	100.00	47,399
Widows' Pension	—	—	115,310	100.00	115,310
Total Pensioners	414,573	30.78	932,501	69.22	1,347,074

Over two-thirds of Social Security pensioners are women. Two categories of payments are made exclusively to women in recognition of their dependent status – widows' and wives' pensions (formerly known as wives' allowance). The largest number of payments and the most expensive item of expenditure of the Social Security budget is the age pension. The greater number of women receiving the pension, more than twice the number of male pensioners, is related to women's greater longevity and earlier entitlement to the pension. However, among persons eligible by age, a larger proportion of women receive the pension. Shorter-term benefits paid by the Department of Social Security reveal an entirely different distribution of payments.

Benefits are seen as a short-term measure to tide families and individuals over the loss of income through unemployment or

Table 2

Pensions and Benefits Paid by Commonwealth Social Security on 30 June 1974 by Sex

(Number and percentage distribution)

Type of Payment	*Male*		*Female*		*Total*
	number	*percentage*	*number*	*percentage*	*number*
Unemployment Benefit	20,080	62.73	11,929	37.27	32,009
Sickness Benefit	17,408	79.00	4,628	21.00	22,036
Special Benefit	704	13.63	4,460	86.37	5,164
Total Benefits	38,192	64.50	21,017	35.50	59,209
Total Pensions & Benefits	452,765	32.20	953,518	67.80	1,406,283

temporary disablement of the breadwinner. Married women are not normally eligible for unemployment benefits. Although a wife's income may mean a man is ineligible for unemployment benefit, should both marriage partners be out of work the husband receives payment for himself and his dependents. Special benefits are paid to unmarried mothers during the pre- and post-natal period for up to eighteen weeks. Of the 1974 figures nearly two-thirds of special benefits were paid for this purpose and most of the remainder were paid to persons (women) caring for invalid parents or other near relatives.

Although the ratio of men to women receiving social security benefits is the reverse of the ratio of male to female pensioners, because benefits are relatively few in number, the overall picture of Social Security payments is little altered by their inclusion. More than twice the number of women as men depend on the State for their basic income.

The single woman's greater economic vulnerability in disability is revealed in an analysis of the marital status of pensioners.

In a survey in May 1973, by the Department of Social Security of characteristics of pensioners in NSW and Victoria, the

Table 3
Marital Status of Age and Invalid Pensioners, NSW and Victoria, May 1973 (Percentage distribution)

Marital Status	Single		Married		Total
	Male	Female	Male	Female	
Age Pensioner	9.9	47.1	20.1	22.8	100
Invalid Pension	31.7	31.6	25.5	11.2	100

proportion of married to single age pensioners between men and women was almost exactly reversed. Twice as many single as married women relied on the State's income maintenance programmes. Men who had the responsibility of a wife were twice as likely to require assistance as single men.

Women and Poverty

As well as merely recording the numbers and characteristics of women dependent upon the State for their basic income, there are other indications of women's vulnerability to poverty.

In 1970 the Federal Government introduced the Subsidized Health Benefits Plan to assist various low-income groups with the costs of health insurance, and to provide reduced pharmaceutical charges. The plan's complexities and its dependence on individual initiative in enrolling in medical insurance schemes have kept participation rates low. However, an analysis of the characteristics of low-income families enrolled in the plan in November 1972 revealed a familiar pattern of the concentration of women in the low-income bracket. Families with a female head were the largest proportion of participants and were found in the lowest income group.

An income and expenditure survey conducted in Melbourne by a research team headed by Professor Ronald Henderson discovered that some 7 per cent of income units surveyed were in poverty, and estimated at least 4 per cent of income units in Melbourne in 1966 were 'in need'.

Table 4

Characteristics of Low-Income Families Enrolled in Subsidized Health Benefits Plan, November 1972 (Percentage distribution)

Total Weekly Income	*Under $51.50*	*$51.50 to $54.50*	*$54.50 to $57.50*	*Total*
Males	33.7	69.2	73.0	36.6
Females	66.3	30.8	27.0	63.4
Total	100.00	100.00	100.00	100.00
No. of families	26,200	1,400	1,200	28,800

Income units were analysed by disabilities like old age, female head, large family, recent migrant, sickness, accident and unemployment, and it was found that 'the families most vulnerable to poverty are these headed by an aged person or a female'.[1] The research team commented:

The low incidence of poverty among the families with non-aged male heads, both with and without dependent children, is a reflection of the fact that almost all adult males are able to secure employment incomes that are sufficient to keep their families out of poverty.[2]

Fatherless families were found to have the highest incidence of poverty. More than a quarter fell below a stringently defined poverty line and one in three was regarded as being in marginal poverty at least. Other studies here and overseas have called attention to the economic plight of fatherless families. In England a study of single-parent families on National Assistance concluded:

Fatherless families are poor because they lack a man's earning power, and the mother's earning power is diminished by her children's needs for her care. In the long run, therefore, the poverty and dependence of the fatherless family can only be eliminated by the attainment of sexual equality of social and economic status in society and by the provision of ancillary child-care services.[3]

Just as a larger proportion of aged women are dependent on Social Security Pensions for income, so poverty amongst the aged is more likely to occur for women than men. The Melbourne Poverty Survey revealed that while families headed by an aged male were more likely to be very poor, more families with an aged female head, normally single-person income units, were below the poverty line. Aged single women in the survey were found to be less likely to have significant means additional to their pension.

The disadvantages and inequalities suffered by women during their working lives result in economic hardship in old age. A cross-national survey of Britain, USA and Denmark of the association between labour market participation and poverty among the old, found that widowed and single aged women were over-represented at the bottom of the income scale, due to women's limited entitlement to contributory occupational pensions.[4]

If a woman has worked in the past, her lower rate of pay will mean she has had less opportunity to secure herself against the eventual loss of earned income. Her savings and other assets will be low or non-existent. Women's lower status employment and low wages have normally excluded them from superannuation schemes. The Melbourne income survey found that just over half of the men at work contributed to superannuation and/or insurance schemes, while barely 20 per cent of women employed outside the home contributed to such schemes.

Woman's Image in Welfare

Woman's image in welfare varies only marginally from the feminine stereotype. Women are seen almost exclusively as wives and mothers, the only apparent difference being that the State or voluntary welfare agency takes on the role of husband and provider. Day care services have been regarded as second best to the mothering provided in the single-income, two-parent family. It is only since the late 1960s that significant numbers of persons active in the welfare field have begun to question the ideal of the nuclear family.

In the face of social and family breakdown, welfare workers have maintained the myth of the 'intact' family and upheld society's traditional values. Welfare's strongest self-criticisms have been reserved for those services which treat social problems on an individual basis divorced from the family situation. This almost obsessive concern for the family emphasizes women's nurturing role and reinforces the traditional stereotype of women as child-rearers and homemakers.

Governments' failure to provide income payments to single-parent families headed by a male discriminates against lone fathers, and reinforces the rigid division between masculine and feminine family responsibilities. It also represents a realistic assessment of the differential between male and female wage rates. At the end of 1973 the widows' pension for a family of four with child(ren) under 6 years amounted to $44 per week, which was not so far below average award rates paid to female process workers, but was well below the male minimum wage.* Similarly, in his study of fatherless families in Britain, Marsden noted that the low rate of women's pay caused up to three-quarters of the women interviewed to find living on national assistance economically preferable to working.

Implicit in the conditions governing eligibility for payments to single parent families is the notion of woman's ultimate dependence on the male provider. A universal feature in all Australian social welfare law is the requirement that a mother applying for financial assistance take maintenance proceedings for herself and her children. Regulations regarding the effect of a woman cohabiting or having sexual relations with a man other than the father of her child are usually at the discretion of the government department making the payment. The Commonwealth Department of Social Security excludes from the widows' pension and its new supporting-mothers' benefit women who are living with a man 'on a bona fide domestic basis'. In interpreting this condition, the officers of the department are expected to

* A recent decision of the Arbitration Commission has made women eligible for the minimum wage, but considerable differences in actual earnings between men and women remain.

take into account the total domestic situation rather than its moral aspects. In spite of this proviso, it is clear that the department upholds society's view that a sexual relationship implies the responsibility of the man for the financial support of a woman and her dependent children.

Much of the inequality suffered by women is the result of her inferior position in the economic system, and society's failure to recognize, monetarily at least, her traditional contribution of child-rearing and housekeeping. The social services, valuing woman's role as mother, apparently redress the balance in guaranteeing income to unsupported mothers, and in maternity allowances and child endowment.

Recently the Commonwealth Government examined a proposal for a mother's allowance or financial assistance to families with children. The rationale behind this proposal included providing women with the opportunity to take on full-time motherhood, to prevent children suffering maternal deprivation, and a means of preventing economic deprivation in single-income families.[5]

A basic feature of the proposal is its unquestioning acceptance of woman's place in the family situation. There was no suggestion that fathers would be eligible for the allowance. The sum under consideration for the allowance, $20 per week, was less than half the lowest amount a woman could expect to earn outside the home, working shorter hours. It is indicative of society's real opinion of the worth of woman's work that such a payment should be regarded as a welfare matter rather than a case for economic justice.

Women as Service Providers

From the other side of the fence, in the area of welfare service provision, women again dominate. Characteristic of the welfare field is its reliance on the unpaid labour of women. Originally welfare services were based on charitable relief dispensed by women from the upper economic classes. As governments gradually assumed responsibility for providing some minimum social services, a duality emerged of voluntary agencies based on unpaid woman power and statutory programmes and services administered by male government officials. The 1940s and 1950s saw the growth of professionalism in the welfare field, with volunteers regarded as aides to social workers. The view that voluntary lay personnel can provide a valuable service in their own right is now re-emerging. What has remained constant in this cycle, has been the composition of the volunteer workforce.

A study of volunteers in social welfare agencies in 1972 found that women are still traditionally seen as the major personnel resource for voluntary agencies.[6]

Sixty-one per cent of the agencies studied estimated that 80 per cent or more of their volunteers were women. Over half the public hospitals and well over a third of all agencies used only women volunteers, and only 2 per cent of them had no female volunteers.

The nature of welfare work, based as it is on the 'feminine' values of feeling and nurturing, encourages the participation of women – both professionally and unpaid. Voluntary welfare work is an attractive alternative to women who are normally underpaid, in boring and often futile jobs. The cultural norm of women's low participation in the workforce creates a large reserve of unpaid female labour for worthy causes.

Social work has been and still is one of the few professions where women outnumber men. The male component of the profession is, however, increasing rapidly. A survey of social workers in Victoria in 1972 reveals a significant change in the composition of the workforce in the five years since 1967.[7]

Table 5

Social Workers in Victoria 1968 and 1972 (Percentages in brackets)

	1968			*1972*		
	Male	*Female*	*Total*	*Male*	*Female*	*Total*
Class I	34 (14.1)	207 (85.9)	241	46 (14.1)	281 (85.9)	327
Class II	13 (24.5)	40 (75.5)	53	36 (27.1)	97 (27.9)	133
Class III	13 (33.3)	26 (66.7)	39	24 (38.7)	38 (61.3)	62
Class IV	7 (35.0)	13 (65.0)	20	21 (50)	21 (50)	42
Total	67 (19.0)	286 (81.0)	353	127 (22.5)	437 (77.5)	564

Male social workers increased by 90 per cent while females increased only by 53 per cent. The most dramatic growth in male participation rates occurred in the most senior administrative positions. Thus, while the present balance between the sexes in the profession overall in Victoria is 23 per cent male to 77 per cent female, at no level in the professional scale is this average achieved. Male social workers are under-represented at the lowest level of the profession and over-represented at every other level.

It is suggested that the reasons for the lower proportions of women in the higher grades of social work are similar to those that keep women under-represented in other professions and in the higher echelons of government and business. The causes include employer preference, reluctance of women to apply for senior positions, and retirement or interruption of a woman's career because of family responsibilities.

More realistically, the growth in the male component of the profession can be seen as both a cause and result of the increasing professionalism of the welfare field. An English social worker commented on the implications of this development:

> The turning of social work into a male career rather than a do-gooding vocation for women, encourages an authoritarian structure because it is based on competition. The women's movement is potentially an onslaught on authoritarianism. That it has had so little effect on even radical social work is amazing and must be significant.[8]

Notes

1. Ronald F. Henderson, Alison Harcourt and R. J. A. Harper, *People in Poverty: A Melbourne Survey*, Cheshire, Melbourne, 1970, p.37.
2. Ibid.
3. Dennis Marsden, 'Fatherless Families on National Assistance', in Peter Townsend (ed.), *The Concept of Poverty*, Heinemann, London, 1970, p.215.
4. Dorothy Wedderburn, 'A Cross National Survey of the Standards of Living of the Aged in Three Countries', in Townsend, op. cit.
5. John Mahoney and John Barnaby, 'Assistance to Families with

Children', *Social Security Quarterly*, Winter 1973, Canberra, pp.6–14.

6. Jean Hamilton-Smith, 'Volunteers in Social Welfare Agencies in Victoria', Technical Paper no. 6, Institute of Applied Economic and Social Research, University of Melbourne, 1973, pp.58–9.

7. Estelle Malseed with Gerard Schuyers, 'The Demand for and Supply of Professionally Trained Social Workers in Victoria 1972 to 1982', Technical Paper no. 5, Institute of Applied Economic and Social Research, University of Melbourne, Melbourne, 1973.

8. Elizabeth Wilson, 'Women Together', *New Society*, London, 14 September 1972.

Eight
Aboriginal Women: The Means of Production

As a general rule if the female sex were completely subject to the male, no problem would be posed by the principle of male dominance. It could be enforced ruthlessly and directly wherever it applied. This seems to be what happens among the Walbiri. For the least complaint or neglect of duty Walbiri women are beaten or speared.

Mary Douglas, *Purity and Danger**

This attitude to Aboriginal women in their traditional world was one of the main humanitarian arguments on which missionaries and others based their claims for smashing Aboriginal culture. The men were violent brutes, the women abject pawns in games of male political power. Young and innocent girls bestowed upon lecherous old greybeards! Pregnant females carrying all the family's worldly goods as they meekly followed their lords and masters across the harsh countryside! A race divided by sex into masters and slaves! Anyone could see that one of the best reasons for raising the savages to civilization was to ease the dreadful burden that their womenfolk bore.

The purpose of this chapter is to see how accurate this view is, and to examine what effects contact with white society has had for one group of Aboriginal women. The community I am discussing is Maningrida, a government settlement in north-central Arnhem Land.† It was established in 1958 by the Northern Territory Administration in an attempt to stop the extensive movements of Aborigines towards Darwin and other white centres following the Second World War. However, the great majority of people who moved to Maningrida in the years

* Routledge & Kegan Paul, London, 1966, p.141.

† The research on which this chapter is based was supported by the Australian Institute of Aboriginal Studies, and carried out in 1967–68.

following 1958 had hitherto been living a tribal life in the bush. They were not totally untouched by outside influence since European goods, especially steel tools and containers, had entered the area well in advance of the Europeans themselves, while Indonesian traders from Macassar and Japanese pearlers had been in the area also. All these outside contacts had left some mark, since both the Indonesians and Japanese 'borrowed' Aboriginal women during their Arnhem Land sojourn and provided goods, tobacco and food in return.

The essential difference between these earlier contacts and those from white settlement is that, whereas the Macassans and Japanese were casual visitors interested only in exploitation of resources, the whites came as bearers of a new way of life, for the benefit of the Aborigines, in humanitarian concern for their well-being. In the early phase this was very different from the situation in the rest of developing Australia – where the whites came as pastoralists to use the land, and the Aborigines became either a useful source of labour or else a native pest. Initially in Arnhem Land the whites came with no thought of material gain to themselves; the only reason they were there was to help the Aborigines. (Of course the mining and timber industries today are a different story.)

Why did the Aborigines need help? There can be no question about the genuine concern which motivated the thrust into Arnhem Land. Leprosy was rife and threatened to affect all the Aboriginal population. Certain unscrupulous whites were making incursions into Arnhem Land, shooting buffalo and crocodile, and exploiting the Aborigines on the way. Some of the men were drifting in towards Darwin, where they were drinking heavily and contracting venereal disease. It seemed necessary to offer a stable point of non-exploitative contact with white society, away from the worst dangers it had to offer. This was the philosophy which brought Maningrida into existence.[1]

When I first went to Maningrida in 1967 there were over a thousand Aborigines, drawn from thirteen different language groups, in more or less permanent residence. There were also over one hundred whites, engaged in a variety of welfare pursuits – teaching, nursing, maintenance and administration; plus a forestry station and its workers. Houses for the white staff were built by teams of builders from Darwin, and a variety of other whites came and went. Nonetheless, Aboriginal contacts with the whites were slight, arising mainly from employment. Physically the settlement mirrored the social segregation – substantial houses for the white staff laid out in a neat grid pattern on the northern section, with Aborigines for the most part living in galvanized iron and bark humpies on the southern side. No one used English except in dealing with whites. Strung out along the white sandy beaches and mangrove strands of the Liverpool River estuary, with the vastness of the Arnhem Land savannah on all sides and the open sea a few miles away, the settlement reflected the whole paradox of white intervention in Aboriginal tribal society; a neatly mown white Anglo-Saxon suburb dropped by a twist of fate at the very edge of the last of wild Australia.

In spite of their small numbers, the philosophy backed up by the power of the whites imposed drastic changes on the black population, while affecting the whites very little. The Aborigines welcomed the whites as guests bearing gifts, but soon found that accepting the gifts entailed accepting a vast and complex superstructure and a state of permanent occupation.

The specific question here is, what are the effects of this confrontation on the Aboriginal women? Does that part of the white way of life to which they are exposed in Arnhem Land in fact offer them a rise in status, better opportunities, a more egalitarian environment than the old ways? I think that white observers have substantially misunderstood the position of Aboriginal women in traditional society because they have attempted to use a Western model of male-female relationships which is inapplicable. By trying in action to make Aborigines conform to this model they have brought about a significant loss of status for the women – both in relation to the closed world of Aborigines on settlements and missions, and in relation to the white world beyond them.

In white Australian society generally women survive at second hand – men support them and their children. While few men have any control over the means of production, they none the less have access to survival through the wages they earn. When women demand equality they are basically demanding that they no longer be dependent on a man in order to ensure the survival of themselves and their children. Feminist theory assumes that once women have equal access to the means of production men will evaluate them differently, and need them differently, and that a unified social system of equality, both real and internalized, will emerge. This need not follow, however. It is possible for women to have access to the means of production, to be acutely needed by men, and still to be classed by men as something less than men, and I think Arnhem Land society offers a case in point. But it's not a simple matter of women being in some global sense 'inferior'. Women are inferior because they are *valuables*, not because they are valueless.

The debate over the status of Aboriginal women has failed to take into account two fundamental factors: first, that women had access to a livelihood that was independent of men, and second that for men, women themselves were the means of production. Women as mothers, wives, dancers, technologists and sexual partners, were not inferior to men, although they often operated in different spheres; but women as the means of production were clearly not of the same order as men. Women's power lay in their capacity as collectors and converters of energy in the form of food and children. Men also acted as the collectors and converters of energy, but they were primarily concerned with psychic energy, and they specialized in religious and philosophical production to this end. Within the belief system, neither could function without the other, and both were equally necessary to survival. But because women's productive skills were needed to reliably support the community while men engaged in pursuits which they considered intrinsically more important, women as a group were subject to control and manipulation by men, as objects of value.

We are familiar with the view that 'primitive' women, because of their biology and in the absence of countervailing technology, were totally bound to home and hearth. The stereotype of hunting societies is of the men running about catching game while the women wait hopefully at home, tending the children and keeping the home fires burning. The recent interest in quantification and ecology has brought to light the fact that in all hunting and gathering societies outside the Arctic and sub-Arctic zones, women's contribution to the food supplies was substantial and reliable. Most groups depended for their daily sustenance on what the women produced. This is especially true of the Aborigines. In the fertile coastal areas such as Arnhem Land women provided a wide range of both protein and carbohydrate foods, in most cases with consistent but fairly little labour. Arnhem Land women traditionally produced so much that their menfolk worked only sporadically and spent much of their time in artistic and ritual pursuits. Women viewed what they produced as largely for themselves and their children. They ate their fill daily, shared with their female relations, and brought back whatever was left over to their husbands. Men, on the other hand, were obliged to contribute most of what they caught for distribution to others, especially to their mothers-in-law and mothers. A husband did not provide for his wife – what she received of the hunter's catch came to her from her mother, not from her husband.

Women were essentially independent in their daily life. In consultation with other women they decided where to go, what to gather, how much to collect; they made communal child-care arrangements, carrying their small children with them to work and bringing the older ones along if they wanted to come. But if a woman didn't want to go, if she was ill or felt like a rest, then she stayed in the camp and her female relatives fed her. Her husband or father did not control her daily activities, nor could a man apply sanctions against a woman by attempting to cut off her food supply. In the matter of survival a woman was substantially independent.

The one aspect of Aboriginal women's life in Arnhem Land which aroused most white concern is that of marriage. Traditionally, women were betrothed before birth, usually to men much older than themselves. This occasionally meant that an old man of sixty, already with several wives, took a young girl of twelve or fifteen years. Girls were married at or before puberty, and their sexual experiences began at a very early age. Polygamy was practised, men having as 'promises' a number of girls who became wives as they matured. Young men, on the other hand, were deprived of wives for a considerable time, and a young man's first wife was likely to be an older woman inherited from a deceased older brother. All of this strikes whites as repulsive if not immoral. No freedom of choice! Poor girls married to horrible old men! (Deep-seated anxieties by whites about the virility of blacks?)

Even sympathetic white (male) observers seem to feel this is a fundamentally bad situation which must be changed. Nurcombe, writing of Elcho Island, a community near Maningrida, says:

> The anachronism of polygamy and the promise system is one of the points of acculturation at which stresses between the old and the new, the traditional and the changing, is maximal. Perhaps there should be instituted a system of worthwhile stipendiary rewards for all men who, having one wife, relinquish their extra promise girls to young men who have none.[2]

Nurcombe is impressed with the overall lack of sexual pathology or disturbance among the Elcho people, although he maintains that the women suffer from 'erotic inhibitions and apathy towards intercourse in marriage'.[3] I find it hard to assess the reliability of such a conclusion without a great deal of evidence from women on this point, and it is not the kind of evidence to be collected by visiting men, scientists or not.

Of course, from a Western standpoint it makes sense. We expect a woman to be sexually excited by her marital partner, since marriage is supposed to be lifelong and monogamous, and if you don't enjoy doing it with your husband then you'll never enjoy doing it at all. But a woman's sexual life doesn't begin and end with the first flush of young love, and the great virtue of the Aboriginal system is that it takes this into account. Women in Western society are not a scarce resource, and in general they are valuable only while they serve as desirable sex objects. It was very different for the Aboriginal woman in tribal society. Because women were the most reliable producers of food, and the only producers of children, they were always valuable. Because older men monopolized the younger women, the older women had access to the younger men. A woman's first husband was seldom her last, and although as a young girl she has no freedom of choice, the older she gets and the more children she has the more able she is to make her own decisions and influence the decision of others.

I would argue that in Arnhem Land society, men viewed women, as a class, as 'inferior' primarily because they were the means of production and therefore were subject to men's political manipulations. But women were not dependent on men for survival, and they exercised considerable autonomy over their own lives. What then happens to women when contact with white society imposes drastic economic, technological and social changes?

Without doubt the transfer from a nomadic food-gathering economy to a cash-based European one is the change with the most dramatic implications for all Aborigines. I suspect that it is even more important for the women than for the men in the early stages of contact; if women as food-producers are the means of production, and therefore of intrinsic value to men, the transfer to a cash economy immediately makes them redundant. Today the people of Maningrida rely almost entirely on food purchased from the store, while in 1967–68 they were still being fed in the communal kitchen arrangement then favoured by the Northern Territory Administration. At one blow the whole economic significance of Aboriginal women was removed. Where the possession of three wives and many children once made a man strong and independent, it now made him, in relation to the new sources of energy and power, no more than a pauper. The white stereotype of men hunting while the women sat at home made it inevitable that efforts to employ Aborigines were directed at male employment, not female. Women were employed as domestics of various kinds, but a woman was not thought to be *entitled* to employment; the white administration on the other hand made strenuous efforts to ensure that all men willing to work were given jobs, no matter how menial or trivial. Suddenly men had all the bargaining power and women had nothing. Child endowment payments were made directly to mothers, and at Maningrida as elsewhere it was understood as the woman's equivalent to the man's wage. The fact that it amounted to only a dollar or two a week, while the men were receiving considerably more than that, was interpreted to mean that the Government considered it possible to support several children on this amount. Since men were traditionally obliged to make payments to the wife's parents, most of whom were receiving old age pensions in any case, they saw the balance of their wages as their own to spend as they pleased, and bitterly resented their wives' and children's demands for extra money.

The white economic system is based on the nuclear family as the consumption unit, where the husband supports the wife and children. The Aboriginal economy is based on a network of rights and obligations throughout a group of kinsmen, on a secure foundation of daily subsistence provided by women. When the white system was superimposed on the Aboriginal economic structure it resulted immediately in a massive imbalance of power and great confusion for all.

Wherever they could, the women of Maningrida continued to gather food from the bush; but with a population of a thousand and no vehicular transport there was little to be gathered near enough to the settlement, and what there was represented a picnic rather than a regular source of supply. Before the whites came, food was there to be harvested abundantly every day; but the white system was based on time, a future orientation and an assumption of scarcity which was in opposition to all traditional Aboriginal notions. This in itself placed a heavy strain on women attempting to care for their families. Wages, pensions, and endowment money occurred reliably but at intervals; hoarding up resources to stretch over a two-week period was virtually impossible, not only because the resources themselves were so slender but also because the behaviour involved in such a process was a subversion of the Aboriginal mother's self-image. The good mother was the woman who gave freely to her children whatever she had; who fed them whenever there was food and searched for food when that was gone. A fortnightly pay check meant that mothers almost automatically had to become bad mothers – for if a woman gave freely of what she had today, there would be nothing for tomorrow; while there was no legitimate way of getting more tomorrow except by saving up today. The women's passion for card-playing, which equalled the men's, is probably related to the need to feel that money can be obtained at times other than pay-day. Card-playing gives everyone in the community a chance of a windfall in the times between pay-day, without putting pressure on the already strained kinship relations through which people traditionally made requests for sustenance. Of course, card-playing for money is illegal and disapproved of by whites, who see it as an irresponsible and time-wasting diversion from the serious business of working for a living.

The impact of education has been to reinforce the dependency and powerlessness of women which the white economic system introduced. Women gathering food were not only participating in an economic activity, they were also acting as educators. The detailed territorial knowledge required by both women and men was founded on the actions and explanations which women gave their small children while out gathering. The intricate details of the Arnhem Land bush, its springs and water-courses, the precise location of the vast shell-fish beds, the whereabouts of yams and likely spots for tortoises, formed a body of knowledge necessary for everyone's survival. People did not wander about picking up whatever looked likely – they went to specific places in search of specific things, and knew that they could rely on this knowledge passed down initially through women. But once the children are in school, and these days in pre-school as well, such knowledge can be transmitted at best spasmodically and unreliably. On the other hand, children are now acquiring knowledge which their mothers don't have – they can speak English, understand money, read magazines, write each other letters. The world of the whites is available to the children, even if at second hand through school books; but it is not similarly available to their mothers. The children naturally aspire to the values that schooling gives them, and are less able to value the special skills of their mothers, especially since the whites do not recognize these skills as significant or relevant. Mothers, who once were good because they fed you and good because they taught you, now can do neither. These consequences of education do not hit the men so hard, since their ceremonial and spiritual knowledge is still maintained and is something which the whites cannot equal.

A further consequence of the education system is the continual breakdown of traditional marriage patterns. When girls went to their husbands before puberty they accepted it as a fact of life. But girls now are encouraged to remain at school for several years beyond puberty. Their heads are filled with dreams of the white man's world and erotic stimuli from the weekly picture show. When they refuse to marry their promised husbands the whites support them. There seems to be a tacit agreement that girls can expect protection from the whites at least until they leave school. But this doesn't mean that they forgo sexual activity, with partners of their choice. The inescapable consequence is illegitimate births to school-children, and a deep sense of confusion among adults as to what to do with the 'long-grass girls' – especially since they seem to choose boy-friends in the wrong kinship relationship, to whom they can never be married. This also places a heavy strain on the girls' mothers, since men expect the women to keep an eye on their daughters; in any case they need scapegoats to protect themselves from accusations of breach-of-promise by men to whom the girls were originally betrothed.

Finally, there is the question of health services. The most dramatic impact on Aboriginal women has been the increase in the number of children surviving infancy, and the repeated pregnancies at short intervals which the women maintain is a new phenomenon. It is impossible to locate any single cause of this, but certainly the survival rate has increased as a direct result of medical intervention. A secondary by-product is the sad state of health of surviving children. Where once the sickly baby died and the healthy one survived, now all survive and almost all are sick, and the burden on the mothers is vastly increased. Aboriginal child-rearing techniques foster early physical development and free, autonomous exploratory behaviour in older children. But when children are born only two years apart and three out of four have some illness simultaneously (gastroenteritis, respiratory infections, otitis media etc.) it is virtually impossible for the mother to handle the emotional needs of the children, quite apart from the lack of physical facilities such as tap water and heating of any kind.

But there are even more subtle anxieties generated by the health services. Just as the good mother is one who gives freely to her children, so she does not hurt them. There is no acceptable physical chastisement of children, and the mother who beats her child can expect to be beaten in turn by an irate husband. Traditionally, illness was the concern of the 'specialist' (medicine-man) who utilized certain physical and spiritual techniques of healing. The good mother took her child for attention, and comforted it if it was frightened or hurt; but she did not do things to it herself, and she did not hurt it or make it cry. Yet white medical theory assumes a range of behaviour to be proper to mothers for the purpose of caring for children – washing, cleaning, insisting on them eating properly, even dressing wounds and cleaning out ears. If children cry and are frightened, that's unfortunate but mother knows best since it's for the child's own good. The fact that Aboriginal mothers don't handle children in this way is seen as a sign of their inadequacy, laziness and ignorance, not as a function of their being good Aboriginal mothers. Hence medical staff tend to become aggressive and impatient with Aboriginal women, implicitly condemning them for their hopelessness and treating them like naughty children. Now the Aboriginal mother knows she can't really be a good mother any more by her own standards, since she is no longer an economically independent person. When whites confirm that she is not a good mother by their standards either, what else can she do but agree that she is not a good mother and give up?

If the economic system makes women and their children a burden on their menfolk instead of a valuable asset; if the education system makes them useless as teachers and unable to communicate with their children; if young girls are encouraged to grow up exploring their fantasy worlds instead of the real world they live in; and if the health services produce a self-definition for women as bad mothers while at the same time making them mothers more often and more continuously than ever before, how is it possible for the Aboriginal women of Maningrida to be anything other than an inferior class by all possible criteria?

The image of the lawn-mowing middle class seems to be the image towards which white intervention programmes in Aboriginal Australia are directed. It was once accepted that this would somehow take place in the capital cities – that Aborigines would leave their homelands and disappear into urban Australia. It is becoming clear that this is not happening, certainly not as fast as the whites hoped. Presumably the ideology is still operating, and whites feel that they are doing Aboriginal women a favour in changing their physical and social environment in such a way that they too can participate as equals with their menfolk in the joys of suburbia. But if my analysis of the status of women in pre-contact times is correct, then Aboriginal women have been given the toughest deal in the game. Where once they were ideologically inferior to but substantially independent of their menfolk, they have been made both dependent and inferior, with little hope of aspiring to anything more than the supposed egalitarianism of the nuclear family in suburban white Australia. But even this is illusory – isolation, lack of employment, large families, poverty and illness see to that. Certainly there is the escape hatch of marriage to a white man, but short of this there seems to be no way out. For Aboriginal women are not only in a relationship with their own menfolk, they are also in a relationship with the white world outside – both the real white world, and a mythical model based on the very atypical behaviour of the few white government servants who live beside them, plus a collectivity of images and fantasies experienced in tangential encounters with the mass media. The one thing they do know is that, for the white world, being what they are is not good enough, while that same white world has made it impossible for them to be what they were. Liberation for Aboriginal women cannot be achieved only by liberation from their men; first and foremost there must be liberation from an alien social system which promises an illusory equality in exchange for complete subservience to a white-controlled economy and the brutalizing value system which supports it.

Notes

1. For a full account of Maningrida's history see L. R. Hiatt, *Kinship and Conflict*, ANU Press, Canberra, 1965.
2. B. Nurcombe, 'Sex Training and Traditions in Arnhem Land' in G. E. Kearney et al, *The Psychology of Aboriginal Australians*, John Wiley, Sydney, 1973, p.403.
3. Ibid., p.413.

Nine
Migrant Women

In sociological research, women often seem to be regarded as invisible, and perhaps the most invisible women in Australia are immigrants. Despite the massive scale of migration into Australia, particularly since the 1950s, there is minimal information about the thousands of women who are trying to make Australia their new home.

I cannot, therefore, offer a summary of available research on the subject. But I can suggest several problem areas that have become apparent to me over the last five years. My own experience covers mainly Southern European women who are relatively recent migrants, unskilled workers and/or the wives of unskilled workers. My information comes from (a) personal observation, especially in the course of a study of the Greek community in Sydney; (b) discussions with teachers, social workers and others in frequent contact with recent migrants; (c) piecing together of snippets of information contained in reports about education, the workforce, the family and social services.

On the basis of this heterogeneous collection of data, I make the following observations.

Working Conditions

There is no question that many immigrant women are being exploited as a source of cheap labour. Sometimes this means minimal payment for piecework done at home, sometimes work in factories where neither conditions nor pay would be acceptable to British-Australians. For women with children, the situation is complicated by the near absence of adequate child-care facilities. Costly private kindergartens are out of the question for poorly paid women who must work to meet the costs of housing and feeding a family in our expensive cities. Subsidized child-care centres are rare, especially in New South Wales. The resulting compromise in arrangements for child-care is likely to be unsatisfactory for both women and children. I have talked to women whose concern about their children clearly aggravated the psychological and physical fatigue engendered by a long day of repetitive work, the journey to and from work and the constant pressure of household chores.

Social and Cultural Dislocation

Closely related to the problems of child-care and the maintenance of the household is the question of social and cultural dislocation. Many families are virtual islands in large anonymous cities where they may understand only a little of the language and few of the customs. Southern European women, more restricted and usually less educated than their male counterparts, often find that they are the most isolated members of such families. Several Greek women have told me that they tolerate poor working conditions in factories partly because they have found at work some of the companionship they were accustomed to in a Greek village.

Cultural differences are also important, particularly where women see their children taking on strange, even distasteful, cultural traits. But perhaps most important to women from rural villages is the fact that they no longer have a sense of control over important areas of their own and their family's lives. In a Greek village, for example, the family is an economic, religious and social unit. Family members interact with other villagers in a number of different spheres of activity, so that villagers develop multiple ties with each other. In every sphere of activity, the mother is extremely important, supervising religious practice, providing children with domestic and agricultural education, familiar with the local church and school, and knowing personally all the families of their children's playmates. As a result, women are genuinely involved in decisions about their families.

In a city like Sydney, however, women find that they must give up their children to an alien educational system, conducted in a foreign language, according to unfamiliar principles. Even the church is relatively impersonal, centrally organized and offering only a partial substitute for personal contact with the village priest. Work is completely dissociated from home in that it is labour for wages, rather than the cultivation of inherited land.

Consequently, the family's various spheres of activity are now separated rather than overlapping. In this situation, mothers feel they have lost control. Many of their anxieties over the children's schooling, health and playmates are related to this general feeling of insecurity. Some women react by placing stricter controls on their children within the home.

These brief notes are inevitably superficial, and touch only a few of the problems of migrant women. The category 'migrant women' is much too broad, of course – the experience of a wealthy American migrant will differ radically from that of poor Turks. The topic, however, is a fascinating, often disturbing one that deserves wider investigation.

Notes

1. R. Johnston, 'The assimilation of immigrant women in the workforce', *International Migration Review*, vol. 4, no. 2, 1966, pp.95–9.
2. P. Lynch, *The woman's role in immigration*, Immigration Reference Paper, Government Printer, Canberra, May, 1970.
3. J. Martin and C. Richmond, 'Working women in Australia' in *Anatomy of Australia*, Duke of Edinburgh's Study Conference, Sun Books, Melbourne, 1968.
4. A. Thodey, 'Migrant unmarried mothers', in N. Parker (ed.) *Focus on migrants*, Australian Council of Social Services, Sydney, 1973, pp.23–7.

PART THREE

The Acquisition of Sex Roles

The Acquisition of Sex Roles

One is not born a woman one becomes a woman.
Simone de Beauvoir

Men and women become social beings in the course of their interaction with their physical and social environments. The physical and social environment varies enormously between individuals. It is affected by one's social class, by one's parents, one's occupation and one's education and by personal idiosyncracies but more importantly, and over-riding all the preceding factors, it is controlled by one's biological sex. Definitions of what is masculine and what is feminine therefore set clearly-defined boundaries for behaviour between individuals. The notion of one's self (or, who I am) develops out of this interaction with others and within the limits defined as normal behaviour for one's sex.

Much of the behaviour of young children is a re-enactment of adult behaviour which is going on around them. Children copy. The girls play at mothers and the boys at fathers. The constant reinforcing of division of labour along sex lines begins in infancy. From their birth we use different vocabularies to girls and boys. Girls are told they are sweet, pretty, dainty whilst boys are told they must be tough and handsome. To generalize, girls are expected to be clean, quiet and helpful round the home while dressed in pink, frills and bows. Boys, on the other hand, are permitted to be dirty and noisy, are dressed in practical clothes and encouraged to be brave, 'a little man', often to act aggressively.

This process, the regulating of behaviour to fit in with society's demands, is known as socialization. It is, however, a lifelong process, from birth to death. In the early years, ways of behaving and the rationales for such behaviour are largely mediated through those close to one, both by example (mothers care for children, fathers work); by children's books and toys (boys tend to be given trains and girls dolls); and by verbal reasoning (girls don't fight). Later the child has greater contact with institutions outside the home, all of which reinforce sex roles and offer ideologies and belief systems which explain and offer rationalizations for people behaving differently according to their sex. None of these ideologies and belief systems is grounded in 'fact'. The second chapter in this book, 'Biology and Human Behaviour', was concerned with the most popular explanation of all, namely that biological differences between men and women result in distinct behavioural differences. It is this particular belief which is used as a rationale for the idea that a woman's prime role is in the home and that her first responsibilities lie in subjugating herself to the needs of her family.

The family is probably the most effective inculcator of values. It is certainly extremely effective today in isolating women and rendering them powerless outside it. One of the false theories surrounding the family and bolstering it up is a firm belief in the existence of a maternal instinct, that is, that there is something innate in women which makes them the most suitable rearers of children. Somehow the biological possibility of giving birth is supposed to endow all women with an ability to rear children in our complex society. Despite the fact that the idea of a maternal instinct is no longer considered valid by psychologists, individuals define as unnatural those women who do not wish to stay full-time with their young children. Similarly, any male who wishes to care for young children is also seen in this light; apparently his lack of a womb makes him an unsuitable permanent figure for a baby or young child to identify with constantly. All of this is nonsense. Such theories persist and with such intensity to reinforce the idea of the inferiority of women and their dependence upon men. Chapter 10, 'The Motherhood Myth', examines this notion in detail.

The other chapter on the family, Chapter 11, 'Husband and Wife Interaction in the Australian Family', is concerned with problems of social science research. Social science, like the physical sciences, reflects and reinforces the basic norms of liberal capitalism. Both in its theory and its methodology sociology reinforces the power and superiority of men. For example, functionalism as a theoretical perspective warns at an abstract level of the disaster of revolutionary social change. At an empirical level, the basic propositions and assumptions on which most sociological research is based largely determine the results. Research on the family, for example, reinforces the traditional division of roles along sex lines within the family. Thus the legal patriarchal, nuclear, single-career family unit is defined as normal, other variations being seen as deviant and in need of special explanation. Similarly, psychologists study maternal deprivation but not paternal deprivation. Chapter 11 looks critically at three studies of the Australian family.

While the family sets the scene in terms of the males' assumed greater intellectual competence, the school rapidly reinforces it. Different facilities and courses and attitudes to 'bright' girls carry on the socialization process. Chapter 12 on the school is concerned with some of these problems but also with the question of whether girls really want equal rights with boys in the present hierarchical, competitive system. The chapter on childrens' books illustrates how both stories and school readers emphasize differences of behaviour based along sex lines.

Although many writers have commented on increasing secularization not only in Australia but throughout the world, the Christian church still plays an important part in reinforcing not only the family but other divisions of labour along sex lines. The writings of the church, particularly the Bible, contain many explicit statements about a woman's role, her sexuality and the sanctity of the family. Neither the idea of women as property nor the notion of the legitimate sexual abuse of women is unrelated to church teachings. So the minister asks 'who giveth this woman to be married to this man'; and Paul stated in the First Epistle to the Corinthians, 'This for men, get yourself a sexual receptacle and call it a wife.' (VII: 9) Elsewhere Paul again stresses the inferiority of women: 'Wives, submit yourselves unto your own husbands, as unto the Lord. For the husband is the head of the wife . . . Therefore as the Church is subject unto Christ so let the wives be to their own husbands in every thing.' (Ephesians V: 22–24)

Chapter 14 looks briefly at some of the accusations levelled at the church concerning its role in establishing and maintaining sexism in Australia, and also at the role of the church in the socialization process, especially in providing all other institutions with an overall rationale for their discrimination against women.

While institutions such as the church invent an all-encompassing belief system around which a whole society must revolve, other institutions such as the mass media exist in order to emphasize, reinforce and give information on the acceptable limits for the behaviour of individuals. Television, women's magazines and advertising glorify motherhood and present unattainable ideals. The ideal woman is either married with two clean children, has a puritanically clean house and looks as if she has just walked out of a beauty parlour, or she is a chic, sexy stenographer. Both are told they are less than complete. The married woman is never allowed to think that she fulfils her role perfectly but is constantly told that if she is to be a true woman she must ensure, for example, that her family's garments are washed in a particular product. A whole range of consumer items are defined as necessary. Thus her role as mother is never complete or even possible without a wide range of male-defined artificial needs. Similarly, the single girl is told that she will never 'catch' her man because of what she is but must increase her marketability by using this or that beauty product. The real person is submerged beneath a mass-produced stereotype.

The position of women without men is portrayed in jokes, in plays, in TV comedy and drama series, in films and in stories. Their situation is portrayed as deviant because in our society the role of woman is defined as relative to man. The spinster is seen as being incapable of catching a man and therefore frigid; the divorcee as the woman who couldn't keep one; and the single mother as the temptress who got her just rewards. Lesbians are defined out of existence, for emotional fulfilment especially sexual fulfilment, for women without men, cannot be acknowledged to exist by this male-dominated society.

Social ridicule and ostracism are therefore directed at those women who do not accept the stereotypes laid down for them by men. From birth, pressures are exerted on individuals to persuade them to control their behaviour within the acceptable confines of masculine and feminine. This process of socialization, of the repression of the individual to conformity, is explored in this section.

Ten

The Motherhood Myth*

Thus when the ruling class grows sanctimonious about the preservation of the family they mean in fact the need to preserve the division of labour which best secures profit. When they wax eloquent on the 'natural' role of women, they mean the ideal of naturalness which capitalism manufactures for itself as it makes an increasingly unnatural and polluted world in which human beings are bred to produce rather than production organized in the interests of human beings.

Sheila Rowbotham, *Woman's Consciousness, Man's World*†

The emphasis on the class struggle in revolutionary thinking has obscured the significance of traditional sex roles and nowhere is this more apparent than in the mistaken belief that child-rearing is, of necessity, the responsibility of women. In fact, other than the optional first few weeks or months of breast feeding, there is no biological connection between the bearing of children and their rearing. Women both in and outside the Women's Liberation Movement are busily mouthing this radical idea, but it is evident that as far as their own lives are concerned, and in their attitudes to others, it remains an empty ideal.

The fact that women everywhere are oppressed is not here in question. Many women have come to terms with their oppression by internalizing it; they do not know that they are oppressed. Others knowingly embrace it. Thus a woman will be pleased if she's whistled at in the street and, more seriously, will defend her right to make a man, *her* man, happy at the expense of her own happiness. This is more than sacrifice; when she projects her ambitions and aspirations on to her children and

* This article is reprinted from *The Spokesman*, no.15–16, 1971, and *Australian Left Review*, no.34, March 1972.

† Penguin Books, 1973, p.58.

her husband and when their achievements are embraced as her own, she is signing away her life, suspending it on an illusion which the first puff of wind will blow away. She is living vicariously, her personality atrophies and ultimately she suffers total loss of identity. Women who recognize this state of affairs for what it is and who therefore attempt, however feebly, to reject it in their own lives, are almost certainly doomed to failure for the simple reason that it is impossible to escape the ideal of motherhood. Childless women who see no need for Women's Liberation are living in cloud cuckoo land, first because their notions about their autonomy are as illusory as the married women's who believe that sharing the housework and the decision-making means liberation; and secondly, because they feel they ought, one day, to have a baby.

Motherhood is society's golden carrot. It is a super-human woman who can live her life without a backward glance, wondering whether she can really be fulfilled or satisfied with only relationships, a satisfying job and whatever else she wants out of life, without having a child somewhere along the line. And why? Because of this one central assumption which underlines everything that pertains to women, that a woman's true purpose in life and the pinnacle of her fulfilment is motherhood. The professional planners of industrial society – the psychologists, educationalists, doctors, sociologists, advertisers and the media, using the different means at their disposal, magnify and elevate the importance of the mother/child relationship. And the amateurs who tread reverentially in their wake translate these assumptions, prejudices and dubious findings into conventional wisdom, so that no one will be allowed to miss the point. Thus we arrive at this supposedly self-evident truth; a child needs its mother and, by implication, a mother needs her child.

In actual practice, of course, a mother is not regarded highly. If she were all the special things that these people would have us believe, then surely they would take her needs into account. But this is not the case. The mother with prams and push-chairs isn't in the forefront of the planners' minds when they design every new building with flights of narrow steps. Even in what is regarded as the woman's domain, like department stores, high rise flats, etc., women with young children are simply not catered for. In fact, every aspect of our environment is designed with one thing in mind, the adult healthy male; mothers, along with the physically disabled and the very old, are ignored. This is just another of the ways in which society operates a double standard. But this one has perhaps some of the most far-reaching implications, the burden of which has to be borne by the mothers.

Caring for children is a difficult and important job of work, but considered in the commodity producing terms that we are conditioned to value the mother contributes nothing of market value and as a result is not recognized economically. It must not be forgotten that it is *cheaper* for the establishment to recognize the woman's job in spiritual rather than economic terms and for this reason, if for no other, it is in the establishment's interest that the *status quo* be maintained. The most damaging way in which this is illustrated is in the desperate lack of day nursery and pre-school nursery facilities. It is worth noting here that the 1967 Plowden Report on Primary Education in Britain recommended that one of the major priorities for the Ministry of Education was the setting up of state-run nursery schools for three- to five-year-olds. That was four years ago and very little has been done. The most effective way of saving the State's money, of keeping children at home with mothers until they are five, is to emphasize over and over again the exclusivity and significance of the mother/child relationship. We are bombarded with this stuff from every corner and no woman is immune to it. From Bowlby to *Woman's Own*, it is everyone's prerogative to state with absolute certainty that a child needs its mother, and, deprived of her constant and exclusive care and attention, the child will suffer unmentionable difficulties and will probably turn out to be a delinquent.

Dr John Bowlby is the arch perpetrator of this. In his own words:

> It appears that there is a very strong case indeed for believing that prolonged separation of a child from his mother (or mother substitute) during the first five years of life stands foremost among the causes of

delinquent character development and persistent misbehaviour. (1947)

What is believed to be essential for mental health is that the infant and young child should experience a warm, intimate and continuous relationship with his mother (or permanent mother substitute) in which both find satisfaction and enjoyment. (1952)

Partial deprivation brings in its train acute anxiety, excessive need for love, powerful feelings of revenge and, arising from these last, guilt and depression ... Complete deprivation ... has even more far-reaching effects on character development and may entirely cripple the capacity to make relationships. (1952)

He admitted in 1956 that he may have overstated his case, but this was only in relation to the long term effects of institutionalization (or what he called 'maternal deprivation'). However, in 1958, in a letter to the *Lancet*, he asserted that, contrary to general professional opinion, his position remained unchanged.

Several writers have attested to the widespread influence of Bowlby's views. In the words of Professor Yudkin and Anthea Holme, in their book *Working Mothers and Their Children:*

There can be little doubt that among the major contributing factors to the general disapproval which our society extends to mothers of young children who work outside the home, and the corresponding guilt of the mothers themselves, are the theses of Dr John Bowlby. Bowlby's hypotheses continue even now to provide both official and unofficial bodies with supposedly irrefutable evidence in favour of such money-saving projects as closing day nurseries.

Grygier et al., in their work *Parental Deprivation: A Study of Delinquent Children*, state:

The responsibility for the emphasis on the mother belongs to John Bowlby, a leading authority on the results of maternal deprivation who has had a powerful influence on lay and professional people.

In view of the vested interest in keeping mothers at home, we begin to understand why it is that Bowlby's views attract world-wide attention while his many detractors, who have presented a wealth of evidence which does not support his thesis, remain in relative obscurity. These investigators are only read by other investigators; they are certainly not read by those people who popularize scientific findings. If these findings were published the threat to the social order would be too great.

But the threat to the social order is as nothing compared to the threat to the mothers themselves – the basis of their lives – their conviction that they are not only the main ingredient in their child's life, but the only *essential* ingredient. In other words, women have embraced the mythology so wholeheartedly that it is they themselves who constantly reinforce it. If really pushed, they would admit that their children could do without their fathers, grandmothers, school, peer group, etc., but, deprived of their mothers, the children would fall apart. If we are to believe that women yearn for security, then they must go some way towards satisfying this need in making themselves indispensable in this way. The most pathetic way in which this is demonstrated is when a mother is ill. She staggers on relentlessly, often refusing offers of help. She might otherwise discover that her children can manage perfectly well without her. Similarly, it frequently happens, when a child falls over and is comforted by whoever happens to be there at the time, that the mother rushes up, whips the child out of that person's arms and says, 'There, there, Mummy's here'. Such women are reinforcing the child's mother-dependence and are thereby postponing the realization that they are, in effect, dispensable as mothers.

The end result, of course, is what is known in all the text books as the normal small child, that is, a child neurotically dependent on its mother. She, being the model mother, has brought this perfect child into being by constantly reinforcing every sign of dependence on her that it displays, firstly its physical needs and then for its emotional needs. She puts it to bed at 6.30 p.m. so that it only sees its father for half an hour a day, she rarely, if ever, leaves it with anyone for more than an hour or so, and she reserves her ultimate contempt for any mother who does not conform to this ideal pattern.

When a child brought up in these conditions is parted from its mother and suffers distress, the social scientists, instead of throwing up their hands in glee at yet another example of maternal deprivation, might be better employed at critically examining the pre-separation experiences of the child.

These social scientists might also be better employed if they turn their attention to fathers. Margaret Mead stands alone in recognizing that the separation and insignificance of fathers is not biologically ordered but is a direct result of industrialization. At the third meeting of the World Health Organization Study Group on Child Development, she said:

In very simple societies, such as the Australian Aborigines, many South Sea island societies, and some African societies, the male takes a great deal of care of the young infant. But with every society that we have any record of, with the onset of what you call civilization, division of labour, class structure, hierarchies of authority etc., one of the first things that has happened has been the separation of the human male from his own baby until any point up to two years, four years, six years, twelve years. I think one of the things that we may want to discuss here is whether this is not a *condition* of civilization, and whether one of the origins of creativity in males has not been this preventing them from having anything to do with babies.

Such subversive views about the role of fathers will not be found in the conventional literature on child care. As can be imagined, Bowlby has very different views. This is what he had to say about fathers:

In the young child's eyes father plays second fiddle and his value increases only as the child's vulnerability to deprivation decreases. Nevertheless, as the legitimate child knows, fathers have their uses even in infancy. Not only do they provide for their wives to enable them to devote themselves unrestrictedly to the care of the infant and toddler, but, by providing love and companionship, they support her emotionally and help her maintain that harmonious contented mood in the aura of which the infant thrives. In what follows, therefore while continual reference will be made to the mother-child relation, little will be said of the father-child relation; his value as the economic and emotional support of the mother will be assumed.

What Bowlby gives us is a beautiful woman's magazine image of the contented mother dispensing harmony to her thriving infant with father coming home on Friday night and smiling as he hands over the economic support, and if by chance he kisses his wife he is not demonstrating his affection but only providing her with emotional support so that the child can continue to thrive. Like Bowlby's views on motherhood, this image of the paternal role has filtered down into popular mythology. It is not difficult to see why this has happened. Just as it is in the establishment's economic interest to keep the mother of young children isolated at home, so it is to keep the father alienated at work. The system needs his labour, which is of course his time, and he needs the money he earns by that labour to buy the goods he makes, so he is advised only to *participate* in parenthood. He is not essential, like the mother, but useful in an also-ran kind of way. None of the lay books on baby care that I have consulted make any reference to father although I am told that one does have a 'note to fathers' at the end which suggests that he persuade his wife to bath the baby in the evening when he is at home so that he can watch. Some of the professional books on child care deny the father's role completely; when he is referred to, he is seen only as an occasional substitute *mother*. Dr Spock makes a valiant effort when he addresses himself to 'parents' at the beginning of his book *Baby and Child Care*, but he does not keep it up, and all subsequent references are to 'mother'. Thus, in all the serious and popular literature the father's role as a parent, in contrast to the mother's is drastically under-emphasized.

To turn now to the evidence for and against maternal deprivation. In the first place, all the original work was done on children in institutions and the reason is only too obvious; it is virtually impossible to find children brought up in motherless families, so that the evidence, such as it is, had to be gathered from the very extreme cases where the children were totally removed from their own homes. In other words, these children were deprived of many things besides their mothers, not least their fathers and love. This fact alone should be sufficient to dismiss Bowlby's evidence. As Grygier et al., have pointed out, what Bowlby and his followers were studying was not the effects of maternal deprivation but the effects of institutionalization. These effects can be, but are not always, harmful.

It must not be forgotten that every child in an institution is there for a reason, such as death of a parent, break-up of a home, or simply that the child is not wanted. Not one of these reasons can be regarded as being conducive to the child's healthy development. None of Bowlby's findings takes any of these points into account. The only criticism he does anticipate is the one least likely to be thought of. That is that the children he observed in institutions may have come from 'poor stock, physically and mentally', so that heredity alone might account for their backward development. He goes on to refute this with devastating logic by citing the case of twin goats, one of which was separated from its mother and became 'psychologically frozen' when lights were flashed on and off. He concludes this with the following statement:

> This is ample demonstration of the adverse effects on maternal deprivation on the mammalian young, and disposes finally of the argument that all the observed effects are due to heredity.

Bowlby is full of such glaring errors of judgement, gross over-simplification and dogged single-mindedness. For instance, he warns observers not to be taken in by children in institutions who are, in his own words, 'quiet, easy to manage, well mannered and even appear happy' because their adjustment can only be 'hollow'. In view of what he has to say about goats and fathers, I hope I have demonstrated that his writings do not warrant serious consideration, except insofar as they affect general attitudes.

Before turning to the other evidence it is worthwhile to refer to what Grygier et al. have to say about the workability of hypotheses in an area as emotionally loaded as maternal deprivation. These authors stand alone in questioning the validity of employing scientific method on human beings:

To determine the effects of parental deprivation a workable scientific model must be used and at the present stage of scientific development this would be an experimental model. Assumed causes must be manipulated experimentally to see how often they produce the hypothesized effects, otherwise the preconceived cause may be merely an association . . . The obstacles to the use of the experimental model on human beings weaken the predictive power of hypotheses in the social sciences, which, when compared with those of the physical sciences rank less as laws than as educated guesses . . . An hypothesis may be confirmed because it has been stated, not because it is true.

A perfect example of a hypothesis being confirmed because it has been stated is found in a widely quoted study entitled *Working Mothers and Delinquency* by Glueck and Glueck, who are prolific workers in this field. The subject was 500 delinquent boys matched pair by pair with non-delinquent boys of similar age, cultural background, etc. The employed mothers were divided into two groups, those regularly employed and those sporadically employed, in similar types of work (cleaning, shop work, etc.). Of the delinquent boys 54 per cent had mothers who were full-time housewives, compared to 46 per cent whose mothers worked, so a slightly higher proportion of the delinquent boys had full-time mothers. However, when the authors turned to the sporadically employed mothers, many of whom had themselves been delinquents, and whose husbands were frequently unemployed and where both parents were lacking in 'self-respect', they found a higher proportion of delinquents. With the singlemindedness of a scientist intent on finding causal relationship between maternal employment and delinquency, and thereby proving the hypothesis, the authors disregard the other potent factors which contribute to the waywardness of these children and conclude:

We already have sufficient evidence to permit of at least a guarded conclusion that the villain among working mothers is the one who seems to have some inner need to flit erratically from job to job probably because she finds relief thereby from the burden of home-making.

Note that there is no mention that this 'inner need' might be financial, owing to the husband being out of work. In their conclusions, the authors drop their guard to reveal the moralizing assumptions and cliched attitudes which underlie their work:

As more and more enticements in the way of financial gain, excitement and independence from the husband are offered married women to lure them from their domestic duties, the problem is becoming more widespread and acute. It is a problem that should be discussed freely and frankly in all communities by mothers, fathers, clergy, psychiatrist and social worker.

When these authors use terms like 'villain', 'luring', 'enticement', 'independence from the husband', their scientific objectivity must be called to serious question. Similarly, their conclusion that there is a causal relationship between the sporadically employed mother and delinquency is highly dubious. Besides the many other factors at work in the families of these boys, the authors have studiously ignored the fact that the fathers were also sporadically employed.

Many of the studies into the effects of the working mother suffer from the same lack of detachment as the Gluecks' study. Margaret Broughton in her paper *Children with Mothers at Work* suggested:

. . . for mothers who work because they are bored or lonely probably the answer would be to provide crèches or day nurseries where mothers could leave their children for a few hours so that they could take part-time jobs. An occasional morning or afternoon a week would probably keep many women mentally happy.

Despite their lack of detachment, none of the studies yet undertaken has succeeded in finding a correlation between delinquency and maternal employment. In fact, as mentioned previously, the Gluecks found a higher proportion of delinquents from homes where there were full-time mothers. So also did Ferguson and Cunnison in their study of delinquents in Glasgow.

In 1965 Warren and Palmer looked into the backgrounds of 316 juvenile offenders and found that 98 per cent were without a father or father substitute compared with a mere 17 per cent who lacked a mother figure. As Grygier et al. pointed out: 'Paternal deprivation can no more be seen in isolation than the maternal variety.'

In fact, it would seem patently obvious that no study of delinquency can be undertaken without full regard of all the factors – economic, social, educational, etc. – which together contribute to the child's development. The nearest that any investigator has come to admitting this is Andry who, in criticizing Bowlby, remarked that he did not take account of 'interacting multi-causation', which is a roundabout way of saying that delinquency has many causes.

In an exhaustive review undertaken by Lois Stolz of all the published evidence on the effects of maternal employment on children, she had this to say on the subject of delinquency: 'The studies reviewed tend to deny the contention that children of working mothers are more likely to be delinquent than children of mothers who remain at home.'

Nevertheless, the popular image of working mothers and consequent delinquency, latch-key children, etc., still prevails. The following quotation from a pamphlet entitled *Mothers at Work* by Sylvia Pearson is a typical example: 'The child needs the sense that there is a person who is the provider of food, comfort and general well-being . . . without this initial foundation . . . the child easily develops a defiant attitude which leads to delinquency.'

I recently heard it seriously suggested in a letter broadcast on the BBC programme 'You and Yours' that married women should not be given jobs in view of the widespread delinquency which results from mothers going out to work. It is clear that the mother who goes out to work has been seized on and been made into a scapegoat for the many social and environmental factors which contribute to delinquency, as that term is understood.

In all the studies reviewed, there is an implicit assumption that maternal employment and maternal neglect are synonymous.

Of course there is no connection, just as there is no connection between maternal presence and what Yudkin calls 'loving attention'. It hardly seems worth saying that the harassed mother who stays at home only out of a sense of duty to her children is as much of a threat to their well-being as the mother who reluctantly goes out to work and is dissatisfied in her job. If the investigators want to continue in this field, they might try assessing the effects on the children of the dissatisfied full-time housewife versus the satisfied working mother. Another area for research might also be the effects on children of *fathers* going out to work. Such a study might yield very interesting results; but as the function of most studies is to confirm prevailing ideologies rather than to further the cause of scientific research a study on the effects of paternal employment will not be forthcoming.

Despite all these points, the doubt will still linger that the mother who works outside the home, particularly while her children are small, is causing them irreparable damage. A typical example of the kind of statement that abounds in the media is this one by the actress Prunella Scales, reported in the *Guardian:* 'It's a *physical* fact that a mother ought to be with her children for the first five years of their lives.' This is stated as though it were an immutable law of nature. One wonders what magical thing overtakes the child on its fifth birthday that it can go to school and do without its mother for six hours a day five days a week.

What is the basis for this 'physical fact'? In fact, very few studies of note have been undertaken on the effects of maternal employment on the under-fives. Lois Stolz suggested in her review that the reason for this is that it is generally assumed that mothers with infants do not work. One study which she and several other writers refer to was undertaken during the war when the need for women's labour in the munitions factories and elsewhere resulted in a rapid increase in the numbers of young children attending day nurseries. The study is tortuously entitled *The Eating, Sleeping and Elimination Habits in Children attending Day Nurseries and Children cared for in the Home by their Mothers*, by Netta Glass. This is the only study I have found which used a control group who were cared for at home rather than an institutionalized group. Again, unlike other studies, the author investigated home environmental factors, personality and attitudes of the mother, marital situations, etc. When she studied the habit disturbances she found that 29 of the home children were affected compared to 33 of the day nursery children. The difference is not significant. However, the author states that the mothers of the day nursery children who presented problems themselves had 'difficult personalities', fathers were more frequently absent among the nursery children and living conditions were generally worse. The problem children were, in fact, associated with certain parental attitudes and types of personality and not with whether the children did or did not attend day nursery. The author concludes that:

> There was no evidence to suggest that children cared for in a day nursery are more likely by reasons of communal care to present developmental problems than are children cared for at home by their mothers. There was in addition no confirmation of the belief that nursery care for children under two is especially harmful.

A study was undertaken by Perry in 1961 in Washington and dealt with children aged three to five years, of 104 employed mothers. These children were cared for during their mothers' absence by relatives, child minders with formal training and the like. The children's adjustment, as measured by nervous symptoms, anti-social and withdrawing tendencies showed no correlation with any of these factors, and Perry concludes that: 'results failed to support the views of those who oppose the separation of children from their mothers.'

Another study was undertaken by Heinicke in 1956. This was a small explorative study. It dealt with thirteen two-year-olds, seven of whom attended day nursery while the rest were temporarily placed in residential nurseries while their mothers were in hospital. The author found that the residential children, after the first two days of initial adjustment to the new routine, did present disturbed behaviour, such as seeking affection, frequent crying, loss of bowel control, etc., while the children who returned home each evening presented no problems. The only point that was brought in connection with the day nursery children was that they more frequently wet themselves, although the author admits that they indulged in more water play than the residential children. The author draws no conclusion from this study as it was so small and only covered a period of nineteen days. However, Yudkin's view is that Heinicke's results: '... suggest that young children may fairly quickly adjust themselves to a new routine and to maintain a close relationship with mother during the parts of the day when they are together.'

Bowlby unwittingly provided his opponents with valuable evidence when he quoted a study by Simonsen:

> Simonsen compared a group of 113 children aged between one and four years almost all of whom had spent their whole lives in one of some twelve different institutions, with a comparable group who lived at home and attended day nurseries. The mothers of these children were working and the homes often very unsatisfactory. Even so, the average developmental quotient of the family children was normal – 102 – while that of the institution children was retarded – only 93.

Now Bowlby gives no indication that he has appreciated the full implications of this evidence. In a paper designed to stress the harmful consequences of maternal deprivation he makes no attempt to account for the normal development of the day nursery children who were deprived of their mothers for eight or more hours a day.

The emphasis in all these studies, much as their findings support my case, is always biased towards the possible harmful effects of partial separation of the child from its parents. I would have been greatly relieved to have come across a study which set out to investigate the *benefits* of partial separation for the under-fives. No less important would be a study of the effects of maternal over-protection. An interesting point to consider here is mentioned in Professor Edward Strecker's book, *Their Mothers' Sons*. He stated that the percentage of mother-fixated neurotic GIs in the last war was 'catastrophic'. A study into the effects of maternal over-protection should prove as interesting as one on the effects of working fathers. Myrdal and Klein, in their book, *Woman's Two Roles*, had this to say:

> So much has been written and said in recent years about the vital needs of children for maternal affection, and about the dangers of neglect, that many parents, in particular those who take an intelligent interest in the emotional development of their children are becoming over-anxious on this score. Very little attention has, in comparison, been paid to the effects of over-protection, though these may also cripple the psychological development of the child.

I don't feel that, in the present climate of opinion, much research will be done either in the direction of maternal over-protection or the benefits of day nurseries, nursery schools, etc., although concessions are gradually being made towards the idea of nursery schools for deprived children. No one in authority has yet reconciled the idea that partial separation from the mother is beneficial to the deprived child while it is harmful to the 'normal' child.

In reviewing the evidence for and against maternal deprivation, I have referred to the major works published. Most of the work was done in the late 1940s and throughout the 1950s, when the subject was 'hot', but so effective was the dissemination of the case for maternal deprivation that it moved out of the realm of controversy into the realm of acknowledged fact; as a result very little work has since been done.

Before moving on to a statement of my own position, I will refer to Margaret Mead's study entitled *Some Theoretical Considerations on the Problem of Mother Child Separation.* Unlike other workers she is able to look at the subject dispassionately and brings it admirably into perspective:

> At present the specific biological situation of the continuing relationship of the child to its biological mother and its need for care by human beings are being hopelessly confused in the growing insistence that child and biological mother or mother surrogate, must never be

separated, that all separation even for a few days is inevitably damaging and that if long enough it does irreversible damage. This . . . is a new and subtle form of anti-feminism in which men – under the guise of exalting the importance of maternity – are tying women more tightly to their children than has been thought necessary since the invention of bottle feeding and baby carriages. Actually, anthropological evidence gives no support at present to the value of such accentuation of the tie between mother and child. On the contrary cross-cultural studies suggest that adjustment is most facilitated if the child is cared for by many warm friendly people . . . It may well be, of course, that limiting a child's contacts to its biological mother may be the most efficient way to produce a character suited to lifelong monogamous marriage, but if so, then we should be clear that this is what we are doing.

This article began with the statement that there was no biological connection between having babies and rearing them. Mothers are no more essential to their children than are fathers, grandmothers, or indeed anyone who loves them with the right kind of care and understanding. By the term 'love' I don't, of course, mean 'mother love', a sentiment which masquerades as the most pure and ideal form that love can take and is so ably characterized in the media by the young mother whispering sweet nothings to her picture book child as she washes up. In its extreme form the term 'mother love' implies the kind of sacrificial commitment which is thought to be seen in the animal world, with mother defending her young. (It appears, however, that among the higher primates, it is often the father who defends the young in cases of extreme need. In addition, there are several species where the father cares for as well as protects the young: see *Discussions on Child Development*, WHO Study Group, 1955.) Instead of recognizing this for what it is – the protection of the young for the perpetuation of the species – we have applied it to human female behaviour and sentimentalized it into a travesty of love.

Thus, the 'good' mother is the one who wraps her child in a blanket of love, attends its every whim, thwarts its wishes only when there is physical danger, prepares it well in advance for every possible little upset and anticipates all its needs. She sincerely believes that she is doing everything in her power to produce a happy child and then wonders where she went wrong when the child sucks its thumb, wets its bed, attacks other kids and finally, in adolescence, turns against her. The other side of the same coin may be the child who is chronically timid and so dependent on its mother that even she recognizes that something is wrong. This dependency may be carried over in the adult who finds difficulty in functioning independently and who constantly seeks reassurance and confirmation of its identity in other people. Certainly this kind of upbringing is widespread and keeps the child guidance clinics very busy.

Perhaps the most lethal aspect of such 'good' maternal care is the conscious anticipation of the child's needs. There is confusion over the need for an *awareness* and understanding of the child's needs, at each stage of its development, with the *anticipation* of them. The mother who consciously provides for each need as or even before it arises is living the child's life for it. Instead of allowing the child to discover the world around it for itself, the mother becomes the mediator, the provider of that world. All that the child is learning is how to conform to its mother's expectations.

It should be possible to challenge all of these basic beliefs about what constitutes good parenthood without presenting a wholly negative picture. Germaine Greer suggested in her book *The Female Eunuch* that children don't need 'bringing up'; given that their physical needs are met, they grow up anyway. It would seem axiomatic to most people that children need the active intervention of adults in the growing up process. This is what 'bringing up' is supposed to mean. What it should mean is the presence of several 'warm friendly people' who are ready to *respond* to the child's needs as and when they arise. This would require a conscious stepping back by the adults so that the child is allowed to determine for itself the quality and extent of the adult/child relationship. Such an approach may well result in a child who really does use its home like a hotel, giving and taking only what is necessary to live its own life in a totally independent and self-reliant way.

This method of child-rearing is not an empty and unattainable ideal. It is practised *unconsciously* in many families and in its mildest form has been described as 'healthy neglect'. As the term suggests, it consists more of what it is not than what it is. The essential point about it is that it avoids all the dangers of an excessive mother/child attachment. The child is thus freed from many of the burdens that a supposedly well brought up child has to bear – the responsibility of fulfilling its parents' expectations, of returning their love and sacrifice and of compensating them for their inadequacies. Instead of being bullied into being a credit to its parents the child is allowed to be a credit to itself.

For those essentially middle-class parents who have eagerly embraced the whole mythology – the strong attachment to the mother, the child's yearning for love and security, its need for constant understanding and guidance – to be told that they give too much attention to their children would be intolerable. Similarly, these people will defend to the last the myth that the basic requirement for the child's healthy development is security.

The pursuit of security must in part explain the strange behaviour that afflicts previously enlightened people when their first child is born. They no longer live in the present, taking from each day as much as it can offer; they start planning for something called the future. They buy a house, build a solid wall of insurance around it, they start thinking about a second child, not necessarily because they want one but to provide a companion for the first, and in order to keep this unwieldy edifice in repair the father's job and the prospects that go with it begin to assume an inordinate importance. In the name of providing their children with security these parents are denying them the raw material on which our experience is based, namely the unpredictability of it. In fact, security is another of the tools manipulated by society to make you stay where you are and work hard.

Security is commonly believed to be strengthened by consistency. In dealing with children many parents are preoccupied with presenting a consistent and rational front. This is characterized by those inane conversations where the adult is conscientiously explaining the reasons for his actions, treating the child as though it were a miniature adult, capable of full-reasoned thought. This is the modern equivalent of 'not in front of the children, dear', our parents hissed at each other when they should have had a row. Their belief in doing everything nicely and respectably matches the present belief in the efficacy of reason. Both types of parents could learn something from the one who gets cross with the kids simply because they are being naughty. That parent does not dress himself up in special clothes whenever he deals with his kids.

The respectable and the consistent parents are disguising their real selves in order to present their children with an idealized version.

The following quotation from the World Child Welfare Congress of 1958 exemplifies the attitude to child-rearing which should be strenuously rejected:

> ... our most important task in regard to every child with whom we are concerned is to give him maternal and personal love ... we must be there for them. In fact, if we are not the visible and tangible centre of their world and if we are not the stable hub of every change all our efforts are in vain.

Is it loving a child to make yourself the centre of its universe? And is it really love that compels parents to protect and defend the child against all the minor upsets it encounters outside the home instead of allowing it to come to terms with them in its way? Most of what goes under the guise of good parental care is an elaborate rationalization of gross possessiveness. It attempts to bind the child to the mother and provides a manipulative object whereby the parents rationalize their personal dissatisfactions. This is often consciously expressed by well-meaning parents who boast that they are giving their children what they themselves lacked. What is understood as 'loving' children is, in fact, using them.

Laing, in his book *The Politics of Experience*, expressed this point very forcefully:

From the moment of birth . . . the baby is subjected to these forces of violence, called love, as its mother and father have been and their parents and their parents before them. These forces are mainly concerned with destroying most of its potentialities. This enterprise is on the whole successful. By the time the new human being is fifteen or so we are left with a being like ourselves. A half-crazed creature more or less adjusted to a mad world. This is normality in our present age. Love and violence, properly speaking, are polar opposites. *Love lets the other be*, but with affection and concern. Violence attempts to constrain the other's freedom to force him to act in the way we desire, but with ultimate lack of concern, with indifference to the other's existence or destiny. We are effectively destroying ourselves by violence masquerading as love. (my emphasis)

So love lets the child be with affection and concern. A mother isn't letting her child be when she makes herself indispensable in its eyes, neither is she when she concentrates all the care in herself instead of sharing it with others. And she isn't letting it be when she projects her concern for its welfare on to it, making it feel responsible for *her* feelings when it 'fails' to fulfil her expectations. The woman who cuts and trims her poodle into a travesty of a dog, takes it proudly out on a leash to show off to the neighbours, only allows it to play with other poodles, is not a far cry from the mother who professes to 'love' her child.

When we have learnt to disengage ourselves from the children that we care for, liberating them from the pressure to conform to our image of them, we will be loving them without violence. In the process we will be going some way towards liberating ourselves.

Eleven

Husband and Wife Interaction in the Australian Family: A Critical Review of the Literature

One latent meaning . . . of the image of a value-free sociology is this: "Thou shalt not commit a critical or negative value judgement – especially of one's own society".

Alvin W. Gouldner, *For Sociology**

Recently a new questioning of sociological writings on husband and wife interaction has become evident, particularly in the USA. It had been widely accepted that the egalitarian family had been achieved, and some writers seemed to imply that such a state of dynamic equilibrium had been reached that automatic adjustments to new situations would maintain this distribution of power. R. O. Blood, for example, concluded from a study of working wives, that 'a spontaneous re-allocation of the balance of power occurs when the wife goes to work, increasing her power regarding decisions relevant to her new role and decreasing it in decisions relevant to the housekeeping role she is partially forsaking.'[1] However, such views have been maintained side by side with the view that it is the husband's occupational role which exerts major control over the family.[2] As Lois Hoffman expresses it 'the person who receives wages in exchange for services has more control over his money than other family members; and this control can be used implicitly or explicitly, to wield power in the family.'[3] Ralf Turner makes the additional and very perceptive point that the husband/father may himself feel constrained by his occupational role so that from his point of view it may not 'feel' as if *he* is exercising power over the family.

The paradox involved in such conflicting views of family interaction has only recently been squarely faced, with Constan-

* Allen Lane, 1973, p.14.

tina Safilios-Rothschild making the most systematic reassessment. She goes so far as to suggest that the 'egalitarian family' is a type which exists mainly and almost exclusively in the minds of family sociologists.[4] The reason for the perpetuation of the myth is partly due to the researchers' own value commitments to such family equality, and partly to the simplistic conception of power they mostly have applied.[5] Those who concluded that the American family had equality of power between husband and wife were generally looking at family relationships independently of the family's integration into the wider social structure.

It is not difficult to grasp the reason why such sociological reassessment should occur at this time. Social scientists are products of their own times, influenced by current views at the same time as they influence those views. Thus at a time when the cause of equality of the sexes appeared to have been won we should not be surprised to find research which supported this view. When the question of equality is again thrown into doubt we find a different type of analysis. The whole of this book obviously can be seen as part of the requestioning of sex roles in society, which in its turn will have some influence on the views that are held.

The findings of social scientists about the Australian family can be reviewed from the same critical perspective that Safilios-Rothschild has focused on the American literature. Here I shall be concerned with only three Australian studies – those of Herbst and his colleagues, Fallding and Adler.[6] These three studies have been chosen because they are directly about husband and wife interaction and they approach their research from different perspectives and to some extent come to different conclusions. This of course is intriguing in itself, but it also allows us to gain insight into different approaches to power and to see that similar data can and will be interpreted differently according to the researcher's own position; and finally shows how another broadly feminist perspective will again alter the interpretation. It is unfortunate that these studies were all carried out fifteen or more years ago but there have been few other published studies directly on husband and wife interaction, and certainly none which breaks new ground. Before attempting to interpret the results of these studies I shall briefly outline their major relevant findings.

Still probably the best known and most extensive of Australia's few family studies is the UNESCO study carried out by the staff and students of the Department of Psychology of the University of Melbourne between 1947 and 1950.[7] It was as part of this study that Herbst developed the 'Day at Home' technique, a research method which has been widely used since. By this technique, school children are asked who carries out and decides about a range of family activities which fall into four broad areas, housework, child control, economic and social activities. A further question attempts to tap the amount of disagreement between husband and wife about 'when and how (something) is to be done'. The questionnaire with its thirty-three items was administered to 86 twelve-year-old children at school, and it was found that housework activities fell into three sub-categories, some of which were virtually exclusively the wife's (e.g. ironing, cooking, washing), some of which were predominantly the husband's (e.g. household repairs, mowing lawns), while there was a common area (e.g. shopping, doing dishes) in which both tended to participate. Both participated in child-control activities but these were 'predominantly controlled by the wife'. Social activities were 'generally engaged in and decided about by both husband and wife' as were economic activities.[8] However, in simple numerical terms wives clearly made most decisions and carried out most activities. Overall, the most common pattern for household activities was for the husband or wife to decide and act independently of each other (i.e. autonomic), with wife dominance being the second most common pattern, where the wife decided and the husband or both acted. A 'syncratic co-operative' pattern in which both decided and acted was almost as frequent as the wife-dominant pattern, while the fourth pattern of husband dominance was quite infrequent. The least amount of general family tension was associated with a 'syncratic co-operative' family structure, the most with a 'husband autocratic' structure.[9]

Of these three Australian studies Fallding's is next in chronological sequence, although different in technique. He made an intensive study of thirty-eight families in Sydney during the early 1950s. Each family had at least two children and they were all visited from four to seven times for a full evening on each occasion. Interviews were conducted with each family member and with the family as a group. He found that generally 'husbands and wives divided authority for family control between them in the traditional way, accepting the customary responsibilities of bread winner and homemaker respectively.' In none of the families did the mother work full-time and when she had a part-time job her income was seen as 'additional and never required'. While the division of family tasks was fairly uniform and almost always on traditional lines, there was greater variety 'in matters of family management'. Fallding found that in 55 per cent of the families, 'the fathers could be said to be in effective control', in 11 per cent the 'mothers were in effective control', and in 34 per cent there was 'partnership in management'. In a majority of cases in which the husband was in control the patriachal situation was considered 'rightful' by both husband and wife but in no cases was mother control seen in this way. In the few cases where the mother had control this was seen to have occurred by default. The vast majority of the partnership families saw their joint arrangement as the right and proper way to deal with family affairs.[10]

The Australian data for Adler's study was collected in 1957–8. He used a modified version of Herbst's 'Day at Home' questionnaire which was administered to 1525 twelve-year-old children at school, in five different states. Adler, like Herbst, found that mothers were very active in all areas except for the traditional male household duties. He found the mother's action role to be 'only a little less developed than her decision role' and found them both to be pervasive. This lead Adler to coin the term 'matriduxy' to denote the mother's powerful leadership functions. He eschewed the use of the more common term matriarchy since the basis of the Australian mother's power is 'not a function of inheritance, legal structure or formal social organization'. Comparison of the Australian family pattern with Adler's own data for Mexico and the USA highlighted the role of the Australian mother. In Mexico, fathers are quite clearly seen to be major decision-makers within the family while in the USA much more co-operation was found. In Australia, the mother made 50 per cent of the decisions and carried out 40 per cent of the forty-four questionnaire items (the figures in the Herbst study were 50 per cent and 30 per cent), whereas for the American mother the figure was only 40 per cent for decisions and 30 per cent for actions. The Australian father's participation was consistently lower and in no cases did Adler find an Australian father who participated in all or all but one of the areas covered by the questionnaire, whereas 90 per cent of the American fathers did. The comparable and conflicting figure from Herbst's study was 30 per cent of fathers who participated in all areas or all but one area.[11]

So much for a resume of the findings of these three studies. It is of some interest to note that two other studies using the 'Day at Home' technique have produced results broadly compatible with those of Herbst.[12] Now we must ask what conclusions we should draw about the family and about women in Australian society from these three major studies?

The outstanding finding is undoubtedly the key role of women in family decisions and activities. All the studies agree on this and it seems clear that the Australian wife/mother maintains a large measure of autonomy within the traditionally defined female realm. The husband/father apparently also maintains a large measure of autonomy in the household realm traditionally considered male, but the number of tasks he is involved in is relatively few.

While all the studies agree as it were on 'the facts of the matter', they do not agree on how the situation should be interpreted. We find Adler opting for matriduxy in Australian society while Herbst and Fallding accept a strong leavening of male authority within the family situation. The reason for these differing conclusions would seem to lie in the scope of the studies. Adler is content to add up a series of disparate tasks and decisions and assign leadership according to gross scores. That is, he tends to assign equal weight to the tasks in his questionnaire and takes no account of antecedents to the current arrangements or ideological differences between families. This is clearly a problem with the 'Day at Home' technique or any technique which questions children only. The problem was to a large extent overcome by Herbst, because the questionnaire was utilized as part of a much larger research project which did involve interviewing parents about a variety of topics although not directly on the area covered in the children's questionnaire. In both Herbst's and Fallding's studies we find a much more complex view of the family power structure.[13] We can see this quite clearly in the fact that Fallding recognizes a similar distribution of activities in his patriachy and partnership families but separates them on the basis of the couple's conception of family power and the way they rationalize the family's distribution of tasks. Thus, for example, the husband's predominance in economic activity would be justified in terms of the rights of the male head in those families espousing a 'patriarchy' conception while it is explained in terms of convenience and on the basis of expertise in partnership families.

Safilios-Rothschild's main contention about studies of family power in the USA is that they have over-simplified what is essentially a complex situation,[14] and Adler's pronouncement of matriduxy is a clear example of this. Nonetheless, his conclusion is understandable when we consider that he was confronted with the task of having to explain why Australian women should score so highly on his albeit over-simplified measuring scale. He concludes that his findings put the lie to the myth of male dominance in the Australian family. However, it is not clear that this has been the stereotypical picture of Australian families, and it is difficult to see how Adler could have believed that his circumscribed study could be said to throw light on male authority, or myths about it, in general. A more reasonable total explanation is suggested by Encel who points out that 'the strongly masculine texture of "public" social relations is balanced by the dominance of the mother in "private" social life within the family'.[15] We can see here that the explanatory emphasis shifts from the process of mother dominance to the wider societal pattern of power relations in general and female exclusion from public life. Thus the fact that husbands and wives co-operate more in the USA could be equally taken as a sign of greater general female power as it can be as a sign of less, which is the way Adler sees it.

In broad terms one must also ask what value is placed on the family before any general statement about female power can be made. We see recent recognition given to the fact that the housewife role has been little valued, in suggestions for payment to mothers who stay at home. It is no doubt significant that the translation to a 'valued' role should be sought through offering a monetary payment. This is itself reinforces the view that it is occupational roles which are paid, that we are most highly valued and therefore likely to afford advantages in power terms. Thus while the term matriduxy may be a useful descriptive term for the Australian family situation, its broader implications about female power are misleading. We see the fallacy of analysing one section of the social structure in isolation, a practice which has made so much family research of only minor relevance at best or misleading at worst.

Two of the three Australian studies were largely restricted to non-working women, but Adler's sample included 29 per cent of women who were employed. He found that in these cases husband participation was greater and that there was more disagreement about the activities. He concludes that apparently 'matriduxy is the acceptable way of family life in Australia and that alteration in the mother's role accompanied by increasing father participation tends to be disruptive and tension producing'.[16] A more detailed study of families in which the mother worked supports Adler's conclusion about the 'acceptability' or at least the degree of entrenchment of the traditional female family role. This study, carried out in Melbourne in 1959, compared fifty-two families in which the mother worked, with a matched pair sample in which the mother was not employed. When husband participation in household activities was considered it was found that husbands did participate more, in the working group. However, on closer examination this was found to be the case only when the mother's working role was seen as temporary. When the wife intended to work permanently the husband's contribution was only equivalent to that of the husbands of non-working wives. Thus we see evidence of a rigidity in sex-role definitions. Apparently these roles will bend somewhat in the face of short-term pressures, but permanent alterations are not readily made.[17]

Studies of dual-career families have recently become popular as such families are seen as likely to come closest to an equal distribution of power between husband and wife.[18] Safilios-Rothschild makes the point that

> . . . in both family textbooks and mass media it is taken for granted not only that the wife's lesser development and non-working status are compatible with a companionate marriage but even that they are conducive to such a marriage. But in fact can a marriage of two unequal people blossom into a companionate relationship ? Does not the very notion of a companionate marriage presuppose the union of equals . . ?[19]

Nonetheless the degree of alteration of traditional patterns in dual-career families remains limited. Garland studied fifty-three families in the USA in which both husband and wife possessed what could be considered equal professional status in terms of objective criteria. Even so, in only one case did he find what he considered to be an 'egalitarian' family type and in almost all cases the husband's occupation was construed as the primary one and the wife's career was seen by the husband as of secondary importance to her domestic role.[20] Thus even in what appear to be ideal circumstances for a redefinition of sex roles we come up against the fact that these are very deeply entrenched in society. This suggests we also need to be wary of definitions such as 'partnership' or 'syncratic co-operative' in relation to family interaction patterns. Such definitions are obviously of some value and may signify comparative differences between families but they are unlikely to measure up to the definition of sexual equality which a feminist would propose.

It has been suggested that American family sociology is really 'wives' family sociology'.[21] We might comment that Australian family sociology has tended to be 'children's family sociology'. When we consider that the interaction patterns in Fallding's 'patriarchal' families could be very similar to Adler's 'matriduxy' we must ask whether there is any value in asking children about these patterns. The arrangement, actual or by default, by which a parent makes certain decisions is likely to have been established years earlier; thus the reasoning may not be apparent to the child. Even more importantly, children are unlikely to realize the intricacies of parental ideology and of such processes as the 'non-decision'. The 'non-decision', an aspect of power relationships discussed by Bachrach and Baratz, is the process by which people in powerful positions are able to control the area of decision-making and decide which issues will be heard.[22] When we start thinking of these complexities it becomes obvious that we must be wary of 'children's family sociology' (or that of wives) and generally of simplistic procedures when they are used to investigate complex phenomenon. This is not to suggest that we should opt for Fallding's conclusions about Australian families – rather that we should recognize his method of study as more likely to produce insightful results. Fallding has not escaped, and cannot escape, criticism. It has been suggested that he was too influenced by what he expected and hoped to find, so that his conclusion that the partnership family is challenging the patriarchal family may well be more of a reflection of his own values than those of his subjects. Also it does not require a great deal of radicalism to suggest that his 'partnership' families might be better designated 'neo-traditional'.

To conclude on a not very satisfactory note, it seems we must accept that we do not really have any studies of family interaction in Australia which take cognizance of the complexity of the situation, or any which use a radical definition of equality. We have some interesting leads from previous studies and the investigation of the link between the exclusion of women from public life and their apparent primacy in domestic roles in particular would make a fascinating topic for study. Local studies of dual-career families would throw some light on this question and provide data for comparison with overseas material. Whatever studies are done must, however, employ a far more comprehensive view of family power than we have seen so far and must make quite explicit the way in which they are defining such terms as equality, partnership or female dominance.

Notes

1. R. O. Blood, 'The Effect of the Wife's Employment on the Husband-Wife Relationship', in J. Heiss, *Family Roles and Interaction: An Anthology*, Rand McNally, Chicago, 1970, p.268.

2. See Ralf H. Turner, *Family Interaction*, Wiley, New York 1970, pp.263–6.

3. Lois W. Hoffman, 'Effect of the Employment of Mothers on Parental Power Relations and the Division of Household Tasks', *Marriage and Family Living*, vol.22, February 1960, p.32–3.

4. Constantina Safilios-Rothschild, 'Family Sociology or Wives' Family Sociology', *The Journal of Marriage and the Family*, vol. 29, no. 2, May 1969, pp.345–52.

5. C. Safilios-Rothschild, 'A Study of Family Power Structure: A Review 1960–1969', *Journal of Marriage and the Family*, vol. 32, no. 4, 1970.

6. P. Herbst in O. Oeser and S. B. Hammond (eds) *Social Structure and Personality in a City*, Routledge and Kegan Paul, London, 1954, chapters 9–12.

H. J. Fallding, 'Inside the Australian Family', in A. P. Elkin (ed.) *Marriage and the Family in Australia*, Angus and Robertson, Sydney, 1957.

D. Adler, 'Matriduxy in the Australian Family', in A. F. Davies and S. Encel (eds), *Australian Society: A Sociological Introduction*, Cheshire, Melbourne, 1965.

7. Oeser and Hammond, op.cit.

8. Oeser and Hammond, op.cit., p.120–121.

9. Oeser and Hammond, op.cit., p.167.

10. Fallding, op.cit., p.60–66.

11. Adler, op.cit, 149–155.

12. R. Taft, 'Some Sub-Cultural Variables in Family Structure in Australia', *Australian Journal of Psychology*, vol.9, no.1, June 1957; L. Bollman, 'Australian Urban Family Structure: A Brisbane Sample', unpublished B.A. thesis, University of Queensland.

13. The concept of power is many faceted, and by some definitions in at least some families there may be no 'power' structure – only influence, authority, etc. Power is generally taken to be exercised in a situation in which there is some conflict over values or action and one person complies with another because of fear of sanction. See P. Bachrach and M. Baratz, *Power and Poverty*, Part 1, Oxford University Press, New York, 1971.

14. Safilios-Rothschild, 'A Study of Family Power Structure', p.345.
15. S. Encel, 'The Family', in A. F. Davies, and S. Encel, Second Edition, *Australian Society: A Sociological Introduction*, Cheshire, Melbourne, 1970, p.283.
16. Adler, p.155.
17. G. B. Sharp and L. J. Bryson, 'The Family: Maternal Work and the Internal Division of Labour'. Paper read to the Sociological Association of Australia and New Zealand, 1965.
18. See Rhonda and Robert N. Rapoport, *Dual Career Families*, Penguin Books, 1971.
19. C. Safilios-Rothschild, *Towards a Sociology of Women*, Xerox College Publishing, Lexington, Mass. 1972, p.64.
20. T. Neal Garland, 'The Better Half? The Male in the Dual Profession Family', in C. Safilios-Rothschild, *Towards a Sociology of Women.*
21. Safilios-Rothschild, 'Family Sociology or Wives' Family Sociology' p.346.
22. Bachrach and Baratz, op.cit., p.8–9.

Twelve

School and the Oppression of Women[1]

This chapter attempts a fusion of two separate currents of radical social criticism. The institution of school is under attack, as distinct from previous demands which were limited to educational reform. The radical education writers such as Illich, Holt and Freire question the wisdom of devoting an increasing and seemingly never-ending proportion of society's resources to schooling.[2]

On the other hand school is coming under attack from the Women's Liberation Movement as a sexist institution contributing to the oppression of women. Sexism in this chapter is taken to mean 'organizing people according to sex and sexual behaviour, and attributing various behaviour, personality and status traits to people on the basis of sex'. It does not necessarily mean a patriarchal society. 'It could equally well mean a matriarchal society or bisexually dominated (bisexuarchy) or a society in which the sexes have equal power and influence providing that their spheres of action are different and defined and enforced as different.'[3]

There are at least three excellent articles which taken together, establish that school oppresses women.[4] This chapter, instead, concentrates on an explanation of *how* school initiates and perpetuates sexism and briefly considers what might be done about it.

The hypothesis proposed here (and which is largely based on Illich's analysis of school) is that school oppresses both women and men, and that one of the forms this oppression takes is sexism. Illich has drawn our attention to what he calls the hidden curriculum – the collection of assumptions that underpin the formal ritual of school. As graduates of that system we are all indoctrinated with these beliefs: that to know anything it has to be learned at school, preferably from a book or a teacher;

the only things important enough and worth knowing were the subjects we sat at examinations and were graded on.

The implications of this process were quite clear to us, even at an early age. Unless we passed the examinations, were graded on our performance and awarded a certificate, we would be unfit for any but the most menial, low status position in adult life.

By contrast the *official* explanations and justifications for school do not spell out anything like this. They talk about changing society, transmitting culture, helping children grow into fully autonomous adults, even national and economic development. The best contemporary example of this other reality is contained in the Report of the Interim Committee for the Australian Schools Commission. It details the special purposes of school as,

> . . . the acquisition of skills and knowledge, initiation into the cultural heritage, the valuing of rationality and the broadening of opportunities to respond to and participate in artistic endeavours . . . the giving to individual children the experience of being a member of a diverse group through which he may come to feel concern for others and to develop his own sense of identity.[5]

The value of the radical education writers is that they penetrate this myth, uncovering the actual process. Freire proposes that 'neutral' education cannot occur. Education's purpose is either for domination or for freedom. Most schools domesticate and pacify the masses through a 'prepossessed and pre-digested reality' divorced from both its origins and its uses. Illich sees schooling as 'knowledge capitalism' – a ritual of accumulating knowledge, just one more consumer commodity which can be produced by research, packaged into curricula, and transmitted by teachers and machines. Within this framework a person's worth is measured by the level of consumption on the international scale of twelve school grades.

The Nature of School

The transference of a pre-digested reality, or the accumulation of knowledge capital is a far cry from the development of critical thought and understanding! But the former perspectives on school have been empirically confirmed. John Holt's observations reveal that the classroom situation actively discourages thinking and intellectual risk-taking. Instead students learn different strategies for success in meeting the school's demands. They mumble, guess, pluck answers out of the air and give replies aimed at teacher approval. Silberman empirically confirmed Holt's classroom observations and found a correlation between fifth graders' desire for teacher approval and their rejection of intellectual challenges.[6]

Other studies suggest that children are often more aware of institutional demands than of the requirements of learning itself. For example White found that elementary school pupils had no 'cognitive map of content' to help them see connections between subjects, but they did have a 'map of school experience' – that is, of the work and evaluation demands placed on them by teachers.[7] A comparative study of elementary schools in four urban neighbourhoods by Leacock found that children consistently reflected a stronger emphasis on 'good behaviour' than on 'good work' when asked what they thought their teachers wanted.[8]

In Australia, with 79 per cent of children attending centrally controlled government schools, 'the school experience' is common to all children. Why is it then, that the end result of schooling is an uncanny regurgitation of children according to their sex, class and race characteristics?

As Jencks states in his important and scholarly evaluation of the effects of compensatory education programmes, 'the character of a school's output depends largely on a single input, namely the characteristics of its entering children. Everything else – the school budget, its policies, the characteristics of the teachers – is either secondary or completely irrelevant.'[9]

School reproduces the social structure almost as if it had been programmed by an invisible computer. Middle-class, white, urban, English-speaking males tend to succeed in the education system. The rest don't. A similar pattern has been reported overseas and appears to be well established.[10]

Part of the answer to this puzzle according to Miller lies in developing a true sociology of education which includes an attempt to build a sociology of *educational knowledge*. It would study what is taught and learned in school, (and beyond) how knowledge is produced, distributed and controlled and how these processes are related to the organization of education and the wider cultural and social structure.[11]

School Knowledge is Sexist

The beginnings of such an analysis have been made by Illich. He begins with a definition of knowledge as

> . . . not a commodity, but a concrete, unrepeatable and surprising part of a man's life. Knowledge is a person's understanding of the context into which he places the information which surrounds him. It is his insight into the meaning this context has for him . . . Knowledge thus understood as an existential life-experience is learning, and this learning is the goal of education.

In other words, knowledge is not the same as a skill. Nor is it a thing that can be delivered to any person, for example by a teacher, a programmed instruction course or a computer. Laing puts the same proposition in a slightly different way.

> I cannot experience your experience. You cannot experience my experience . . . My experience of you is always mediated through your *behaviour* . . . Our behaviour is a function of our experience. We act according to the way we see things.

It is comprised of personal experience and therefore cannot be taught or pre-constructed in any way.[12] But this is exactly what school attempts to do. The 'knowledge' handed down in the school, both in the formal and the hidden curriculum, is clearly very different from the kind of experience which Illich believes constitutes learning. I will distinguish it as 'school knowledge' for the purposes of argument.

Let us examine school knowledge. What is its content? How has it been transmitted and what are its effects?

As it has been handed down, school knowledge is a particular interpretation of the world. It is predominantly a male, white and Anglo-Saxon interpretation, and it has permeated our consciousness to the extent that we are prepared to accept it as the 'truth'. Women are therefore either denigrated or ignored by school knowledge. For example Marjorie U'Ren in her study of Californian school texts discovered that Madame Curie was depicted in one book as, 'little more than a helpmate for her husband's projects. The illustration that accompanies this section even portrays Madame Curie peering mildly from behind her husband's shoulder while he and another distinguished gentleman loom in the foreground, engaged in a serious dialogue.'[13]

The other major tactic used against women has been tokenism, the creation of special women – heroines – who have demonstrated within a framework of male reality and standards, what women can achieve. Daisy Bates 'the eccentric' and Caroline Chisholm, the strong mother figure and family supporter, are two examples commonly used in schools.[14]

School knowledge concerns itself with the public arena, the world-out-there inhabited by politicians, scientists, adventurers, humanitarians. It is no coincidence that they are predominantly male. The public domain belongs to men. While writing this paper, the author received a copy of the 'Secondary Teachers' Notes – English', published by the Education Department of Western Australia to help teachers with classes who listen to the ABC school broadcasts. The July 1973 issue is an excellent example of school knowledge as mainly concerned with the world of men – the public world. Its contents include notes on broadcasts about violence (and the perpetrators are all depicted as boys); the myth of Beowulf, the great adventurer; war; a series with the subtitle 'A Man Speaking' which includes poet Robert Frost, author Joseph Conrad and playwright Arthur Miller. The novels and authors considered on television broadcasts are D. H. Lawrence, George Orwell and *Huckleberry Finn*. Not one broadcast dealt with the daily world women inhabit – children and the family, the home, supermarkets, love and romance.

Curthoys applies the same distinction in her discussion of the ramifications of sexism in the university.

I think the sexism of the university is a function of, and is needed by, a society which requires a division of kinds of work between its members. Roughly the *public* positions, both powerful and powerless, in the areas of production go to the males, while women work in the private or domestic sphere . . . the university maintains this division of labour between the sexes not only in its membership but in the kinds of theories it produces.[15]

In the school system the *public* positions of principal and all the promotion positions, as well as the people downtown at the Department of Education head office tend to be male. The *private* positions of child-minders and attendants – that is the teachers – are taken by women. (See Table 1 below.)

Table 1

Women Teachers as Proportions of all Teachers and Persons in Promotion Positions: N.S.W., Qld and S.A., 1972[44]

State	*% of Primary Persons* (d)	*% of Promotion Persons, Primary*	*% of Secondary Persons*	*% of Promotion Persons, Secondary*
N.S.W. (a)	68	38	45	19
Qld. (b)	58	8	49	23
S.A. (c)	73	18	46	26

(a) From 1972 Annual Report of N.S.W. Minister for Education.
(b) From Annual Report of Minister for Education and Cultural Activities, 1972.
(c) From S.A. Education Department, 'Women in Education' 1973 figures.
(d) Includes infants.

The stuff of learning in Australian schools and universities does not include the validity of personal experience. In March 1973, Ms Helen Garner was dismissed from her position as an English teacher at Fitzroy Girls High School in Melbourne for using 'four letter' words in a general studies lesson. She made the mistake of approaching the subject of sex, which had been raised by the students, in a straightforward way, without the airy-fairy trappings of Victorian modesty. The language she used was familiar to the students but it was foreign to the bureaucrats at the Department of Education. Similarly, the reasons behind the initial refusal of Sydney University's Professorial Board of the women's course in philosophy was its emphasis on the politics of experience.

> ... the fear is that this respected public institution is going to be invaded by subject matter which is essentially trivial and feminine. Yet to see what we wish to do as devaluing the activity of the university is to reflect the judgement that what 'naturally' belongs to the public sphere is valuable, while that which belongs to the private sphere is valueless.[16]

As long as school does not concern itself with the area of private experience we are all, women and men, alienated from our learning, according to Illich's definition. In addition school alienates us from the self by denying the validity of that private, 'unrepeatable and surprising part of a man's life'. And now we must emphatically, include 'a woman's life' in our definition too.

School knowledge presents a *Weltanschauung* including men (at least in the public domain) so boys are better able to understand and place it in a personal context than are girls. The hidden curriculum includes the sexist message that women do not belong in the Real World (that is outside the home). I have described this effect elsewhere.

> Our teachers reminded us again and again until we accepted it unconsciously, that we should behave like little ladies, that we should be neat and tidy and obedient, that we should be sweet and feminine, and not too smart in case we scared the boys away. We got the girls' jobs like taking the principal's morning tea into his office and the boys got the boys' job of moving the chairs and tables and carrying heavy loads of books for the teacher.

We knew that no matter how hard we worked at our English literature and logarithms our destiny was motherhood and household slavery. Like the sword of Damocles that future lay before us. It subverted our consciousness so that we seemed to have absolutely no freedom of choice about our own lives. It sapped our energies away from the serious business of getting an education.[17]

In this way school prepares children for their adult sex roles. It is commonly described in the 'neutral' language preferred by conservatives as fitting children to enter adult society, helping them mature or assisting their self-development. The New South Wales Minister for Education, Mr Willis, recently put it this way; 'Our education system is the medium by which a common culture is transmitted to each new generation.'[18] To speak of a common culture is to be in cloud-cuckoo land. What he means is that the school system is the means by which the *dominant* culture is transmitted. And in Australia, as in most other Western industrialized English-speaking countries, the dominant culture is that of white English-speaking males. In any analysis of women in Australian society the yardstick used is invariably whether they have penetrated the male dominion of work (outside the home) and power as expressed for example in the fields of education, politics and the law.[19] Instead of confronting stereotyped sex roles the school accepts and actively transmits them, just as it fails to challenge any other aspects of society. John Holt eloquently sums up the futility of separating school and society.

I am saying that truly good education in a bad society is a contradiction in terms. In short, in a society that is absurd, unworkable, wasteful, destructive, secretive, coercive, monopolistic, and generally anti-human, we could never have good education, no matter what kind of schools the powers that be might permit, because it is not the educators or the schools, but the whole society and the quality of life within it that really educate.[20]

In other words a sexist society inevitably has sexist education. One measure of the extent to which our sexist society has perverted the school system is the latter's refusal to even recognize sexism as a contentious issue. Education Departments do not collect statistics by sex. They appear to be blithely unconcerned that 36 per cent of fourteen-year-old students and 46 per cent at sixth form level are still in single sex schools.[21]

A plethora of studies on co-education has failed to demonstrate any educational or social advantages for single sex schools. On the contrary, Dale, in a massive study showed that both girls and boys seemed happier and better adjusted in co-educational schools.[22] Here again, the omission of co-education as a contentious issue, by education pressure groups in favour of sex education, class size and teacher qualifications, can only be interpreted as resulting from a failure to examine the sexist nature of school and society. It has been suggested by Martin that the education system's refusal to collect such information and use it to examine sex differences, is its over-readiness to identify factors outside the system, such as community and parental attitudes, as responsible for sexual inequalities, for example the higher drop-out rate of girls.[23] Husen makes a similar point.

> For a long time it has almost been a professional disease among educators to regard school education as though it operated in a social vacuum and to disregard the incompatibilities between school and society. This attitude provides a very efficient defence mechanism against demands for educational change that would bring the educational system into line with changes in society at large.[24]

The Effects of Sexism in Schools

By denying everything outside the formal curriculum, everything outside school as not worth learning, school alienates children from learning about themselves. It denies them a sexual identity except the one laid down in the stereotyped sex roles that society and hence school accepts.

It is important to note that the notion that sex roles have changed and become more flexible – for example since 1946 when Mirra Komarovsky first studied the female sex role – is a piece of popular mythology.[25] Broverman et al. using a questionnaire administered to almost a thousand subjects, concluded that a strong consensus still exists about the differing characteristics of women and men irrespective of the subject's age, sex, religion, marital status and educational level. The characteristics attributed to men are positively valued more often than those attributed to women. The sex role differences were considered desirable by college students, healthy by mental health professionals and ideal by both women and men.[26]

On the one hand says Levy, girls' sex role is even more incompatible with the institutional demands of school than boys' sex role. They are forced into a conflict-ridden, schizophrenic position. They are asked to study hard while at the same time both school and society send out cues saying 'Girls aren't supposed to be too intelligent and successful'. The prevalence of role conflict and intellectual under-performance amongst girl students is the result. Crandall et al. for example report that the brighter the girl the *less* well she expects to perform.[27]

On the other hand, Levy points out that school reinforces girls' training for obedience, social and emotional dependence, and docility. Even the way they learn has been compared unfavourably with the cognitive processes involved in boys' learning. Widdup claims girls are reinforced for passive learning while boys are encouraged towards independent learning that involves breaking set.[28] The independent, active behaviour of boys conflicts with the authority ethos of schools whereas girls submit as part of their sex role socialization. This explanation of the cause of teachers' preference for girls and of the discipline problems associated with teaching boys has also been suggested by Levy. She points out that the values of school – all quintessentially middle class – neatness, punctuality and order, are important values for girls, as they are specifically relevant to their future domestic role.[29]

A study of adolescent attitudes in Victoria led Edgar to say: 'The education system, it seems to me, is one of the major institutional bases for the social production of incompetent, dependent, self-denigrating females.'[30] He found that girls score significantly higher than boys on self-deprecation scales, that they are more likely to perceive self-limitations, such as lack of ability in educational achievement, that they are considerably lower on self-confidence, and that they perceive their parents and teachers as having consistently lower expectations of their educational achievement than boys.

His conclusions are supported by Taylor's findings that test anxiety for girls interfered more with their school performance than it did for boys.[31] Connell also reports that a much greater percentage of girls than boys in a study of 8,000 Sydney adolescents, said they were anxious about exams. (See Table 2.)

Table 2

Percentage who report 'a great amount' of anxiety about exams

Age	*11–12*	*13–14*	*15–16*	*17–18*
Boys	29	32	33	28
Girls	41	47	50	48

Source: R. W. Connell, 'You can't tell them apart nowadays—can you?' Paper presented to ANZAAS, Sydney, 1972.

In the competition for knowledge capital girls lose out to boys. They do not win as many certificates and their parents are not apparently as willing to spend as much on their education.[32] (See Table 3.) As an adult a woman has an impossible task catching up since her full-time work includes the primary responsibility for child-rearing. Thus, even if she has an independent income, a woman finds it relatively more difficult than a man to study part-time.

A study of family responsibilities of working women conducted by the Department of Labour and National Service in 1971 found that more than half of the household tasks were carried out exclusively by women, and another third by women with some assistance. Only one in ten tasks was performed exclusively by others in the household. Child-minding facilities in Australia are minimal and only accessible to a limited number of mothers. The two groups who use child-minding most are women who through economic circumstances must work and middle-class women who can afford to pay high fees. The first group cannot afford either the time or money to enrol in courses leading to qualifications. This is one explanation for the predominantly middle-class characteristics of the women who attend adult education courses and part-time advanced level courses.

In any case the monopoly of knowledge capital – that Illich says is a natural consequence of treating knowledge as a consumer commodity – acts as an effective barrier against former 'drop outs' re-entering the school system.

Table 3

Age Participation, All Schools, Australia (a)

Age	*1961*	*1966*	*1971*	*1973*
Boys				
Age 14	90.1	96.9	98.3	97.8
15	65.3	75.2	83.2	83.4
16	34.6	46.4	57.7	56.5
17	14.9	21.2	32.8	32.3
18+ (b)	5.5	6.8	11.8	11.4
Girls				
Age 14	87.0	96.3	98.3	97.6
15	56.5	69.7	79.8	81.1
16	26.3	37.6	49.5	52.2
17	8.8	13.4	24.8	27.6
18+	1.8	2.6	5.8	6.4

Source: Australian Department of Education[44]

(a) With the exception of 1971, which is based on the June 1971 Census, all the other years are based on population estimates at 30 June.

(b) Students aged 18 years plus are shown as percentages of the 18 years age group.

A unique survey by the Australian Bureau of Census and Statistics in 1968 showed that 6.1 per cent of the total population aged fifteen and over were enrolled in courses of study or training other than full-time secondary school. A breakdown by sex showed that males in non-school study courses constituted 8.3 per cent of the male population while the females enrolled were only 3.9 per cent of the female population. Seventy per cent of the persons enrolled at universities, colleges of advanced education and teachers colleges were male. Persons enrolled for technician level courses in technical, commercial and other fields were 62 per cent male, while persons in trade courses were 92 per cent male.[33]

Within the school curriculum women are degraded by the treatment they receive in texts by the discriminatory channelling of girls into certain 'feminine' subjects and sports, future careers, and unfortunately by the attitudes of teachers.[34]

The information surrounding girls and boys in school comes mainly from the curriculum and the teachers. Studies of children's books, pre-school readers and texts show how women are depicted in small numbers, mostly inside a house, in a service or glorified servant position, passive and accepting. Men on the other hand are generally shown in disproportionately large numbers, as active, intelligent, displaying initiative, strong, brave and independent. Florence Howe sums up the position this way, 'The school girl knows that for her life is one thing, learning another . . . She cannot find herself in history texts or as she would like to see herself in literature, yet she knows she is not a male.'[35]

In a study of factors influencing choice of subjects in fifth form in NSW schools, Humphreys found that of all the factors she expected to find, sex was the most significant. She writes, 'The sex of the pupil is the only single factor apparently playing a significant role in determining reasons for choice of subjects and this seems particularly so with respect to the reason for choice of economics, French, mathematics and science in that order.' She goes on to say that for boys' career choice was the main reason given for choice of subjects. For girls' subject choice is made for reasons of liking and interest, achievement and school organization. She also found that family advice was the main influence in choice of a career which suggests that the Australian family is still sex-role bound in its view of women.[86]

In terms of learning by experience, both sexes learn at an early age that women are inferior through the practical examples of the power structure of schools and the distinction made between boys and girls in discipline practices.

The notion that boys are tougher and stronger than girls is reinforced in every Australian school by the distinction made between the sexes in corporal punishment. Queensland, Victoria and South Australia forbid the corporal punishment of girls under any circumstances. In Tasmania girls may be beaten 'in extreme cases of open defiance of teacher authority'. In NSW and Western Australia corporal punishment for girls over twelve is forbidden and only in extreme cases may girls under twelve be punished in this way. For boys, all states allow the use of corporal punishment although there are slight differences in the means adopted.[87]

The women who continue in the education system are made aware of an even more marked division of labour in the universities and colleges – the professors and lecturers are male, and their handmaidens, the tutors and research assistants, are female.

Madge Dawson calculated that in 1970 there were nearly a thousand women on the teaching staffs of Australian universities, representing 14 per cent of the total. At the bottom of the academic hierarchy, that is tutors and demonstrators, 33 per cent of the teaching staff were women, and at the top, that is professors, only 2 per cent were women. This is again hardly surprising when academic positions depend increasingly on the possession of a higher degree. Only 13 per cent of Ph.D and 19 per cent of Masters enrolments in 1971 were women. Women are concentrated in untenured positions and constitute the highest percentage of irregular appointments outside the 'real' system, for example, as part-time research assistants, part-time tutors and lecturers.

Women have less knowledge capital so they accept their subordinate position – after all, their husbands and men friends have more training and more education. (Though the growth of the women's movement has meant that an increasing number of women are struggling against their oppression and no longer accept their decreed inferiority.)

Girls start school knowing that they are not as important as boys and this realization is maintained and reinforced by the school. Little wonder then that girls leave school in greater numbers (see Table 4), and attend university and colleges in fewer numbers than boys (see Table 5). School reinforces women's minority status.[43]

Table 4

Percentage of Form 1 Enrolments Remaining in the Final Year in 1967, 1969, 1971, 1973, All States, By Sex.

	Government Schools							
	Girls				*Boys*			
	1967	*1969*	*1971*	*1973*	*1967*	*1969*	*1971*	*1973*
ACT	37	52	49	55	54	70	63	60
NSW	17	21	24	28	24	30	33	34
Vic.	16	22	25	27	20	23	25	24
Tas.	7	10	14	20	11	14	21	21
SA	11	16	20	24	18	23	29	31
WA	15	18	20	25	20	22	25	28
Qld	—	20	21	25	—	25	26	27

	Non-Government Schools							
	Girls				*Boys*			
	1967	*1969*	*1971*	*1973*	*1967*	*1969*	*1971*	*1973*
ACT	41	47	52	63	67	71	63	71
NSW	21	27	31	37	36	44	48	49
Vic.	31	37	43	50	50	56	61	69
Tas.	15	17	23	28	27	31	39	41
SA	25	37	46	54	54	68	74	76
WA	39	41	40	48	48	53	49	52
Qld	—	38	41	45	—	58	60	56

Source: Australian Department of Education[44]

Table 5

Students at tertiary level by sex, 1972

	Females	*Males*	*Persons*
Colleges of Advanced Education—Total	12 016	40 379	52 395
Colleges of Advanced Education—Teacher Education	2 582	1 264	3 846
Teachers Colleges	18 264	8 300	26 564
Universities	42 128	86 540	128 668
Totals by percentage	34.9	65.1	100
Totals	72 408	135 219	207 627

Source: Year Book, Australia, 1973, pp. 649, 654, 657.

Possibilities for Change

The study of the sociology of education is littered with research into equality of educational opportunity. The classical liberal response to the social stratification caused by and resulting from school, has been the notion of compensatory education for the so-called deprived children – blacks, the poor, rural and immigrant and handicapped children. However, evaluative data on compensatory education programmes indicates very small tangible results for the massive resources expended. According to Illich the War on Poverty in the United States cost one billion dollars a year for three years – close to a quarter of the Federal budget – with the result that the education gap between rich and poor widened and educators discovered they needed an additional $10 million for newly discovered underprivileged groups. He concluded that even the very rich nations cannot afford to keep escalating schooling. After a wide-ranging evaluation of compensatory education programmes, Jencks says that poverty is best attacked directly by economic changes and not through schools.

Miller depicts compensatory education as a form of cultural imperialism: '. . . the interventionist policies derived from the scholarship which engendered widely held deficit-hypotheses have frequently involved – at best – a culture-centric paternalism and at worst psychic violence to the doubly-bound "disadvantaged" dependents.'

The deficit hypothesis approach, particularly its theoretical precepts, is not very useful.[39] Perhaps because it fails to come to terms with the sexist, racist and class-based nature of school. Instead of focusing on this, the liberal approach is to force the child to assimilate to the school and particularly to the WASP values it perpetrates.

In the case of women and girls the traditional liberal response has been to try and entice or even force girls to stay on at school. Macleod and Wykes are good examples of the liberal response. 'How can we persuade more girls to stay longer at school and to prepare through some form of higher education and training to enter a stimulating, creative profession?' asks Wykes.[40]

But if school is a sexist institution women will continue to be further socialized into the traditional female sex role. The Women's Liberation Movement has suggested, and in some cases successfully implemented, rewriting of texts and readers and the introduction of women's courses.[41] These tactics appear to be valid and useful means of exposing and challenging the hidden curriculum. Women's demands for courses where they can learn about themselves, their psychology, their history and their experiences cut right across the hidden curriculum.

A logical next step for feminists is to join the move to end grading, streaming and tracking, which are the institutional props for school knowledge. And after that it is clear that women's demands should turn to finding alternatives to school. Florence Howe provides strong justification for this view.

'Before one can begin to change a condition one must believe in the possibility of change. To prevent such belief is the purpose of the education of women, even in 1970.'[42]

Therefore women must bypass school and escape from its pernicious effects. This can only be done by establishing alternatives to school.[43] The establishment of the Grapevine learning network in Melbourne in mid-1974 was the first such step by Australian feminists.

Notes

1. 'School' is used as a generic term and includes schools, colleges and universities.

2. C. E. Silberman, *Crisis in the Classroom: The Remaking of American Education*, Vintage, New York, 1971;
S. Repo (ed.), *This Book is About Schools*, Pantheon, New York, 1970;
I. Illich, *Deschooling Society*, Calder and Boyars, London, 1971;
J. Holt, *How Children Fail*, Penguin, 1969; *How Children Learn*, Penguin, 1970;
P. Freire, *Pedagogy of the Oppressed*, Penguin, 1972.
Freire developed a spectacularly successful method of teaching illiterate Latin American peasants to read and write, based on his analysis of education.
See for example, J. Harper and D. Heath, 'Separate and Unequal – Boys and Girls at School', *Dissent*, no.28, Winter 1972. (Special Issue on Women.)
M. Greeland, *Education*, Women's Liberation Movement, Sydney 1970.

3. Hobart Women's Action Group 'Sexism in the Women's Movement', *Refractory Girl*, no.5, 1974, p.30.

4. N. Cooper, 'The Education of Girls', in D. McLean, (ed.) *It's People that Matter*, Angus and Robertson, Sydney, 1969;
J. Martin, 'Sex Differences in Educational Qualifications', in R. J. W. Selleck (ed.), *Melbourne Studies in Education*, 1972, Melbourne University Press, 1972, p.96;
B. Levy, 'The School's Role in the Sex Role Stereotyping of Girls: A Feminist Review of the Literature', *Feminist Studies*, vol.1, no.1, 1972, p.5.

5. Interim Committee for the Australian Schools Commission, *Schools in Australia*, Canberra, 1973, p.14.

6. M. L. Silberman, 'Classroom Rewards and Intellectual Courage', in M. L. Silberman (ed.), *The Experience of Schooling*, Holt, Rinehart and Winston, New York, 1971.

7. M. A. White, 'The View from the Pupil's Desk', *The Urban Review*, vol.2, 1968, pp.5–7.

8. E. Leacock, *Teaching and Learning in City Schools*, Basic Books, New York, 1969.

9. C. Jencks et al., *Inequality: A Reassessment of the Effect of Family and Schooling in America*, Allen Lane, 1972; Penguin Books, in press.
Schools in Australia, Chapter 3, on Equality of Educational Opportunity, has a good summary and discussion of the latest Australian evidence (pp.16–22).
See also T. Roper, *The Myth of Equality*, Heinemann Educational, Mel-

bourne, 1971, for a run-down on the following disadvantaged groups – inner-city and rural children, migrants and Aboriginals, women, handicapped children and pre-school children.

10. In Britain:
The Newsom Report, *Half our Future*, London, HMSO, 1963;
The Plowden Report; *Children and their Primary Schools*,
London, HMSO, 1969;
J. W. B. Douglas, *The Home and the School*, MacGibbon and Kee, 1964.
In the United States:
J. S. Coleman et al, *Equality of Educational Opportunity*, Department of Health, Education and Welfare, Washington, 1966;
G. W. Mayeske et al., *A Study of Our Nation's Schools*, U.S. Department of Health, Education and Welfare, Office of Education, Washington, 1972;
J. Henry, 'Education of the Negro Child', in J. Henry, *Essays on Education*, Penguin, 1971.
Internationally:
T. Husen, *Social Background and Educational Career – Research Perspectives on Equality of Educational Opportunity*, Centre for Educational Research and Innovation, Organization for Economic Co-operation and Development (OECD), Paris, 1972.

11. This approach accords with the assumption of the author, that *what* is learned is of lasting import, not the certificates and consequent employment opportunities.
A. Miller, 'Social-Cultural Theories of Education and the Sociology of Education', Paper presented at the Sociology of Education Conference, Melbourne, November, 1972, p.6.

12. I. Illich, 'On the Necessity to Deschool Society' in *Alternatives to Schooling*, AUS, Melbourne, 1972, p.6.
R. D. Laing, *The Politics of Experience*, Penguin, 1967, pp.16, 22, 24.
See also Max Charlesworth on deschooling in *Dissent*, no.30, Spring 1973 for an extended discussion of the radical education stance on knowledge.

13. M. B. U'Ren, 'The Image of Woman in Textbooks', in V. Gornick and B. K. Moran, *Woman in a Sexist Society*, Basic Books, New York, p.222.

14. For a different view see M. Murnane, 'Mystification in Feminine Biography, Daisy Bates Exhumed', *Refractory Girl*, no.1, Summer, 1972/3, p.19; and K. Jennings, 'Founding Mother's Dirty Faced Children', *Nation Review*, July 6–12, 1973, p.1188.

15. J. Curthoys, 'Sexism and the University', Mimeograph, University of Sydney Philosophy Department, June 1973, p.5.

16. Curthoys, op.cit., pp.7–8.

17. D. Humphreys, 'Conform you little bastards, or else', Paper to First Women's Electoral Lobby National Conference, Canberra, January 1973 in *The WEL papers*, National Journal of the Women's Electoral Lobby, 1973/74.

18. E. A. Willis, 'Teaching calls for Dedication', *Sydney Morning Herald*, Tertiary Education Guide, 8 January, 1973.

19. R. Stephenson, *Women in Australian Society*, Heinemann Educational, Melbourne, 1970.

20. J. Holt, *New Schools Exchange Newsletter*, no.60.

21. Figures are from J. P. Keeves, 'Sex Differences in Science and Mathematics Courses', Paper prepared for Sociology of Education Conference, Melbourne, 1972.

22. R. R. Dale, *Mixed or Single Sex School*, Routledge and Kegan Paul, London, 1971.

23. J. Martin, op.cit., p.123.

24. Husen, op.cit., pp.156–157.

25. M. Komarovsky, 'Cultural Contradictions and Sex Roles', *American Journal of Sociology*, November 1946.

26. I. K. Broverman et al., 'Sex Role Stereotypes: A Current Appraisal', *Journal of Social Issues*, vol.28, no.2, 1972, p.61.

27. See also V. C. Crandall, 'Sex differences in expectancy of intellectual and academic reinforcement', in C. P. Smith, (ed.), *Achievement-Related Motives in Children*, Russell Sage Foundation, New York, 1969, pp.11–45. M. Horner, 'Fail: Bright Woman', *Psychology Today*, vol.3, November 1969, pp.36–38.

28. D. Widdup, 'The Great Mathematical Inequality', Dip. Ed. Thesis, University of Tasmania, 1972.

29. Levy, op.cit., pp.8–9.

30. D. Edgar, 'Competence for Girls?', *The Secondary Teacher*, June 1972.

31. F. G. Taylor, 'Some Aspects of Test Anxiety, Self Concept and Academic Achievement in 6th Grade Boys and Girls', M. A. Thesis, University of Newcastle, 1968.

32. An *Age* opinion poll published in August 1972 found that 62 per cent of women and men agreed with the statement, 'If a choice had to be made, a boy should receive more education than a girl', The *Age*, 7 August 1972.

33. From *Survey of Non School Study Courses*, Australian Bureau of Census and Statistics, ref. no.13, 11 August 1968, p.2.
See M. Fogarty, R. Rapoport and R. Rapoport, *Sex Career and Family*, Allen & Unwin, 1971, p.121–129 for a discussion of the international situation of female lower qualifications.

34. D. Bradley and M. Mortimer, 'Sex role stereotypes in children's picture books', *Refractory Girl*, 1, 1972/3.
L. Weitzman, D. Eifler, E. Hokada and C. Ross, 'Sex role socialisation in picture books for pre-school children', *American Journal of Sociology*, vol.77, no.63, 1972.
Dick and Jane as Victims – Sex Stereotyping in Children's Readers, Women on words and images, Princeton, New Jersey, 1972 (National Organization of Women, New Jersey chapter). National Organization of Women, *Report on Sex Bias in the public schools*, New York Chapter, NOW.

35. F. Howe, 'Sexual Stereotypes start early', *Saturday Review*, 16 October 1971.

36. G. M. Humphreys, 'A study of factors influencing the choice of courses and elective subjects by form V pupils in departmental schools selected from the Warringah Shire in N.S.W.', M.Ed. Thesis, University of Sydney, 1968.

37. *Discipline in Secondary Schools in Western Australia*, Report of the Government Secondary Schools Discipline Committee under the Chairmanship of Mr H. W. Dettman, Perth, December 1972, p.65.

38. H. Hacker, 'Women as a Minority Group', *Social Forces*, vol.30, 1951.

39. See for example, S. S. Baratz and J. C. Baratz, 'Early Childhood Intervention: the Social Science Basis of Institutional Racism', *Harvard Educational Review*, vol.40, no.1, February 1970, pp.29–50.
N. L. Friedman, 'Cultural Deprivation: A Commentary on the Sociology of Knowledge', *Journal of Educational Thought*, vol.1, no.2, August 1967, pp.88–99.
H. Ginsberg, *The Myth of the Deprived Child*, Prentice Hall, 1972.
D. C. Morton and D. R. Watson, 'Compensatory Education and Contemporary Liberalism in the United States: a Sociological View', *International Review of Education*, vol.17, no.3, 1971, pp.289–307.

40. J. Macleod, 'Where have all the Young Girls Gone?', *The Secondary Teacher*, February 1965, p.11; and O. Wykes, 'Have Women the Same Chance?' *The Secondary Teacher*, February, 1965, p.16.

41. See *The Witch of Grange Grove*, a non-sexist book for children published

by the Women's Movement Children's Literature Co-op in Melbourne; and P. Ryan (ed.), *A Guide to Women's Studies in Australia*, Australian Union of Students, Melbourne, 1974.

42. F. Howe, 'The Female Majority', in P. Lauter and F. Howe, *The Conspiracy of the Young*, World Publishing, New York, 1970.

43. This is argued in more detail in D. Humphreys and K. Newcombe, *School's Out*, Penguin Books, 1975.

44. From research in progress for interim report to Schools Commission on 'Social Change and the Education of Women' by D. Torsh.

Thirteen
Sex Stereotyping in Children's Books

What a person does and what she believes herself to be will in general be a function of what people around her expect her to be and what the overall situation in which she is acting implies that she is.[1]

The world, as it is presented to children, is a world of men, and for men. Our language and media reinforce rigid sex-role stereotyping upon our children from the moment of birth. The most important and earliest social role that children learn is that of 'female' or 'male'. Having made a decision in early childhood (based on a simple physical reality judgement) that they are male or female, children spend the next several years crystallizing the implications of this and learning the 'appropriate' sex-role behaviour and values. Girls progress through the education system from a weak base of 'equal but different' to an early realization of their inferior status.

What children learn comes from a variety of sources – in particular the family, peer group and the school. To this can be added the influence of the media which offers idealized models of behaviour which children are encouraged to emulate. Groups struggling to present alternative models (for instance migrants or blacks attempting to maintain their culture in the face of Anglo-Saxon Australia; or role diversity on the part of adult males and females) have to contend with the all-pervading values presented in the media.

Children's books are effective in transferring these values which are predominately bound up in presenting a white, male, middle-class ideal. As these books are used to introduce children to written language, it is not surprising that they have come under attack in recent years. Articles have appeared on the racist nature of Australian children's books, and recently, two studies have appeared in Australia on the sexism contained in readers.[2]

The two studies, examining picture books for young children and readers for primary school children, have yielded similar results to the studies of children's books overseas.[3] The portrayal of Madame Curie as assistant to her scientist husband, and a story about eight-year-old girls organizing a beauty contest – to be judged by boys – to see which of them has the loveliest feet, are two of the more obvious ways that children are reinforced into sex-role stereotypes. This article attempts to summarize some of the more significant findings of the Australian studies – to examine more closely the types of sex-role values our children are subjected to in the schools.*

Perhaps the most striking fact of all in the books studied, is that females were simply ignored or neglected. Males outnumbered females by two to one. Males frequently appeared without females – whilst females rarely appeared without accompanying males – and males appeared in many more varied situations.

The implication for a child reading these books is that the world is peopled mainly by males and that as a consequence, males are more worthy of documentation than females. There is also the strong implication that males do – and are expected to do – more things more frequently and in more varied situations than females.

Women and men

Adult characters in children's books are important in two ways. Firstly they provide the reader with models against which to measure her parents and other familiar adults and secondly they give her a model of acceptable behaviour to which she can aspire as she grows older. The adults, both male and female, in the children's books studied, were generally presented as active, independent and knowledgeable persons. However, there was a significant and important difference in the area of activity for male and female adults. The female adult was typically shown as

* Some of the books discussed were for example *No Roses for Harry; Babar; Little Toot; Fish Head; The Cow who Fell into the Canal; Borka; Where the Wild Things Are* and *Madeline.*

acting capably and authoritatively within the home and as putting the interests of family, friends and those-in-need-of-care, before her own. Motherhood was thus idealized, and homes shown as secure places where mothers answer questions about cooking, listen to problems and are always helping others around them. The adult male, by contrast, was typically shown as acting capably and authoritatively within all areas of the wider community and as pursuing his own self-interests. The apparent contradiction in values – 'good' people co-operate and help others, yet 'good' men help themselves, is overcome by appealing to basic ideas about the intrinsic roles of female and male. The message is clear – back into the home with the unselfish female, and out into the world with the self-seeking male.

To reinforce this image, virtually all female adults were portrayed as mothers or other members of a family, whilst men were most frequently shown as workers or adventurers. Thus whilst the male adult was most frequently defined in terms of his activities in the community (i.e. worker), the female adult was defined in terms of the family. Despite a high and ever increasing female workforce where over 60 per cent are married, women were rarely shown outside the home in employment. Given that the authors could not adjust to this piece of social reality, it is not surprising that housework was not portrayed as 'work'. Generally, mothers were shown to be untiring, endlessly preparing meals and cleaning. Only on one occasion was there acknowledgement that there might be some challenge in what women do in houses – where the children (the older girl attempting supervision of younger brothers) look after the house one day when their mother is sick. Needless to say they find it impossible, and gladly hand it all back to their mother when she makes a quick recovery by nightfall. The image of women then is a tightly confined one: to remain in the home as wives and mothers at all costs; and paid employment is for men only.

Girls and boys

The child characters in the books were even more markedly, and even less realistically differentiated by sex. As child characters in books offer greater opportunities for reader identification, this is of particular importance.

Girls were shown as significantly less active, less creative, less inclined to initiate, less knowledgeable and more oriented to domestic activity than boys. They were twice as likely as boys to be uninterested in learning and were markedly less likely to possess significant skills.

The girl was usually shown as a passive onlooker or follower who did very few interesting things within the confines of home. Girls looked after their younger brothers and sisters, found new friends when skipping near the house, cared for animals, or were saved from numerous incidents by boys. Boys were usually shown as active, creative, and doing more interesting and exciting things normally far from home. For instance boys were involved in such activities as riding in aeroplanes, persuading developers to delay a building project to save a family of birds in a tree, earning money, riding dolphins, and saving a girl (who constantly cries) from kidnappers.

Of course, there were a few exceptions where girls were shown in a more adventurous light, but these were generally stories set in fantasy or history – rarely did they occur in everyday life. Moreover, stories which showed girls in this light usually had them acting together with adults or boys. Girls are thus never presented in the here and now acting autonomously and independently.

Towards a liberation of children's books

Books for children should reflect those aspects of social reality which are in opposition to traditional sex-role typing, for example, the fact that many mothers work. Also, they should not present images which reinforce traditional notions of what is masculine and what is feminine. Rather they should challenge existing world views and suggest alternative ones which are not based on inequality. Australia does consist of migrants, blacks, rich and poor, single parents, old and young, men and women – despite what children's books would have us believe. And the trouble is that most of us still believe many things contained in those books, so successful has the process of absorption been.

While rewriting children's textbooks will not bring about the smashing of sexism it is a necessary step towards liberation from sex-role stereotypes. The struggle for more liberal, more realistic children's books will bring the sexist issue into debate. Teachers can use existing texts to point out the more blatant examples of sexism, and rely upon new books to give girls a more positive image. A group in Melbourne has already written and is publishing five non-sexist children's books.[4] A few American communities have already begun organizing workshops – with parents, teachers and librarians – to investigate the ways in which sex stereotypes in books affect their children, and ways of challenging these values.

As Denis Bradley and Mary Mortimer conclude in their study, 'Children's books, it would seem, are ripe for revolution.'[5]

Notes

1. Naomi Weisstein ' "Kinder, Kueche, Kirche", As Scientific Law: Psychology Constructs the Female', in *Sisterhood is Powerful*, Robin Morgan (ed.), Vintage, New York, 1970, p.219.

2. Denis Bradley and Mary Mortimer 'Sex Stereotyping in Picture Books', Unpublished paper, School of Librarianship, University of New South Wales, September 1973.
'Sex Role Stereotyping in Children's Picture Books', *Refractory Girl* No.1 Summer 1972–73. The study examined ninety-three picture books appearing in at least three State School Library Service lists of recommended books. Patricia Healy and Penny Ryan, 'The Female Image: A Context Analysis of Sexism in NSW Primary Level Texts', University of NSW Union, Sydney, 1974. The study examined three sets of reading material frequently used in NSW primary schools: *School Magazine*, NSW Department of Education, Part 1 and 2, 1971 and 1972; SRA Reading Laboratory Cards and SRA Readers – Books G.H.I.J., Science Research Associates, Sydney; Young Australia Readers, Books 13, 14, 15, Nelson, Melbourne, 1971.

3. Numerous articles have appeared during the last few years, but in particular see, Marjorie D'Uren 'Images of Women in Textbooks', in V. Gornick, *Women in Sexist Society: Studies in Power and Powerlessness*, Doubleday, New York, 1971.

4. The Non-Sexist Children's Book Co-operative has five books due to be published by Wren, Melbourne, in 1975.
5. Denis Bradley and Mary Mortimer, 'Sex Role Stereotyping in Children's Books', op.cit.

Fourteen
Religion, Socialization and the Role of Women

The church is one of the most influential institutions in the socialization process. It provides a total belief system, a whole world view. Our social organization, our political-legal system, and our morality are all derived from Christian theology. Because it is all-pervading, religion provides a 'legitimate' rationale for discrimination against women not only for the church but for all institutions. The teachings of the church reinforce the power of men through reference to some supernatural being. They present the role of woman – as wife and mother living through her husband – as inevitable and ordained by God.

As an examination of the relationship between religion, socialization and the role of women in Australia, this chapter can do no more than point to some areas which need far more discussion, research and clarification. The paucity of information on the way in which religion establishes and reinforces the oppression of women is due in large part, of course, to male neglect. There is also the fact that what little information does exist on the 'sociology of religion' is descriptive rather than critical of selected aspects of church organization and teaching. For example, Blaikie says that definitions of religion – what people choose to define as the object of study – which take a value position lie 'outside the field of social science'.[1] He goes on to claim that there are two sociological perspectives available – either 'functionalist', which focuses on what religion *does* (descriptive not critical for criticism is value-laden and thus not sociology), or 'substantive', which focuses on what religion consists of, on the nature of religious beliefs and practices and again is descriptive not critical. Since to talk of oppression or discrimination is to be critical, such 'dynamic' aspects of religion are ignored in favour of a safe concern with the nature of beliefs about God and existence or with the relationship of the church as an institution to other institutions. Of course, since to challenge religion is to challenge the whole fabric of society, including the male academic's comfortable place in it, the academic maintains his status through a convenient 'objectivity' which defines as sociologically irrelevant the sort of enquiry which would challenge his world. 'Discussion' of belief systems is left to theologians who, as they are also comfortable academics, concern themselves with minute problems of interpretation rather than with the practical value positions that those teachings imply. But even descriptive studies are rare, for merely to touch the sacred is dangerous.

The first part of this chapter deals with specific criticisms which have been directed at Christian theology by feminists around the world and in Australia. These criticisms come both from within the church and from without. This first part looks at those beliefs which are particularly important in reinforcing the present expected role of women, and at the discrimination encountered within the church's own structure. The second part is concerned with how these views are instilled into society at large. The church can most successfully imbue practising Christians with its teachings, and the fact that 90 per cent of all Australians are prepared to acknowledge on the census form allegiance to one or other of the Christian denominations is an indication of the legitimacy accorded to the church throughout Australia. Thus non-practising Christians rarely object when the church enters the political arena. In fact since the majority of people who frame and carry out the laws operate according to principles derived from Christianity, even the non-Christian, in obeying the dictates of the so-called 'secular' government, behaves in accordance with the teachings of Christianity.

Western thought and culture have to a large extent been fashioned on Christian theology. The Western view of women and the social institutions which reinforce this view and circumscribe her life are derived from this tradition. There is considerable disagreement about the degree to which the church is either initially responsible for, or contributes to the maintenance of, oppressive and discriminatory attitudes towards women in

Australian society. But in spite of an ever-increasing world-wide secularization and a general decline in the crucial role played by the church in politics, there seems sufficient evidence to suggest that within Australia at least, religious factors vitally influence everyday life. In particular they have contributed in no mean part to a discrimination against women which is rampant throughout society. The influence of religion is felt not only in the running and organization of major institutions such as government, schools and the family, but in the circumscription of our day-to-day actions; for example, our drinking laws, Sunday as a day of 'rest', and enforced restrictions on what we are allowed to read and view. All contribute to the formation and maintenance of the restricting, stereotyped roles which women are expected to play.

Religion is concerned with the problem of meaning, with how individuals make sense of the world around them and how they see themselves in relation to others. Religious belief systems are not versions of, or ill-defined types of, scientific knowledge for they do not seek to explain sequences of events, the cause and effect relationships between events, but rather to provide an ultimate reason for events, in fact for everything. To quote Sharrock:

> . . . they show that this world exists in some kind of relationship to a supernatural world and that the fate of men depends in part upon the forces or beings which inhabit the supernatural realm. The distribution of fortune is seen within the context of this relationship, its allocation to individuals and groups being seen as a consequence of the degree to which their conduct conforms to the moral standards sanctioned by the supernatural world.[2]

Again the fate of women is ignored. For example, from an early age children accept the importance of the family and the authority of the father over the mother. The rationalizations for such patriarchal attitudes are clearly evident in Judaeo-Christian teachings.

Religion therefore not only provides a system of meaning but acts as a form of social control, a supposedly divinely ordained world view, a fact which is critical for understanding the development of an individual's view of herself and her relation to others. The very language of the church makes it patently clear where the power lies. The commonly-used phrase in the Christian church 'forgive me father for I have sinned' clearly designates men as masters just as does the general term 'mankind', subsuming women with the general category of man. So, too, we have 'man and wife'. Religion is a major source of shared values and norms within society, a means by which these and other forms of social control are legitimated or sanctioned in society. It works as an agent of social control in two ways. Firstly by socializing individuals into notions of what is wrong and what is right, an internalization of norms which promotes conformity. For example, the notion that the male is head of the household is taken for granted in most families. Secondly, as socialization is never complete or uniform, external constraints such as laws and regulations are often deemed necessary for the maintenance of social order, those which can be interpreted as in accordance with sacred teachings being strongly supported by the church;[3] many, such as marriage and divorce laws, are derived straight from canon law.

Feminist Critique of Christianity

What then are the charges being directed at the church with regard to the subjugation of women? Criticisms levelled at the Judaeo-Christian tradition fall into two categories. The first is criticism from secular feminists who while seeing the church as one of the most important influences in the development of a patriarchal society and the consequential subservience of women, do not regard reform of the church's practices and teachings as sufficient to bring about the vast social changes which are necessary if we are to achieve equality in relationships between women and men. The second is criticism from within the church, particularly within the Roman Catholic church but to a lesser extent within Protestant (and Jewish) faiths as well. Women's Liberation has aroused in many female theologians, particularly in the United States and Europe and to a lesser extent in Australia as well, and also in the occasional male theologian, the need to re-analyse the Christian tradition.[4] These writers are highly critical of the culturally-defined sexual stereotypes which have been handed down over the centuries and of the way in which institutionalized religion has manipulated its teachings to constantly reaffirm and reinforce male superiority.

Criticism of the secular feminists

What are some specific arguments which have been directed against the church? Simone de Beauvoir's monumental thesis on the secondary place of women in society cogently looks at the church as an agent of oppression.[5] She shows how the church has ensured the inferiority of women, an inferior position dictated from Genesis onwards but an inferiority particularly reinforced in the New Testament by Paul and by the cult surrounding the Virgin Mary. She also points to the fact that there is no evidence that God is male! She argues that where there was a very strong and direct relationship between church and state the church was able to control the legal status of women. This was done by defining woman as man's property and equating her status in the eyes of the law with that of a minor. The lack of political power also meant a lack of private rights, and so as the civil legal status of women has improved the church has had to alter its attitude from one of legal constraint to that of psychological constraint or deception. Thus women are told to forget their present situation and concentrate on the rewards to come in the after-life. In this sense religion justifies the inertia of women. They are expected to live through others by love or religion. Similarly, because all creatures are equal in the sight of God women are deceived into believing that equality already exists. Furthermore, the very teachings of the church itself tell women of the inferior status of their sex. Thus Paul states in his First Epistle to Timothy:

> Let a woman learn in silence with all submissiveness. I permit no woman to teach or to have authority over men; she is to keep silent: For Adam was formed first, then Eve: And Adam was not deceived,

but the woman was deceived and became a transgressor. Yet women will be saved through bearing children if they continue in faith and charity and holiness with sobriety.[6]

Simone de Beauvoir points out that although the inferior status of women is told in a variety of ways from Genesis, it is in the subservience of the Virgin Mary, particularly to her son, that the inferior status of women was cemented. She shows that the cult of the Virgin has been particularly harmful to female sexuality. Mary, whom all females were supposed to emulate, was seen not only as subordinate to all males, including her son, but also as pure and chaste. It is little wonder that women have been confused about their sexuality for so long, when at one level women are seen as evil seducers and tempters and at the same time are placed on a pedestal as mothers and guardians of morality. This ambiguity is reinforced by many of the notions of female impurity which are the subject of church ritual. For example, the 'churching' of women after childbirth characterizes childbirth as a polluting experience – that very experience through which Paul said women will be saved. Fears about a woman's pollution during menstruation are common in Western society.

During the Victorian era there was widespread and violent oppression of female sexuality, all in the name of Christian puritanism. For example, numerous clitorectomies were performed on women to remove all possible pleasure from sex, stressing that salvation was child-rearing while sexual pleasure *for women* was damnation. Not so for men. This double sexual standard, where it is accepted that men have sexual needs but women do not and where women but not men must be virgins on marriage, has of course resulted in prostitution, seen by the church as a necessary evil and in the past financed by the church for its 'celibate' males. In the thirteenth century, Cardinal Hugo said to the people of Lyons who had been hosts to a council of the church for ten years, 'We have made great improvements since we have been here. When we arrived we found three or four brothels. We are leaving only one behind us. We must add, however, that this one brothel stretches from the east to the west gate.'[7] The refusal of certain religious groups to permit contraception and the refusal of almost all religious institutions to allow abortion are further examples of the church, as a male-dominated institution, assuming the right to control a woman's body. Control over one's body, to enjoy its sexuality voluntarily, and to compete mentally and physically with men, are necessary if women are ever to escape from the slavery of their present situation. The church directly opposes such control. Finally, the church also reinforces the inferior status of women by excluding them from their institutional hierarchy. Thus God, Jesus and the disciples are male, and so are the Pope, the priest and the vicar.[8] Men are the mediators between a woman and her God. The church places women in an inferior position, provides a 'divine' explanation for that position and reinforces patriarchal attitudes through its emphasis on the family.

Feminist movements within the church

The realization that the church is patriarchal has lead to a feminist movement within the church which is demanding the equality which the church has hypocritically preached for so long. The feminists within the church differ from the secular feminists in believing that the church is an institution worthy of reform. They argue for a return to the original teachings of Christ, which they see as pure and non-sexist, to rid the church of its current sexist attitudes. These reforms vary from those which merely aim at equal pay and job opportunities within the church and outside it, to those which challenge the whole institutional structure of the church and its current teachings.

In Australia, feminist activity within the church was non-existent until 'Christian Women Concerned' was formed during Lent of 1968. Twelve women from six denominations organized a seminar which had a discussion of the role of women as part of the main topic. In May 1973 the journal *Magdalene* was produced. The editorial stated, 'We believe that women have a vital role to play in the renewal of the Church and the World'. Also in May 1973, a Commission on the Status of Women was set up by the New South Wales State Council of the Australian Council of Churches in response to requests from female members of the Australian Council of Churches and the Roman Catholic Church. Some of its aims are to 'investigate the status and role of women in church and society and to promote action to remove discrimination on the grounds of sex'.[9]

Outside Australia, the first widespread acknowledgment of the need to question the role of women in the church came at the Second Vatican Council (1962–5) when the Council was asked to reconsider the theological and professional status of women. These requests, given added poignancy by the adverse publicity accorded the biased treatment of women at the Council, led to some 'progressive' statements from Pope John. Recently, Pope Paul VI has set up a special commission to examine the role of women in the church and society, the purpose of the commission being to study 'the specific role of women in society and man-woman relationships on the basis of the radical equality of men and women, but also in the light of the way in which they differ and complement each other.' The Vatican went on to say that an analysis 'of the happy and unhappy situations of women in the world and their aspirations and frustrations should make both men and women more aware of the obstacles and possibilities connected with woman fulfilling her role in the different social communities, family, profession, city and nation.' However, at the first meeting of the International Vatican Commission, Pope Paul not only called for caution in the discussion of the role of women but also stated that the 'feminine values' of women must be considered as well as their fundamental rights.[10]

The position of women was a little better in Protestantism, a few denominations having allowed women equal rights for nearly a century. But it was not until 1950 when feminist activity from within the Protestant Churches in the USA resulted in the World Council of Churches agreeing to a study into the status of women in member churches that the situation improved slightly. Since then more denominations have granted the right to ordination and a few have some seats on their governing bodies reserved for women. But in most of the churches in Australia there are few if any women occupying decision-making positions. For example, in the NSW Methodist church less than 6 per cent of 816 members of Conference Committees are women.[11] The only committee with several women is the Historical Records Committee, while many others, such as the powerful Board of Finance, have no female members at all. In part this is due to the fact that many senior posts are open only to the clergy, but there is also a tendency for women to be channelled into traditionally female areas of activity.

The problem of whether or not women can be ordained arises in all religious groups with the exception of the Congregationalists, the Baptists and the Methodists. The first female Congregationalist minister was ordained in Australia in 1926. Since then seven more have been ordained. Four of these eight have now retired. In Victoria, the Methodist church has six ordained female ministers out of a total of over 300. In the Baptist church it is theoretically possible for a woman to be ordained but this has not occurred yet. Ordination is still impossible within the Anglican and Presbyterian churches, although the latter discussed the question of ordination of women at its last General Assembly, in Melbourne in May 1974.[12] Ordination of women within the Catholic church is forbidden by canon law and as with the Anglican church there seems to be little likelihood of change at present. Similarly, very few women take theology degrees. The Melbourne College of Divinity has had one female graduate but no full-time female faculty member. However in 1974 two other colleges began to accept female students for this degree course.

With little opposition, the institutional church in Australia remains practically an all-male enclave. It is fairly clear that within the church there is widespread discrimination against women both in terms of professional opportunities and decision making. Thus in terms of its own organization the church practises what it preaches on the status of women. It presents virtually an all-male front to society and therefore as the symbol of ultimate authority it manifests that authority as male. People are urged to look to the church for guidance and so when women feel dependent on the church they are dependent yet again on men.

Women and Religious Beliefs in Australia

We now consider further the role of the church as a major agent in the socialization of sexist attitudes by examining first the relationship between the church and the 90 per cent of Australians who acknowledged allegiance to a denomination of the Christian church; and second the way in which the church affects the lives of non-believers. The first aspect is concerned with the degree of authority women and men attribute to sacred teachings and the degree to which they accept these teachings. This involves consideration of just how religious a nation Australia is and especially what differences there are between the sexes with regard to religious observances and beliefs. The second aspect involves consideration of the extent to which the social organization of Australia is based on Christian thought and teachings. If the laws coming from a 'secular' state can in fact be shown to be based on beliefs and attitudes which are distinctly Christian, then all citizens, whatever their religion, must behave according to the dictates of the church.

To date there has been little research into religion in Australia, and what there is pays little attention to the relationships between sex differences and socialization in relation to religion. Is the family the most important agent for religious socialization? Do females tend to be more obedient to parents? Are they more likely to accept parental values and if so why? These are the sorts of vital questions which to a large extent must remain unanswered as long as the research findings that are available continue to dwell on figures for church attendance rather than on the dynamics of family life, and depend on statistics rather than people. But what does the available material on religion in Australia tell us about women and religion?

First, what do the available statistics tell us about religious habits and activities in Australia? Table 1 shows the breakdown of Australia's population by religious denomination and sex as given in the 1966 and 1971 censuses. With regard to the distribution of the population through different denominations, what clearly emerges is a continuing increase in the proportion of Catholics, by 6 per cent from 1947–1966 and by a further 13

Table 1

Population: Religious Denominations, By Sex, Australia Censuses 1966 and 1971

Religious denomination	*Census, 30 June 1966*			*Census, 30 June 1971(a)*			*Increase 1966–1971*
	Males	*Females*	*Persons*	*Males*	*Females*	*Persons*	
Christian—							
Baptist	78,443	87,779	166,222	82,877	95,482	178,359	12,137
Brethren	7,491	8,180	15,671	9,731	10,891	20,621	4,950
Roman Catholic and Catholic undefined	1,532,930	1,509,577	3,042,507	1,718,360	1,722,057	3,440,416	397,909
Churches of Christ	48,566	54,694	103,260	42,647	51,431	94,078	−9,182
Church of England	1,933,567	1,951,451	3,885,018	1,956,749	2,026,093	3,982,842	97,824
Congregational	35,933	40,689	76,622	32,554	37,587	70,141	−6,481
Greek and other Orthodox	135,623	119,877	255,500	175,880	161,465	337,345	81,845
Jehovah's Witness	n.a.	n.a.	n.a.	14,919	19,179	34,098	n.a
Lutheran	91,279	88,554	179,833	100,560	98,280	198,840	19,007
Methodist	549,751	577,209	1,126,960	524,903	569,980	1,094,882	−32,078
Presbyterian	513,019	532,545	1,045,564	501,082	532,025	1,033,108	−12,456
Salvation Army	27,188	29,497	56,685	29,441	33,550	62,991	6,306
Seventh-day Adventist	17,175	20,877	38,052	17,954	22,009	39,963	−1,911
Protestant (undefined)	53,028	52,346	105,374	114,461	121,197	235,658	130,284
Other (including Christian undefined)	64,663	68,481	133,144	87,529	88,542	176,070	n.a.
Total Christian	*5,088,656*	*5,141,756*	*10,230,412*	*5,409,646*	*5,589,767*	*10,999,413*	*76,900*
Non-Christian—							
Hebrew	31,303	31,972	63,275	29,204	29,515	58,719	−4,556
Muslim	n.a.	n.a.	n.a.	12,955	8,497	21,452	n.a.
Other	8,804	4,843	13,647	8,851	5,822	14,673	n.a.
Total non-Christian	*40,107*	*36,815*	*76,922*	*51,011*	*43,834*	*94,845*	*17,923*
Indefinite	19,905	16,645	36,550	17,253	12,924	30,177	−6,373
No religion	61,623	34,517	96,140	515,996	336,756	852,752	756,612
No reply	631,297	528,177	1,159,474	419,013	364,505	783,518	−375,956
Grand Total	5,841,588	5,757,910	11,599,498	6,412,918	6,347,786	12,760,704	1,161,206

(*a*) Preliminary, based on a sample.

Source: Australian Bureau of Census and Statistics

per cent from 1966–1971, so that they now comprise 27 per cent of the population. While their numerical strength and also that of the Greek Orthodox Church are increasing, the proportion of the population belonging to the Anglican Church is declining. In 1966 approximately 33.6 per cent of Australia's population belonged to the Anglican Church but by 1971 this figure had reduced to 31.1 per cent. There are two reasons for this. Firstly, migration rates show a statistical bias towards Catholic immigrants, but secondly, and more importantly for understanding how religion affects women in Australia, the greater number of Catholic women of child-bearing age and the higher birth rate within the Catholic group compared to the rest of Australia, make it a trend which is likely to continue. Figures from the 1966 census showed that 57.2 per cent of Catholic women aged between fifteen and forty-five had children in the under four age group, in contrast to 44.4 per cent for Anglican women.

The census figures give little information about religious practices in Australia and it was not until 1965 that a preliminary study of religion in Australia began to examine the question and then only at a shallow, exploratory level.[13] One indicator of participation in institutionalized religion which was measured is church attendance. Mol's study found that only 23 per cent of Australian Christians never went to church while 39 per cent attended regularly. When the figures are broken down according to denomination, 70 per cent of the Catholics went at least once a month, compared with only 20 per cent of Anglicans. Also in all denominations more women went to church than men. It was also found that of those who attended church regularly 95 per cent also said that they prayed. Among those who attended church irregularly slightly less than 75 per cent of the sample claimed to pray regularly. As with attendance figures, all Catholic proportions were higher. Similarly belief in God and belief in the church as a necessary and useful institution were found to be held more strongly by Catholics.

The statistics that are available become more significant if differences between the sexes are examined. The women not only go to church more regularly, but they were found to be more likely to pray daily, to hold traditional beliefs about God and the church and to support stricter moral values, particularly with regard to pre- and extra-marital sex. If one considers that these differences between the habits of the sexes occur not only for all denominations but are most marked among Catholics, it would appear that much of the feminist criticism directed against Catholicism may be very relevant in Australian society, since according to the traditional Australian way of life it is women who are expected to play a major role in the rearing, and therefore in the socialization of children.

The fact that the religiosity of Catholics is greater and that Catholics are becoming numerically more dominant in Australia is a definite threat to feminism and is thus being highlighted here. Catholicism, more than any other Christian denomination, directly concerns itself with the everyday lives of its flock and preaches a more sexually oppressive morality. Also, Catholicism is more directly concerned with holding political power and in line with this takes a dictatorial attitude towards the morals of Australia as a whole. The recent opposition by the Catholic church to abortion law reform showed them to be an extremely effective political lobby.

Church and family

The role that women in early Australia played in making religion an integral part of Australian life has been well documented, particularly the pressure that was put on young females to participate in church activities.[14] But from the evidence given above it appears that Simone de Beauvoir's comment that 'there must be religion for women; and there must be women, "true" women to perpetuate religion' is as true in Australia today as it was in the past. Images of the Australian family and of the place of women in it remain traditional and hard to change. The expected 'normal' family unit is the nuclear family and social psychologists and sociologists have stressed it to be predominantly the concern of the Australian female, some even classifying the role of the father as vestigial,[15] though Adler commented, 'Australian men and women believe the husband to be the real head of the household'.[16]

The church reinforces strongly the notion that the expected role of a woman is in the home caring for her children and husband – the private sphere is her domain and the public sphere is his. An extreme example of this is found in the Catholic magazine *The Magellan – Champion of the Family.* In an article entitled 'A True Apostolate', Doctor Don has the following to say:

> Looking for an apostolate? . . . Would you like to do great things for God before you come to judgement . . . ?
>
> There is one delightful, rewarding, wonderful apostolate: that of the modern housewife. You can retain your favorite armchair, watch TV, have your kitchen full of electric gadgets, stay warm and snug in the winter rain and go off to the beach for picnics in summer. All you have to do *is sit at home and have a few kids* whom you will teach to know and love God. Not an excessive number: just one or two *more* than the average Australian/New Zealand household. All the equipment you need is love, *a burning sense of justice, purity* and *perseverance to stick at it* day after day *for twenty or thirty years* . . . With increasing rapidity contraception, abortion and sterilization will eliminate those who follow self not Christ . . . Stick to the Faith, follow the Pope, trust in God. Do this and you will play a vital role in saving your native land.[17] (my italics)

This article, as well as reinforcing the mainly reproductive function of women in our society also stresses the notion of purity, the need for women to emulate the mother of all time, the Virgin Mary. In the same journal, another article 'For Husbands and Wives' states, 'Sex has two purposes which are equally important: to generate children and to unite the parents of those children'.[18] But despite the repressive role such a magazine portrays for women it must be born in mind that with a circulation of approximately 65,000 in 1973, *The Magellan* is probably only read in one out of every fifty households in Australia, and subscribing to the magazine does not necessarily mean the readers accept its views. However, such magazines do express the teaching of the church and approximate to much that is preached from the pulpit, thus playing a vital role in the socialization of Catholic Australians.

Mol's evidence would seem to suggest that religion does play an important role in the development of world views and value systems, particularly of women and to a lesser extent of men in Australia.[19] But the church is not alone in pushing the traditional image of the Australian housewife, for it is solidly backed up by the mass media, in particular by advertising, and by the economic organization of our society where employment of women is seen as secondary to that of males.[20] The lack of child-care facilities and often no provision for maternity leave merely compound the problems of discrimination in employment. Although organizations such as the Women's Electoral Lobby, Women's Liberation and Women's Media Action Group have brought sufficient pressure to hasten certain changes – for example, in December 1972 the Commonwealth Conciliation and Arbitration Commission adopted the principle of 'equal pay for work of equal value' – it seems likely that the greater proportion of women in Australia still see the role of wife and mother as of primary importance. The church plays no small part in maintaining these perceptions, but to what extent do major institutions other than the family both reflect and show that they are influenced by Christian value positions? How far does the influence of the church extend through institutions other than the family?

The church in education

The schools organize education, a major institutional activity in which all Australians spend much of their lives between the ages of five and fifteen. Despite the fact that the influence of the school as a socialization agent is overshadowed by the family, its influence on the values and behaviour of Australians cannot be ignored. Particularly relevant is the fact that one of the major ways the church has sought to effectively pass on its beliefs and practices has been by taking responsibility for the education of the young. It has done so for centuries throughout the world and historically Australia is no exception.

The early years of the development of the education system in Australia were characterized by heated debate over whether Australia should have a secular or non-secular education policy.

Initially it was argued that because education was intricately associated with moral and religious training, responsibility for it should lie with the church. This view was reinforced not only by the penal nature of the early settlement but later by fortune-hunting, materialistic free settlers. However, the financial burden proved too great for the church and many children had little or no schooling. Coupled with this was the growing view that education should be 'free, compulsory and secular'. The role of the state in education became one of the most contentious issues in nineteenth century Australian politics and has become so again and again right to the present.[21]

In the early nineteenth century the Anglican church presumed, unchallenged by the Government, that it was the official church with prime responsibility for the education of the young, and it received financial support for its schools. This view was not popular with other groups, particularly the Presbyterians and Catholics, who felt they too should have financial support for their schools. Meanwhile public schools were being set up throughout the country and by 1870 the number of denominational schools was declining, with the Anglican church gradually accepting a state-run system. But following the condemnation of secularism, liberalism and democracy by Pope Pius IX in 1864 the Catholic hierarchy renewed its efforts to establish its own education system. The Education Acts of the 1870s and 1890s led to the removal of state assistance to denominational schools and the acceptance of a secular education system, with provisions for some general religious instruction and some by clergy. But these moves only reinforced the efforts of the Catholic church which now told its flock that those who failed to send their children to Catholic schools were living in a state of sin. Large numbers of Catholic children were withdrawn from public schools until, by the end of the century, over half the children of Catholics were attending church schools.

Recently, although the proportion of Catholic pupils attending Catholic schools has remained relatively constant (approximately 20 per cent) the proportion of Catholic children in the community has risen considerably. If one also includes those who attend Protestant schools, slightly under a quarter of Australia's children are educated in denominational schools. The important question then, is the extent to which such an education affects the belief and value systems of an individual. Again the only evidence available is that from Mol's study, which found that there are differences of belief and behaviour between Catholics who attended church and state schools in terms of church attendance, prayer, belief in God, and attitudes to sex, contraception and the family. Consequently we can conclude that in Australia the influence of the Catholic church is much stronger than it would have been had it not established its own schools. Mol found that no such differences are immediately apparent in relation to Protestant schools. Differences between their pupils and those who attend non-denominational schools appear to be more closely related to political, educational and occupational factors.

The church in politics

What of church and state? Much of the present legal system, particularly that which denies a woman equal status and rights in the eyes of the law, can be traced back to church law. But what influences, if any, do the churches exert over the democratic processes of government? Is it possible for a minority group to exert political pressure through the church? How pluralistic a society is Australia? The Federal Constitution states that 'The Commonwealth shall not make any law for establishing religion, or for imposing any religious observance, or for prohibiting the free exercise of any religion, and no religious test shall be required for any office or public trust under the Commonwealth.' But despite this there is state aid to denominational schools, Christian religious festivals are public holidays and blasphemy is a crime. And the churches act as effective pressure groups on the political scene.[22]

In the past the Catholic church urged its flock to both join and vote for the Labor party, it opposed conscription, and opposed changes in the laws relating to abortion, obscenity and divorce. More recently the flock were urged to vote for the

Democratic Labour Party (DLP), were urged to actively oppose proposed reforms to provide abortion on request, were warned of the dreaded dangers of Communism (this resulted in little opposition to conscription for the Vietnam war from the Catholic church), and warned of the dangers of divorce law reform. Despite unsuccessful attempts in the past to set up denominational parties,[23] it was the two issues of conscription and state aid to church schools which firmly established the church in politics. The influence of Archbishop Mannix who established the National Secretariat of Catholic Action in 1937 which became the National Civic Council under the control of B. A. Santamaria, has been well documented.[24] Although these bodies were primarily concerned with saving the country from Communism, the resultant split in the Labor Party with the formation of the DLP has given rise to the development of a party which assumes the role of women to be virtually that portrayed in Catholic theology. The DLP is not isolated in propagating such views but is simply more extreme than the rest.

In 1970 Phillip Lynch, the then Federal Minister for Education, and a Catholic, said:

> As in other economically and socially advanced countries, women's role in Australia extends beyond the family. Certainly the family is their primary responsibility. But it is not regarded as women's sole responsibility . . . As a group, Australian women take a generous view of their responsibility. A wide range of social welfare and other community service activities is utterly dependent on their voluntary work . . . There is a long history to this, a tradition dating back to the earliest days of settlement: Australian women have always stood beside their menfolk . . .

And finally, in an appeal for more voluntary, unpaid social service work with the partial aim of solving the loneliness of migrant women, he concluded, 'And only you – the women of Australia who are already doing so much, can do this . . . I offer you in return no material rewards – only the challenge of conscience: for you, I know that this will be enough.'[25]

One hardly needs to point out the similarity between such statements and the church's view on the role of women. More recently, the attempt to alter the laws relating to abortion resulted not only in a conscience vote on the part of male politicians who were not expected to put the views of the electorate whom they supposedly represented, but were allowed to express their religious biases to make it illegal for women to have control over their own bodies. We were treated to a multitude of hysterical speeches from a group of men who appeared to fear not only an erosion of their authority over women but the power of the church to lose them their jobs.

Therefore within the political sphere, the church acts in two ways. The first way is the easier to observe, document and appreciate, – that is, when it acts as a direct pressure group. The second is indirect and much harder to document – that is the influence the church exerts through its members who are parliamentarians and public servants, and whose attitudes affect the framing of new laws and policies.

Conclusion

There seems to be little doubt that within Australian society religion provides much of the rationale needed to explain the subjugation of women as normal or natural. It preaches a doctrine which stifles and oppresses women in the name of humanity. Within its own hierarchy it practises a policy of discrimination against women which is repeated in all other institutions. Despite recent moves from women within the church to question the patriarchal nature of our society, the church has nothing to offer women's liberation. The church, like other institutions in society, is so grounded in male chauvinism that it is impossible for women to be truly liberated within its structure. It seems ludicrous to even suggest reform of a belief system designed by men precisely to legitimate the oppression of women. Indeed is there any need for a God of any kind to justify a belief in equality?[26]

Notes

1. N. W. H. Blaikie, 'Religious Groups and World Views' in F. J. Hunt (ed.), *Socialisation in Australia*, Angus and Robertson, Melbourne, 1972.
2. W. W. Sharrock, 'The Problem of Order' in P. Worsley (ed.), *Introducing Sociology*, Penguin, 1970, p.350.
3. See Chapter 5, 'Women and the Law'.
4. See for example M. Daly, *The Church and the Second Sex*, Chapman, London, 1968; Sheila D. Collins, 'Towards a Feminist Theology', *The Christian Century*, no.89, August 2, 1972, pp.796–99.
R. Scroggs, 'Paul and the Eschatological Woman', *Journal of the American Academy of Religion*, no.40, 1972, p.283–303.
'Woman in Theological Education: Past, Present and Future', *Theological Education*, no.8, Summer, 1972. See B. Thiering, *Created Second*, Family Life Movement of Australia, Adelaide, 1973.
Magdalene, A Christian Newsletter for Women.
L. Swidler, 'Jesus was a Feminist', *Catholic World*, January 1971.
5. Simone de Beauvoir, *The Second Sex*, Penguin Books, 1972.
6. The Holy Bible, First Epistle of Paul the Apostle to Timothy, Chapter 2, V.11–15.
7. Quoted in J. Kahl, *The Misery of Christianity*, Penguin Books, 1971, p.80.
8. There are some exceptions to this, e.g. Congregationalists and Baptists have ordained female ministers and the first female Presbyterian minister was licensed on 19 August, 1974. In general, arguments against ordination seemed to rest on the assumption that the sex of Jesus was more important than his teachings. For a reactionary discussion of this problem see Appendix: 'The Ordination of Women' in B. Thiering, op.cit.
9. Quoted in *Magdalene*, no.2, July 1973, p.4.
10. Quoted in *Magdalene*, no. 3, September 1973, p.7.
11. Ibid., p.7.
12. The General Assembly of the Presbyterian Church reversed the decision banning women from ordination. See above.
13. H. Mol, *Religion in Australia*, Nelson, Melbourne, 1971.
14. Ibid., p.27.
15. D. Adler, 'Matriduxy in the Australian Family' in A. Davies and S. Encel (eds), *Australian Society*, Cheshire, 1965.
16. Ibid., p.149.
17. *The Magellan*, October/December 1971, p.38.

18. Ibid., p.29.

19. For similar conclusions see Blaikie, op.cit.

20. See Chapter 15 'Women and the Australian Media' and Chapter 4, 'Women and the Australian Labour Market'.

21. For a discussion of the place of religion in education see P. H. Partridge, *Society, Schools and Progress in Australia*, Pergamon, 1968, and A. G. Austin, *Select Documents in Australian Education, 1788–1900*, Pitman, Melbourne, 1963.

22. See L. Oakes and D. Solomon, *The Making of an Australian Prime Minister*, Cheshire, Melbourne, 1973.

M. Richards and M. Edwards, 'Guardians of Eternal Truths: the League of Rights and the Election', in H. Mayer (ed.) *Labour to Power*, Angus and Robertson, Sydney, 1973.

See also articles on the Democratic Labour Party in Mayer, op.cit.

H. Herbert, 'The Churches and the Election' in Mayer, op.cit.

23. Mol, op.cit., p.282.

24. See for example L. Overacker, *Australian Parties*, Cheshire, Melbourne, 1968,

P. Ormonde, *The Movement*, Nelson, 1972.

25. P. Lynch, *The Women's Role in Immigration*, Government Press, Canberra, May 1970, p.6.

26. See J. Kahl, *The Misery of Christianity*, Penguin Books, 1971.

Fifteen
Women and the Australian Media

Every day all over Australia people switch on radios, read newspapers and magazines and watch television. Few fail to come into contact with some form of mass communication. Are the media an all-powerful force which shapes our ideas and behaviour? Are we brainwashed, persuaded, coerced by them? Are women especially pressured?

These questions are difficult to answer. Research into the topic suffers from the inability to control for other influencing factors and the problems of isolating the impact of mass communication; this is true for both academic research and marketing research.[1] Can we say anything at all about the influence of the mass media on Australians in general and on female Australians in particular?

I think we can by looking at the available evidence, drawing upon knowledge of psychological and social processes and examining the content of the Australian media. It becomes clear, when these factors are considered, that media communications don't 'cause' behaviour in any simple way. The processes of influence are subtle and complex. For example, it has been demonstrated that the availability of pornographic literature does not induce sexual offences, and may even reduce them.[2] Despite dark predictions, the Scandinavians have not lapsed into libidinous degradation, but appear to be largely oblivious to the pornographic communications freely available to them. Again, studies of voting patterns show that political advertisements have little effect on voting behaviour.[3]

However, it does seem that the media tend to reinforce existing values and practices and to have the most effect where there is no certain opinion.[4] Children are much more open to media influences than are adults, as the latter have more firmly established sets of values and opinions; thus, the child of a staunch Labor voter might be persuaded by a television advertisement for the DLP but his parents would undoubtedly 'set him straight' should they be present. The primary group and face-to-face contacts are much more influential in forming or changing opinions than are the more impersonal media, and so established attitudes, particularly those supported by the peer group, are very resistant to media persuasion.[5]

While people may not be directly persuaded by the media to change their life patterns and opinions, it should also be recognized that very little of the content of the Australian media activity proselytizes in favour of a particular opinion. A great deal of what we see and read is factual reporting, fiction and music. Yet, taken as a whole, the Australian media give a consistent message overall of what is and what should be. A model form of behaviour is assumed; one ideology is accepted, but without the viewer/listener being aware, usually, that a point of view is being expressed. This point of view pervades the music we hear, the selection and reportage of news, advertisements, the fiction we read, hear or watch. With the exception of a few printed or broadcast debates on controversial issues, the media act as arbiters of public opinion.

Mass media appear to operate in two ways – in the reinforcement of existing opinions and the approval of existing behaviour patterns, as well as the more limited function of actually setting new standards for ideas and actions. In the first case, the current standards of conformity are enforced and justified; alternatives are attacked or ignored. These assumptions usually go so deep as to prevent any real moral, philosophical or political issues from being aired, either as fiction or public debate. In the second case, the mass media seem to be capable of affecting public opinion in areas where opinions are vague and people uncertain, a factor of importance where new issues are concerned. Therefore, as more and more new ideas and practices arise in the society the media's power as opinion leaders is increased. As traditional norms become inapplicable, the media become more influential in determining new norms.

Charles H. Cooley is well known for his work on identity.[6] Cooley's concept of the 'looking glass' self is particularly interesting. We see ourselves and form our self-concepts according to the way others react toward us; by their actions others are holding up a mirror which says to us 'This is you'. Of course, this mainly occurs in face-to-face contacts with family, friends or even strangers, and we learn to fuse, reconcile and adapt to these reflections of ourselves. But does this phenomenon have to rely on face-to-face communications?

Let's suppose we're watching a television western and the hero is just about to take revenge by shooting the villain, whereupon the village priest admonishes him not to do it, pointing out that if he does, he's no better than the villain.

Now this actually has two effects; firstly, it stresses the norms of mercy and compassion, but it also lets us see, vicariously, how others might react to vengeful intentions. Add to this the phenomenon of 'identification': assume that because of the actor's appearance or because of a script written to help us identify with the hero, we feel a sense of empathy with him, an affinity of selves. Emotionally we're also ready to kill the villain. The effect of this strong sense of identification which is common among audiences will be to make the priest's remarks even more effective, especially if the hero accepts his opinion. This is a fairly obvious example, but most of us do have a predilection for putting ourselves, in fantasy at least, into an action which we observe. In this way, we experience vicariously a wider range of situations and through this process work out for ourselves attitudes and opinions. We tend to think, 'If *I* were Scarlett O'Hara, I'd have . . .' The 'soap opera' serials are well known to involve the viewers in the plots to the point where the actors are identified with the characters they play. Incidents of actors being accosted in the street and berated for their actions on television have been reported and television channels regularly receive letters bitterly complaining about things occurring in serials as if the fictional actions were real-life events. A study of 'soap opera' fans also shows the intense involvement with the fictitious proceedings and the identification with the characters.[7]

To sum up, the media have the following effects. They reinforce existing norms and values, thus having the potential for inhibiting change. They can help establish new norms and values, especially in areas where clear standards did not previously exist. They provide a vicarious learning context for the viewer/reader which can impinge on his identity and opinions, especially if he identifies with the characters; this provides an arena for 'working out' ideas, problems and even behaviour.

Women and the Media

We have already mentioned the fact that children are more prone to accept media communications than are adults. They have less well-developed cognitive systems, less experience to be used in validating or rejecting the communication, more tenuous self-concepts, and identities which are not fully formed or independent. Adults with these characteristics have been shown to be especially susceptible to the media;[8] and for a variety of reasons it would seem that the media impinge more on the adult female than on the adult male.

Women in Australian society, as in most of the world, are taught to accept the views and authority of others. The independent, opinionated woman has never been one of our heroines. Success for the Australian woman is measured in terms of social acceptibility rather than professional or economic achievement. In other words, we tend not to laud women for breaking world records, inventing new machines or climbing to the top of the corporate ladder, but rather for being pleasing, accepting, charming and presentable. Our ideal tends to be a model, beauty queen or loving mother. The approved areas of success are the arts, fashion or being an important someone's wife. Of course, women do other things. They work in factories, teach school, heal patients, write books, etc. The point is that these activities are seen as being of secondary importance to the idealized role for women, in which the un-comely female brain surgeon is less desirable than the pretty hat-check girl. Nonconformity in women is unacceptable to a far greater extent than for men, for whom the term 'maverick' is a welcomed label. Thus, this measure of acceptability makes women more dependent on the 'looking glass', less able to ignore what others think of them and this leads to an unstable, easily attacked self-concept. And so, like the child, the woman is susceptible to messages from the same media which are engaged in the wholesale propagation of just these ideals! Whether one watches the late-night movies or the afternoon cartoons, the image of female success remains the same.

Another factor which makes women particularly susceptible to the media is their pattern of media exposure. Women would be more likely to watch afternoon television while doing the ironing than would their husbands; there are special programmes aimed at them during the day. The names drawn out of the barrel to receive prizes on various afternoon quiz shows are invariably female as are the contestants. The advertised products are those particularly associated with conventional female roles; such as prepared foods, laundry detergents, cosmetics. Women's magazines, which are examined later, are another example of the ease with which women can be isolated and presented with specialized, narrow and generally sub-standard material.

Rather than opening up new vistas of achievement, success, social contribution and personal fulfilment, these woman-oriented segments of the media are especially enthusiastic in supporting the most myopic and traditional views of woman's role, far more so than media segments where the audience includes men.

Women are also sensitized to the media, and especially to advertisements, by their consumption role within the family. As a housewife, whether she has a job or not, the Australian female has the task of getting goods from the shops to the home. She makes consumer decisions, does the major portion of the shopping and as often as not manages the household budget. It is her responsibility to allocate income to the best possible advantage and she takes this responsibility seriously. Therefore, portrayals of consumption patterns or admonitions to acquire some new item have a receptive audience among women. Moreover, in a high consumption society like Australia, where material accumulation is almost considered an art form, the pressure on the woman (particularly the wife) in this role is increased. In order to keep up with the spiralling consumption expectations caused by fashion changes and the growing 'standard package', she must put in more time and effort and keep her eye constantly on current trends. Of course one of the main movers of this accelerating involvement in consumption is the media, especially advertising. This does not mean that women can be persuaded to buy anything at all, and the issue is quite different from that of false or misleading advertising; but the result is that the woman is more likely to pay attention to media items that concern consumption – whether she buys or not – than is her husband who is not expected to engage as much in consumption activity. This makes her more susceptible to the media, less likely to shut off or maintain her distance.

So for the Australian woman the forces which allow the impact of the media on everyone are exacerbated by her weak, dependent self-concept, her particular pattern of exposure to the media and her role as consumer within the family. She starts out more vulnerable than the male and is given back the information that the traits which make her vulnerable are the ones she should cultivate.

The content of the Australian mass media, both locally-produced as well as imported, not only includes choice misogynist bits but in fact has little else. The achieving female, the important female, the contributing female is ignored in favour of a solid diet of wives, mothers, glamour girls, supportive side-kicks and the occasional judo-chopping spy who always cuddles up in the end anyway. The vicarious learning situation constantly presented shows that females who don't accede, who demand too much, who aren't self-effacing are undesirable. The un-beautiful, the un-slim and the un-young are likewise rejected. The ad or story or article all say the same thing: measure up to this monolithic standard of female attractiveness; accept only this standard from others.

The norm is stated and supported and the media 'looking glass' flashes back terrifying warning images of the nag, the frump, the mother-in-law, the blue-stocking, the frustrated spinster. We are invited to laugh at the homely woman looking at herself in the bedroom mirror (while her dissatisfied husband fantasizes her into a lovely blonde with a Lifesaver). We are induced to scorn the woman who is particular about her tea and to be delighted that she is taken in by a Lipton tea bag. The older assertive woman is invariably caricatured as unpleasant, a notable example being Dorrie Evans of 'Number 96'. The ad may not have sold the product, the story may be soon forgotten, but the lesson remains. For the girl or woman who is ambitious or adventurous or dissatisfied there are few places in popular culture to base her identity, and almost nothing to inspire or support her.[9] Therefore, she is obliged to follow her inclinations alone unless she has a very sympathetic peer group (and since they probably watch and read the same things, their standards are unlikely to differ much). What most often happens is that the woman who ventures beyond the stereotype finds it necessary to play both sides at once, so that after hours she is a perfect mother, a superb cook, a gracious hostess or an elegant dresser. Unlike a man who can merely get on with the job of doing whatever he considers important, a woman must constantly reassure herself and the rest of the world that she is acceptably feminine by the standard portrayed in the media.

Australian Women's Magazines

To date there are some twelve major Australian women's magazines on the market. The original ones were the *Australian Women's Weekly*, *Woman's Day*, *New Idea* and *Home Companion*[10] which were all aimed mainly at the housewife and mother and concentrated on fashion, knitting, information on child care, gardens, homemaking. They have been popular among all age groups.[11]

In the past few years we have seen the advent of the 'new' women's magazines: *Pol*, *Dolly*, *Belle*, *Cosmopolitan* and *Cleo*. These magazines are glossy and glamorous with heavy emphasis on an idealized girl who represents the magazine. ('*Dolly* is a girl like you.' 'You'll find yourself in *Belle*.') The vicarious 'looking glass' is brought in and we find that the message is substantially the same as before. The image is one of a pretty, acquisitive, sociable girl mainly interested in clothes, men and spending money, the difference being the obsession with fashion and the consumption of fashion goods. In fact, the chief purpose of publishing both *Dolly* and *Belle* was to provide a medium for advertising which reached the young consumer.[12]

The *Dolly* story is an interesting one. Launched by Sungravure, its target was the sixteen- to twenty-four-year-old female. Careful planning and marketing made *Dolly* an instant success and won it the Hoover Marketing Award for 1971. The first issue sold 120,000 copies which exceeded the original sales estimate by 41 per cent.[13] Obviously, Australian girls had been more sensitized to mass consumption and fashion and more willing to buy a guide to expenditure style than even the marketers had realized. What made *Dolly* so attractive? It sold to the public purely on image appeal, an image which reinforced the traditional notions about females with an overwhelming emphasis on consumption. Although it is read by one in three girls in the sixteen to twenty-four age group,[14] it offers no widening of horizons for its readers. 'The magazine [*Dolly*] was going to recognize the fact that Australian girls, like girls everywhere else in the world, were interested in one thing mainly – boys, how to get them and how to keep them. The editor kept this in mind for every feature of the magazine.'[15]

The young girl reading *Dolly* receives the information that dates, clothes, beauty, parties and men are not only the core of existence, but that these are the only things that should matter.

Dolly's older sister *Belle*, aimed at the nineteen to twenty-six age group, was launched in 1972 using the same strategy.* The $2 billion spending power of that age group was its main attraction to advertisers and the editors promised that *Belle*'s features would blend nicely with a consumeristic orientation: major areas of interest were entertaining, home-making, cooking, fashion, beauty and travel.[16] The consumption role is stressed more, but otherwise the ideas are much the same as those of the old home-service magazines. *Belle* and *Dolly* have both taken the advice that '*Dolly* must move with its market, be in close touch with its fads and whims, and be entirely flexible

* This, like *Pol*, was originally a monthly but is now published quarterly.

in its operation. In short, the publishers must be wholly consumer-oriented. So publishing is just like any other fast-moving consumer goods business . . . and should be treated as such.'[17]

Little has been said here about the other glossies *Pol*, *Cleo* and *Cosmopolitan;* their overall ethos does not differ from the rest. The benefits of having magazines which extol a high rate of consumption are obvious for the industries involved. The benefits for the female reader are much more dubious. Her original vulnerabilities, viz. her dependent self-image and her responsibilities in consumption, are exploited even in the non-commercial material, which is also geared to justify and promote greater buying.

To sum up, the media in Australia which might possibly help and encourage women to explore and achieve their potential because it can devote its whole attention to them, instead feeds off them by exploiting their role as consumers. It can no longer be seen as an innocent quirk that the material is shallow and one-sided but, as I have tried to show, a cynical and well-planned operation to involve Australian women increasingly in consumption and the inane life style conducive to it.

Women may glean courage and support from novels, biographies and male success stories but they still find little in the Australian mass media to recognize them as diverse, autonomous human beings. The 'looking glass' still says they are acquisitive and ineffectual, dependent and accepting, pleasing and unmotivated. As long as this situation remains, the chances for social change are impeded.[18]

Notes

1. J. Tunstall, *The Advertising Man*, Chapman & Hall, London, 1964, Chapter 7.
2. *The Report of the Commission on Obscenity and Pornography*, Bantam Books, New York, 1970.
3. Joseph T. Klapper, *The Effects of Mass Communication*, The Free Press of Glencoe, Illinois, 1960, pp.16–17.

4. Ibid., p.74.
5. Ibid., p.50.
6. Charles H. Cooley, *Human Nature and the Social Order*, Chas. Scribner and Sons, New York, 1902.
7. Klapper, op.cit., p.204.
8. Klapper, op.cit., p.75.
9. The few exceptions to this rule only go to prove that this stereotyping procedure isn't necessary to produce good, believable, interesting fiction. An outstanding example of what can be done was Tony Morphett's original 'Certain Women' series which began on ABC-TV on 1 March 1973.
10. *Australian Financial Review*, 7 November 1972, p.37.
11. National Committee of the Hoover Awards for Marketing, *Australian Marketing Projects*, Sydney, 1971, p.8.
12. *Australian Financial Review*, 10 August 1971, p.36.
13. *Australian Marketing Projects*, op.cit., p.27.
14. *Australian Financial Review*, 10 August 1971, p.36.
15. *Australian Marketing Projects*, op.cit., p.16.
16. *Belle* pre-publication circular. The current emphases of the magazine, now called *New Belle*, are home-making and interior design.
17. *Australian Marketing Projects*, p.31.
18. For examples of the sexist way women are exploited by the mass media see *Media She*, Patricia Edgar and Hilary McPhee, Heinemann, Melbourne, 1974.

PART FOUR

Women Labelled as 'Deviants'

Women Labelled as 'Deviants'

The previous section, 'The Acquisition of Sex Roles', emphasized those processes at work in society which are geared to conformity, which result in men and women modifying their behaviour to conform to the stereotypes of 'masculine' and 'feminine'; which are geared to the maintenance of social stability and antagonistic to change. However, socialization is never total or complete. Individuals have the potential to actively decide whether or not to accept a particular value position. In practice many do not, simply because one set of beliefs is presented as if it is the *only* set of organizing principles around which to order one's behaviour. In Australia, the role of wife and mother and the accompanying economic dependence on a man is offered without a viable alternative for the majority of women. But what of those who either don't accept the roles others wish to force upon them or who are encouraged to perform roles within society which are labelled as necessary but immoral, as necessary evils, by the wider society? What of the women who fail to act in accordance with society's norms and therefore become labelled 'deviant', to be ostracized by society and treated as dangerous, odd, mad, to be pitied, or sick, depending on how much they are seen to challenge the social order? These women are condemned to even greater isolation than the already isolated suburban housewife. The housewife who merely rejects her role while staying in it is defined as sick and becomes subject to a barrage of psychoanalytic theory and treatment which is designed to help her see that the fault lies in her rather than in the role she is expected to perform.[1] Similarly, a lesbian is defined as in need of aversion or hormone therapy.

Sociologists in particular have been involved in the study of deviance, partly as a reaction to the original idea, still rampant in law and criminology, that all deviants are criminals, but most of all as a means of understanding those forms of behaviour which are regarded as wrong, since the evaluation of right and wrong behaviour can be seen to change constantly. The study of 'deviance' has enabled sociologists to demonstrate that morality is relative, that it varies not only over time but from culture to culture and even between sub-cultures within the one society. This perspective has been developed recently by those sociologists who have adopted what is labelled a 'symbolic interactionist' or 'phenomenological' approach in the study of society, an approach which seeks to understand society in terms of its individual members' conceptions of their own reality, in terms of society's own categories rather than in terms of categories predetermined by the sociologist which are supposed to reveal processes which the individual cannot hope to conceptualize. The symbolic interactionist perspective stresses that there is nothing inherently deviant in a piece of behaviour but rather that what behaviour is labelled as deviant depends on those in power. Consequently, any behaviour by women which deviates from the traditional sex role is likely to be seen as socially undesirable from a male viewpoint because it challenges their comfortable position.

The symbolic interactionist approach to the study of deviance, an approach considered 'radical' in sociological circles, is outlined in Chapter 16. It is an approach which, because of its central concern with the individual's own definition of reality coupled with the stress that morality is relative, has been adapted by Women's Liberation consciousness-raising groups to present a female view of reality in opposition to the 'respectable' male view. But taken to its logical conclusion the approach poses a problem which is sinister in its implications. It allows the social scientist to opt out of taking any social responsibility. By conceiving of all views of reality as equally viable it ignores the subtle way that socialization manipulates people into unwittingly supporting their own oppression and exploitation by lulling them into a false consciousness of happiness and leaving no other socially acceptable options open. An example of the dangers of the symbolic interactionist perspective is provided by Chapter 20,

'Life as a Prostitute', where the male author who recorded the views presented in the chapter promotes a pluralistic view of society which regards the prostitutes as moral in their terms, and their way of life as a viable one. He doesn't begin to consider the way in which the buying and selling of access to the female body devalues and degrades not 'sex', an abstraction, but women, real people. The notion that supports prostitution is that *men* need their sex, not that they need people. So they get it by exploiting women even more blatantly than in the 'moral' society; by pushing them into the dark corners of society to use them but condemn them. It does not matter who they are, simply that they are available and hopefully happy, ensuring that sex remains an assured commodity. The prostitutes perform a role demanded by but also condemned by society and their views are presented via a male sociologist only because no other material was available.

The other three chapters present the experiences of women who also are doubly discriminated against for not only are they female but they do not fit into any of the acceptable female roles, not even those regarded as necessary evils. Unlike the prostitutes whose views are presented, the other three authors are fully aware of their oppression with no vestiges of false consciousness.

Because the groups dealt with in this section are seen as 'deviant' by Australian society they have been grouped together. The problem is that by doing so, notions of what is 'deviant' might be reinforced. However it is important that the book highlight the mechanisms by which society attempts to ensure conformity in the interests of the powerful. Also, the experiences presented in this section indicate how the individual can oppose convention. The ability of these women to challenge the *status quo* is a first step towards social change in the direction of liberation. The final section of the book examines the effects on Australian society when these challenges to convention are made by women who, by banding together have defused the label of deviance so that it no longer acts as an effective social sanction.

Notes

1. For example see: J. B. Miller, *Psychoanalysis and Women*, Penguin Books, 1973; N. Weisstein, 'Psychology Constructs the Female' in A. Koedt, (ed.), *Radical Feminism*, Quadrangle, New York, 1973; K. Millett, *Sexual Politics*, Abacus, London, 1972.

Sixteen
Women and Deviance

The general aim of this chapter is to examine the relationship between sex, or more accurately gender, and social deviance. To this end, a brief outline of the main elements of a sociological approach to deviance is presented; and then some of the more important implications for women of drawing a distinction between persons according to their sex, are discussed. In talking of deviance, one cannot, of course, avoid the fact that deviance and its opposites, conformity and respectability, are inter-dependent and closely inter-related aspects of the same basic phenomenon: morality.

Each society contains a number of social customs, conventions and beliefs about how people should conduct themselves in their work, their play, their religious worship, their personal relationships, and so on, which are to a greater or lesser extent unique to that society and which constitute its 'culture'. The members of a society endow these rules of preferred behaviour with moral qualities: they are not only convenient, sensible, customary or expedient ways of doing things, but they are also intrinsically good. It is in relation to these standards or norms that deviance is defined.

The fact that a highly industrialized society may appear to run according to standards of technical, scientific or economic worth does not mean that morality has been supplanted. Rather, to the extent that such criteria as efficiency, rationality or economic utility provide the bases on which decisions between two or more alternative courses of action are made, they have themselves become moral values: that is, such societies are operating on the assumption that it is *morally desirable* that these should be the kinds of criteria used.

Though it is probably true that, in modern Western societies, it has become less fashionable for leading citizens and others to make public pronouncements of a 'moralizing' nature about the wide range of issues of general social concern facing these societies, this does not mean that individuals are not constantly engaged in subjecting the ideas and actions of their fellows to moral scrutiny and in passing moral judgements on others. Indeed, one of the most effective ways of dismissing the arguments of others is not by reason, fact or logic but by morally discrediting the authors of the views – casting doubt on their motives, intentions, intelligence, state of mind, moral character, ideological affiliations, etc. So, despite the fact that 'most moral judgements made in our society are understood – not stated – or else are stated indirectly, even insinuated, and not stated pontifically',[1] i.e. they are taken for granted until called into question, they nevertheless constitute an ever-present element in our mental attitudes to, and perceptions and evaluations of other people and their opinions, practices and personalities. In other words, other people are not just considered to be different from ourselves, they are better or worse, superior of inferior, to be emulated or despised. 'We daily reaffirm our moralities and value structures by placing ourselves apart from others whom we regard as deviant.'[2]

Morality is not, however, wholly a personal matter. As the comparative study of morals in different places and times shows, it can be seen as part of the culture of a group or society and, as such, is linked to particular social conditions, interests, opportunities and experiences. Morality is perceived by individuals as 'external to themselves, as given to them' and as 'necessary'.[3] In two main ways, values including moral values are products of society: firstly, individuals acquire moral standards as part of their overall assimilation of the culture of their group or society (i.e. as part of their socialization); and secondly, morality is one component element of an individual's world-view, his way of making sense of or giving meaning to the world as he experiences it and his own place in it, which in turn is determined by his general social location, relationships, experiences, background, and so on.

Although each person's set of moral values is complex, internally inconsistent, subject to change over time and unique to that individual, there is still some general moral consensus over at least some issues even in pluralistic societies. The *degree* to which norms and values are shared and the *nature* of the consensus is, however, an empirical question in each particular case. Thus, it makes some sense to ask which rules 'society' seeks to enforce and how 'society' deals with offenders, but only if it is remembered that 'society' means in practice particular groups and individuals and not necessarily even a majority of the population.

Even if it is impossible to define a universal morality (irrespective of time and place) or even a single set of moral standards within a particular community, it is still true that certain sorts of behaviour are likely in most societies to arouse strong moral feelings, of both a positive and a negative kind. Each culture contains a wide range of 'folk types' which function as moral examples and object-lessons: heroes, villains and fools, saints, sinners and devils.[4] At the interpersonal level, deliberate infliction of violence and etiquette in interaction between persons of different age and sex and, at the societal level, patriotism, heroism and treason – those actions which advance or retard the collective good – always figure prominently in the moral code of a community. Different actions and individuals will be regarded with varying degrees of approval, tolerance and condemnation by the members of the society as a whole or by various groups within society. Thus, although each individual can and does receive praise and blame from others for his or her various actions, in each group and in society in general at any one time all possible acts can be placed somewhere on a hypothetical moral continuum ranging from highly commendable to totally reprehensible. It may happen, however, that an individual receives a label for one of his or her acts which then dominates his or her life; deviant labels in particular tend to exhibit this quality. Various writers have drawn attention to the way deviance acts as a 'master status' or a 'pivotal' identity.[5]

However, not only can total moral consensus never be assumed to exist, but also norms are rarely, if ever, uniformly and consistently enforced. Sub-groups in a population to some extent decide which norms they regard as binding and which optional, and certain (mostly biological) characteristics are recognized as conferring differing degrees of moral responsibility, such as sex, age, race, mental capacity and even social position.

Deviance, therefore, is behaviour which departs significantly from the norms set for an individual or group so as to provoke a response from others. Sociologists of deviance usually concentrate on the sorts of deviant conduct that meet with a negative reaction, a practice which will be followed here. Deviant behaviour for the present discussion is behaviour which society, the majority of the population or a significant, articulate or powerful minority attempts to control, prevent or eliminate.

A full understanding of deviance, conformity and social control requires the independent investigation of three main aspects of the whole phenomenon:

(1) What are the norms or rules which members of a group or a society are expected to observe and how do they come to be defined?
(2) What sorts of people under what kinds of conditions violate these norms?
(3) How and on whom are the norms enforced, how are detected rule-breakers treated and what are the consequences of social and societal reaction to deviant behaviour?

The second question (which deals with the incidence and causes of deviant behaviour) has been the traditional concern of criminologists, sociologists, psychologists and others. However the first and the third (the social control aspects) have increasingly been regarded as of equal importance, particularly in what has come to be called the 'labelling' or 'societal reaction' approach to the study of deviance.[6] Its basic postulate is that:

> [Deviance] is not a property *inherent in* certain forms of behaviour; it is a property *conferred upon* these forms by the audiences which directly or indirectly witness them.[7] (original emphases)

At the level of a single and total society, such a basis is found in the dynamics of what proportion of a society, how well organized and how powerful, are fearful of, and feel threatened by, some other portion of the society. Organized social life can be viewed as a game in which actors and collectivities defend themselves against distrusted and suspected others.[8]

One major consequence of taking such a view is that power becomes a factor of central importance, since it is power that ultimately determines who labels whom deviant. 'Deviance is a conflict between at least two parties: superordinates who make and enforce rules, and subordinates whose behaviour violates those rules.'[9] Alternatively, as Buckner has put it, we should re-define the field of deviance as 'the politics of subreality conflicts': at the most fundamental level, the designation 'deviant' emerges when two or more conceptions of 'reality' (as well as of morality) are in direct conflict.[10] But ultimately the 'production' of deviance will be subjected to moral evaluation by sociologists and others.*

This perspective on deviance is therefore a morally relativist one, since the sociologist defines deviance only in terms of the norms, values and expectations of actual people and groups. He sees the answer to the question 'what norms?' not as an established, self-evident or easily discovered 'fact' but as an empirical but problematic matter. In any particular instance, the prevailing norms are the outcome of negotiation between sets of people who subscribe to different moral and social standards and who represent different interests in the society. It is also a largely 'subjectivist' approach since the investigator attempts to understand the phenomenon from the standpoint of the various parties involved in the production of deviance: those defining the rules, those breaking them and those seeking to enforce them. However, a truly interactionist perspective attempts to move beyond a description simply of the making of rules and of the reactions of society to rule-breakers by locating deviance and conformity within the total society and by analysing the whole process of deviance production at all levels (personal,

* For further comments on the responsibility of sociology in this process see the introduction to this section of the book, and Chapter 27 'A Beginning'. (*Editorial note*)

situational and societal) as an ongoing, everyday human activity.*

This should not be taken to imply that particular deviance writers do not in fact hold very definite and often differing views themselves about their subject of study. Claims have recently been made that sociologists of deviance should explicitly define their field as the sociology of violence or of oppression, thereby demonstrating where their sympathies lie and where they place the main responsibility for the suffering incurred by the 'underdogs' of our society.[13]

It is now proposed to look at some of the insights into the socio-cultural differences between men and women that can be gained by studying deviance under the following headings:

Definitions of deviant behaviour

Basically, females may attract the label of deviant for three different reasons: (a) simply by virtue of their sex, females may be regarded as different and inferior sorts of human beings in whatever they do; (b) certain types of female behaviour may offend the standards set specifically for members of that sex to observe (e.g. the 'double standard' of sexual morality); or (c) some women may violate norms which are not sex-specific and which regulate the conduct of every member of a society or group, the most obvious example of such norms being the laws of the land.

Causes of deviant behaviour

Whether male-female differences are due to genetic and biological endowment, to psychological and personality factors or

* Interactionism and labelling theory are not in fact identical in their approaches to the social reality of deviance. Some writers claim that essentially an interactionist perspective is appropriate only in the analysis of micro-social factors and processes and that, therefore, it must be supplemented or replaced by a theoretical framework which gives due weight to the historical and structural aspects of deviance production[11] (see, for example, Taylor, Walton and Young 1973). This writer, however, denies that interactionism is *necessarily* or *inherently* limited in this way and argues this case at greater length elsewhere.[12]

to cultural conditioning and social influences, the unquestioned sex differences in experiences, desires, attitudes, expectations, frustrations and lifestyles must play a major part in leading the members of each sex to resort to various forms of rule-breaking behaviour (mental illness, crime, drug-taking, sexual deviance, social protest, etc.) with varying degrees of frequency and often for different reasons.

The processing of deviant individuals

Not only may the standards of expected and approved behaviour differ for the members of the two sexes, but even where the norms are defined as binding on males and females alike, the enforcement procedures and social control mechanisms may differ to the advantage or detriment of either sex.

At root, the argument here is that in line with the general sociological conception of deviance described above and in view of the undoubted differences in social status and role between men and women in modern industrial societies, it is justifiable and meaningful, in exploring the part played by sex-related factors in deviance, to interpret one form of the conflict between 'subordinates' and 'superordinates' which results in deviance in sexual terms.

> Differences in the ability to make rules and apply them to other people are essentially power differentials (either legal or extralegal). Those groups whose social position gives them weapons and power are best able to enforce their rules. Distinctions of age, sex, ethnicity, and class are all related to differences in power, which accounts for differences in the degree to which groups so distinguished can make rules for others.[14]

It cannot, of course, be maintained that sex differences (particularly in relation to power) are the only significant factors in female deviance or are necessarily, in any given case, the most important determinants, but simply that they are often relevant, have frequently been neglected and are obviously worthy of study.

Clearly age, for one, is of importance in many ways. Turk approaches juvenile delinquency from the angle of conflict between age-groups, thus bringing out similar processes to those involved in the relationship between sexual politics and female deviance.

> It seems apparent that delinquency is, from an operational standpoint, not actually a class or combination of classes of behaviour, but rather a definition of pre-adults by those in a position to apply legal sanctions ... While problem behaviour is variously defined and variously handled, the fact remains that it is something about the behaviour of pre-adults that provokes age-specific enactment, interpretation and enforcement of laws.[15]

Although deviance writers are alert to the crucial role played by class and status differences in relation to pretty well every area of social life and every sort of social deviance, it is still the exception rather than the rule to find the same close attention given to sex, despite the fact that sex is surely as fundamental a determinant as class of people's life-chances, attitudes, values and interests.

It must be recognized that 'conflict' need not, and usually does not, involve an open or violent confrontation between the two parties; conformity to prevailing standards of conduct is mainly achieved through socialization and persuasion rather than by coercion. The power of the patriarchal type of society lies in the effectiveness with which it succeeds in internalizing in each new generation a particular conception of what is natural, normal and desirable female (and male) conduct.

> A disinterested examination of our system of sexual relationships must point out that the situation between the sexes now, and throughout history, is a case of that phenomenon Max Weber defined as *herrschaft*, a relationship of dominance and subordinance. What goes largely unexamined, often even unacknowledged (yet is institutionalized nonetheless) in our social order, is the birthright priority whereby males rule females ... However muted its present appearance may be, sexual dominion obtains nevertheless as perhaps the most pervasive ideology of our culture and provides its most fundamental concept of power.[16]

What this means has not yet been systematically investigated by sociologists. Since sociological concepts and theories are male-oriented and male-inspired, they contain a consistently biased and partial picture of social reality. We need, therefore, a thorough-going sociology which explores all aspects of the social world from the standpoint of women – politics, work, the family, education, leisure, religion and, of course, deviance. One of the intentions of this paper is to suggest some of the directions this might take in the field of social deviance.[17]

Any attempts to 'liberate' females (and males) need to be directed as much at the sex-role stereotyping and socialization, and at the underlying ideology, as at direct or forcible methods of ensuring compliance from unwilling individuals.

We will now examine in more detail the question of women and deviance using the framework outlined above.

Definitions of Deviant Behaviour

(a) Women, like children and like blacks in America, are accorded a social status to some extent inferior to that of the adult male. This is a function of the overall culture and social structure of most societies, in which the sexual division of labour results in the more socially valued tasks being performed by males and/or in males doing the more valued jobs. In all patriarchal societies, the sexes are not only seen as being 'objectively' different in their abilities, aptitudes, and biological, psychological and social attributes, but these perceived differences are differentially evaluated in both social and moral terms.

The attitude taken towards females has something in common both with attitudes to ethnic minorities (they are viewed as inferior types of beings) and with attitudes to children (they are seen as dependent and somehow immature). Women can be entrusted only with less responsible and demanding duties and must be protected from 'bad' influences and from their own weaknesses.

Hacker has explicitly examined the situation of women as a

minority group, not obviously in the numerical sense but in terms of discrimination. She points to a number of similarities, specifically the caste-like status of both blacks and women.[18] Obvious differences also exist: while racial and ethnic minorities can and sometimes do live their lives almost entirely among their own kind, women to date have been reared and pass their adulthood in the company of males in almost every sphere of life. Shulamith Firestone makes the point that this can be a distinct advantage when it comes to trying to exert an influence on the rest of society: 'a revolutionary in every bedroom cannot fail to shake up the status quo'.[19] In this connection it is important to note that certain lesbian groups are now establishing indepen-ent, self-sufficient social communities from which all males (and most other females) are totally excluded, reflecting presumably a similar philosophy and strategy towards the rest of the population to that found in the black separatist movement in America. Other writers from within the feminist movement have stressed the parallels between economic or occupational and sexual stratification in modern society, linking sexual liberation to the overthrow of capitalism.[20]

It is at the level of 'cultural revolution'[21] that the Women's Liberation Movement has primarily been operating: to challenge the taken-for-granted assumptions of male superiority in the areas of life which carry most power and prestige in our society (and in the case of some authors to query whether these are the most important areas anyway) and to question these traditional conceptions of what is 'real', 'necessary', 'natural', 'normal' and 'desirable' about the respective roles and status of men and women in the social order, these being the key elements in the social production of deviance. Others, who subsume the sociology of female oppression under a broader Marxist critique of modern capitalist society, attempt to trace the connections between attitudes to sex, sexuality and the family and the economic needs and institutions of a certain type of social structure. At this point, the analysis of male homosexuality and of female deviance raises similar issues. Both can be seen as responses to social injustice in the form of social discrimination and a repressive attitude to sexuality and the Gay Liberation and Women's Liberation movements in part are both attacking the same underlying conditions and advocating similar kinds of social change.

(b) A different moral continuum of behaviour, ranging from the 'saintly' to the 'sinful', may be said to exist for males and for females. What constitutes extremely wicked and highly laudable conduct varies in the public mind according to the sex of the actor. Our images of heroism and villainy tend to be sex-specific and are a product of people's conceptions of the roles, capabilities and personalities of males and females. Although no single role model can adequately encompass all the varied life-styles currently found among men and women in Western societies, the traditional assumption of the domestic sphere being the proper place for the woman and the occupational world being for men is still widely held.

Sex-specific forms of rule-breaking can, therefore, be defined in relation to sex-specific norms. Indeed, women and children can be punished for behaviour that, in an adult male, is entirely legitimate or even mandatory. The most serious sorts of female deviance are believed to be those which offend the standards society sets for women as wives and mothers: pre-marital chastity; marital fidelity; devoted, full-time and self-denying motherhood; full responsibility for the physical and emotional welfare of children; and subordination of personal interests and modes of self-expression to the demands made by husbands for support and assistance in pursuit of their (male) goals and in satisfying their (male) needs. So, working mothers (especially those who cannot arrange to be in their homes at all times when their children are not at school or who do not work from economic necessity), unmarried mothers, unfaithful wives, deserting mothers, prostitutes, mothers who are cruel to or neglect their children and, in fact, though to a decreasing extent, single women over a certain age are all regarded as serious cases of female deviance because such behaviour threatens aspects of the ideal form of the family, to which society has attached its own judgments of high moral worth and within which women are expected to live a contented life.

This is not to deny that females who violate other norms, who steal, engage in homosexual acts, commit suicide, go mad or fight for a new and better society are not also regarded as deviants, or to suggest that such women are not treated with as great or greater a severity than the equivalent males. It is simply to observe that, since women are entrusted with greater responsibility for the moral character of family life than are men, female deviance in this sphere arouses greater alarm and consequently greater social and moral condemnation.

A further illustration of this pattern of sexual discrimination may be found in the sorts of social and personal characteristics which are particularly emphasized when male and female deviance of various sorts is under discussion. For instance, the mass media usually give much greater prominence to the marital and familial status of women than they do in the case of men when reporting acts of an unconventional, unusual or disreputable kind. Thus the Press apply this principle indiscriminately whether women are being condemned for committing a criminal offence (drug-possession, theft or assault) or being commended for achieving some high office or public honour. When men are concerned such information is only consistently featured when directly relevant (such as where a father is convicted of attacks on children). For instance, newspaper headlines of the following kind are commonplace: 'Pregnant Mother on Drug Charge' or 'Probation for Mother of Seven'. On the other hand, when a woman's appointment to the Commonwealth Conciliation and Arbitration Commission was announced in December 1972, the Melbourne *Sun* carried this headline: 'Mother of Two is Wage Judge – an Evatt' (December 16). Her origins (an Evatt) and current familial status are clearly regarded as being of far greater interest than her own qualifications for the job. To be fair, the Melbourne *Age* of the same day handled the news in the same kind of way as it usually reports such events when they involve men.

This raises the whole question as to how far the existence of sex-specific norms (like age-specific ones) simply reflects an exercise of the greater power held by a superordinate group (men) to the disadvantage of a weaker group (women). Such forms of discrimination and oppression can and have been analysed either as a more or less conscious exploitation of women by men or as one of many consequences of a certain type of social structure and value system. In other words, the root of the problem may be seen as sexism or capitalism or as large-scale bureaucratic society. However, which of the various alternative explanations one chooses has important consequences for the understanding of the various forms of female (and male) deviance.

(c) Even where a particular kind of rule-breaking is regarded as equally serious whether committed by a male or a female, the types of behaviour which qualify an individual for a particular sort of deviant label may vary according to sex. Two important examples are juvenile delinquency and 'mental illness'.

Whereas both boys and girls (though far smaller numbers of the latter sex) are charged with property offences, truanting from school, fighting, drinking under age and joy-riding in cars, girls are far more likely than boys to be taken to court for being 'wayward', 'beyond parental control', 'in moral danger' or sexually promiscuous. In America this is particularly striking.

Cavan, for instance, has shown that of the 1959 court cases 69 per cent of girls and 34 per cent of boys were charged with 'conduct' offences, compared with 15 per cent of girls and 48 per cent of boys prosecuted for property offences.[22] It is less marked in England, but even there, although under one-third of all girls in court in 1967 came into this category of 'incorrigible' or 'sexual' offenders, this involved ten times as many girls as boys.[23]

This differential cannot be explained in terms of the greater incidence of these forms of delinquent behaviour among females. Studies of self-reported delinquency, where individuals are asked for a full account of any offences they have committed, whether or not they have ever been caught, demonstrate that the types of offences engaged in by boys and girls are far more similar than the official statistics (based on convicted cases) suggest, at least as far as thefts, juvenile offences connected with cars, alcohol and curfew regulations, sex and ungovernability are concerned. Indeed, one writer goes so far as to say:

In sum, the question which should guide theorizing about girls' delinquency is not 'Why do girls rather than boys run away from home, commit sex offences, and seriously misbehave at home?' A more valid question is 'Why do girls commit less delinquency of all kinds compared to boys, with the exception of running away from home and striking their parents?'[24]

In a recent book, it has been argued that a similar sort of sexism operates in the field of psychiatry with respect to what comes to be perceived as 'mental illness' in men and women. Chesler claims that female mental health and social adjustment is defined in terms of women's conformity to the *traditional* concept of the female role and temperament and that women who find difficulty in fitting themselves into the conventional patterns for their sex are likely candidates for diagnosis as mentally sick or disordered.[25] An alternative and more sociological interpretation would be that they are part of a process of social change and are simply trying to conform to one of the other role models that are available to women and one which *in itself* is no more or less 'healthy' than the traditional one.

In both these cases any changes to sex roles are likely to have significant effects on how 'deviance' of this type is perceived and therefore produced. Feminism, in seeking in the short-run to gain social acceptance for women to adopt lifestyles similar to those already enjoyed (?) by men and in the long term to establish a whole range of alternatives which are equally open to and approved for males and females, directly challenges the sorts of assumptions which underlie current conceptions of female delinquency and mental illness and every other type of female non-conformity.

Causes of Deviant Behaviour

Though women have been largely ignored by criminologists, at some time or another almost all the observed differences between the sexes – biological, psychological and social – have been advanced as causes of the relative lack of female involvement in law-breaking activities. At one extreme, this has been attributed to female timidity, innate moral superiority (women as saints), biologically determined passivity, greater skill at duplicity and deception (women as temptresses and devils), and physical weakness and, at the other extreme, sex-role conditioning and fewer opportunities. One writer – Otto Pollak – is famous for his theory that females have in fact committed more crimes than have males but have been more successful in concealing the evidence. With the striking and obvious exception of prostitutes and, to a lesser extent, mental patients, female deviants have been seriously neglected. Even Laing, as Friedenberg has observed[26], does not explore the consequences for women particularly of his analysis of schizophrenia in terms of the politics of the family, despite the fact that all his illustrations are of female patients.[27]

On the whole, sociologists have assumed that because the traditional female role insulates women from the harsh (male) world of economic, political and social competition and conflict and the stresses and strains of occupational advancement, few females have any need to resort to deviant practices, and those who do are probably psychologically disturbed anyway. Such thinking, of course, itself provides an interesting example of sexism at an intellectual level. Though, theoretically, recent sociologists of deviance have attempted to come to a greater understanding of the phenomenon through an 'appreciation'[28] of the viewpoint of the deviant, this has not prevented most writers from continuing to exercise a bias in their choice of topics to study in the first place which has resulted in the perpetuation of a predominance of males among the subjects of deviance research. For example, all the contributions to Cohen (ed.) 1971, and Taylor and Taylor (eds)[29] 1973, made by members of the National Deviancy Conference in Britain deal with aspects and types of deviance which are either exclusively male or are non sex-specific.

In the past, the approaches adopted by psychologists, sociologists and other criminologists did not even include this 'subjectivist' orientation: the population was seen as comprising two basic sub-categories of persons – a majority of conventional, law-abiding 'normals' and a minority of anti-social 'deviants'. The moral stand taken by researchers was the same as that of society or of its social control agents and deviance was measured against what was assumed to be a single, widely shared and unambiguous moral code. In its extreme form,

> The traditional sociological perspective on deviance has, then, assumed that deviance takes place in a social world that is unproblematically meaningful, based on moral consensus, homogeneous, stable, closed, and deterministic.[30]

Consequently, deviance was seen as being caused by factors located in the individual or in his or her immediate social environment, particularly the family, so that even if the individual was not regarded as being to blame the presumption has been that he or she needed to be changed or re-formed so as to fit 'better' into society. The possibility that societal factors and processes may be responsible, that individuals can be put into intolerable situations with conflicting demands made upon them, with 'reality flaws'[31] between their expectations and their experiences (between 'subjective' and 'objective' reality), which only deviance of some kind can resolve, has been recognized until recently by only a small minority of writers and workers in this field. Certain social groups, whose social needs and interests are not adequately served by the dominant institutions and values of a society, are particularly vulnerable to this kind of societally induced rule-breaking: for example, women, blacks and other ethnic minorities, the young and the lower socio-economic groups. The ultimate solution in the case of deviance of this sort is to change the society, not to punish or reform the individual.

The Processing of Deviant Individuals

How rule-breakers are treated once their deviance has been discovered is partly a function of current social conceptions of the causation of deviant behaviour and partly of the prevailing moral evaluations of the relative seriousness of various forms of deviance, as we have just seen. The individual 'sinner' model has, to a large extent, given way to a 'social disease' model in most Western societies, individuals 'in trouble' being given training, re-education, behaviour therapy, etc.

Although there seems to be some evidence that the community as a whole and social control agents take a less punitive attitude to female rule-breaking (for instance, police are more willing to give cautions and courts lighter sentences), this is by no means always the case and anyway can be partly accounted for in the case of crime and delinquency by the fact that women and girls tend to commit less serious offences and far more often are appearing in court for the first time than is the case with males. On the other hand, when it is a question of determining parental custody of children it seems the mother can be required to satisfy far higher standards of personal morality and social responsibility than the father; in England deserted wives may lose their social service entitlement if officials suspect that because they have visits from men they may be receiving financial support.* In another area, rape, the legitimate rights of women are tied to their presumed moral integrity measured in terms of their past or present sexual behaviour. Shulamith Firestone makes the perceptive and relevant comment that the 'rhetoric of sexual revolution' has greatly weakened the position of women and only strengthened that of men. Women have either lost or surrendered the traditional defences of innocence, purity and lack of sexual drive, but in the final analysis are still expected to live up to these ideals and, to a large extent, are only treated 'fairly' when they attempt to do so.[32] Thus advocates of the significance of victim-precipitation in causing crimes have succeeded in convincing many, particularly the police and the courts, that 'true' rape rarely occurs. The situation now seems to be that, in order to get her account accepted (where there is no

* A similar situation exists in Australia where if the Department of Social Services decides that the deserted wife has set up a 'domestic relationship' with a male (which may or may not involve his residing with her) she then loses her entitlement to a pension.

independent corroboration or incontrovertible evidence), a rape victim must be of impeccable moral character, preferably single and a virgin or, if married, an exemplary wife and mother. All, or nearly all, the academic criminologists in America and elsewhere (including an Australian priest who recently talked to the newspapers about a study he had undertaken on the subject in Melbourne among prisoners) seem to subscribe to this general view. The only real challenge has come from women, and particularly those who have themselves been victims of rape.*

One of the major insights of the recently developed alternative approach to the study of deviance which has been outlined here is that the way in which society and other people treat an individual who is regarded as 'deviant' may in fact contribute to that individual persisting in his or her deviance. At a certain stage, societal reaction (involving stigmatization, deprivation of various kinds and maybe incarceration) may itself become a crucial causal factor in the production or maintenance of norm-violating patterns of behaviour. In a classic example, it was suggested that a group of boys may become increasingly antagonistic and destructive as society expresses more and more hostility to and discrimination against them for their anti-social delinquent acts.[33] At a more general societal level, the amount of any given type of deviance is directly related to the level of tolerance for and the perceived degree of threat posed by persons engaged in such behaviour. A recent example of how community reactions (and the media in particular) can in a sense manufacture a deviant phenomenon can be found in Cohen's account of the 'moral panic' associated with Mods and Rockers in England in the mid-1960s.[34]

This is also the case with the feminist movement where women who try to change traditional, patriarchal attitudes and practices using conventional democratic channels, find themselves ridiculed or penalized, and are forced to employ less 'respectable' or 'legitimate' methods of achieving the desired social changes: protests and demonstrations, direct action of

* See for example, an article published in the *The Times*, London, 3 December, 1973.

various kinds, and the establishment of alternative institutions and services (medical, familial, welfare, and so on) run by and for women and irrespective of whether in some cases they are technically against some law. The resort to more radical or 'deviant' tactics must be seen in relation to the reception given by the community in general and by particular interested and powerful groups (and, again, the media) to the initial legal efforts to bring about some improvements in the status of women. In the early stages, though the ends sought might be regarded as more or less suspect by many sections of the population (including some women), the methods used conform to what is usually considered acceptable in a 'democracy'. However, at the later or secondary stage, both the means and the ends of the feminist movement are deplored because its members (like those of the black separatist movement) advocate a new and different type of society and morality, and hence every effort is made to discredit and outlaw those subscribing to such revolutionary and dangerous ideas! An analysis of social and societal reaction to organized feminism along these lines would be of benefit both to the women's movement and to the sociology of deviance.

Finally, to sum up the main argument put forward here, we cannot and must not regard the questions of what constitutes female rule-breaking and what society should do about it as straightforward, factual issues which simply require empirical investigation or expert advice. Defining certain behaviour as deviant and treating those responsible in a particular way are political acts. Differences of opinion on moral and social matters (such as working mothers, abortion, illegitimacy, middle-aged suburban neurosis and single parenthood) reflect the different experiences and sectional interests of various groups and individuals in society and the decisions made have serious, unintended and often unjustifiable social consequences for the people whose circumstances and actions are being criticized.

Notes

1. J. D. Douglas, 'Deviance and Order in a Pluralistic Society', in J. C. McKinney and E. A. Tiryakian, (eds), *Theoretical Sociology*, Appleton-Century-Crofts, New York, 1970, p.380.
2. N. K. Denzin, 'Rules of Conduct and the Study of Deviant Behaviour: Some Notes on the Social Relationship', in J. D. Douglas (ed.) *Deviance and Respectability*, Basic Books, New York, 1970, p.121.
3. J. D. Douglas (ed.), *Deviance and Respectability*, Basic Books, New York, 1970, p.10.
4. See O. Klapp, *Heroes, Villains and Fools*, (Prentice-Hall, Englewood-Cliffs, N.J., 1962), for a systematic treatment of the role of folk types; there is also a brief discussion of this topic in S. Cohen, *Folk Devils and Moral Panics*, Paladin, London, 1972, pp.11–18 and in P. Rock, *Deviant Behaviour*, Hutchinson, London, 1973, pp.33–38.
5. See D. Matza, *Becoming Deviant*, Prentice-Hall, Englewood-Cliffs, N.J., 1969, pp.165–180; J. Lofland, *Deviance and Identity*, Prentice-Hall, Englewood-Cliffs, N.J., 1969, pp.124–144; and E. M. Schur, *Labelling Deviant Behaviour*, Harper and Row, New York, 1971, pp.52–65. See also L. T. Wilkins, *Social Deviance*, Tavistock, London, 1964, p.46, and T. J. Scheff, *Being Mentally Ill*, Weidenfeld and Nicholson, London, 1966, p.191, for attempts to conceptualize the range of kinds of behaviour possible.
6. This approach is associated originally with the work of H. S. Becker, *Outsiders*, Free Press, New York, 1963, and E. M. Lemert, *Social Pathology*, McGraw-Hill, New York, 1951, and *Human Deviance, Social Problems and Social Control*, Prentice-Hall, Englewood-Cliffs, N.J., 1967. For a brief summary of its main features, see E. Rubington, and M. S. Weinberg, (eds) *Deviance: the Interactionist Perspective*, Macmillan, New York, 1968, pp.1–12, or S. Cohen, (ed.) *Images of Deviance*, Penguin Books, 1971, pp.9–24.
7. K. T. Erikson, 'Notes on the Sociology of Deviance' in H. S. Becker, (ed.) *The Other Side*, Free Press of Glencoe, 1964, pp.10–11.
8. J. Lofland, op.cit., p.13.
9. I. L. Horowitz, and M. Liebowitz, 'Social Deviance and Political Marginality: Towards a Redefinition of the Relation between Sociology and Politics', *Social Problems*, vol.15, 1968, p.282.
10. H. T. Buckner, *Deviance, Reality and Change*, Random House, New York, 1971, p.429.

11. See for example I. Taylor, P. Walton, and J. Young, *The New Criminology*, Routledge and Kegan Paul, London, 1973.
12. See the Introduction to A. R. Edwards and P. R. Wilson, (eds), *Social Deviance in Australia*, Cheshire, Melbourne, forthcoming.
13. See A. W. Gouldner, 'The Sociologist as Partisan: Sociology and the Welfare State', *American Sociologist*, vol. 3, 1968, pp. 103–16; A. Liazos, 'The Poverty of the Sociology of Deviance: Nuts, Sluts and Perverts', *Social Problems*, vol. 20, 1972, pp.103–120; and A. Thio, 'Class Bias in the Sociology of Deviance', *American Sociologist*, vol. 8, 1973, pp.1–12.
14. H. S. Becker, *Outsiders*, Free Press, New York, 1963, pp.17–18.
15. A. T. Turk, 'Towards Construction of a Theory of Delinquency', *Journal of Criminal Law, Criminology and Police Science*, vol. 55, 1964, p.216.
16. K. Millett, *Sexual Politics*, Abacus edition, Sphere Books, London, 1972, pp.24–25.
17. The only previous attempt to examine female deviance from a comparable theoretical viewpoint is F. Heidensohn, 'The Deviance of Women: a Critique and Enquiry', *British Journal of Sociology*, vol. 11, 1968, pp.160–175.
18. H. M. Hacker, 'Women as a Minority Group', *Social Forces*, vol. 30, 1951, pp.60–69.
19. S. Firestone, *The Dialectic of Sex*, Paladin, London, 1972, pp.43–44.
20. Juliet Mitchell in *Woman's Estate*, Penguin Books, 1971, talks of woman's 'estate' and Shulamith Firestone, op.cit., describes women as a 'sex class'.
21. Millett, op.cit., p.362.
22. R. S. Cavan, *Juvenile Delinquency*, Lippincott and Co., New York, 1962, p.278.
23. The question of sex differences and juvenile delinquency is discussed in some detail in the writer's unpublished Ph.D. thesis – A. R. Edwards, 'Adolescence and Delinquency: a Sociological Analysis of Sex and Area Differences', Ph.D. thesis, University of London, 1973.
24. M. Gold, *Delinquent Behaviour in an American City*, Brooks/Cole Publishing Company, Belmont, California, 1970, p.64.
25. P. Chesler, *Women and Madness*, Doubleday, New York, 1972.
26. E. Z. Friedenberg, *Laing*, Fontana, London, 1973, pp.19–21.
27. See R. D. Laing, and A. Esterson, *Sanity, Madness and the Family*, Penguin Books, 1970.

28. D. Matza, op.cit.
29. S. Cohen, (ed.) 1971, op.cit. and I. Taylor, and L. Taylor, (eds), *Politics and Deviance*, Penguin Books, 1973.
30. J. D. Douglas, 1970, op.cit., p.371.
31. For a more detailed account of this concept see H. T. Buckner, op.cit.
32. S. Firestone, op.cit., pp.135–138.
33. J. I. Kitsuse and D. C. Dietrick, 'Delinquent Boys: a Critique', *American Sociological Review*, vol. 24, 1959, pp.208–215; and L. T. Wilkins, op.cit., chapter 4.
34. S. Cohen, op.cit.

Seventeen
Black Women in Australia – A History

A young black girl about ten years old crept timidly towards the missionary who controlled the Reserve on which she lived. She would not have come forward were it not for her mother's insistence.

'Walking in the bush, sir,' she began quietly, hysteria submerged beneath nervousness, 'and a white man on a horse punched me and fucked me.'

The missionary smote the girl a stinging blow which caused her to reel and fall.

'Do not use that sort of language around here, girl, or God will punish you', said the holy man.

* * *

The twist of fate which causes an infant to become, before birth, a boy or a girl, is a cruel blow to the infant who is born into an oppressed group. Throughout history, the 'spoils of war' have always included the 'carrying away of the women', and men – who have hitherto been the writers of books and of history, not to mention also the instigators of those wars – have glossed over the fate suffered by women in such circumstances.

Following the invasion of Australia by the British, though 'war' was not officially proclaimed, similar 'state of war' circumstances prevailed – at least for the blacks. During the era which began with the arrival of the very first boat-load of convicts from England, the white man shot down the black, took his land, poisoned him, set down steel traps to ensnare him so that he might more easily be clubbed to death, wiped out his source of food and water, and mounted raids upon his tribes – and, of course, *took his women.* Armed with guns, and without the availability of women of his own colour, the white man used and abused the indigenous woman, often in front of her entire family, who were held at bay by threat of death. And thus began the miscegenation of the black Australian race.

Occasionally the white man took for himself a *de facto* black wife, and in the main he treated her reasonably because he knew that she would run away if he did not. Sometimes the 'marriage' lasted the mere length of his stay in the area, or for the shearing season, or for a few days only while passing through. Inevitably, offspring would be born, and seldom did the white man claim his heirs, and even less frequently any responsibility towards the children. Though he was apt to boast to his mates of his virility, proof being the number of half-caste children he had left scattered behind him, rarely did he keep track of these children, and – if he passed that way again in thirteen or fourteen years time – chances are the light-skinned beauty who attracted his eye and his sexual attention would be his own daughter.

The attitude of the broader white community, however, was that lighter-skinned blacks generally constituted a much graver 'problem'. They were, in many areas, not wholly accepted by their full-blood tribal brothers. In fact, in more outback areas, light-skinned infants were killed at birth – because they were living visual proof of the outrage which was being perpetrated against the tribes, and undeniable proof that the black man was not able to defend his woman against this outrage. And, for obvious reasons, the half-caste was not 'acceptable' to the white community.

On rare occasions a relationship between a white man and a black woman assumed some degree of permanence, and the 'wife' would be trailed along behind the man, an object of ridicule for the white community, and an object of scorn for her own people. However, when opportunity of any description presented itself, the white man would take his 'wife and *her* piccaninnies' to the hills and abandon them, or perhaps just never return from a trip into town for supplies. Without doubt, though the relationship may have endured a number of years, the appearance of 'kin from the Mother Country' would provide motivation for a hasty abandonment, as would the chance – no matter how remote – of marrying a white woman. The 'gin' or 'lubra', as a black woman was called at this time, was no more than a mere receptacle to be used until something better, anything better, appeared on the horizon.

Perhaps more relevant to today's attitudes are the many racist laws which were passed, ostensibly for the 'protection' of the Australian black, but in reality these laws were misused and abused to further allow rape and miscegenation to occur. Government Reserves, set up over the entire country as supposed areas of protection from the encroaching whites, stripped the black community of any rights which they may have utilized, the right of defence when attacked being perhaps one of the most important. Unable to speak the language, or to present any sort of defence of his actions, and unable to comprehend the white legal structure, the black man who defended the honour or virtue of his wife and/or daughter was, of course, a killer, and abo-hunts were mounted and whole families and tribes slaughtered in retribution. 'Justice' was a word never heard by – and certainly never applied to – the black Australians.

On each of these protected areas, these government Reserves, was installed a white Protector or Manager, who distributed the handouts of meagre rations, restricted movement of the black population, and had the power of life or death over those in his custody. Often the Manager's idea of 'protecting' ran to taking his pick of the available black women for himself, and also making women available for prominent men in his area by way of gaining their favour, and also for passing officers of the law who were, even then, not above receiving their graft in human traffic.

Parallels in history, of course, are the black American female slaves, who were beaten and killed if they refused the favours of the white master, and were 'loose, and for the taking' if they did not refuse. In many country areas the belief that the half-caste made the better worker was prevalent, and it was acceptable to 'breed your own' to ensure a continuous supply. It was not until the number of half-castes (without corresponding figures of inter-marriage, naturally) in the country became a problem complicated by over-all unemployment due to an economic depression, that the white population became concerned. And so laws were passed which prohibited sexual intercourse between white man and black woman, and – in the West – between Asians (who were slipping along imitating the white powers) and black women. Laws, then, were passed, but *not enforced*, relating to racial miscegenation, for who would enforce them when the agents of the law themselves were often the most notorious gin-jockeys in their area?

The sexual abuse of black women continued, with the balance of life or death remaining in the hands of the white community, and the black woman's existence could only be assured by her continued availability for the white man's sexual demands. Many early white explorers and writers noted that the Australian black was dirty – obviously *she* was not *too* dirty!

Along with tuberculosis, leprosy, and diseases such as measles and chicken pox to which the white race had built up a tolerance through their continued exposure, but which caused the death of many thousands of blacks when they swept across the country, the white man also brought his venereal diseases. The white man withheld from the black communities treatment for these new diseases, but of course he called in white doctors for himself and his family when occasion arose.

V.D. untreated raged rampant through the black community, with the white rapist infecting the black woman, and the woman infecting her own men, and also infecting other white rapists and seducers. However, these white men sought and obtained medical treatment, but not so the black woman. Instead, she was forced to bear syphilitic children, diseased children, and to spend her entire life in heartbreak and pain. The rapists and seducers from the white community, on the other hand, merely skirted the problem by choosing as their victims increasingly younger girls, until sexual abuse of youngsters from age seven became a common occurrence.

Further complicating the issue for black women through the years of white oppression is the type of verbal 'belief' professed to be held by the power, the white man, as opposed to his practices. Missionaries, who were given wide powers to govern and control the Mission/Reserves, often 'steeped themselves in sin' to the detriment of black women, from Monday to Saturday, and then spent Sunday telling the entire black community to 'turn the other cheek'. The Bible becomes an ominous weapon of suppression when viewed in this light.

The black communities had no avenue of escape, no means to bring about changes in their situation, other than by death – and until the period prior to the Second World War death was often chosen as the lesser of the two evils. The black race was dying out. Everyone knew it. Humanists went out into remote areas to find blacks, in order to soothe them as they lay dying.

'And what happened then?' you might well ask. Until now, no one *has* asked. Does it not strike you as strange that since a complete reversal has been effected within the last fifty years, no one has questioned why – or how?

While the white community accepts, apparently without question or in divine faith, the fact that the black community spread right across a country which covers almost three million square miles 'changed its mind' about dying out, and has become instead the fastest growing section of the entire population in this country today, the black community does not. We do not deny the trend reversal, but we do not accept that it happened by some miraculous chance.

Remembering that the black communities consisted in the main of hundreds of little scattered groups, severely weakened by a diet of flour, sugar, and tea rations, and their movements restricted by the white managers, it is not feasible to suggest that someone went from group to group, breaking into and out of Reserve barriers, entering areas geographically inaccessible except by boat or plane, carrying a message. It is just as unlikely that a message attempting to co-ordinate the revitalization of these black groups could have been somehow worded, understood, and acted upon. And yet the reversal *did* occur, and it occurred simultaneously across the country within an extremely short time. All of which might suggest what the white community calls the 'supernatural', but which the black community considers to be as natural as breathing.

This is perhaps, historically, the most important aspect and exposes the lack of communication and cultural understanding on the part of the white community. Earlier omissions on the part of the white community, cultural blocks and ignorance, are partially understandable because there were so few whites at that time in this country. Now however, eleven million white people, many 'trained' observers and scientists, witness a phenomenon among a black people whom they consider mentally inferior.

At least, no one will deny that the black community has indeed taken on a new lease of life, in more ways than one. Playing her part in this reversal of population figures, the black woman has assumed an awesome burden of responsibility. She is the vessel through which the multiplying must be done, and she is the one who then must tend the young, despite all odds, despite the common incarceration of her mate, despite her white rapist, despite the leer of the white community at her plight. She has overcome – despite the continued negligence of the white government, despite the world's highest infant mortality rate, despite the many diseases which strike at the root of her chore. She is carrying the black community to population levels never before achieved since the first white man set foot in this country.

Yet her just place in society is as far, if not further, from her grasp than ever before. Burdened down with the complexities of bringing up children in this sophisticated and complicated society, she remains an object of sexual fulfilment for the white man, and an 'invisible' woman to her white female contemporaries, especially the 'establishment' of Women's Liberationists who chatter on about sexual oppression and the competitive orgasm, and who spare not a thought for the true object of sexual oppression in this country today.

A few women's organizations have made overtures towards a few black women, particularly those black women who have become something of a community spokeswoman or figurehead, and again there is lack of understanding of the reasons why black women do not wish to join these groups. That there has been no common experience is perhaps the most obvious reason, and on what other ground could these white women expect black women to *want* to join them? Black women do not seek to be patronized, nor to be made 'token niggers'; they have their own, and very different, experiences, and black women will join black women's groups on this basis.

White women seek, amongst other things, sexual freedom. Black women have had 'sexual freedom', if that's what it can be called, forced upon them. The 'freedom' that the white woman seeks sexually is the right to say 'yes', without condemnation from society, without lowering herself in the process. The black woman seeks the right to say 'no', to explode the myth of the over-sexed black woman, and she has to overcome not just the barriers of sexism to reach her goal, but – and more importantly – the barriers of racist attitudes.

An indication of the overall lack of interest in the real problems in the heart of the black community by these white liberation groups can be seen if we examine the reaction (or rather, the lack of reaction) following the publication and wide circulation of a leaflet by a Canberra-based organization called Joint Women's Action. The leaflet, and the fact that it was not seized or an outcry raised, constitutes an indictment of Australian society in general, and established Women's Liberation groups in particular. Written by several black women, the leaflet read in part: 'If you are black and a woman and in your early teens, you have probably been raped at least once. If you are black and a woman and in your early twenties, then you have probably been raped two or three times.' Investigation into any group of young black women in this country supports the awful truth of this leaflet. Worse still, police are most commonly named as the offenders – those stalwart officers of the law to whom white women actually report sexual offences which have been committed against them. To whom, then, does the black woman turn?

The black community turns inwards. But even now there is a rising indication of a turn of events. Motions passed by those 'Advisory' groups called together by the Government give whole-hearted support for investigation into rape of the black communities. Motions being passed all over the country by groups such as the National Council of Aboriginal and Island Women, call for urgent enquiry to be made. Registering simultaneously with the motion is the knowledge that 'nothing gets done unless we do it ourselves', reinforced by the practical experiences of the community-controlled Aboriginal Medical Service, Aboriginal Legal Service, and the Redfern Black Urban Development programme. Black women realize that they are going to have to develop these projects themselves, and they are going to get little, if any, help from the white community.

It is necessary to look beyond the straight analysis of what constitutes 'rape', to recognize it in its every aspect, in order to be able to counter it. What then is 'rape'?

Is rape the forcing of sexual attention onto an unwilling party? Is rape accompanied by coercion and/or threats against the person? Can rape also be accompanied by threats made against another person, such as a nearby child? Can rape also be accompanied by threats against an entire community, such as a police officer could make, threatening harassment and arrest of other members of the family and community, immediately or in the near future? Could not these threats also be 'implied', instead of going through the monotony of speaking them each time, especially if both parties are aware that the other knows the lines?

If the above analysis is correct, and I maintain that it is, does not then the situation of the white community and the establishment in this country constitute an unspoken threat to every black woman in this country? It might then be queried that natural progression would mean that rape of black women could become the norm . . . which is exactly where we started, because rape of black women with impunity has become the norm, which is borne out not only in the urgency of the motions passed by our organization, not only in the desperation evidenced in the Joint Women's Action leaflet, but in the visual evidence of the increasing number of light-skinned children in the black community – and still without corresponding numbers of white marriage partners to account for them.

Rape is an ugly subject. Rape is also an ugly experience. Yet, burying our heads in the sand will only leave our backsides in the air, which is a dangerous position in more ways than one. There is a marked reluctance in the white community to confront the subject of rape, regardless of who is the victim. In the white community, even among their own, the rape victim becomes somehow 'guilty', and is further victimized by even her closest associates, and more particularly by her husband if she is married. No one ever admits to having been raped, or that anyone in their family has undergone this harrowing experience. Despite the ever-rising rates of this crime, there appear to be no victims at all. Rape, therefore, always happens to 'somebody else', or perhaps it is just something that occasionally crops up in books or in nasty movies.

With attitudes such as these towards rape in their own community, the attitude of the white community on the subject of rape of *black* women becomes a matter of near hysteria and schizophrenia. Black women are *never* raped, they are over-sexed and therefore welcome this type of attention. Rape of the very young is often countered with the information that 'black girls *mature* earlier'. It has even been argued in this context that it is easier to educate and to assimilate the lighter-skinned child, therefore justifying the continued practice of rape of black women. White women notoriously remain ignorant of the fact that the children who live on stations in the outback are also becoming progressively lighter, and the white women who live on these stations refuse to comment on these conditions – because they are denying to themselves even that the children are being fathered by their husbands, sons, brothers, and employees.

The black women then who seek to liberate themselves from racial and sexual oppression have before them the almost impossible task of overcoming not just the erroneous preconceived ideas of the white community in every detail pertaining to themselves, but to do so without causing further injury to the black man, who has also borne the physical and mental brunt of oppression on a racial basis, and who, too, is labouring against similar, but different, myths regarding his sexuality.

Eighteen

An Australian Housewife: A Disillusioning Experience

I was born in 1927, too late for the Suffragette Movement and too soon for Women's Liberation. I regretted having missed the former fight, which I naively imagined to have been won before my time, and long before the second wave of feminism broke I had succumbed to my Irish Catholic conditioning. I accepted the family as the basis of society and the mother as the linchpin of the family. From this it followed that any limitations placed upon woman in her role as mother were justified in the interests of her family and of society and were amply compensated by the rewards of the job. So, whilst earning a frugal living in a variety of ill-paid secretarial and clerical positions I never doubted that my real career would eventually be marriage and that I would make a splendid success of it. Thrusting aside the overwhelming evidence in the life of my mother and sundry other female relatives that marriage for a woman is not all it is cracked up to be, I marked time in the workforce waiting the right candidate to present himself – when my real life would begin.

I was twenty-six years old when I came to Australia to get married and in the fullness of time to have a family – four, I thought, would be nice – who would reflect great credit on their parents and their country. Now, twenty years and five children later, I have to own to a failed marriage which has not so much broken up as dissolved into total disillusionment, and whether the children reflect any credit on anyone is a moot point. Although charming in their way, up to now the best that can be said of them is that they are amiable young savages.

In considering the gradual development of my disillusionment I can only marvel at the thoroughness of the indoctrination which convinced me, and evidently many like me, that I could look to marriage to provide all my social, intellectual and emotional needs, and which led me to blame myself when the reality of my situation fell so far short of the theory. I must have expected my husband to give meaning, purpose, emotional support, intellectual stimulus, economic security and total enrichment to my life. This, of course, was a tall order for a young man, who for his part had a separate and in many respects contrary set of expectations, mostly centred round the enhancement of his lifestyle and personal comfort. But if marriage and family are to be all of a woman's life, these are the expectations she must bring to it. Neither I nor anyone else marries to be miserable.

Tradition has it that the wedding day belongs to the bride. This is *the* day in a woman's life when she symbolizes glamour, beauty, achievement – but alas her reign is of one day's duration. I certainly found that immediately after the honeymoon some subtle Law of Diminishing Returns began to operate in my life. With my change of name came a completely new lifestyle. I became a housewife. The scant respect society paid to my role of homemaker rankled rather, but lack of status was easier to bear than economic dependence, which I found humiliating. I still do.

As might be expected of a working girl, I knew little more about the craft of housewifery than did my husband. I had had to do my share of routine chores at home, as he had, but total responsibility for cleaning, catering, cooking and laundry did not come naturally, as apparently it is supposed to, being after all 'woman's work'. I learned, as I suppose most brides do, in the hardest and most wasteful way possible, by trial and error, feeling not a little inadequate in the process. As I floundered it occurred to me that since I and many like me do not just naturally fall into 'woman's work' perhaps there is nothing specifically female about the household chores after all.

I did in time become an accomplished housewife but even this is not without its hazards. Opting for a fairly high standard of neatness and order I was often chidden for being houseproud. It does seem hard that the housewife may be married to the damn house but on no account be proud of it. I fretted over the injustice of this situation but stuck doggedly to my right, as the one who did all the mopping up, to set the standard to be maintained. Houseproud, I realized, is a term of opprobrium applied only to the female, most usually by other users of her premises who find her standards inconvenient. It is irksome to have to bear the criticisms of slovens with lower standards but there is no defence against them. Nagging, of course, is a similar and often related female phenomenon. Men may make repeated but legitimate demands concerning their tools, cars or other paraphernalia; their wives who may be sensitive to muddy stains on carpets or gross untidiness in the bathroom are held to be nagging when they voice their views on these subjects. Gossip is yet another unpleasant vice held to be specifically female, which falls into the same category of traits which exist in the eye (or ear) of the beholder and against which there is no satisfactory defence. Men converse; women gossip. Of course men have the advantage here. We women run into our friends around the shops and with children in tow we stop to pass the time of day and such news as might be of interest, or we maintain contact with seldom-seen friends by lengthy telephone calls; our husbands have a few drinks with the chaps in the pub or even sit down over lunch to conduct the same sort of social intercourse. Frankly I would rather converse their way than gossip our way if time, money, opportunity and children permitted. They do not, so the housewife is a sitting duck for attack on this and the other two counts mentioned above. I know, I have been through it all.

Another chapter in my personal saga opened with the first pregnancy and another ego-eroding process it proved to be. Notwithstanding a confident, positive approach, a regime of exercises and proper diet, Grantly Dick Read and the rest, I felt very sick all through pregnancy and childbirth was the most shattering experience of my life. Doctors, nurses and visitors all told me briskly how well I was as I lay half-stunned by the agony of it all and dreaded going home in charge of the voracious little monster whose sucking at my tender breasts was nothing short of torture. Of course, I was delighted with my little son and so was my husband, but I knew he had no idea what it had all cost me, emotionally, physically and psychologically. Furthermore he had no fears of my proving inadequate to the task of rearing the child whilst I was silently very apprehensive on this score. After all up to this point so many of my expectations had gone unrealized that my self-confidence was losing ground steadily. But somehow I could not discuss my fears. There appeared to be a conspiracy in society to treat pregnancy and childbirth as female concerns of small importance which are always good for a laugh. How could I be such a rotten sport as to spoil the joke for everyone?

Like housekeeping, childcare has to be learned by trial and error which is doubtless why my beloved firstborn was the most difficult – the trials we both survived, the errors left their mark. I had not expected his determined attitude of non-cooperation nor his immense strength of will. Much later I realized that most parental failure results from the child's ability to outstay the adult in any contest of wills. I learned this bitter lesson over the matter of feeding and I am paying for it still as the firstborn's food fads have been copied by subsequent children. If he pronounced it to be yuk, yuk it was, right down the line, and of course nothing would have been yuk in the first place if I had not been so concerned that he should eat his carefully balanced meals. All too late I discovered that the secret of success is to avoid confrontation unless absolutely necessary and then stick to your guns at all costs. My fifth child has reaped the benefit of my hardwon wisdom and I have high hopes of his growing into a well-rounded personality, but who wants well-brought-up children in the ratio of one to four as against the other kind?

In the fog of fatigue in which I passed the first weeks as a new mother I often wondered at the cruelty of a supposedly humane society, exalting motherhood as it does, which habitually abandons the inexperienced, isolated and weakened young mother to the none too tender mercies of a first child and expects her to know by instinct how to go about 'mothering' it. In spite of all the ballyhoo about maternal instinct my husband knew just as much about care of the newborn infant as I did, which was precisely nothing. And the fact of bearing the child conferred no special expertise upon me whilst it did leave me tired and weak and less able to cope with new and difficult tasks. If 'fathering' as a desirable concept were fostered it would be of enormous benefit at this crucial juncture in the life of the family. As things stood, and neither of us new parents considered any other way, the care of the baby was solely my concern.

The father's life went on as before. He maintained his sporting interests; he became more absorbed in his work as he advanced in his job. He even had opportunities to travel overseas which I tried hard not to envy as I found that my whole life revolved round my new responsibility. Nothing could have prepared me for the total loss of liberty this involved. The needs of the baby influenced my every decision, my every movement. I have a recurring nightmare, originating at about this time, in which I am separated from the children and I know they need me desperately but I cannot reach them and not only am I anguished by the situation but I feel guilt-ridden as well that I should have allowed myself to be separated from them in the first place. Evidently, waking or sleeping, the responsibility weighed heavily upon me and especially so during the nine-month breastfeeding period which followed each birth. Naturally as a conscientious mother I could not tolerate any other way of raising a child, even if I wore myself out doing it, which I did.

Well-wishing friends and neighbours jollied me along by telling me things would be better when the baby ... slept through the night ... was weaned ... was walking ... out of nappies ... off to school ... Maybe so. But was I to wish my life away? And what of my life's work? Wasn't this it? I had an uneasy feeling that I must be failing somewhere as I was very very tired and although I adored my baby I did look forward to better times ahead when I would get more sleep and he would be more reasonable.

It took ten years and four children before I finally admitted to myself that it was no use pinning my hopes of personal fulfilment on my wife/mother role. With the arrival of each new baby my gains in efficiency were outweighed by an increase in work so that I was endlessly looking forward to better times ahead when my own personality, totally submerged in domesticity, might reassert itself. For it was undeniable that my personality was submerged. The 'enriching' experience of marriage and motherhood was diminishing me. Whilst my husband's horizons widened, mine contracted. As I snatched my peanut butter sandwich off the end of the draining board, I would ponder the contrast between our lifestyles, knowing him to be lunching at a good restaurant with congenial associates. Similarly with sport: my sporting interests ran to a couple of sets of tennis once a week when I would set off for the courts laden with babies, pushers, toys, playlunches, spare parts and the certain expectation of having to hold up the game to attend to emergencies off-court. My husband could pick up his golfing equipment and drive off to spend most of the day on a pleasant round and some light conversation and refreshment afterwards. Of course he could only do this on Saturday or Sunday but no matter what the day, wherever I went the children had to go too.

I loved the children and put their welfare, as I saw it, before any other consideration but I certainly did not feel myself to be growing as a person, rather the reverse.

My confident expectations of measuring up well as a mother did not long withstand the erosion of doubt either. Even amongst my own acquaintances I noticed a wide range of differences in child-rearing practice, from the neurotically over-protective to the frankly neglectful. I, aiming at perfection, became less and less sure of my goals and of the possibility of reaching them but taking my responsibility as seriously as I did I personally assumed the guilt for anything that went wrong. If they fell ill, I felt it must be through some negligence on my part; if they needed dental treatment, who but the one responsible for their diet could be at fault; if they had poor peer relationships, were judged immature or precocious by their teachers, behaved badly on social occasions or did not measure up in some other way, who could be responsible but the one with whom they had spent all their waking hours? One or two of them even bit their nails occasionally which oppressed me dreadfully as evidence of some untraceable maternal omission or commission. Compared with this responsibility it did not seem to me that the rat-race of business could be too hard to deal with, but my husband was very inclined to compare the difficulty of his lot with the ease of mine and to expect endless sympathy on account of what he saw as his relatively disadvantaged position. But in business he could only lose money: on the success of my fumbling maternal ministrations depended the future well-being of four small children.

Everyone, experts, amateurs, relatives, friends, critics, carried on about the vital importance of the mother/child relationship, but why, oh why, did they all assume it to be so natural and easy?

What the experts do not seem to realize is that bearing a child is one thing, rearing it is quite another, and neither has much to do with the third aspect of the woman's role, housekeeping, although all three functions are lumped together as though they comprised a single entity. I found housekeeping and child-rearing to be mutually antagonistic pursuits. As housekeeper I was concerned with order, cleanliness, general maintenance and the provision of meals. Child-care involved meeting the child's reasonable demands, providing an environment which stimulated him and allowed freedom of movement, and above all relating to him in a meaningful way, all of which were demanding of time, patience and attention. Even with judicious management of my time and the sacrifice of my personal interests, I found housekeeping demands often necessitated pushing the child aside, or vice versa, a situation that was exacerbated by poor design of both house and furniture, which are full of hazards for little children. The onus was on me, the mother, to protect the children from the traps set for them by shortsighted architects and designers whose business it should properly be to foresee and supply family needs. Since they do not, an unconscionable amount of maternal energy is wasted on mere surveillance, to protect the young from danger and not infrequently to protect furniture and equipment from the ravages of the same young. The unfortunate truth is that the suburban house is rarely geared to the needs of children, which is absurd, since the only reason for setting up house in this elaborate way is to raise children.

Still convinced that I had a full-time job, although by now rather less convinced of its attractions, time came for my eldest child to go to school, which he did with extreme reluctance. No doubt his very limited experience of people other than his family made it a very big and frightening experience. He did eventually settle down and then I noticed a significant change. Instead of 'my mummy says' when he needed to cite an expert it became 'sister says so'. Obviously, with the major part of his education handed over to the school, my nurturing function was all but ended. Even with three to follow, in a few years 'looking after' my family would amount to being no more than their servant, the simultaneously revered and despised 'Mum' who does the chores that a family could well do for themselves because that is her job and she has no other.

I emphatically did not want to be a Mum, an endearingly idiotic moron whom the children would have to protect from knowledge of their more offbeat exploits; whose sensibilities the censor would have to consider before releasing films and books, who would be the target of that nauseating annual charade on the second Sunday in May; for whom TV and radio would air their most puerile programmes, the Admen their most insulting campaigns; whom politicians, clergy, encyclopaedia salesmen, disc jockeys, motor mechanics and the rising generation would feel entitled to patronize; whose very real problems and frustrations would be the butt of ridicule and whose contribution to the GNP would be counted as NIL.

With rising panic I took stock of my situation and took no comfort from it. I began to count the number of times I heard women describe themselves as 'only a housewife'. I became acutely conscious and resentful of the lack of facilities for young children – ramps for prams, child-sized lavatories, changing/feeding facilities for babies, over-high bus and tram steps, difficult-to-open train doors, restrictions on taking prams on public transport, rigid shopping hours which forced mothers to take children along if they could not afford or find a babysitter. The family might be the basic unit of society but clearly no one wanted to know you if you were accompanied by a few of the unit's component parts. Society was all too evidently organized around the requirements of the unencumbered, able-bodied, adult male. At about this time I even voted against the ALP because their campaign harped so on 'the workers' and I knew full well they did not mean me, in my middle-class suburban home, who worked harder and longer than any of them. I had at last come to the realization that I, the housewife, was the most despised, neglected and exploited member of society.

When my husband began to notice that I was ill-at-ease, which he did not until I was threshing round fairly frantically in my domestic cage, he counselled me to be like normal women who were happy in their role as a support and comfort to their husbands and who enjoyed the things and people their husbands enjoyed. Asked how he knew all this about normal women, he assured me it was a self-evident truth. My keener observation of other women led me to quite different conclusions. I saw them developing 'suburban neurosis' as they approached middle age, not because of the onset of that universal scapegoat the menopause, not for regret at their passing youth, but quite simply because with the longer portion of their lives still ahead of them they found themselves with no other justification for living than rendering menial service to their husbands and children. Since all good parents realize that they can measure their success by the thoroughness with which they work themselves out of a job, it is obvious that any service habitually performed for a child which he is capable of performing for himself is retarding the desired end, independence. Is it not ridiculous therefore for a mother to fetch and carry for growing children to the extent that is accepted as normal in our culture?

I did not take to drugs, drink or doctors, although I have every sympathy with those who do. Instead, I took to education. I embarked upon a university degree course and began to be me again. As my involvement in my new interest became more serious, several surprising things happened. When my self-esteem began to grow again people actually started to listen to my opinions with some respect; my husband unaccountably seemed to resent my enjoyment of the new experience, the more so when success attended my efforts; the schools' mothers' clubs got off my back, accepting my excuses where previously they had used standover tactics to blackmail me into activities I hated – you owe it to your children to support this or that or the other fund-raising effort – and most gratifying of all, as I demanded more self-reliance and co-operation from the children, their response was far better than it had been to the fewer demands I had previously made. In the light of my experience I am convinced that 'looking after' children is grossly overdone in our society. I've overturned this concept in our house and we are all the better for it. My husband had been too well indoctrinated to relinquish his male privilege of being looked after. He has retreated into resentful sulks, feeling very hard done-by in drawing such an unnatural wife in the marriage lottery. The children take an inverted pride in telling their friends what a tough mother they've got, who will not do for them the things other mothers do for their kids as a matter of course. The four who are old enough are all developing reasonable skill in the domestic arts. The one who was unexpectedly added to the family after my metamorphosis will never have known a housebound mother and in spite of this shows himself to be a perfectly satisfactory specimen of humankind. We are all very pleased with him.

It may have taken twenty years but I believe I have at last crawled out from under the burden of misconceptions which my expectations of the Woman's Role laid upon me. I have recovered some of my eroded self-esteem and personality. I am no longer hoping for good times ahead, I am living now. I sincerely hope that my generation of women will have been the last to accept such a very unjust deal in terms of loss of freedom, self-determination and public respect in return for the very mixed blessings of marriage and motherhood. My hopes are tempered somewhat by the continuing relentless pressure from schools, media, church and government on the young to conform to the rigidly defined sex-role stereotypes which have up to now served society so well. My good wishes go with the girl who would buck her conditioning – she will need them.

Nineteen
Life as a Lesbian

In our society any sexual relationship between women is labelled 'lesbian' and is generally considered to be unnatural, perverted, sick, immature, wrong, sinful or deviant. The woman whose primary sexual orientation is to her own sex is labelled 'a lesbian' and is *a fortiori* unnatural, perverted, sick, immature, wrong, sinful or deviant. There is a stereotype of the lesbian as man-hating, masculine in appearance and tastes, ugly and frustrated. Any woman who sleeps with another woman, or wishes to do so, must somehow come to terms with these social attitudes. She will ask herself, am I unnatural, perverted, etc.? Am I really a lesbian? Do I conform to the stereotype? There are many possible answers to these questions, and the same woman may give different answers at different stages of her life. In the first part of this article I shall try to describe the slow process by which I arrived at the answers I give to those questions today.

Becoming a Lesbian

I call this process 'becoming a lesbian'. Of course, I do not mean to suggest that some sort of metamorphosis took place. 'Identifying myself as a lesbian' might be better but it is rather clumsy and longwinded. Women often say that they have *been* lesbians all their lives but did not 'realize' it; however lesbianism is a relationship between a woman and the rest of society, and naturally it changes from time to time. As the American Radicalesbians say, 'It should first be understood that lesbianism, like male homosexuality, is a category of behaviour possible only in a sexist society characterized by rigid sex roles and dominated by male supremacy.'[1] In other words, it is sexism which makes an issue of homosexuality.

When I told my mother that I was a lesbian she asked, 'Where did we go wrong?' Most accounts of becoming homosexual (more often called the deviant career or the aetiology of homosexuality) set out to discover where homosexuals or their parents 'went wrong'. That is a non-question. Love between women does not need an explanation. Instead I shall try to explain social attitudes to lesbianism and the way in which they interact with the feelings and behaviour of individual women.

I went to a girls high school and I had 'crushes' on some of the girls there. I also had 'crushes' on boys. I started going out with boys when I was seventeen. Later that year I met a very beautiful girl called Anne. I never got to know her very well but she haunted my mind for many years. I used to talk about her all the time. One of my girl-friends, perhaps a little bored by these conversations, asked me bluntly, 'Would you sleep with her if you could?' I had not slept with anybody at the time, and my sexual fantasies were rather vague, so I needed time to think about it. When I had thought about it, the answer was 'Yes'.

Through one of my boyfriends I met a group of homosexuals who belonged to that aesthetically-oriented homosexual subculture which Susan Sontag describes so well.[2] I did not become involved with any of the women in that group but I was influenced by the group as a whole. I admired them and wanted to be accepted by them.

I did not feel any guilt about being attracted to Anne and I was not shocked by anything my homosexual friends said or did. I did not think that homosexuality was wrong. And yet I demurred when one of my girlfriends suggested that we sleep together. There were two reasons: firstly, I did not feel strongly attracted to my friend, I was still preocupied with Anne, and, secondly, I was afraid that I would not know what to do in bed, and she would not know either, so that it would be an embarrassing failure.

I started sleeping with men. (No need for anxiety there – men tell you what to do!) Over the next few years I had affairs with a number of men and I continued to think about Anne. None of my affairs with men worked out well. At the time I had no idea why. I know now that it was because the roles we were trying to play were confused and conflicting – intellectual and good housekeeper, 'nice girl' and sexy chick on my part, leader and guide, great lover and free, untamed male on theirs. I began to wonder if a lesbian relationship would work out better. However, the only lesbians I knew were living in jealous, exclusive couples, and I was afraid to approach any woman who was not clearly labelled 'lesbian'. Eventually I met a woman I liked, and was not afraid to approach her because she looked like the stereotype of a butch lesbian.

For a time, although I was sleeping with women and thought of myself as a lesbian, I still slept with men occasionally. I did so for various reasons – because I had slept with the man before and found it hard to say no, and because it was easier to meet men and I did not have to take the initiative in sexual relationships with them. I found that my relationships with women meant much more to me than my relationships with men, and I ceased to sleep with men at all.

I became part of a group of lesbians who had a party every week at someone's house. I had little in common with these women; nonetheless I looked to them for my definition of a lesbian and hence my definition of myself. Usually when a woman finds that she is sexually attracted to other women she goes around trying to find out what a lesbian is, that is, what other people expect her to be. It would be more rational to ask herself exactly what she feels, and to create her own definition of herself, but we are all so dependent on other people's opinions of us that it hardly ever happens that way.

At the beginning I accepted the assumptions of the group without question. They assumed, for example, that lesbianism had to be concealed from everyone in the outside world except very close friends, and that it involved some playing of 'butch' and 'femme', that is, masculine and feminine roles. After a while I began to have doubts about the need for secrecy and role-playing but these doubts did not really take shape until after I had joined Women's Liberation and Gay Liberation.

I was involved in the Women's Liberation movement in England from its early days, but at first my position was a dishonest and painful one, because I was afraid to tell the other women in my group that I was a lesbian. I knew from things they had said that they did not want lesbians in the movement. I remember once talking to one of the members of my group and her boyfriend about lesbians. She said she did not know any and he replied, 'You probably do but they're pretending to be real people.' Because of the prejudice against lesbians which I found in the women's movement both here and in England, I dropped out for a while.

I joined Melbourne Gay Liberation and began the process of 'coming out', that is, telling people that I was a lesbian and proud of it. My life had been divided into compartments – on one hand, my daily life as a lesbian and, on the other, my interest in radical politics and feminism, my work, my public 'front'. Now that I have started to break down those divisions, and I still have a long way to go, I am able to lead a more satisfying, honest life.

I felt more at home in Gay Liberation than in any other group I had ever belonged to, but I began to feel uneasy about the fact that it was dominated by the men. They were learning to take a pride in their homosexuality but they were not learning to question the roles and stereotypes they had taken over from the heterosexual world. Again and again the men assumed that their experience was *the* homosexual experience, the norm. They were not interested in what the women had to say but they found it convenient to have token women representatives in Gay Liberation. For these reasons the women in Melbourne Gay Liberation established a separate women's group in January 1973. And through the Gay Women's Group I have come to change my definition of a lesbian and my definition of myself once again.

We began to work with the women's movement as well as Gay Liberation, and I found that while I had been away the climate of opinion had changed. Lesbians can now work openly in the women's movement. In fact there is no longer a clear division between lesbian and heterosexual feminists. The more radical feminists feel that the taboo on lesbianism is just one of the devices which are used to divide women from each other.

How Lesbians Are Oppressed

'Coming out' is important but it certainly cannot solve all the problems a lesbian faces. We are oppressed in many ways, and all the different forms of oppression work together, reinforcing each other.

I have not completely 'come out' at work. When I do, I may lose my job. Recently a Melbourne television station made a short programme on homosexuality. As a result of appearing on that programme two homosexuals were evicted from their flat and another lost his job. A fourth was warned by his employer (a government department) that he would lose his job if he appeared on the programme and so he decided not to do so.

My present job is one of the few which have equal pay but my income is low and my chances of advancement are worse than those of a man. Because of my low income I find it almost impossible to save money, and even if I managed to save enough for the deposit on a house, I know that, as a single woman who does not have a good job, I would not be able to get a bank loan.

Although some homosexual couples live together for a lifetime homosexuals are always assumed to be single. And to be single is a disadvantage because in our society everything is geared to the nuclear family, everything conspires to force people into marriage. Banks and insurance companies, welfare agencies, hospitals and the law, sometimes recognize *de facto* marriages, but they all pretend that homosexual relationships do not exist. And there are many social occasions where the only alternative to taking a partner of the opposite sex is to go alone.

People often ask if homosexual relationships are less stable than heterosexual relationships because they are not socially recognized. It depends what is meant by stability. Heterosexual couples may continue to live together because of social pressures but no amount of social recognition can breathe new life into a dead marriage. The lesbian is free to end a relationship as soon as it breaks down.

Most lesbians have had some heterosexual experience[3], as I have. Some are divorced, others still married. Some are single mothers. Thus the oft-repeated question, 'Don't you wish you could have children?' is rather absurd. Lesbians can and do have children. The real problem is, how can the single lesbian survive and bring up her children on a tiny pension? How can she find time to work or rest when child-care facilities are everywhere inadequate? Some married lesbians do not leave their husbands because they fear that they will not be able to support their children alone. Indeed, if a husband complains in the divorce court that his wife is a lesbian she may lose custody of the children.

I mentioned that one of the reasons that I refused when a friend asked me to sleep with her was that I was afraid that I would not know what to do. Passivity and self-doubt are part of the traditional female role. I still find it hard to take the initiative in a sexual relationship with a woman, or even ask another woman to dance. Until recently I made a sharp distinction, as many women do, between sexual relationships and (asexual) friendship. That distinction now seems to me false and restrictive. It meant that my sexual relationships, whether with women or with men, were jealous, exclusive and short lived. Whether or not men are actually involved, all women suffer in their personal relationships from the fact that they have been trained for a system of reciprocal role-playing in which males are dominant and females submissive.

Perhaps because homosexuality was scarcely mentioned in my religious and family training, I have never felt guilt about being a lesbian. However, I have often felt embarrassment. Gay Liberation has a slogan, 'Gay is just as good as straight!', but to some degree we have all internalized the idea that it is not, and we have to work to overcome that idea. The very fact that she conceals her sexual preferences every day of her life creates a doubt in a lesbian's mind.

There have been a few times in my life when I thought of going to see a psychiatrist, never because I was a lesbian, but because of depression or problems in specific relationships. I always decided not to go. I remembered friends who had received psychiatric treatment and instead of being 'cured' had come to believe in their own 'madness'.[4] And the more I heard and read about psychiatrists' attitudes to homosexuality the more difficult I found it to respect people who did not respect me or my way of life.

Whatever the problem being presented, many psychiatrists will insist that a lesbian's main difficulty is being a lesbian and will treat her either by the barbarism of aversion therapy or by reinforcing in psychotherapy any guilt, anxiety or self-hatred she may feel. There is a myth that treatment is always voluntary but homosexuals are often forced into it by their parents, the courts or the doctors themselves. Both forms of treatment are based on a notion of human sexuality which is so perverted and degraded in the fullest sense of those words, that it is not surprising that they are rarely successful. Even psychiatrists who do not attempt to 'cure' homosexuality suffer from the limitations of their personal experience, and the pernicious influence of their training. The bulk of psychiatric literature is simply heterosexual prejudice and male chauvinism raised to the level of an ideology. If the therapist is a man he will probably feel the traditional male resentment of a women who prefers her own sex to his. In any case a woman cannot learn to be strong and self-loving while deferring to a male expert.

Although other forms of oppression may have had more serious consequences for my life, the experiences which have disturbed me most have involved direct personal conflict. Earlier this year the parents of a girl I was living with threatened me with violence and attempted to blackmail me. In 1968 I went to a political demonstration with a woman friend and some of our fellow demonstrators decided, apparently on the basis of our appearance, that we were lesbians. They harassed us with a stream of insulting remaks of the 'Do you use a dildo?' variety, and when the demonstrators began to link hands the men around us refused to link hands with us. They treated another woman in the same way, then noticed that she was with a man and apologized to her.

Like any single woman who has to travel alone at night I am constantly aware of the danger of physical violence. And even at social gatherings men often react with violence to women who make it clear that they prefer each other's company to the company of men.

There are penalties for being a homosexual in our society and so homosexuals conceal their preferences in order to escape these penalties. But concealment, dishonesty and fear are the worst penalties of all. I used to go to great lengths to conceal my homosexuality. One of the reasons I went overseas when I did was that I felt that people were gossiping about me in Melbourne. I quarrelled with one of my closest friends because she had told someone I was a lesbian without getting my permission first.

The liberal argument that it is no concern of anyone else what people do in their bedrooms only perpetuates the torment of secrecy. First of all, you cannot do anything in your bedroom except masturbate, unless you have first gone out and found a sexual partner. Secondly, homosexuality is not simply a matter of contact between two sets of genitals, it involves two people who like or love each other, and therefore want to spend a large part of their time together, show affection in public, and so on. No one can lead a good life while putting most of her or his energy into fear and deception.

Female and Homosexual

Some of the experiences I have mentioned, for example, feelings of passivity, and difficulties with promotion and credit, will be familiar to heterosexual women. Other experiences, for example the suffering involved in keeping one's sexual preferences a secret, are shared by homosexual men. However, in my experience all these things have been woven together. A lesbian is not divided into two sections, a female section and a homosexual section. To put it another way, there is nothing essentially male about homosexuality, and being a woman does not mean being a heterosexual.

Social attitudes to homosexuality and to women are so bound together that it is impossible to separate them. The American Radicalesbians say, 'Lesbian is the word, the label, the condition that holds women in line . . . Lesbian is a label invented by the Man to throw at any woman who dares to be his equal, who dares to challenge his prerogatives (including that of all women as part of the exchange medium among men), who dares to assert the primacy of her own needs.'[5] Similarly, the man who steps out of line, who refuses to play the male role, is called a homosexual, a poofter, a pansy. At the same time male homosexuals are accused of being effeminate. Lesbians are said to be mannish but there is a subtle difference. Being a man is assumed to be a good thing, and the lesbian's trouble is that she is not successful, she is not a *real* man, she lacks a penis, the symbol of male power.

These accusations and sexual insults are heard every day in the street and the pub, and they are very significant. Behind the insults we find the assumptions which form the basis of our sexist society. Firstly, it is assumed that a man is superior to a woman, and a heterosexual to a homosexual; thus a lesbian is doubly inferior. Secondly, the sex act is seen as an act of aggression and mastery: it symbolizes all relationships of dominance and submission. Thus male homosexuality is seen as one man mastering another, with the loser being demoted to a woman. That is why many men have a deep dread of homosexual advances. In the case of lesbianism, however, two inferior beings actually seem to prefer each other. Some men find this very insulting and may attack the woman they think is playing a male role in an attempt to prove their superiority. Other men cannot take lesbianism seriously, they feel that women cannot really prefer each other, either they have been rejected by men, or they are just filling in time until a good man comes along. The law itself does not take lesbianism seriously; there are many crimes relating to male homosexuality, including the 'abominable crime' of buggery, but lesbians are usually prosecuted under the catch-all heading of 'offensive behaviour'.

The Future

How then do I see the future for myself and other lesbians? I have made it clear that I believe that our society is based on sexism. I think that more and more lesbians will come to realize that it is necessary to totally transform society. On the one hand this means coming out in the general community, publicly and proudly acknowledging that we are lesbians, and fighting discrimination against female and male homosexuals. On the other hand, it means turning inwards to build alternative institutions which are supportive and warm. It also means turning inward to eradicate sexism in our own minds and power games in our relationships with other people. It is easy to set these goals but hard to live by them. As Robin Morgan says,[6]

To learn to love one's woman-self
has been made to seem
both intolerable and difficult.
To learn to love another woman
in one's self is both, and also
worth it.

Notes

1. Radicalesbians, 'The Woman-Identified Woman', *Come Out!: Selections from the Radical Gay Liberation Newspaper*, Times Change Press, New York, 1970, p.50.
2. Susan Sontag, 'Notes on "Camp"', *Against Interpretation and Other Essays*, Dell, New York, 1966.
3. See Alfred C. Kinsey, et al., *Sexual Behavior in the Human Female*, W. B. Saunders, Philadelphia, 1953, pp.473–4.
Del Martin and Phyllis Lyon, *Lesbian/Woman*, Glide Publications, San Francisco, 1972, Chapter 5.
4. See Thomas Szasz, *The Manufacture of Madness*, Routledge and Kegan Paul, London, 1971.
5. Radicalesbians, pp.50–51.
6. Robin Morgan, 'Lesbian Poem', *Monster*, Random House, 1972.

LESBIANISM: A SELECT BIBLIOGRAPHY

General Books and Articles

Sidney Abbot and Barbara Love, 'Is Women's Liberation a Lesbian Plot?' in Vivian Gornick and Barbara K. Moran (eds), *Woman in Sexist Society*, Basic Books Inc., New York, 1971. *Sappho Was A Right-On Woman: A Liberated View of Lesbianism*, Stein & Day, New York, 1973.

A Boston Gay Collective, 'In Amerika They Call Us Dykes', in The Boston Women's Health Book Collective, *Our Bodies: Ourselves*, Simon & Schuster, New York, 1971.

Anonymous, 'Lesbian London', in Hunter Davies (ed.), *The New London Spy*, Corgi Books, London, 1967.

Anonymous, 'Lesbians' in Susan Kedgley and Sharyn Cederman (eds), *Sexist Society*, Alister Taylor, Wellington, 1972.

Anonymous, 'Sexuality and Reality', *Shrew* (London Women's Liberation Newspaper), vol. 5, no. 2, April 1973.

Ingrid Bengis, *Combat in the Erogenous Zone*, Wildwood House, London 1973.

Come Together: London Gay Liberation Newspaper, Lesbian issue, no. 7, January 1972.

Donald Webster Cory, *The Lesbian in America*, Tower Publications, New York, 1971.

Gene Damon, 'The Least of These: The Minority Whose Screams Haven't Yet Been Heard', in Robin Morgan (ed.), *Sisterhood is Powerful*, Vintage Books, New York, 1970.

Simone de Beauvoir, *The Second Sex*, Book 2, Part 4, Chapter 4, Jonathan Cape, London, 1953; Penguin, 1972.

Raymond de Becker, *The Other Face of Love*, Neville Spearman & Rodney Books, London, 1967; Sphere Books, London, 1969.

Farrago (Melbourne University), Gay Pride Week issue, 20th July 1973.

Jill Johnston, *Lesbian Nation*, Simon & Schuster, New York, 1973.

Alfred C. Kinsey, Wardell B. Pomeroy, Clyde E. Martin, Paul H. Gebhart et al., *Sexual Behaviour in the Human Female*, W. B. Saunders Co., Philadelphia & London, 1953.

John I. Kitsuse, 'Societal Reaction to Deviant Behaviour', in Earl Rubington and Martin S. Weinberg, *Deviance: The Interactionist Perspective*, Macmillan, New York, 1968.

Anne Koedt, 'Lesbianism and Feminism' and 'Loving Another Woman', *Notes from the Third Year*, P.O. Box AA, Old Chelsea Station, New York, N.Y. 10011, 1970.

Anne Koedt, 'The Myth of the Vaginal Orgasm', in Leslie B. Tanner (ed.), *Voices from Women's Liberation*, Signet, New American Library, New York, 1970. Also appears in The Radical Therapist Collective (ed.) *The Radical Therapist*, Ballantine Books, New York, 1973.

Lesbians Speak Out and *Lesbians Speak Out II*, Free Women's Press, 1018 Valencia Street, California, 94116, 1971 and 1972.

Del Martin and Phyllis Lyon, *Lesbian/Woman*, Glide Publications, San Francisco, 1972.

Melbourne Feminist Collection I, 50 Little La Trobe Street, Melbourne, July 1973.

Robin Morgan, 'Lesbianism and Feminism: Synonyms or Contradictions?', *Amazon Quarterly*, vol. 1, issue 3, May 1973, 554 Valle Vista, Oakland, California, 94610.

Rabelais (La Trobe University student newspaper), Gay Pride Week issue, 12th September 1973.

Radicalesbians, 'Woman-Identified Woman', *Come Out! Selections from the Radical Gay Liberation Newspaper*, Times Change Press, New York, 1970.

Nanette Rainone, Martha Shelley and Lois Hart, 'Lesbians Are Sisters', Leslie B. Tanner (ed.), *Voices from Women's Liberation*, Signet, New American Library, New York, 1970.

Refractory Girl, Lesbian issue, Summer 1974, 25 Alberta Street, Sydney, 2000.

Martha Shelley, 'Lesbianism', The Radical Therapist Collective (ed.), *The Radical Therapist*, Ballantine Books, New York, 1973.

Martha Shelley, 'Notes of a Radicalesbian', in Robin Morgan (ed.), *Sisterhood is Powerful*, Vintage Books, New York, 1970.

Valerie Solanas, *SCUM Manifesto*, Olympia Press, New York, 1970, Olympia Press, London, 1971.

Marty Stephen, 'Bitch: Summer's Not Forever', in *Come Out! Selections from the Radical Gay Liberation Newspaper*, Times Change Press, New York, 1970.

Tharunka (Sydney University student newspaper), Gay Pride Week issue, 8 to 16 September, 1973.

The *Digger* (Melbourne monthly newspaper), Gay Pride Week issue, no. 22, 8 September to 6 October 1973.

Kay Tobin and Randy Wicker, 'Phyllis Lyon and Del Martin', 'Barbara Gittings', 'Ruth Simpson' in *The Gay Crusaders*, Paperback Library, New York, 1972.

Fiction and Literary History

Vera Mary Brittain, *Radclyffe Hall: A Case of Obscenity?* Femina Press, London, 1968.

Rita Mae Brown, *The Hand That Cradles the Rock*, (Poetry), New York University Press, New York, 1971.

Colette, *The Pure and the Impure*, Secker & Warburg, London, 1968; Penguin Books, 1971.

Cyril Connolly, *The Rock Pool*, Penguin, 1963.

Maureen Duffy, *The Microcosm*, Panther, London, 1967.

Lillian Hellman, 'The Children's Hour', *Collected Plays*, Little, Brown and Co., Boston and Toronto, 1972.

Louise King, *The Day We Were Mostly Butterflies*, Michael Joseph, London, 1964.

Louise King, *The Velocipede Handicap*, Michael Joseph, London, 1965.

Violette Le Duc, *Therese and Isabelle*, Farrar, Straus and Giroux, New York, 1967.

K. A. McKenzie, *Edith Simcox and George Eliot*, Oxford University Press, London, 1961.

Sappho, *Sappho: A New Translation*, translated by Mary Barnard, University of California Press, Berkeley, 1958.

Australian Periodicals Which Often Print Articles by and about Lesbians

Boiled Sweets, Dr Duncan Memorial Bookshop, P.O. Box 12 North Adelaide.

Camp Ink: The Journal of the Campaign Against Moral Persecution, Box 5074, GPO, Sydney, 2001.

Mejane, 25 Alberta Street, Sydney, 2000.

Melbourne Gay Liberation Newsletter, Melbourne University Union Box 85, Melbourne University, Parkville, Victoria, 3052.

Melbourne Women's Liberation Newsletter, 50 Little La Trobe Street, Melbourne.

Refractory Girl, 25 Alberta Street, Sydney, 2000.

Overseas Periodicals

Amazon Quarterly, 554 Valle Vista, Oakland, California, 94610.

The Lesbian Tide, 373 N. Western, Room 202, Los Angeles, California, 90004.

Women: A Journal of Liberation, 155 W. 15th Street, New York, N.Y. 10011.

Note

This bibliography was selected on the basis of content and availability. I have omitted some well-known works like Charlotte Wolff's *Love Between Women* and Bryan Magee's *One in Twenty* because they seemed to me to be on the whole misinformed or prejudiced. I had to omit other titles which sounded promising because they were not available to me.

Twenty

Life as a Prostitute*

The Social Context: Views Concerning Prostitution

Rarely has the prostitute been understood and studied from a viewpoint which stresses her role as primarily that of a woman – an individual – capable of choosing, deciding and planning courses of action in an attempt to attain her independence, happiness and self-fulfilment.† This is due to the fact that not only has a great deal of the written work been formulated from

* This chapter is concerned with those women in society who illegally sell the rights of their body to a man. It is not concerned with legal prostitution, namely the legalized right of every husband to sexually abuse his wife (see Chapter 5). *Editorial note*

† To reiterate what was discussed in the introduction to this section, viewing prostitution entirely through the prostitute's eyes fails to utilize the insight gained from a knowledge of the way socialization manipulates people into supporting their own exploitation and oppression (see also the introduction to Part 3, 'The Acquisition of Sex Roles'). The present chapter supports prostitution as a way of life without mentioning the exploitation of women. It does not start to consider the way in which the buying and selling of the female body devalues and degrades the people regarded simply as sex objects for the provision of a commodity – sex. The notion current in our society is that *men* need their sex, not that they need people, so they get it by exploiting women; by pushing them into the dark corners of society to use them but condemn them, and even then not as people but as abstractions of themselves, as sex objects. It does not matter who they are, simply that they are available and happy so that sex remains an assured commodity (see Chapter 26 for an alternative conception of social reality to that presented in this chapter). The advantage of this chapter is that it does present the views of women who have been thoroughly socialized to accept their oppressed position in society. *Editorial note.*

a male viewpoint, but also a lot of the material on this subject treats the prostitute as a deviant, as a degenerate with a deranged mind. The widespread use of 'negative' stereotyped images in reference to the label 'prostitute' indicates an author's value orientation. It also, however, leads him to mystify and obscure what a more accurate or realistic picture of a woman labelled a prostitute would be, if the prostitute's own viewpoint were included. This paper will therefore attempt to illustrate the inadequacies and biases of many of the traditional conceptions of prostitutes, by presenting the prostitutes' viewpoints on a wide range of topics covering their occupation and moral code.

The negative status of the term prostitute with its concomitant value bias is manifest in many areas of society, in particular in academia and in the law and its enforcement.

In the academic sphere, the social sciences have generally treated the topic of prostitution as a 'social problem'. In psychology, for instance, the prostitute is often treated as the female form of deviance which is said to be caused by faulty personality development stemming back to early childhood experiences. That is to say, the prostitute is said to have a 'sick personality', and consequently to be in need of 'treatment'. Therefore, due to the inherent assumptions as to what constitutes a social problem, as well as the preconceptions governing what is to be considered aberrant behaviour, research in psychology, psychopathology, psychoanalysis and in sociology, is inadequate for the pursuit of an understanding of the prostitute's experience of prostitution.*[1]

In Australia prostitution is officially condemned, with legislation in every state prohibiting soliciting on the part of the

* Also, sociologists and others have failed to examine the social context of prostitution, the socialization and oppression of women which leads some to consider prostitution a viable way of life. The fact that the author of this chapter has failed to realize this aspect is due not only to his socialization as a male but also to the inadequacies of his phenomenological approach which sees all behaviour as relative in moral terms and therefore supports the notion of 'equal but different' which has been the main ideological support for discriminatory behaviour. Exploitative *relations* are ignored. *Editorial note*

woman and the keeping of brothels. While this legislation is primarily geared to keeping prostitution hidden from public view, thus removing it from the experience of those to whom it may cause offence,* prostitutes are to be found both on the streets and clandestinally through some nightclubs, hotels, health studios, photographic and model agencies, not to mention the availability of call-girls to those 'in the know'.[2]

Official condemnation is further evident at the administrative or police level. For example, Detective-Sergeant Bill Walters (former chief of the Victorian vice squad) was reported to have said that 'One of the biggest bogies the squad has to face is that a lot of people think we are censors. We're not. The law is there . . . made by the representatives of the people. And we carry it out. The role of the vice squad is to act as professional evidence gatherers.'[3] And also, '. . . we are not the custodians of private morals . . .'[4] In relation to the *actual operations* of the squad, Detective-Sergeant Walters gave us further information when he stated that '. . . normally these women (prostitutes) have one or two regular clients and can't see that they are doing anything wrong. *We try to tell them that it is wrong morally*, but they argue that they need the money.' (my italics)[5] The administrative application of existing legislation can therefore be seen as an exercise in the maintenance *and* the active endorsement of a particular set of morals or values. Therefore the police action *can* be seen as a form of censorship.†

The foregoing accounts indicate that prostitution is generally

* Rather than prohibiting the sexual exploitation of women for money. *Editorial note*

† They are however quite prepared to go along with a double form of morality (see below). The police appear to regard prostitution as a necessary evil to be controlled. They do not condemn it outright for they are the guardians of a system in which women are required to make their bodies available for the satisfaction of men on demand. When notions of legalizing prostitution arise the main rationales are that men need their sex and that venereal disease might be better controlled by registering the prostitutes, by registering the women. There is no thought of registering their users. The identity of the men remains secret. *Editorial note*

seen as a deviant activity in the Australian community. However, merely stating that a certain type of behaviour is labelled deviant in a society, does not necessarily indicate how those persons labelled deviants define their conduct. Thus in order to illustrate the existence of differing sets of values or the politics of the situation, the viewpoints of the so-called deviants need to be examined. The next section will outline the ways in which some prostitutes view their world.

Prostitutes' Views of Prostitution[6]

Why prostitution exists

Prostitution exists because there's mugs [clients] willing to pay money for it, and girls willing to take it. It's been going on for years and years.

Why become a prostitute

To get some money. I realized I was giving it away free on ships and that, so I thought I may as well get some money for it.

Going on the batter [becoming a prostitute] then, made me more independent. I didn't go on it because I wanted to do what the others [prostitute friends] were doing. That's not what prompted me to go on the batter, it was the fact that I needed money. For some reason I could survive in Sydney without hardly any money. You can survive without being on the batter, without even working. But in Melbourne it's harder. It was even easier here before, but that was because there were lots of ships here. And then, if we were hungry we'd just hitchhike down to the ships and go on there for dinner and they'd give us fags and that sort of stuff. And then we were living down Dalgety Street and it didn't matter if we paid our rent or not there. In Sydney it was pretty much the same. But these days, when there's not many ships coming around, you have to do something to earn a crust.

We're basically lazy, you see. When you're on the batter you've got no strict hours or anything. You don't have to work if you don't want to. It's a reason for not getting a nine-to-five job, or anything like that. This way you've got the comforts and things money will buy without having to go out and earn it . . . It's easier than getting a job and worrying about bosses, and doing work you don't like. So, going on the batter was a good way of getting money. If we have to go shopping or something, we just sort of think, 'Oh well, we'll go out and work and get about twenty dollars each to spend.' That's all we do.

Becoming a prostitute

When I was living with my parents, you would hear it from other girls that there are girls that go with men for money. I used to think I could never do it.

Then, before I was going on ships, when I was knocking around the Cross and that, there was this girl there that did it [prostitution] every now and then. She didn't do it full time, but when she needed money she would go out and do some jobs somewhere. I used to think, I wish that I could fucking do it.

When I came to Melbourne and found that I needed the money, I thought that I'd go on the batter to get some. Sylvia [a middle-aged pro] said she'd show me what to do and where to go. There was really nothing to learn – anyone can do it. I mean, there's nothing you do really, just lie there. You really only need moral support, that's all! Though I did ask if the mugs put the french letters on themselves or if I had to do it, and stuff like that. Sylvia also told me that when you're getting a mug, you don't put on any airs. You just ask them if they want a girl, and if they say 'yeah' you tell them the price and everything, and that's it. You don't have to know much – it just comes natural.

Prostitution as an occupation

Going on the batter is just a job, nothing more! You don't have to get involved in your normal job. No, I don't get involved in it at all; you don't sort of sit down and work out new tactics, or study it or anything.

Alternative employment to prostitution

We've thought about it a couple of times, like when we've had a bad run or something, well then we thought about getting a part-time job. But you know quite well, even when you say it, that you won't do anything about it.

As far as other good paying jobs go, there's only things like dirty photographs around, isn't there.

Going on the batter is the best [money-wise] we can do. I can't see or think of the day we won't be on the batter. Because every time you got no money you just realize how easy it is to get some. Actually, that's the only thing wrong with it, you know. I reckon once you do it you realize how easy the money is, and then you never sort of give it up.

The effect of prostitution

I was pretty naive when I went to Tech. Just coming down from the country and all; meeting people, city people, that's when I changed. I left Tech. and found a place of my own to stay. Then I started knocking around with all these other kids that didn't work and all they did was smoke grass and that. I got a job as a salesgirl, but I threw that in. It was only a couple of months after that that I began going on ships. And then my life really broadened! Going on the batter wasn't much of a change – it was just sort of a decision that was made, that's all. Before I made the decision though, I thought for years and years that I couldn't do it. Now that I am on the batter though, I'm more independent, you know, better pay, more freedom. If anything has changed it's our attitudes to men, but to the better. You appreciate a good man now, after seeing all them useless bastards. I'd hate to be married to any of them, relying on them for a fuck.

'Visibility' as a prostitute

The majority of people we know now, know we're on the batter and everything. But they don't say anything. You don't get people standing in corners and pointing at you. We haven't lost any friends because we went on the batter. There are a couple of guys though, 'Tom Cat' and Allen, who think that when we go with a mug it's a real screw sorter. John and Mick though, are all right. They know quite well that we don't class it [intercourse with 'mugs'] as a fuck or anything. It's just a job, isn't it? We don't get any pleasure out of it. The only pleasure we get out of it is spending the money.

Their first arrest

I thought, 'Oh well, it's finally come'. You know, just sort of resigned myself to it. I knew I was going to go [get arrested]. Because we talk about it all the time. The other girls [those who have had previous encounters with police] tell you what to say and what to do. We didn't even remember, we didn't even think what people had told us to say. We admitted straight out that we were on the batter and everything. We didn't even lie. It was like a matter of course for them and we thought there was no point in telling lies; they were fucking great to us.

The prostitute as a 'marked' person

I reckon the cops know us now, but they'll give us a good run. Because of the attitudes they took and the way they treated us, I don't reckon we'll have any trouble with them. You see, I'm beginning to pay my tax!

I was embarrassed though, standing there with all those young cops, I felt a real cunt. Especially when they pulled a couple of french letters out of my purse.

Anyway, the cops don't make you stop going on the batter or anything. If they wanted to make you stop it, they'd give you all kinds of big lectures. But they don't bother with things like that. Like, when we said to them 'Do you pick up the mugs too?' They said, 'Oh no, if we picked them up you girls wouldn't have any money, would you?' It's just a matter of course. Anyway, it's like Jenny says, 'It's like paying tax.'

Leading a 'double life'

I don't get that feeling, because we never make a secret of being on the batter. Sometimes, though, when you're walking down the pub to do a bit of drinking, well cars come up and guys pester you for a crack; then you wonder a bit, but that's all.

Losing your 'good name'

I don't think I've lost my good name. Because the only people we really have a reputation with are seamen. The majority of them seemed quite surprised when we told them we've been on the batter. They just sort of laugh and everything, they just don't care.

Prostitution as a criminal activity

I don't think of myself as a criminal. But in the eyes of the law I am. But then, even in the eyes of the law [the police] they don't think so. Because when those cops picked us up, I said to one of them something about, 'Oh well, if it wasn't for people like us you wouldn't have a job.' And they said, 'Oh, there's a lot worse than you, my dear.'

And it's not as if we're taking the mugs for their money, because they're all prepared to pay for it. It's not as if we're taking them home and chatting them up or something, and then rolling them [stealing their money].

Opinions on the existing law and the issue of legalization

You can't prevent prostitution! As it is there's a law against it, but you've still got it going on, haven't you. Unless they gave you a real stiff gaol sentence or something, then it wouldn't be worth it. Like I mean, you might work for a few months and get yourself in a pretty good position and then go into gaol and lose it all. They would have to be real heavy fines as well, like two to three hundred dollars, depending on how many times you got pinched. In that case, it wouldn't be worth it for the time we work. We'd just be working for about two weeks to get the fine!

If prostitution was made legal, then I wouldn't crack it. I wouldn't get enough money! You'd probably only get ten dollars more than a normal job. It'd be like being a waitress or something, but you'd probably work twice as hard as you do now. It would only be different because it would be legal then.

I wouldn't mind if they change the present law so that prostitution wouldn't be illegal. I mean, if it [the present working situation] stayed as it is now when it was legalized it wouldn't be so bad. But then you'd still have to pay tax.

But they wouldn't change the law. Because if they legalized it, they would still have to have some control over the money.

Anyway, I reckon that even if they did legalize it, there would still be a lot of people working on the sly. I mean, that wouldn't probably be legal, would it? There'd be a whole lot of people working on the streets – they'd be packed!

Mugs are mugs

I reckon the mugs have got to pay high prices for what they really get. I mean, they've got to work all day to earn ten dollars and then they spend it like that – for a measly five minutes!

The wogs reckon they get their money's worth, but they're real dumb. I don't think any of them have got any intelligence. All the little wogs and things, they're just hot-blooded!

A lot of Aussies don't get their money's worth. Because some of them want all sorts of queer things for their ten dollars, but we don't give it to them, not for that at any rate. Some of them want some real queer things, but with them you just keep the door open in case you get into trouble. There was one mug who wanted to be dominated, you know, he wanted to be told what to do and if he didn't we had to punish him. He paid well, we got forty dollars a go out of him.

Wogs are about the safest of the lot, because all they want is a fuck. If they don't want to use a french letter though, you tell them to fuck off. Then they drive round the block a few times and can't find anyone so they come back to you and say they'll use a french letter. You see, they're pretty desperate! So next week when they're round again they know what's expected.

You get different types of mugs: big dicks/little dicks; fatherly types; big-lovers – they're the worst. They really give me the shits. You don't enjoy it anyway, and they just make it worse. They try to kiss you and think they're going to make you love them. You get some big Cassanovas and they think they're to give *you* pleasure and everything! A lot of them say, 'Are you ready to come [have an orgasm]?' And you say, 'Oh yeah, yeah!' – Just to keep them happy. The good mugs are the ones who are quick and don't try to mess about. Then there are some who try and get away without paying – they're real cunts!

Prostitution and morality

I don't worry about those people that say prostitution is immoral – it doesn't really concern me. I suppose some people do worry about it though. It depends on the way they were brought up. I thought it was pretty immoral when I was younger. But I've never condemned anyone for doing it. I don't reckon it's immoral anymore.

To people with higher moral standards it would seem immoral, but to people like us who haven't the same values it isn't. The kind of people we hang round with also have morals; ours are a bit different, that's all. But I suppose in the eyes of other people they wouldn't call them moral . . . I don't mind being called immoral. I'd rather be immoral anyway!

When I go out with other people, I don't try to put on any false front. Everyone knows you're a ship-mole and that you're on the batter, who cares! And I think that the majority of people appreciate you better if you are straightforward about it . . .

I reckon that prostitution is something completely alien to the average female. It's something that they would never have really associated with. But we're not different, we're just the same as everyone else. At least to an extent. Because I think that everybody thinks themselves different to everyone else. I mean, you may think some people as being good or bad, but you should still respect them because we're all human beings.

Editorial postscript

In a society which relies on the sexual dominance of women by men and where the basic social unit, the family, pivots on an ideal of female chastity (see Chapter 14), the buying and selling of sexual access to the female body must be contained and condemned. Nor in a society where men are socialized to 'need their sex' do they always want to have to 'pay' for it. Therefore women are socialized to regard it as their duty to provide men with their sex, to value their roles as wife and mother as sacred. It is thus not surprising that those most condemning of prostitution are women who see sexuality for its own sake as threatening the roles of wife and mother. But as Lily Gair Wilkinson said:

Lady! What does it mean, this 'lady'? . . . Lady! A slave and bondswoman! She has sold her woman's body for costly accessories and a soft living. She has sold herself into married prostitution. The Christian religion has given to the sale the odour of sanctity, and at the priest's bidding she has promised to love, honour and obey the man who purchased her body in the marriage market . . . These . . . are three types of women in bondage – the lady sold in marriage, the working woman, and the prostitute. The bondage of these three types is different in kind, but the manner of entering bondage is the same in all three cases. All these women enter bondage by selling their bodies; selling them for man's pleasure or selling them for the profit of an employer, but always by selling that sacred thing, a woman's body.[7]

Notes

1. The following list is an example of the kind of material being referred to; there are many other references which take the basic propositions in the following articles as a point of orientation.

K. Abraham, *Selected Papers on Psycho-Analysis*, Hogarth Press, London, 1927.

F. S. Caprio, *Female Homosexuality*, Citadel, New York, 1954.

M. Choisy, *Psychoanalysis of the Prostitute*, Philosophical Library, New York, 1961.

E. Glover, *The Psychopathology of Prostitution*, Institute for the Study and Treatment of Delinquency, London, 1945.

L. Goiten, 'The Potential Prostitute', *Journal of Criminal Psychopathology*, vol. 3, 1942, pp.359–367.

H. Greenwald, *The Call Girl: A Social and Psychoanalytic Study*, Ballantine, New York, 1958.

G. J. Kneeland, *Commercialized Prostitution in New York City*, Patterson Smith, New Jersey, (1913), 1969.

2. P. R. Wilson, and D. Chappell, 'Prostitution in Australia', *Australian Journal of Social Issues*, no. 2, vol. 4, July 1969, p.71. Although prostitution is officially condemned in Australia, it does not necessarily imply that this is also an accurate reflection of Australians' opinions on the subject. Indeed, Wilson and Chappell's study indicates that there is a wide division of opinion on the issue of the legalization of prostitution: 46 per cent of the sample agreed that 'prostitution should not be legal under any circumstances', but a further 45 per cent disagreed with the statement. (Ibid. pp.67–8).

3. The *Herald*, Melbourne, 30 September 1969.
4. The *Herald*, Melbourne, 20 November 1969.
5. The *Age*, Melbourne, 21 November 1969.
6. This needs to be read with a number of features in mind – first, the account has been written and presented as though it were the views expressed by only one girl, when in fact it is a composite of about six girls' views. There is insufficient space to allow for an adequate exposition of a number of individual points of view, and it is easier to read the statements of 'one' person than to read the disjointed statements of many people. No attempt is made to generalize about the views of prostitutes at large. This account is based upon personal encounters with a particular type of prostitute – 'ship-moles'. It is representative of a group of twelve girls aged from their late teens to their mid-twenties whom I came to know over a period of a year (1972–1973). Thirdly, a lot of this material is based upon hand-written notes made after contacts, as well as tape recorded interviews collected originally for a Ph.D. thesis.
7. Lily Gair Wilkinson, 'Woman's Freedom' in *Women in Rebellion – 1900, Two Views on Class Socialism and Liberation*, Square One Pamphlet no. 6, I.L.P. Square One Publications, Leeds, 1973, pp.16 and 19.

PART FIVE

The Politics of Change

The Politics of Change

We have to make ourselves not as a projected abstract ideal, but out of the shapes of here and now. The barriers which confront us are real, not merely the conjurings of our imagination. We cannot bypass the long making of a new society simply by inventing a liberated female culture, intact out of time and space, unaffected by the social relations which exist around us. The movement between conception and action, culture and social revolution, is partial, laboured, and painfully slow. But it is the only way we can heave ourselves into the future.

Sheila Rowbotham, *Woman's Consciousness, Man's World**

The previous section, 'Women labelled as "Deviants"', looked at the problem of the *individual* women who, because they do not accept the white males' definition of their role, are ostracized by the rest of society and hence isolated. But what of those who, while deviant in the eyes of the wider society, rejecting some or all of society's norms, are not isolated but are organizing to fight for change. Recently there has been a resurgence of political groups of women who have again realized the need to critically examine the expected role of women in Australian society.[1] These movements vary greatly in aims, ideology, size and membership. They represent an enormously widespread range of views on the way in which social change might be achieved. The chapters in this section were chosen because of these differences but also to demonstrate that despite these differences, all are motivated by a realization of the oppressed position of women in our society and thus all have basically the same ends in view: their identity in their own right; the right to decide and define for themselves; the right to be autonomous, responsible individuals.

* Penguin Books, 1973, pp.xii–xiii.

Many people claim that our century has been one of far-reaching and rapid social change, but this change has been restricted to particular areas of social life. The new technology which has given us atomic power and *men* on the moon; the motor car, the supermarket, the jumbo jet and the automatic washing machine; has changed the *way* people do things but it has not changed the *relations* between the sexes. Behaviour is still motivated by traditional male and female stereotypes. There may be more women in a wider range of occupations but women continue to be discriminated against *as women.* Chapter 21 examines 'the Sex-Role Ideology' by which our society continues to classify tasks and behaviour according to sex rather than to individuals irrespective of sex.

It is this stagnation in the quality of relations between the sexes amidst an atmosphere of change which has prompted women to ask for, demand, or hope for change, and to organize to promote such change. Some have sought change through the reform of specific 'key' laws. Chapter 22 is a case study of the Abortion Law Reform Association of South Australia (ALRASA), an organization which successfully campaigned for changes in one specific law. Others sought wide-ranging change through the existing political system, organizing as a political lobby. This reform movement, the Women's Electoral Lobby, is critically examined in Chapter 23, presenting arguments for and against its viability as an agent for real change. The chapter also considers a movement, the Women's Liberation Movement, which shuns traditional 'democratic' political action, seeking eventual widespread rebellion by raising the consciousness of women to the way they are oppressed in their relationships with men.

For some women, as Chapter 24 makes clear, the conventional world is to be shunned, not reformed, and so they seek a new life in the 'counter culture'. For others there is no counter culture to escape into, no social life they can slot into, and so they have grouped together to search for a way to change society so that they will be accepted as whole people. They formulate and present a Utopian vision in the hope that it will, as an end to aim for, spark off change. Such is the case with the Melbourne

Gay Women's Group who outline their aims in Chapter 25. Chapter 26 looks not to reform, to the counter culture or to Utopias for change, but rather stresses the need for constant revolutionary action as the only possible way to eradicate the severe sexual oppression which permeates Australian society.

But these are not the only movements towards liberation. The establishment of Women's Studies courses in universities and the establishment of Women's Medical Centres in Sydney and Melbourne are also movements which aim to promote the interests of women by challenging the male biases which have dominated the perspectives adopted by academics and doctors respectively. A growing consciousness of the oppression of women coupled with the willingness of more and more women to stand out against the oppressive norms of society is a constant and growing encouragement for the establishment of women's movements in every sphere of social life, for at the moment sexism is all-pervasive.

Notes

1. For an account of early feminist activity in Australia see V. Goldstein, *Woman Suffrage in Australia*, pamphlet held by the British Museum. Microfilm held by Monash University Library.

Twenty-One
Political Socialization and Women in Australia

Sex-Role Ideology

Throughout Australia's short history it has always remained a mystery why so few women succeed in, or even participate in politics or public life, especially when one considers the opportunities which seem to be available and a national heritage which appears to value freedom of speech and equality of opportunity above all. Therefore it has been customary for individuals to either ignore the question as a non-issue, or to propose simplistic, trite explanations based on prejudice and ignorance – 'A woman's place is in the home'; 'Politics is a man's game'; 'Women are not capable of taking the responsibility, they need men to make the decisions for them!'

However, since the emergence of a highly diverse, rapidly expanding women's movement in Australia in the late 1960s and 1970s, the whole issue of women's role in society has come to be reconsidered and discussed more fully, both within the movement and in popular debate. The core of the debate has been a discussion of the influence of sex-role socialization in modern society, and the analysis of our social structure and culture from a feminist point of view has led to an understanding of the Sex-Role Ideology, a pervasive yet powerful set of beliefs innate in our cultural heritage which has a decisive impact on every aspect of Australian life.

Within the context of the Sex-Role Ideology it is assumed that it is not only right and proper but biologically natural and historically valid that individuals should be primarily classified according to their sex, that biological sex and socially-prescribed gender are contiguous, and that the two sexes have innately different qualities, attitudes and potentialities.

Quite clearly this ideology has both a rational and an emotional component, being based as much on prejudice, mystification and historical tradition as on knowledge and understanding; and it exhibits a remarkable capacity to survive despite changed social conditions and new insights which challenge its basic assumptions.

In her book *Sex, Gender and Society* Ann Oakley distinguishes carefully between *sex* ... 'a word that refers to the biological differences between male and female (i.e. the visible difference in genitalia, the related difference in procreative function)' and *gender* ... 'a matter of culture which refers to the social classification into masculine and feminine', noting that confusion of meaning between the two terms has impaired our understanding about the nature and behaviour of women and men.[1] However, the Sex-Role Ideology specifically links the two aspects together in its key belief that each sex has a separate and different gender, that is, that certain qualities, attributes and types of behaviour are social manifestations of innate male characteristics and therefore designated masculine, while other qualities, attributes and modes of behaviour are seen as innately female and thus designated feminine.

In Australian society the Sex-Role Ideology characterizes the male stereotype as superior to the female stereotype. The masculinity stereotype describes the ideal male as one who is decisive, rugged, virile, strong, unemotional, responsible, ambitious and aggressively self-confident. The femininity stereotype is somewhat more complex, involving the contradictory images of (i) eternal mother earth, that is, emphasizing the qualities of maternalism, nurturance, supportiveness, purity and solidity, and (ii) woman as sex-object, that is, emphasizing the qualities of sexiness, glamour, dependence, passivity, inconsistency and irresponsibility. However, these two 'feminine' images are linked by the underlying assumption of the femininity stereotype that women are basically the weaker, less intelligent, less self-sufficient sex in contrast to the superior male sex.

This rather arbitrary differentiation between the sexes in terms of male and female stereotypes is a convenient but often misleading form of labelling on which to base routinized social interaction. Individuals of both sexes are more often evaluated on the basis of their sex rather than any other characteristic, and this sexist evaluation of human behaviour is expressed in social structures and predominant social values in such a way that stereotypical behaviour is reinforced. Members of either sex tend to act, think and feel in accordance with their assigned stereotype, and the two sexes receive differential treatment in childhood and adulthood, having access to a very different set of opportunities based on the behaviour, qualities and lifestyle thought natural or appropriate to each.

It should be noted that what is believed to be natural for each sex is not universal, but varies between cultures. It can validly be concluded that the ramifications of the Sex-Role Ideology are culturally relative, and that the *cultural mandate* for each sex in a particular society plays a crucial role in creating and maintaining the characteristic, and supposedly natural, inequalities and differences between men and women, by providing unequal opportunities and experiences and imposing structural and normative constraints on conflict or change.

The beliefs of the Sex-Role Ideology have a significant effect on both the nature of Australian society and the participatory role of women in that society. Males and females in Australia are generally channelled into two different streams throughout their lives, not only by the different expectations society has of each but also because of the separate social, educational and occupational experiences available to each sex.

The Australian child may attend a mixed school rather than one of the popular single-sex schools, but even there the school routines and the social choices of the children tend to separate along sex lines, and to be reinforced by the attitudes of the teachers and the administration. In adolescence the pattern is repeated, sex differentiation being typical of the social life of adolescents as well as their educational experiences. At this stage language and sexual behaviour, sports, intellectual and cultural pursuits, and activities in clubs and groups generally have a sex-role connotation attached to them.

Thus the feminine activities expected of adolescent girls include domestic handicrafts, cultural activities, passive timid sexuality, refined language, and organized activities in girls' clubs or groups centering on religion, community service, social or domestic skills or hobbies, or being spectators of masculine activities. By comparison the types of activities expected of adolescent boys include intellectual pursuits, sporting prowess (or at least enthusiastic participation), free language, aggressive or exploratory sexual behaviour, and a lesser amount of organized activity in groups, focusing mainly on sport and male social activities.

In late adolescence and throughout adulthood the individual is faced with an unfortunately limited social environment in which opportunities for natural interaction between the sexes are minimal, especially since the development of modern Western society has precipitated the loss of many of the family home's social functions. Consequently, the pattern of Australian social life tends to reinforce social distance between the sexes, thus perpetuating the traditional sexist types of interaction between men and women.

The influence of sexist belief is even more apparent in a highly specialized division of labour in Australian society which clearly differentiates between the activities and functions considered acceptable or natural for each sex. Characteristically, the female stereotype identifies the domestic realm as the province of the female, and emphasizes the 'feminine' nature of the processes of nurturance, reproduction, social production, socialization, domestic maintenance and domestic consumerism. The male stereotype specifies the world of work, politics and public affairs as the male domain, which typically involves the processes of management and control, economic production and distribution, financial exchange and the acquisition of material goods and services for the home which are large scale, expensive, prestigious or designed primarily for male use.

It follows logically that maintenance of the family and responsibility for the individual's physical and emotional well-being is regarded as a female task, one for which women by their natural and/or socialized qualities are well suited. Similarly, control and development of the political and economic system are regarded as male tasks, men being most successful in and suitable for this role by virtue of their natural and/or socialized male qualities. Consequently, any activity or contribution by the male inside the home or the female outside it tends to be evaluated as less important or deviant – although the influence of male dominance is evident in that it is more legitimate and becoming more acceptable for the male to play a larger part in the domestic realm than it is for the female to enter the world outside on an equal basis.

Within the work force the sexual division of labour is manifested in clearly differentiated male and female jobs, rates of pay, working conditions and status. The entry of women into the work force was bound to challenge both the prescribed male and female sex roles in Australian society, and the prescribed economic roles of male producers and female consumers. However, there has been some adjustment in the economy to meet this challenge, with women being accepted into areas that are in accord with the lower status, lesser importance, 'feminine' qualities and service orientation of the female stereotype. Clearly, changes in economic regulations and employer policies are not sufficient to overcome the entrenched values of the Sex-Role Ideology which support the unequal status of 'male' and 'female' and the belief that woman's place is rightly in the home.

When we consider the political arena it is again evident that the assumptions and beliefs of the Sex-Role Ideology have had a decisive impact, in this case precluding most women from taking an effective or extensive part in public political activity.

The interaction between the values of the Sex-Role Ideology and the values of the economic system produce a situation where status and role articulation and the exercise of power are defined as legitimate for men whereas they are defined as illegitimate for women, for they conflict with woman's primary duty to home and family.

It is taken for granted that there is, or should be, a division between the female private world and the male public world, and that it is not only traditional and functional, but also natural, that men should legitimately exercise power and influence in the public sphere while women should confine the exercise of power or influence to the domestic sphere. Since the domestic unit has limited social and economic resources, a division is effectively created and maintained by which one sex is predominantly powerful and the other is predominantly powerless – the rulers and the ruled. This process can be seen to operate within every socio-economic strata, whether it is reinforced deliberately or unconsciously. It is reminiscent of the division in ancient thought between the 'polis' and the 'household' – between the active males in the free and equal public world and the women and slaves in the sheltered, limited, private world of the household.

In the modern context the isolated existence of the majority of women, involving invisibility, limited scope and domesticity, contributes to their lower status and ineffectiveness in the male world of politics. As long as women in general continue to avoid public disclosure or statement of their existence they can be regarded as not existing or not fully human,[2] and therefore not fully capable of taking an equal part of playing an important role in the public realm of work and politics.

The public acceptance of the idealized dichotomy between masculinity and femininity in Australia is reinforced just as much by unimaginative, stereotyped thinking as it is by the weight of tradition and male-oriented history; for few examples are provided of successful yet ordinary women while undue emphasis is given to the power and achievement of ordinary men. Thus at the public level the belief in separate and different masculine and feminine qualities has not been challenged, even though evidence exists in Australian society of sufficiently varied types of men and women to disprove the generalized validity of such a belief.

Within this context it is clear that the colloquialism 'politics is a man's game' really means that politics, as it has been envisaged by many political scientists and writers and by the majority of the general public, is in fact a construct which centres on and expresses both the masculine stereotype and the belief in the public realm as man's realm. By contrast, and by definition, women's participation is regarded as minimal or ineffective. The masculine mode of participation and success is so much taken for granted in Australian politics that those who do not participate or succeed in this way are automatically labelled as failures or described as lacking the necessary qualities and aptitudes.

Thus the normative framework of the Sex-Role Ideology in Australian society constrains both sexes to remain within the confines of their cultural mandates, male participation in politics, as in work, being facilitated by existing structures, opportunities and attitudes, while female participation is generally not assisted and often vigorously opposed or resisted. In the area of politics, as in work and recreation, we can see that the Sex-Role Ideology places many women in a classic double-bind – they are damned if they do, and damned if they don't! If a woman exhibits 'feminine' qualities, as she is expected to do, she is assumed to be less capable and responsible than a man; but if she exhibits 'masculine' qualities, or refuses to accept the limitations of the femininity stereotypè she is generally regarded as deviant by both men and women. As such deviance is socially unacceptable, the woman is subjected to strong normative sanctions, and is faced with the choice of conformity and acceptance, which means remaining powerless politically by remaining a woman in a man's world, or non-conformity and non-acceptance, which leads to lack of support for active female participation in politics.

Perhaps the most significant consequence of this control process is that it perpetuates a male monopoly over membership and positions of influence in politics and most areas of community affairs, and prevents most women from becoming active participants. To overcome the entrenched structural and normative constraints would require exceptional personal ability and strength of character, or commitment to a cause, which would make it worthwhile to confront the difficulties and frustrations involved. Thus when women are defined as apolitical, conservative, irresponsible or politically incapable they are in fact being defined by a subtle double standard. Female participation, or lack of it, is being explained in reference to masculine standards in a male-oriented organizational framework (this is particularly true of 'male' party politics), even though the distribution of resources and opportunities is patently unequal. Although many Australians are well aware of existing inequalities, the community at large has never been quite conviced that more than a few women have the necessary ability, for so few women have made it to the top in politics or any other field.

The persistence of such an attitude shows clearly how the prevailing situation is a self-fulfilling prophecy. Women who have no visible proof that members of their sex can be successful as local community leaders or in politics and public life are more likely to believe the negative aspects of the female stereotype. They will either limit their aspirations and accept male leadership and power, or be so lacking in confidence, courage and self-esteem that they are unlikely to confront a difficult or challenging situation with any hope of success.

The Early Feminists

The Sex-Role Ideology provides an effective, self-perpetuating system of social control within the Australian socio-economic framework, and in the past its influence was unchallenged, for the basic sexist assumptions were totally taken for granted. However, at the turn of the century awareness of the fundamental social inequality between men and women in Australia generated feminist activity around the issue of gaining 'equality' for women.

It should be made clear that many women's groups at the turn of the century in Australia were conservative in their aims and organization, and could not be classified as 'feminist', for they were frequently more loyal to men and male power than they were to women and women's needs and rights. They generally accepted the traditional sex-role division, and the most common focus of their activities was on the traditional interests and role of women. The Women's Liberal League (1902) and the Australian Women's National League (1904) are excellent examples of conservative women's organizations at this time which expressed a distinctive female viewpoint and established an independent organization, but which strongly upheld the traditional feminine stereotype and a supportive, auxiliary role *vis-a-vis* male party politics.

However between 1880 and 1910 many new women's groups emerged, and a number of these groups expressed the growth of feminist consciousness among women, inspired in part by the debate on female suffrage before the various states extended the franchise to women between 1889 and 1906. Vida Goldstein's Women's Federal Political Association (1903) is an example of the more militant, feminist group expressing radical ideas which challenged the traditional view of woman's role as well as the supposed egalitarianism of Australian society. The aims of this sort of group included female emancipation rather than equality with men, the use of women's votes to support female candidates, and support for non-party feminism which implied that existing parties could only speak for women from the masculine point of view and that therefore non-party women should represent women's interests in the political arena. At that time such organizations had a comparatively short existence due to lack of support or concerted opposition to their aims and values.

The early feminists in Australia did succeed in demonstrating the strength of the dominant male culture and male-oriented party politics, but in retrospect it is evident that they could not succeed in achieving their radical goals for women while they continued to take for granted the basic tenets of the Sex-Role Ideology and the importance of the small, conjugal, nuclear family to the stability and well-being of Australian society.

The New Feminism

The present decade has witnessed a resurgence of feminism in Australia, this time based on a more concrete understanding of sexism and the Sex-Role Ideology, and embodying a series of insights and demands far more revolutionary in their consequences than those of the early feminists. An independent Women's Movement has developed which rejects the assumptions of the ideology of sex-roles and challenges the sexism inherent in Australian society which perpetuates an unequal and discriminatory relationship between the sexes.

It is significant that the new wave of feminist thought and agitation emerged out of a decade of rapid growth and change in Australian society during which fundamental political conflicts were being debated in the public arena, and during which Australian women became more aware of the struggles of contemporary women's movements overseas. Many women were drawn into the arenas of student protest and the anti-war movement, while others began the struggle to gain equal pay in industry and recognition in the trade unions. It was largely from these two areas that the initial members of the independent women's movement came.

Women who were keen to become involved actively in political causes, or in bringing about a successful resolution of the equal pay question soon found that progressive or radical groups and trade unions did not extend their 'radicalism' to the situation of women, and that women were being expected, again, to ignore their own problems and work for the freedom or rights of others. Often they were simply expected to continue serving others in the work place and in political activity, playing a supportive role to male trade unionists and male radicals who were then freed to get on with the *real* work.

As women began to communicate their experiences to each other, and to read the new feminist literature they began to understand that the problems they faced were shared by other women, and that in essence these problems were social or political rather than purely personal. This growing feminist consciousness was reflected in the number of women from diverse backgrounds who attended the first national Women's Movement Conference in August 1971 which focused on the issues of 'Women and Work: Women in the Trade Unions', and the enthusiasm and commitment to Women's Liberation which was generated at that time manifested itself in the proliferation of consciousness-raising groups, project groups and specific campaigns which rapidly developed around feminist issues.

The widespread move to improve working conditions for women, and the increasing numbers of married women being absorbed into the work force made the issues of equal pay and equal job opportunities important ones, and pushed the issue of adequate child care into the public arena. A consideration of the feminine role in Australian society, and the disadvantages of being a woman in the work force, in the professions or in public life brought to light the educational and socializing agencies which perpetuated a negative view of women and which labelled many different alternatives and options as masculine by definition, thereby excluding women. As this process became more clearly understood by women, attention was turned to the ways in which other agencies, such as the mass media, schools, the established church, the family, and the prison system, collectively perpetuate and reinforce the Sex-Role Ideology as an invisible part of Australian culture. Perhaps most importantly there developed, for the first time, a real understanding of the nature of woman's role in the family and the implications of the marriage-family institution in regard to woman's inferior status as a second-rate citizen.

The political activity among Australian women which has been generated by understanding, anger and the demand for change, takes a variety of forms based on different needs or different perceptions of the problems involved.

The Women's Electoral Lobby has concentrated on legislative reform within the existing system, and on the function of educating women through discussion and public debate of relevant issues, while the Women's Liberation Movement has been attempting to develop a total critique of the existing society with the aim of developing alternative structures which will provide a liberating environment for women and children. At the same time the elevation of feminist issues to the level of public debate has helped to motivate a resurgence of interest and participation in a number of other women's groups that have long been dedicated to improving the position of Australian women, for example the Local Government Women's Association the National Council of Women, the Young Women's Christian Association, and the Union of Australian Women.

On the personal level an even greater variety of approaches is evident as women try, individually and in groups, to understand

and overcome the debilitating effects of sexism in their lives. Thus some women are experimenting with alternative lifestyles, or tackling the difficult task of changing personal relationships to reflect newly developing beliefs and attitudes. Others are trying to attain influential positions from which they can assist the women's cause and fulfil themselves, or pushing for changes in the allocation of government finance, in laws affecting women, or in structures and regulations which discriminate against women.

Thus the current growth of the many facets of the women's movement, and the increasingly strident demands for reform and social change reflect the gradual growth of political awareness and feminist consciousness amongst Australian women in the 1970s. We are reaching the stage where it will no longer be possible to convince women that femininity is an adequate substitute for a full, meaningful life, for personal autonomy and political power.

Notes

1. A. Oakley, *Sex, Gender and Society*, Sun Books, Melbourne, 1972, p.16.
2. H. Arendt, *The Human Condition*, University of Chicago Press, 1958, p.38.

Twenty-Two

The Abortion Law Reform Association of South Australia: 1968–73

There have been in Australia five attempts, all in the last five years, to liberalize laws relating to abortion: three in Western Australia in 1968, 1970 and 1972; one in South Australia in 1969; and one in the Federal Capital Territory in May 1973. All five were Private Members' Bills. The South Australian Bill alone was introduced by a Minister (the Attorney-General), was given virtually unlimited time, was referred to a Parliamentary Select Committee of Enquiry, and was ultimately sanctioned by both Houses of Parliament. Two of the Western Australian attempts – 1968 and 1970 – passed the Legislative Council, but were defeated in the Legislative Assembly; the third, in 1972, was defeated on the second reading in the Legislative Council. The Bill introduced in Federal Parliament was defeated on the second reading in the Lower House. South Australia thus made one more piece of social history when on 4 December 1969, after just over one year of not too intensive parliamentary and public debate, both Houses of Parliament passed the Criminal Law Consolidation Act Amendment Bill.

The main provisions of the Act, which is closely modelled on that passed in the United Kingdom in 1967, are that a pregnancy may be terminated where two legally qualified medical practitioners agree that continuation of the pregnancy would involve

(1) Greater risk to the life of the pregnant woman or greater risk of injury to the physical or mental health of the pregnant woman than if the pregnancy were terminated;

or

(2) ... substantial risk that the child ... [if born] ... would suffer from such physical or mental abnormalities as to be seriously handicapped.

In assessing the risk to physical or mental health, 'account may be taken of the pregnant woman's actual or reasonably foreseeable environment'. The Act stipulates that the woman concerned must have lived in South Australia for two months (the residence clause), and that the operation must be performed in a registered hospital. It further provides for the protection of members of the medical profession with conscientious objections to abortion (the conscience clause); and it empowers one doctor only to act in cases of emergency (the emergency clause).[1]

The legislation went into effect on 8 January 1970. In the first three years 6,631 women were granted a legal termination, and 'it may well be that a plateau will be reached close to 3,000 a year'.[2] It is probable that almost as many women were refused a legal termination,[3] and it is impossible to know how many women did not even request termination, given that the situation is well known to be still far from abortion on request. Nevertheless, it is generally recognized by the public, the Press, and medical experts, that the law is working well.[4] With GP's more willing both to perform terminations themselves and to refer women quickly, more pregnancies are being terminated in the safer first trimester period, and the administrative delays caused mainly by shortage of bed space and of practitioners may well fade with the introduction of abortion units within the teaching hospitals.[5]

Prior to the passage of the Act in 1969, the situation regarding the legality of abortion was confused to say the least. At Statute Law, the Criminal Law Consolidation Act, 1935–1966, prohibited the 'unlawful' procurement or performance of an abortion, but never defined 'unlawful'. At common law, it was held that the United Kingdom Bourne case, 1939, had persuasive authority at the most, and in any case the ruling had never been tested in Australia. In this situation, with few doctors caring to find out what was 'lawful', the incidence of notified abortions was low. But the incidence of illegal abortion was known to be high. With estimates varying from a highly conservative 250 to a liberal 8,900 a year, the minimum estimate of the Abortion Law Reform Association of South Australia

(ALRASA) was 5,100 – broken down roughly as 800 backyard abortions, 1,300 abortions performed by doctors in South Australia, and 3,000 done on South Australian women interstate.[6]

Although abortion had hardly been a lively issue in South Australia until the passage of the British Act in 1967, public, press and media discussion became fairly frequent after that, and polls showed that in Australia, as throughout the world, majority public and medical opinion was moving towards liberalization.[7] In October 1967 the Premier of South Australia, D. A. Dunstan, had announced that the Criminal Law Revision Committee set up by his ALP Government might well look at the State's abortion laws, but it was in Young Liberal circles that concrete reform proposals originated. At their Federal Convention on 18 February 1968, they voted in favour of liberalization along the lines of what was to become South Australian law, and forwarded their recommendations to the Standing Committee of Attorneys-General. In June 1968 the South Australian Young Liberals and the Annual Conference of the South Australian LCL both carried resolutions in favour of liberalization. The resolutions were taken up by the LCL Government elected in March 1968, and when a delegation from the newly formed ALRASA went on 18 October 1968 to see the Attorney-General, R. R. Millhouse, to request the introduction of a Bill, it was told that he already had the support of Cabinet for such a move. The Bill, substantially the same as that passed a year later, was designed primarily to clarify existing practices, though extending slightly their scope in the controversial social clause, which was subsequently deleted.[8]

Millhouse's motivation, however, was more complex than the mere desire of a lawyer for codification. As a lawyer, but also as a deeply moral and religious man personally antipathetic to abortion, he was anxious to avoid by legalization both the kind of graft and corruption obtaining in the eastern States, and the social problems engendered by restrictive laws.[9] As a politician, he saw abortion law reform as a key element in the long overdue process of modernizing his party, while on the personal level abortion was possibly the one issue which would allow him 'to leave a mark on law reform as distinctive as [that of] his rival and predecessor, Dunstan'.[10]

The Parliament to which Millhouse introduced his Bill on 3 December 1969 included three women – Molly Byrne (ALP) and Joyce Steele (LCL, Minister of Education) in the thirty-nine member Lower House, and Jessie Cooper (LCL) in the Upper House of twenty. None of them had at that time made any public statements supporting liberalization, although Jessie Cooper was believed to be sympathetic. The Bill passed the first reading on 10 December with the support of both Government and Opposition, and was immediately referred to a Select Committee of Enquiry of five – a non-voting chairman, and two each from the ALP and the LCL. Millhouse, as mover of the Bill, was chairman. The ALP, following its usual practice, balanced its members. R. R. Loveday, former Minister of Education, supported the Bill, while J. D. Corcoran, Deputy Leader of the party and a Roman Catholic, opposed it. Molly Byrne was not considered because of her 'ticklish electoral situation'; and because as a counterpoise to Corcoran she would have been less effective than the 'strong, articulate' Loveday, who was 'capable of probing witnesses'.[11] Of the two LCL members, Joyce Steele 'chose herself'[12] – possibly with a prod from Loveday who had already in September pressed for the inclusion of a woman on any committee which might be set up to investigate the abortion law[13] – while the choice of S. G. Evans was, according to Millhouse, 'haphazard'. 'I didn't know at that stage that he *was* sympathetic: I just wanted someone who would take an intelligent look at the evidence.'[14] 'Haphazard' it may have been, but the composition of the Committee virtually assured a favourable report – particularly as drafted by Millhouse – since throughout, Corcoran found himself in a minority of one.[15] The Committee in fact recommended that the Bill be passed with the addition of a conscience clause.[16] The report was received by the House on 18 February 1969, and the Bill was then deferred until the next session of Parliament. In the meantime both Millhouse and Dunstan, on visits overseas, spent some time gathering information on the situation in Britain and the United

States, and it was in this period that the pressure groups became really active.

The Bill was restored to the notice paper in October 1969, and for three weeks from 21 October was hotly and continually debated. Before overflowing galleries, and assured of extensive media coverage, nearly every Member of the House spoke in what was not only the longest debate ever known in committee stage on any specific issue, but also, according to most Members, the best debate for years.[17] The Bill, without the social clause, passed the third reading in the House of Assembly on 5 November by twenty-four votes to twelve. The Legislative Council then debated it intermittently from 11 November to 4 December when it passed the third reading by twelve votes to six, but with eight amendments. Finally, after long hours of weary debate. compromise, and negotiation on amendments between the two Houses, the Bill was passed in the very early hours of 5 December 1969, the last day of the Parliamentary session.

The Act has twice come under attack since then. There was a minor flurry in November 1970 when, some time after the release of the first six months' figures, Corcoran threatened to introduce restrictive amendments, but did not do so.[18] The major challenge came in 1972 when, urged if not pressurized by the highly active and organized National Right to Life Association and by the Catholic electorate, T. M. McRae, ALP, lawyer and Catholic, announced in May that he would seek to restrict the terms of the Act. The effect of McRae's highly convoluted amendments would have been virtually to restrict abortion to cases of rape and potential deformity. Introduced to the House on 2 August 1972 – a date which had been fixed definitively only ten days before – his Bill was debated in Private Members' time on that day and on the following Wednesday. Finally on the third Wednesday, 16 August, government time was made available in order to bring the matter to the vote that night. Again an unusually high number of Members – twenty-eight of the increased total of forty-seven – spoke. This time the galleries were not so well attended; the media not so interested, and the second reading was defeated twenty-seven to nineteen. Shortly afterwards McRae announced his intention of moving the identical Bill in the next session of Parliament,[19] while in May 1973 he foreshadowed a modified version.

The Abortion Law Reform Association of South Australia was founded in September 1968 as an offshoot of the Humanist Society of South Australia, whose Vice President, Michael Kowalik, had frequently raised the matter of abortion in committee. The Humanist Society had at a meeting in August 1968 recommended that a steering committee be set up to look into the possibility of forming an organization to promote abortion law reform. Two things were felt very strongly – that the organization should *not* be part of the Humanist Society, whose appeal was not considered broad enough; and that it should be headed by women, 'since politicians find it more difficult to talk them down'. So important was this that it was decided to hold out until the right kind of middle class, professional women could be found – a strategy whose success Kowalik feels has been amply proven.[20]

The aims of ALRASA were set out in the constitution adopted at the inaugural meeting held on 26 September 1968 under the auspices of the Humanist Society. These were originally to amend the South Australian law to make all terminations a matter between doctor and patient; or, failing this, to amend it 'at least to the extent of the United Kingdom Abortion Act, 1967'.[21] As amended in September 1970, after the implementation of the reformed legislation, the aims remain:

> To promote by lawful means, more liberal abortion laws, with the eventual aim of repeal of all legislation specifically referring to medically performed abortion. To remove, by lawful means, any obstacles preventing women obtaining abortions which they want and to which they are legally entitled.[22]

Membership, open to anyone subscribing to the aims of the Association, has never exceeded the peak of 200 reached in October 1969, at the beginning of the crucial parliamentary debates. It has always been essentially metropolitan, middle class and professional, and draws heavily on the residential areas of the eastern foothills and North Adelaide. Members have from the outset seemed singularly reluctant to attend general meetings, and have been content to be recipients of newsletters. Government of the Association is by a council of up to twenty-one members elected annually. Initially, this council met weekly, and throughout 1969 at least monthly, but the bulk of the work has been done from mid-1969 by an informal working executive of four or five members of council, meeting frequently and at times of crisis almost daily. Of the seventeen foundation members of council, five remain; and of those five, three have always served on the executive, thus ensuring continuity.

The first President was, as the Humanists had envisaged, a woman – Lilo Weston, social worker, and wife of an Adelaide psychiatrist. Of the four Vice-Presidents, three were women; of the remaining twelve members, six were women, giving a total of ten women, seven men. Council, like the general membership, is essentially middle class and professional – and included initially three academics, two postgraduates, three teachers, an architect, a social worker, two interior designers, an industrial scientist, the wife of a gynaecologist, and the wife of an architect. The medical element was soon enlarged by the co-option of a psychiatrist; and from September 1970 there have never been on council less than one GP, one pathologist and one psychiatrist, while three women council members are also members of the council of the Family Planning Association.

For finances, ALRASA has relied almost entirely on the annual subscription of two dollars, on donations, on payments received for television interviews and conferences, on loans from members, and on the occasional sale of literature.

The scanty resources, both financial and human, of ALRASA were not offset by substantial outside backing. Throughout both campaigns, ALRASA was the only active pro-abortion group.[23] In 1969 it faced a series of uncoordinated anti-abortion groups including the Committee of One Hundred to Defend the Unborn Child, the Society for the Protection of the Unborn Child, the Christian Life Association, the Human Life Research Foundation, and the Moral Rearmament League. In 1972 it faced the much more formidable and cohesive National Right to Life Association backed by the resources, material and moral, of the Catholic and Lutheran churches. ALRASA had no support from and little contact with interstate reform associations, although information was exchanged both through local newsletters and the national newsletter, *ABRA*. But through close contacts with ALRA (UK), ALRASA was able to get up-to-date and often vital items of information on the British and international scenes. One member of the working executive during the first campaign had already worked with ALRA in England, while another member had lengthy discussions with the ALRA executive and with the Birmingham Pregnancy Advisory Service on his visit to England in 1971. ALRASA was also in contact with reform movements in the United States.

If from the outset ALRASA was not operating in a situation where it had to pressure politicians into doing something, nevertheless it still conceived of its task as two-fold: *public*, to educate public opinion to provide both community reassurance and a groundswell of opinion so that the MPs would feel neither isolated nor too radical in voting for the Bill; and *parliamentary*, to provide arguments to those MPs already favourable to reform, to influence the uncommitted, and to keep a close watch on numbers. Given limited energy and finance the MPs were the prime target throughout both campaigns; the public was secondary.

In what is now seen as the pre-campaign period from the formation of ALRASA to the deferment of the Bill in February 1969, the tactical pattern was set. Publicity in the form of regular press releases[24] and a petition appealing for termination of pregnancy at the discretion of a doctor, provided the background for the twin primary tasks of lobbying and preparing for the Select Committee of Enquiry to which ALRASA volunteered to give evidence.[25] Three members spent much of the Christmas break reading widely and producing a written submission which, since it was also destined for public circulation, had not only to read well but to look good. The submission ran to fifty foolscap pages, expensively typed, with a new page for each new topic, the whole bound in thick paper. The arguments used there also set the pattern for the future – namely, that abortion is a social, not merely a woman's, issue; that every child has a right to be born into a loving environment and that, vice-versa, unwanted children are frequently social misfits, thus perpetuating social problems. Since for many MPs the Select Committee Report was 'the most important source of information and the report and evidence had greater influence on their deliberations than did any of the direct lobbying',[26] it is worthwhile listing the various headings of ALRASA's submission:

The incidence of legal abortion in Australia and South Australia; medical consequences of abortion; psychiatric aspects of abortion; the attitude of the public towards abortion; the welfare of children; women's rights; the law and morality; is the foetus a person?; sexual morality; 'preventing a Beethoven'; one law for the rich, another for the poor; the effect of abortion on population growth; what will limit the number of abortions?; recommendations.[27]

In the submission, as in all its activities from January 1969, ALRASA deliberately and in spite of advice to the contrary, used the word 'abortion', rather than 'termination', believing that the more frequently the word was used, the sooner its emotive value would disappear.

The five people chosen by ALRASA to appear before the Select Committee also set the pattern for the expert and professional approach it has always tried to adopt: two men – an obstetrician and a psychiatrist; two South Australian women – an academic and a social worker; and Beatrice Faust, brought over from Melbourne because of her investigations into the area of criminal abortion. Through a council member who was also a member of the Council for Civil Liberaties, ALRASA persuaded the Council for Civil Liberties to send to the Select Committee a submission urging abortion on request, which was a masterpiece of tactfulness.[28]

With the debate adjourned from February to October 1969, and with the experience acquired during the pre-campaign period, ALRASA faced a fundamental strategic decision: to continue to press for abortion on request – unrealizable though that was in terms both of the politicians themselves and, as the opinion polls showed, of majority public opinion;[29] or to support to the hilt the half-way position embodied in Millhouse's Bill. Not without heated discussion in council, the latter course was adopted. Again, in 1972 it was decided to give whole hearted support to the *status quo*, rather than to push for further reform.

The tactics were the same for both campaigns, though, given the time factor, the emphasis was even more on Parliament and less on the public in 1972. First, the public. In 1969, council members spoke at about fifty meetings after letters had been sent to all possible interested groups offering speakers, and took part in a moderately well-attended weekend seminar on abortion run by the Department of Adult Education. In 1972 ALRASA was invited to speak to high school groups, university students, party sub-branches, kindergarten mothers and housewives. Each of these audiences almost entirely lacked the hostile element clearly discernible in 1969. ALRASA welcomed and solicited radio and television debates and interviews, cultivated press contacts to get coverage for feature articles as well as press releases, and made sure either by article or letter that no anti-abortion article or advertisement went unanswered.

In August 1969, 9,000 roneod letters to parliamentarians in two forms – abortion on request or support for the Millhouse Bill – were letter-boxed, and an advertisement to the same effect was put in the Press. The replies were collected, sorted, and sent to each respective MP, with a complete list of figures from all constituencies. But, like the petition organized in January, replies were few – 1,920 signatures in January, 1,660 replies in August, compared with a total of 15,420 anti-abortion signatures – and overwhelmingly from the solid middle class residential areas of North Adelaide, Beaumont and Mitcham. For these reasons, and because politicians themselves set little store by petitions, it was decided not to repeat them in 1972. On the other hand, short carefully-phrased individual letters from constituents are known to be effective, and in both campaigns ALRASA appealed for individual letters. Leaflets listing points to be developed both in letters to MPs and to the Press were circulated not only to ALRASA members, but also through the newsletters of sympathetic organizations such as the Council for Civil Liberties, the Humanists and, in 1972, ZPG (Zero Population Growth), Women's Liberation and WEL (Women's Electoral Lobby).

In the month before the debate resumed in October 1969, one council member organized in a carefully selected 'typical' electorate a survey on attitudes to social questions including abortion. The result – that eight out of ten South Australian men and women favoured the kind of legislation proposed by Millhouse – was used in large advertisements in the *Advertiser* and the *News* in the week before the debate resumed, and also in a series of thirty-second spot commercials on 5KA and 5DN on 13, 14 and 15 October, urging people to 'ring or write to your Member *now*'.[30] The survey, a full report of which was given in the *Advertiser* on 28 October, was referred to during the debates by many Members including Millhouse. In the second campaign, ALRASA encouraged the Congregational Union and Methodist Churches to make public statements[31] and to write to each MP supporting the *status quo*, and asked several of those Trade Union officials known to be sympathetic to abortion to write to all MPs stating their views. Both of these sources were referred to by several Members during the debate.

These activities, whose prime purpose was after all to influence MPs indirectly, through the public, were however regarded as background to the direct approach. Six brief newsletters making one single point of recent interest were sent to all Members of both Houses between 10 September and 20 October 1969, and two newsletters in July 1972, when a precis of up-to-date material and arguments was also sent to all members known to be interested.[32] More information was not sent for fear of over-saturation.

Similarly, since ALRASA had become aware during the pre-campaign period that over-lobbying was counter-productive, in the campaigns proper it adopted a highly selective lobbying technique. Late in the first campaign, each Member of the Lower House was visited once by someone from the ALRASA council whose approach was best suited to the character and views of the Member concerned; and in the second campaign by one of the Executive, again carefully primed beforehand about the views of the particular Member. Only key people and waverers were visited more than once, and on the second visit by a member of the medical profession. Since ALRASA had been told that the Legislative Council was even more sensitive than the Lower House to any kind of pressure, the Council was not approached until the Bill had passed through the Lower House. Each Member was then visited once by a carefully selected medical specialist. All lobbyists were concerned to present a moderate, respectable, reasonable image, since it was considered as essential not to adopt a dictatorial attitude as it was not to over-lobby.

Throughout the weeks immediately preceding the debates, ALRASA was in contact with one or two influential and sympathetic Members on each side of the House, getting constant reports on how the numbers were going, and whom therefore to talk to and how; and giving them in turn feedback from the visits. The Members, different in each campaign, were with one exception men – S. G. Evans and J. S. Freebairn (LCL) and C. D. Hutchens (ALP) in 1969; J. D. Wright (ALP) and Joyce Steele (LCL) in 1972. In addition, although their views did not necessarily coincide, ALRASA was in close touch with the only medical men in Parliament – Dr V. Springett in the Legislative Council in 1969 and Dr D. Tonkin in the House of Assembly in 1972. It was also in contact with Millhouse whose views, as Attorney-General and introducer of the Bill in the first instance, and as Deputy-Leader of the LCL Opposition and guardian of his own Act in the second, carried great weight. In August 1972 ALRASA arranged for Joyce Steele to meet Dr Malcolm Potts, President of the International Planned Parenthood Federation; and to see for herself at first hand, in a morning's interviewing of applicants for abortions at the Queen Elizabeth Hospital, how the legislation was being administered. She drew on both these sources in her speech, while Wright used other material provided by ALRASA. In 1969 ALRASA arranged that Hutchens would move an amendment removing entirely from the sphere of the criminal code abortion done by a medical practitioner (an amendment which, predictably, was defeated seven to twenty-eight). Similarly, in 1972 if McRae's restrictive amendments had not been defeated on the second reading, Joyce Steele, primed with a list of substantive arguments, was ready to move in committee stage abortion on request up to twelve weeks. Both of these were seen as purely tactical moves, to make other Members feel more comfortable in supporting a middle-of-the-road solution.

Throughout both debates, protracted though the first one was, ALRASA so rostered council members as always to have someone present in the House – not merely to show official ALRASA interest or to buttonhole last minute waverers in the lobby, but also to be able to send in immediate information with which to refute an opposition argument. This was vital on one occasion in November 1969 when Corcoran moved an amendment restricting the performance of abortions to registered specialists. The amendment sounded sensible, many Members were clearly swayed by it, but ALRASA realized that since only twenty-four gynaecologists were registered in the metropolitan area and only two in the whole of the rest of the State, then on the official figures it simply would not work. ALRASA therefore talked intensively to key figures in the House, and overnight drew up and sent off to every Member a letter giving these arguments, to which many Members referred the next day. In the event, Corcoran's amendment was defeated decisively. On the other hand, ALRASA decided not to try to do anything about either the newly inserted residence clause, or the social clause – since the one was probably unworkable and unconstitutional, and the other would to a great extent be covered by the environment rider.

After the passage of the Bill in 1969, ALRASA sent a letter to each MP who had voted for it, thanking him and offering continuing information; while the defeat of McRae's Bill in July 1972 was followed up by a letter to each Member of the Lower House, couched in slightly different terms according to his persuasion, urging him to do all he could to increase government support for the Family Planning Association.

In the two and a half years between the two campaigns,

ALRASA deliberately adopted a watching brief, in the belief that the more the legislation was left alone, the more rope its critics were given, the more quickly its largely administrative teething troubles would sort themselves out. ALRASA kept a close watch on the figures, began a dialogue with the AMA (Australian Medical Association), and with the Statutory Committee set up to investigate abortions, drew up a list of sympathetic doctors in the metropolitan area in order to be able to act as a kind of referral service, and sent to MPs a total of five newsletters, each commenting on some specific recent issue, but also to serve as a reminder of ALRASA's existence.

The question remains as to how much difference ALRASA made. In the purely negative sense, in that there had to be some tangible opposition to the anti-abortion groups, ALRASA achieved a balancing effect – and neither Millhouse nor Dunstan sees its influence as any greater than this.[33] On the other hand, by acting as an apparent 'enemy' ALRASA may at least in 1972 have polarized the more emotional anti-abortionists and moved them to counter-productive excesses. Most Parliamentarians consider that lobbyists were 'of little importance, except in supplying information and bolstering stands taken by Members'[34] – but if that is indeed all, ALRASA does not consider it 'of little importance'. Information it supplied on the specialist clause in the first campaign, and information contained in the impartial Furler report, the timely release of which in the very middle of the debate in August 1972 was due in part to ALRASA, were both vital in preventing erosion. A more accurate assessment is perhaps that ALRASA 'could claim credit for directly influencing the outcome of at least one amendment, and for convincing enough waverers that the Bill did not, or barely, extend the grounds for abortion, thus encouraging members to support it'.[35] Equally, in 1972 ALRASA encouraged support for the *status quo* by appealing to pride in the State's progressivism, and by convincing some of the doubtful that the situation was not one of 'abortion on demand', an emotive phrase they still feared.

Admittedly, ALRASA's task was not as difficult as that faced by reform movements interstate. The Bill was introduced of his own volition by an Attorney-General committed to getting it through in some form; it was, although technically a conscience vote, supported by the entire LCL Cabinet; and half the Legislative Council Members viewed it as a government-sponsored measure and treated it accordingly. In 1972 the political situation militated against the prolonged debate which any change in the *status quo* would have entailed. The legislators themselves were on both occasions working in the context of a state with the smallest percentage of Catholic voters, and with a famous if ancient tradition of liberal legislation behind it. Again, in the first campaign ALRASA's opponents were less than united; and in the second they used somewhat cruder tactics than did ALRASA. Indeed, in the immediate aftermath of his defeat, McRae wrote 'I must again deplore the fact that we lost votes because of the blackmail techniques used in letters to MPs'.[36].

On the other hand, ALRASA was in 1969 blazing a trail in an environment where 'abortion' was a much more emotive word than it is now: where there was no tested common law precedent, such as Victoria and NSW now have in the Menhennit and Levine judgements respectively; and where it had, neither Women's Lib as possibly slightly dubious allies, nor help from WEL as parliamentary conscience-prickers. ALRASA must be given credit for husbanding its slender financial and exiguous human resources, for setting the whole argument in a broader context than that of women's rights alone, for deliberately choosing to give priority to short-term pragmatism as opposed to long-term principle, and for creating and maintaining over the last five years an image of informed and moderate respectability (even down to dress) with which MPs and leaders of public opinion alike have not been unhappy to associate. For it may well be that 'ALRASA's greatest asset was apparent agreement with public opinion';[37] but public opinion has to be seen to be expressed, and in an acceptable form. In that sense, ALRASA's greatest asset was the peculiar geographical and social compactness of Adelaide which gave council members a feeling that something could be achieved, and then enabled them to exploit to the full their professional and political contacts in a manner utterly palatable to South Australia's essentially middle class political elite.

Notes

1. S. A. Parliament, *An Act to Amend the Criminal Law Consolidation Act, 1935–1966*, 1969 (No.109).
2. S. A. Parliament, *Report of the Statutory Committee to Examine and Report on Abortions*, 1973, p.2. (Hereafter referred to as the Mallen Reports). The annual figures are 1970, 1,440; 1971, 2,519; 1972, 2,672. Mallen Reports 1971, 1972, 1973.
3. A. F. Connon, 'Medical Abortion in S.A.: the first twelve months under the new legislation', *Medical Journal of Australia*, vol.2, 18 September 1971, p.608ff; and 'Trends in Legalized Abortion in S.A.', *Medical Journal of Australia*, vol.1, 3 February 1973, pp.231–234.
4. Pastor Overduin, who stood for Henley Beach in March 1973 against the sitting Member and Minister for the Environment G. R. Broomhill, as an Independent candidate on the anti-abortion issue, received only 10 per cent of the vote. See also editorials in the *Advertiser*, 4 August, 1972, 7 March, 1973, 10 May, 1973; and the editorial 'Legal Abortion, the S.A. experience', in *Medical Journal of Australia*, vol.1, 28 April, 1973, pp.821–3; I. K. Furler, *An Investigation of Abortion Laws and Practices in Europe and America*, (Report to Cabinet) August 1972, p.58; also the *Advertiser*, 11 May, 1973, where Furler is quoted as saying 'as far as it stands, the Act is quite adequate, it is the administration of it that needs smoothing out'.
5. As recommended in the Mallen Report 1972, p.3, the Furler Report August 1972, p.58; and by Professor Lloyd Cox, the *Advertiser*, 28 April, 1973.
6. Abortion Law Reform Association of South Australia, Submission to the Select Committee on the Criminal Law Consolidation Act Amendment Bill, 1968, January 1969, pp.2–5.
7. Gallup Polls, Roy Morgan and Associates, June 1968, February 1969, and MFI Surveys, 1968, all gave figures of about 63 per cent of the general public in favour of liberalization. *Modern Medicine of Australia*, July 1968, showed 81.5 per cent of Australian doctors in favour of liberalization.
8. The social clause added, after 'greater risk . . . to the physical or mental health of the pregnant woman', the phrase 'or of any existing children of her

family'. S.A. Parliament, *A Bill for an Act to amend the Criminal Law Consolidation Act, 1935–1966*, 1968 (no.80).

9. T. Nicholas, 'Abortion Law Reform in South Australia', unpublished B. A. Hons. thesis, Flinders University, 1970, p.23. This detailed examination of the S.A. abortion campaigns, 1969, is a case study of pressure groups at work.

10. N. Blewett, and D. Jaensch, *Playford to Dunstan: the Politics of Transition*, Cheshire, Melbourne, 1971, p.188.

11. Conversation with Dunstan, 22 June 1973.

12. Conversation with Millhouse, 31 May 1973.

13. S.A. Parliament, *Debates* 1968–9, vol.2, 24 September 1968, p.1310.

14. Conversation with Millhouse, 31 May 1973.

15. S.A. Parliament. Report of the Select Committee of the House of Assembly on the Criminal Law Consolidation Act Amendment Bill, 1968, *Parliament Papers* 1968–9, vol.3, no.105.

16. Ibid, p.5.

17. Nicholas, op.cit. p.30.

18. *News*, 3 November 1970.

19. *Southern Cross*, 20 August 1972.

20. Conversation with Michael Kowalik, 31 May 1973.

21. ALRASA Constitution, September 1968.

22. Amendment to ALRASA Constitution, 29 September 1970.

23. Women's Lib., S.A., founded early in 1970, was too late for the first campaign, and took little part in the second; while WEL, S.A., was not founded until July 1972.

24. It was in fact ALRASA who after its delegation's visit to Millhouse on 18 October 1969, immediately announced his intentions to the Press, *Advertiser*, 19 October 1969. See also Nicholas, op.cit. p.16.

25. A clerk of the House, Mr J. Hull, subsequently stated that if ALRASA had not already volunteered, it would have been called upon to give evidence by the Select Committee; Nicholas, op.cit. p.26.

26. Nicholas, op.cit. p.30.

27. ALRASA, Submission, January 1969.

28. Select Committee Report, 1969: Appendix E.

29. Gallup Polls, Roy Morgan and Associates, February 1969 and April 1972, showed 13 per cent and 19 per cent respectively in favour of abortion on request.

30. ALRASA records.

31. *Advertiser*, 24 June 1972.
32. ALRASA, 'Recent arguments relating to abortion', July 1972.
33. Conversations with Millhouse, 30 May 1973, and Dunstan, 22 June 1973.
34. Nicholas, op.cit. p.106.
35. Nicholas, op.cit. p.106.
36. *Southern Cross*, 20 August, 1972.
37. Nicholas, op.cit. p.107.

Twenty-Three (Part one)

The Women's Electoral Lobby and the Women's Liberation Movement

The History of the Women's Electoral Lobby

Introduction

The first part of this chapter is a shortened version of an article originally published after the 1972 Federal Elections.[1] It is included here to give the reader historical information about WEL before reading the second and third parts. I have tried not to change any of the ideas expressed in the original article since it was written at a time of great optimism when I fully believed that WEL could be a viable agent for radical change through the existing political system.

Re-reading the chapter three years after it was written was a salutary experience. Had I really believed, as is emphatically stated in the conclusion, that non-violent social protest could be effective or even that we could wrest some of the power from men and bring about legislative change which would alter the status of women in society? Had I allowed myself to be manipulated into thinking that submissions to the Government on child care would radically change the oppressive nature of the family; and even foolish enough to be flattered when asked to do surveys for them (free of course, presumably the honour was sufficient reward) while being knocked back for government grants?

Research, government submissions and dealing with reporters for a full year meant that WEL was very much a full-time involvement. Eventually it became clear to me that the very respectability and credibility we had fought so hard to gain was being thrown back in our faces. WEL was not powerful, as I had so idealistically believed, but was being manoeuvred into a convenient harmless position in the establishment. For me social reform was finished, indeed if it had ever begun. There had to be another way.

The History of WEL

In February 1972 two Women's Liberation groups held a joint meeting to consider forming political action groups and Beatrice Faust circulated an article from *Ms* (an American Women's Liberation magazine).[2] Later, on 27 February, Beatrice Faust called a meeting in her own home which ten women attended. A few of these had been at the earlier meeting; the rest were invited because of specific skills. Professions represented included journalism, sociology, psychology, education and law. The article in *Ms* which the group discussed reported a survey by four American feminists of American presidential candidates. How did the candidates feel and think about women? How far did their behaviour rely on the traditional masculine role?

The presidential candidates were mailed questionnaires covering a wide range of issues. They were also interviewed. The information was analysed and the data thus obtained was divided into three major categories, candidates receiving a score in each category. The first category looked at the candidates' political and personal attitudes to women. The second category, relying on historical information, charted candidates' ability to challenge the *status quo* and take action. The third category assessed the candidates' commitment to peace and the degree to which they rejected the traditional male role.

The Melbourne meeting decided to develop these ideas; to find out the attitudes of all candidates in the 1972 Australian Federal Election on women's issues. The meeting adopted a three-stage strategy:

Provide a form guide derived from a *Ms*-style questionnaire plus information from interviews with candidates.

Publish the guide both through the Women's Movement and local and national newspapers.

Campaign for the candidate who was not only the most sympathetic to women's issues, but also the most likely to effect the social reforms desperately needed by women. This of course required a far larger number of women.

Two more meetings were held in Melbourne, and attendance rose to twenty-five. This group divided into smaller working parties of experts. Each undertook to research a particular area of concern to women – such as education, welfare, finance and pollution – and to report back by mid-April to the survey team. Now that WEL was firmly established it attempted to broaden its membership. A public meeting in Melbourne was advertised throughout women's groups and in *Nation Review* and the *Age*.

After its first meeting on 23 April, eighty-five people joined WEL. Most were also members of the Women's Liberation Movement. However, although much of the early membership overlapped with Women's Liberation (a situation which was to change later) WEL soon established itself as an autonomous body. As membership grew so did the necessity for some minimal organizational structure and a constitution.[3]

The structure of WEL varies slightly from state to state. In Victoria a number of specialized committees exist, each with an administrative convenor. There is, for example, a survey team, a publicity group and a broadsheet subcommittee. A co-ordinating committee, which includes at least one member from each subcommittee, liases between these specialized groups and the general membership. Although attendance at any meeting is open to all individuals many members attend the monthly meetings only. At these meetings the activities of various subcommittees are discussed and policy decisions taken. Badges, posters, car stickers and T-shirts provide useful identifying symbols for those not so actively involved. The structure is minimal and merely facilitates the carrying out of WEL's primary aim: social protest.[4]

WEL is a reformist movement which accepts some of the present purposes and methods of the existing order but wishes to modify specific attitudes and institutions. Thus although WEL plays the game both politically and academically through existing structures, politicians find themselves in an unusual situation of being publicly evaluated by a relatively powerless group they had hitherto ignored. Unlike most of the women's movement, which on the whole tends to be inward looking, WEL is committed to interaction with the larger society. Hence it was far less 'threatening' to most women than the Women's Liberation Movement. The majority of middle-class women who formed WEL's initial membership do not want revolution – they have too much to lose. So far WEL has never had to seek members. Women and the occasional male have joined at a rate almost faster than this voluntary organization, with few funds and no benefactors, can manage. WEL is concerned with changing specific legislation rather than with concentrating on raising the level of an individual's consciousness. WEL is committed to non-violent protest activity: the publication of information on candidates, attendance at political meetings, submissions to official enquiries such as the Tariff Board and Equal Pay Case, and non-violent demonstrations.

Given that the organization is voluntary and its members primarily women, many with young children, and that it has no financial resources, how did it become an influence in the 1972 election and what was the extent of that influence?

Because WEL had no direct access to political machinery it had to find a way to influence those who did have the power. This was provided by the communications media which influenced politicians both directly and indirectly: directly through the publication of the form guide; and indirectly by publicizing WEL and its aims. Politicians thus became concerned about WEL's influence with the bulk of women voters. As one Liberal back-bencher is quoted as saying: 'WEL is regarded by most politicians with a mixture of scepticism, apprehension and a little amusement. Most of them think it is a bloody nuisance.' With the prospect of a close election before them, politicians regarded WEL as yet another unknown quantity which could not be ignored. Therefore through the Press, radio and television WEL gained indirect access to the power structure.

WEL had a very wide coverage from all types of media, partly because the Women's Movement throughout the world was news in the early 1970s but also because women have rarely been politically active in Australia. WEL too had distinct differences from other branches of the Women's Movement. It was not as 'threatening' to the establishment as were some of the more revolutionary groups. It operated through established channels using methods acceptable to society at large. For example, the survey used to evaluate candidates' opinions was devised and administered in a way acceptable to conventional social science and thus helped earn WEL respectability in the eyes of the wider society.

Support by women journalists was another important factor in WEL's media coverage. A large proportion of the major articles on WEL were written by women journalists in papers like *Nation Review*, the *Age*, the *Australian*, the *Bulletin*, the *National Times* and the *Australian Financial Review*.[5]

Table 1 sets out the growth of WEL membership in relation to media coverage received and the particular activities in which WEL was engaged for each month of 1972. The Press greeted WEL's arrival in April enthusiastically. The decline of publicity in May and June reflects the concern of the organization with researching areas for the questionnaire schedule and with the development of a loose administrative structure. May saw the start of a nucleus of interstate groups in the ACT, New South Wales and Queensland.

In June publicity increased with the organization of women to make applications to sit for the Victorian Public Service administrative examination which, up to that time, was open to males only. Of the seventy women who applied to sit for the examination, three with ambiguous Christian names received examination numbers. A demonstration in support of those women who were admitted to the examination room was organized in conjunction with the Women's Liberation Movement. The success of two of the women candidates in this examination, together with the WEL tariff submission on contraceptives, coincided with an increase of publicity in July. These activities apparently established WEL's credibility with the Press. The tariff submission was referred to in an *Age* editorial. In August there was an enormous leap in membership, doubtless due to publicity received in July and August. This included articles in *Woman's Day* and the *Bulletin*[6] which attracted members from as far afield as Norfolk Island and Darwin, and also from many country areas.

Table 1

The growth of WEL membership and its relation to the communications media

	Membership		Media coverage*						
	Victoria	Other States	Daily papers	National weeklies	Local papers	Radio	Television	Total	Action
April	85		6	1	0		1	8	First public meeting.
May	65		0	1	2	1		4	Beginning interstate groups in ACT, NSW, Qld and SA.
June	54	30	2	3	0			5	Victorian public service administration examination.
July	51	106	8	2	7	1		18	Start of Tasmanian WEL. Results of VPSA examination. Tariff submission on contraceptives.
August	123	252	13	1	6			20	Interviewing commenced. WEL asked for budget comment. NT WEL commences.
September	58	211	3	1	11	(numerous country broadcasts)		15+	Continuation of interviewing.
October	77	127	6	5	18		1	30	Attendance at political meetings. NSW release of material. WA WEL begins.
November	229	169	13	7	48	3	2	73	Vic. WEL form guide released.
December	75	108†	5	1	not yet complete				
Total	717	1,060							

* Applies to Victoria only. † Each state now keeps its own membership records.

Television and radio also had a significant effect on increasing WEL's membership as well as enhancing its political power. Four current affairs television programmes devoted segments to WEL and numerous radio and regional television interviews were broadcast throughout the year. Publicity was overwhelmingly favourable. Of the 164 press articles published in Victoria between April and November only three were antagonistic to WEL's views.

More important for WEL was the need to know the extent to which its ideas and information had been accepted by women. A survey was carried out in three electorates in Victoria (Bruce, Deakin and Isaacs) one week after the election. In each electorate a random sample of street blocks was chosen, giving ten streets in each. In each street ten women were systematically identified for interview. The electorates were of similar social standing. In each case voting patterns had altered considerably from 1969. In terms of the WEL rating two of the electorates represented extreme scores. The ALP candidate for Isaacs (Gareth Clayton) received WEL's top score whilst the L-CP candidate in Bruce (Billy Snedden) scored the lowest rating given. Deakin was also included because WEL leaflets had been distributed to half the electorate. Some indication of how effective this had been is shown in Table 2.

Table 2

WEL and female voters in three Melbourne electorates

	Bruce	*Deakin*	*Isaacs*	*Total average* %
Number of women interviewed	100	100	100	
% of women who took WEL issues into consideration when choosing a candidate	36	49	31	39
% of women who had heard of WEL	37	49	34	40
% of women who saw the form guide	9	19	13	14
% of women voting according to WEL form guide	3	10	12	9

As is shown here, of the 300 women interviewed in the follow-up survey 40 per cent had heard of WEL. How had these women heard of WEL? Table 3 illustrates the importance of daily newspapers and, in particular, the *Age*. Radio and television are also significant;

Table 3

Types of media through which women voters had first heard of WEL

Daily newspaper	60
Local newspaper	17
Radio/TV	46
Friends/members	11
Posters/car stickers	2
Other	1

These figures exceed the actual number of women who had heard of WEL since ten women checked more than one medium. They were unable to remember how they first heard of WEL.

local newspapers and friends and members are less so.[7] Within the three electorates chosen for study the more 'establishment'-type media are apparently responsible for communication between WEL and the female voter. This is probably partly a function of the social standing of the three electorates chosen, as an analysis of the letters received by WEL requesting membership shows a slightly different pattern. In '*Age* areas' this particular newspaper seems to have been the most important means of contact, but in 'non-*Age* areas' other factors, especially local newspapers and the radio, seem increasingly significant.[8]

The greatest communication barrier was in the publication of the form guide. Of the 40 per cent of women interviewed who had heard of WEL only one in three (or 14 per cent of the total sample) had actually seen the form guide. However, of those who had seen the form guide, 60 per cent (or 9 per cent of the original sample) voted according to WEL's ratings. This is to be expected since, as Table 2 showed, 39 per cent had considered the issues on which WEL rated candidates in choosing whom to vote for.

If we look at the swinging voters – women who said that they do not necessarily vote for the same political party in each election and who in fact switched their vote from the party they voted for in the last election – an interesting pattern emerges. Eighty women in our sample of 300 changed the party they voted for in the 1972 elections compared with the previous election. Fifty-seven of those eighty (that is, 70 per cent) took account of feminist issues when choosing the candidate they voted for. Of those eighty who took feminist issues into consideration, half had heard of WEL. Only eight had actually seen the form guide. Six of those who had seen the form guide deliberately voted a WEL ticket.

One thing which clearly emerged was that feminist issues are important to a very large proportion of female voters. Where individuals had specific data (the form guide or leaflet) which gave information as to where a candidate stood on issues, most chose to vote for the most sympathetic candidate.

Conclusion

1972 saw the rapid development of a political protest group which arose for the specific purpose of making women's issues of national importance. From a small group of ten its membership grew to almost 2,000 in nine months, with branches in all states and one forming in New Zealand. Initially WEL was a group with little access to the power structure in Australia but through the media WEL became an established interest group and a political force almost overnight.

WEL grew out of the Women's Liberation Movement but its subsequent development and concern with reforms has led to its establishment as an autonomous organization. Lack of revolutionary tactics has broadened its membership appeal to many women. Ironically, therefore, it may be more influential in changing the balance of power between men and women than the Women's Liberation Movement. Certainly, as many writers have pointed out and the present Labor Government will discover, WEL will grow in membership and continue to press for social change.

Post-script 1974

This optimism now appears to be unfounded. WEL had little if any effect on politicians or government policies in the 1974 elections and seems to have been absorbed into the establishment. Indeed, some of the advances WEL might have claimed to be influential in, e.g. increased grants for child care, were reduced in the 1974 Budget. Probably the most important function now is in raising the awareness of women to their oppressed position in society. See Chapter 26 for further comments.

Twenty-Three (Part two)

The Women's Electoral Lobby and the Women's Liberation Movement

Where's the Women's Movement Moving To?*

During the past year (1972–3), with the formation of groups like the Women's Electoral Lobby, Media Women's Action Group, Women Active Politically, Joint Women's Action and many other smaller, more specific aim-oriented groups, the Women's Movement in Australia has developed a size and a diversity which has made it a nebulous and rather elusive body whose exact boundaries are very difficult to define. We all share a common feeling that we are somehow different from both earlier feminist groups like the National Council of Women, and from other non-feminist women's organizations like the Housewives' Association, but this has not implied more than a rather tenuous unity among us. We might all use the women's symbol, we can come together for a women's march but beyond that we can hardly agree on our analysis of the position of women in contemporary Australian society, let alone on its causes or how we will act to change it.

The Women's Movement in Australia is just four years old. It has passed beyond the stage of being regarded by many women as a minority lunatic fringe and is now something which involves or at least interests thousands of women and it would seem appropriate at this stage in our development to make an attempt to describe and assess what the Movement is and where it is going. One way in which this can be done is by examining the conferences which have been held each year and where many of us from different groups and different states come together to try and define ourselves and our aims. These conferences are only very imperfect microcosms of our activities during the preceding year but since we bring to them the

* This part of the chapter is a reprint of an article which appeared in *MeJane*, No. 10, March 1973.

problems we have experienced in carrying out these activities, and as the conferences tend to crystallize the major differences between us while at the same time determining our methods of action and organization for the following twelve months, they do comprise a suitable means by which to make judgements about the state of the Movement.

I have attended four conferences in the past three years. Each of them was very different and each, it seems to me, marked a significant stage in the development of both the critique and the theory of change predominant in the Movement at that stage.

The first conference, held in Melbourne in May 1970, was a rather daunting experience. Women from three states came together for the first time but this probably constituted our only achievement. There was much talking and shouting, there were heated exchanges between the protagonists of various 'lines' and those espousing minority views were frequently patronized or even jeered at. One woman abused several of us for wearing make-up (some of us still felt we needed to present a front to all those women we were meeting for the first time), others were castigated for knitting during the sessions, one evening was devoted to an acrimonious debate between the more vocal women and several male radicals. And although I exchanged brief words with quite a few women over those two days, I could not claim to have made one new friendship as a result of that conference. As our first national conference it provided the benefit of allowing us to gain at least a cursory idea of what was happening in other states, it gave us some sense that Women's Liberation was struggling to define itself and that it was developing as a fairly widespread movement, but the ideals of a coherent expression of the oppression of women together with the sisterhood which putatively arose from such a common basis belonged to the distant future.

Twenty-five months later and we had come a long, long way. Despite a national train strike women from all states and from New Guinea came to Sydney for the third national conference in June 1972. (There was a Working Women's Conference in Melbourne in August 1971 which I did not attend and so cannot describe what happened there – for an account see *Mejane* no.5).

And although our meeting hall was cold and badly lit and had shocking acoustics, right from the start it was evident that this conference was going to be very much better than the last one I had been to. It may sound trite to say that the atmosphere was permeated by friendliness and good will but this was how it struck me.

In 1970 we had no formal organization but the fact that papers were delivered to the congregated conference (of seventy or so women) ensured that discussion was limited to those who could, and felt confident enough to, shout. This time no papers were given but instead we broke up into small workshop groups to discuss topics which were either quite specific (child-care, education, abortion etc.) for those who wanted to get down to immediate concrete problems, or else wide-ranging (radical therapy, social attitudes to women) for those interested in broader psychological or cultural phenomena.

Throughout the weekend most of us were able to participate in at least three different workshops, each time with different people. There was sufficient flexibility to enable special groups to be convened quickly and at least three which were not programmed met to cater for needs which had been voiced once we were all together. This enabled people with specific interests related to, say their jobs, to meet. For example, the teachers concerned with sexism in their curricula, and the group composed of women who were either teaching courses or writing about women, and it also allowed for people to circulate papers and to convene small groups to discuss these, e.g. Biff MacDougall's paper 'Women's Liberation and the Left'. To me it seemed that this format overcame the twin evils of most conferences: having to listen to boring papers which do not interest you, and not being able to discuss in depth things which do.

But although not all women were satisfied with these arrangements and (obviously) there were many improvements which could be made it seemed that we had arrived at the right kind of framework for a Women's Liberation conference and that this framework should be defended. For even though we might only hold such conferences once a year, the principles of organization involved can be applied to our activities within each state.

From its inception Women's Liberation has been anti-organization in the sense that we have had no elected officers, no formal membership, no rules or platform to which people must adhere, and no theories determining the relationship of factions or opposition groups to the movement as a whole. We have justified this stance by pointing out that formal organizations is always oligarchical in that it inevitably produces an elite of leaders who cling to their powerful positions more tenaciously than they adhere to the principles of the organization they purportedly represent.

Many of us have had experiences in a variety of organizations from the ALP to revolutionary groups which have demonstrated the truth of this theory, and we have also found that such formal organization acts to curb spontaneous actions to voice our grievances or to attain our ends. Often more time is taken up in fighting other members of the organization than is spent fighting for our goals. In trying to overcome these deficiencies in other modes of organization we have in our own political methods tried to prefigure the kind of social relations which would prevail in the kind of society we are trying to create. I do not think that we can claim to have perfected our practice of anti-organization; quite often *de facto* elites have arisen, the small groups have not known how to cope with incorporating new members and there have inevitably been problems in maintaining continuity of operation without vesting this continuity in particular individuals. There have also been problems of differing interpretations of the 'real cause' of women's oppression and consequently of the means that should be used to overcome it. Some of us have felt that nothing short of a complete overthrow of the existing system will improve things for women; others have felt that they would be satisfied if the existing system worked more equitably for women. In practice these problems have been temporarily solved by people of like theories and ambition forming their own groups and, while perhaps meeting others at monthly co-ordinating meetings, operating mainly on their own.

At a national conference all these varying groups came together and it was a sign that we were still so imprisoned in the old form of political response that many of us felt that this could only be accompanied by conflict and perhaps even open divisiveness. I had approached the June conference feeling rather apprehensive and even pessimistic about our chances of being able to spend three days together without these differences precipitating some kind of crisis. That I was proved wrong and that some 200 of us aged from 17 to 70, some of whom had been fighting for feminist causes all their lives, others of whom had only been to their first meeting weeks before, were able not merely to co-exist but to engage in mutually productive discussion and planning, seems to me to have been a vindication of our methods of organization.

But while it was easy to bask in a virtuous sense of rectitude for a while, a lot of things have changed in the past seven months and we can no longer coast along and ignore things which may have a determining effect on our future. The new Labor Government has shown itself ready to at least listen to demands which affect women and has already made a couple of perhaps small but important changes – abolition of the tax on contraceptives, the introduction of paid maternity leave for both married and single women employed by the Commonwealth Public Service and the re-opening of the Equal Pay Case to intervene on behalf of this principle. (We should not be fooled into thinking that this will automatically ensure that all women receive equal pay but at least some of the legal barriers to it have been removed. It is now largely up to the unions – and us to pressure the unions – to fight for its implementation.) Women's Liberation has been debating the reformist/revolutionary issue since we got started but this choice has been largely pre-empted from us by the rise to national prominence of WEL. Our choice is no longer whether or not to fight for 'reformist' goals, but what stance we are going to take in relation to WEL which is determinedly fighting for them.

The WEL Conference held in Canberra on 20 and 21 January, 1973 was the third women's conference I attended. WEL has in the space of eleven months grown from a group of eleven women in Melbourne to a national pressure group with 1,777 paid-up members. It grew out of the Women's Liberation Movement but was started by, and has since attracted, women who were less interested in the total critique of the relationship of the sexes to Women's Liberation than in trying to effect specific, immediate and piecemeal reforms. It achieved a lot of mostly favourable publicity during its pre-election questioning of candidates and its publication of the WEL form guide to voting. The effect of WEL on the election results is impossible to determine. It may not have swung a single vote – although this seems unlikely – but this was less important than the fact that it managed to at least draw public attention to many women's issues and it probably precipitated the public stances on these issues which the leading parties were forced to take. WEL is claiming credit for the first two of the reforms listed above and it is already planning campaigns to press for other changes.

Four hundred women and a few men attended the WEL Conference. Its differences from a Women's Liberation Conference were apparent as soon as I walked into the opening session and saw the row of 'leaders' facing the hall full of women. The political mood of the weekend was set very early with two papers from experts on lobbying tactics. Dr Thelma Hunter from the Political Science Department of the Australian National University, put forward a very vigorously argued case for the necessity of having a highly structured, efficient national body – the AMA and the RSL were two of the examples she gave – in order to gain access to the Government. She was followed by a description of two of his successful campaigns by a freelance professional lobbyist, Mr Peter Cullen. Their twin performance was terrifyingly convincing and the mutters of hesitation or downright disapproval were drowned in the enthusiastic applause. It seemed to me at that stage that the WEL Conference was going to be like any other conventional political conference. A clear demarcation existed between the organizers and the attendants, with power struggles and secret battles being fought out before a largely uncomprehending audience which was expected to give its meek approval to whatever the elite had decided. In fact the opening and closing sessions were pretty much this from what I, as an outsider, with no access to the inner circle, could gauge. The final, summing-up session in particular seemed to breach every principle of democratic organization yet devised, with motions being put without explanation or discussion, with those reporting back from the various policy sessions (which, because they were held concurrently, we could not possibly attend most of them) having their time tapped out by the chairlady's pencil and with final resolutions on organization, and how they would be actually implemented, being left very much up in the air. A further cause of unease on my part was the way in which the policy sessions were conducted. Certainly these were more democratically run in the sense that participants sat around in a circle and the leader/led distinction was somewhat blurred, but this fine intention was somewhat undermined by the fact that each session had one or more papers presented by an 'expert' in that field. Not that the soliciting of expert advice is especially reprehensible in itself, but I had thought that since WEL had been researching all of these areas of discrimination itself all year that such papers would have been unnecessary and the time could have been spent, with delegates from all groups together for the first time, in working out exactly what kinds of changes they wished to press for.

However these initial misgivings of mine were not completely justified for something of a grass-roots revolt occurred during the conference and if any power-grabbing schemes had been entertained by any group or individual, they were at least modified if not completely subverted. Although there was a strong move for the setting up of a centralized national body to undertake all WEL lobbying at a federal level, there was strong protest against this from women who saw that it would lead to the end of WEL's most valuable component – its close contact with the thousands of women throughout Australia who took some part in the interviewing and other pre-election activities. Also the proposals from the various local groups for future organization all demonstrated some unwillingness to sacrifice their autonomy to a super-lobby somewhere in the eastern states. The New South Wales Group was most outspoken on this:

We are determined to avoid having leaders – (either convenors or permanent spokeswomen – and any form of power hierarchy). Like many other radical feminist organizations, in setting up a structure we want to move on from competitive masculine power politics, involving aggression and backstabbing, to true egalitarianism. All of us in NSW would like to see this ideal carried through to the national structure. If so ... it could be one of WEL's major achievements.

The Canberra group agreed: 'Pyramid power structures are anathema to WEL's basic aim of involving all women.' Some other groups, like the Townsville one, wanted to retain official positions but to rotate the holders of those positions.

A protracted and at times bitter debate raged almost all day on this question. It was eventually resolved to set up a central communications network with a central clearing house for collecting, retrieving and disseminating information to all groups. A series of resolutions guaranteed local group autonomy to lobby on issues of local relevance while Australia-wide agreement had to be obtained before any group could act on a federal level. Most people seemed happy with these proposals, although they had to go back to the local groups to be ratified, and were confident that they had averted the possible threat of any one group obtaining supremacy. While this may be true, much will depend on the actual working of the scheme and the extent to which the groups are prepared to co-operate. So far WEL's short history has already been marked by interstate rivalries and by the presence within its ranks of a seemingly highly organized anti-abortion lobby. The conference itself was characterized by a degree of distrust and even acrimony that totally belied the notion of much sisterhood within the ranks of WEL. Several of the contributors to the organization debate, while they were espousing anti-centralist ideas, were doing so in the most authoritarian manner imaginable. Many of the women there, particularly those from country areas who, presumably, have been less exposed to Women's Liberation ideas, were genuinely puzzled by the anti-organization, anti-leadership slogans being parried at them. Several of them met with abuse, rather than explanation, when they tried to move motions. In such an atmosphere of ill-feeling it was hard to be confident that WEL had solved its organizational difficulties.

One of the endemic problems of a pressure group is that it tends to view self-examination as either a luxury that it has little time to indulge in, or as totally unnecessary. While Women's Liberation is often criticized for being too introspective and thus involving only a relatively small number of women, WEL seems to have adopted the other extreme and this carries many dangers, not only for WEL itself but also for all Australian women.

Several of the 'expert' speakers turned out to be advocates for self-analysis and their contributions were to me among the most important sections of the conference. Dany Humphreys, Madge Dawson and Julie Rigg all warned against the danger of WEL pressing for reforms which would only aid middle-class women. Julie Rigg concluded the conference with a paper on what had been scheduled as 'The Future of Feminism'. She said that she had intended to talk about sisterhood and how this was one of the most valuable things to emerge from the new feminism, but that much of what had happened during the weekend had made her realize that it would be farcical to do so. Instead she concentrated on a gentle, but nevertheless, determined warning to WEL to consider other women's groups when formulating its policies and not to undermine the ideals of the more radical groups, like Women's Liberation, in their search for quick reforms. She urged that the Women's Movement remain pluralist, and tolerant of other parts of the movement. Her words could have been interpreted as a plea to do nothing and this may have been how it came across to some people. It seemed to me that she was urging caution rather than inactivity, and that she was in particular asking WEL to examine its own motives a little more closely before jumping onto the Labor bandwagon: any reforms we achieve now are going to be around for an awfully long time and they need to be thought out very carefully.

Her pleas for self-examination should also, in my opinion, include a look at WEL's political inheritance. Many of the WEL spokeswomen seem incredibly ignorant of the history of women's groups in this country and I have heard several of them claim that WEL is the first such women's non-party lobby ever organized. It isn't – I can think of at least a dozen others. The first ones were formed as soon as women in Australia obtained suffrage and some of these are still going, even if their earlier radicalism has dissipated. Periodically throughout our history new such groups have arisen, determined to ensure that women were listened to. The last major one that I am aware of, Women for Canberra, which existed in all states during the early 1940s was least as big as WEL is now. It is necessary to look at what happened to these groups, and to their demands, when assessing WEL's potential power. Certainly the political climate may be different now and the Government may be a willing listener to women's demands. It is the demands themselves however which must be carefully assessed. Do they really get to the heart of the problem? Even if we get equal education, child-care centres, abortion on demand and the other reforms which WEL advocates (though it equivocates a bit on the last one), are we going to see a necessary alteration in the power between the sexes? Are women going to be treated as people rather than categorized by their sex? Even if that categorization has changed somewhat in content, sexist attitudes can still remain and be even more insidiously entrenched if they are not continually confronted. We could well end up with a situation similar to that existing in several Eastern European countries where legal, economic and social equality exist on the statute books but where fundamental attitudes have not altered one iota.

These questions have always preoccupied Women's Liberation and were again the subject for debate and discussion during the Theory of Feminism Conference held at Mt Beauty during the 1973 Australia Day long weekend. A petrol strike prevented many of the Sydney women from coming (is there some kind of conspiracy among male unionists to stop Women's Liberation conferences from being fully attended?) and only about ninety people attended. There were a large number of papers but these were circulated and none of them was actually read out. It was intended that their writers would speak briefly and then the conference would break into small groups to discuss either the papers themselves or ideas arising from them. This worked well for the first session but then tended to break down as people seemed to be reluctant to leave the main meeting place. This to me represented a reversal of the principles we had established during the June 1972 conference and this was quickly evident when the same people tended to be vocal in each discussion. A large number of those present did not speak out at all during large sessions and probably a great many valuable contributions were lost because of this. Certainly the degree of participation did not seem as great as previously. As the first residential conference ever held by Women's Liberation, we should have expected even greater communication and rapport. I think this occurred informally, in between sessions and during the talks over drinks at night, but I am not sure that it characterized the conference overall. There were a number of heated and at times even hostile discussions which at least temporarily shattered the idea of sisterhood as we were forced by several of the papers to re-examine some of our most fundamental ideas.

I will concentrate on just one of the discussions, the one that I thought was the most important, and the one which raised the most disturbing ideas. This was the paper on Sexism within the Movement given by the Hobart group. The paper argued that sexist attitudes exist within Women's Liberation and that these are illustrated by the treatment of lesbians by many movement women and by the way they are discussed in much of the literature. This accusation was shattering enough to those of us who had comfortably regaled in the notion that it was only men who were sexist. In fact this revelation seemed to be very similar to the situation at the Black Power Conference in Brisbane last year when the black radicals accused the white radicals of being racist. We were now being confronted with the fact that while we might be victims in some situations, we are also oppressors in others. (The 'We' here must include not only heterosexual women but also those bi-sexual and lesbian women who categorize each other in sexist terms.) I think that this, the main point of the paper, did not sink in with a lot of people for in the course of arguing it, the paper attacked the twin pillars of Women's Liberation – sisterhood and consciousness-raising – and said that these were unable to be shared by lesbians. This precipitated both incredulity and hostility from those who either accepted both of these concepts uncritically or who doubted the validity of what the paper was arguing. There was also considerable tension and even reticence generated by the fact that we were discussing lesbianism at all, a further example of our inability to completely escape sexist thinking in ourselves. It became very easy during this discussion to relegate lesbians to the freak category, to see them as *them* as opposed to *us*. The very arrangement of the room reflected this thinking. During all previous sessions we had all sat around in a circle facing the centre. This time practically everyone faced the four women who had written the paper who were sitting together against one wall. One was reminded of a court-room situation. This, and the blatant antagonisms aroused upset a lot of people and we would be kidding ourselves to say that the conference ended on the same euphoric note as the June meeting. I think most of us were deeply disturbed, not necessarily for the same reasons, but quite a lot of illusions had gone and we all realized that many of the pat theories and ideas we had entertained were no longer adequate.

This is not meant to imply that the conference was a failure; it was probably the most successful and certainly the most significant one in terms of developing our understanding of how the mechanics of oppression operate, that we have had so far. But the way ahead no longer seems very clear. Many people are anxious to have an action conference later in the year: at the same time as we were engaging in this lengthy self-analysis there was a growing impatience to engage in some kind of overt political activity.

I was struck particularly by the contrast between the two conferences. Although they were held only a week apart and there was a slight overlap of the same people attending both conferences, the WEL weekend, planning campaigns to agitate for better child-care and reforms in the education system, seemed light years away from the agonized introspection that took place at Mt Beauty. Does this matter? I think it does, and that we must find some kind of connection between them if the Women's Movement is not to polarize around mutually exclusive activities. This is not to suggest that it is simply a matter of WEL becoming more self-analytical and Women's Liberation more activist. I think we have to accept for the moment anyway that many people in each group reject what the other is doing. Many members of WEL have been involved in Women's Liberation and have deliberately rejected consciousness-raising while some W.L. women are impatient or sceptical about the idea of lobbying governments.

But we have to recognize that both groups belong to the same field of opposition to sex discrimination even if we each inhabit vastly different landscapes within that field. The ideas and activities of each group affect the other even if negatively. We have always tried to maintain that the Women's Movement represented a contrast to the competitive ethos of much of the male political scene but so far we have not really begun to work out our relations to each other and the co-operation which we espouse in theory has not always been evident in practice. (Though there are plenty of instances where it *has* existed – but what I am trying to say is that we should perhaps make it more deliberate and long-term.) What we need to do is find some meeting point at which to try and break down the fear and distrust we often have of each other. Obviously there are many differences within both WEL and W.L. too and it is not a matter of two unified groups meeting each other. But if we are interested in trying to secure meaningful changes as opposed to patchwork reforms we have to communicate and, hopefully, co-operate.

One way this could be started would be to ask WEL to participate in the action conference to be held later in the year and if this was done I would suggest a return to the formula adopted by the June 1972 conference. The workshops there were just another variation of our basic unit of organization, the small group, but they were different in that they came together for only a short period of time and that most of us did not know more than a couple of women in each workshop. Although some of them were rather large they still provided a framework in which to work out how we must learn to relate to each other. It is easier to confront differences in a small group situation and such confrontations did occur in several of the workshops I participated in. There was no running away and hiding in cliques, no resorting to slick formulas and no immunity to attack another person's ideas without explaining and justifying what was meant. We were approaching resolution of the problem of how to disagree with someone's ideas without rejecting them as a person; we were forced to accommodate the fact that none of us, no matter how long we had been in the movement, had the 'correct line', none of us held a monopoly of truth. The kind of reassuring security of continually associating with people who agree with us was broken down and this forced us to each have to reconsider very carefully not only whether or not the ideas we had espoused still held good but also how we coped with other women who disagreed with them.

I think we were approaching then, and should try and consolidate now, the kind of dialogical situation which Paulo Freire[9] characterizes as essential for the attainment and maintenance of a revolutionary consciousness. In his theories of the pedagogy of the oppressed, Freire is dealing with the problem of how both literacy and a critical awarness of their environment can be instilled in Latin American peasants, but he also applies his theory to the relationship between leaders and the masses in a revolutionary situation. And although we may have abolished leadership within Women's Liberation, we in the movement do assume something of the position of leaders in relation to those who are still outside it. I think this applies within both WEL and W.L. and so not only do both groups need to work out how to relate to non-movement women, but we also need a means whereby we do not assume either towards each other or towards those not in the movement the arrogance and the lack of critical awareness which all too often characterizes those who see themselves as holding a monopoly of revolutionary truths. The educators themselves need continual educating, and one of the ways this can be done is by dialogue. Leaders of any group are always unpleasantly surprised when the masses they had contemptuously regarded as stupid or unperceptive suddenly display initiative or resistence to leadership directives. This is what happened during the May 1968 Paris uprising, and this is what occurred on a much smaller scale at the WEL conference. We cannot naively expect that such dialogue will invariably lead to agreement but it should produce some understanding of the fears we hold about each other. It should also help perpetuate the pluralism which is necessary to ensure that neither group undermines the ideas and aims of the other. If we want to continue as a movement and not just a series of unconnected groups knowing almost nothing of each other, then we must start to find ways of establishing links with each other. We should not regard the others (whoever they be) as 'less developed' women who 'need' to receive the blessing of our profound insights. This is the kind of authoritarianism which we reject from men. If we begin with the assumption that every woman, inside or outside the Movement, from any group whatever, has insights and experiences as valid and as worthy of discussion as our own, and if we reject the idea that we alone possess the 'right' theory and strategy about Women's Liberation, then some basis for co-operation and real movement sisterhood will have been established.

Twenty-Three (Part three)

The Women's Electoral Lobby and the Women's Liberation Movement Borrowing from Each Other*

Unfortunately a pattern of knocking WEL has developed from within the Women's Liberation movement. With the emergence of WEL, drawing its strength from the suburban family woman, the concept of sisterhood – which once seemed to include all women who were conscious of their oppression – is being revised to include only a revolutionary elite and – from a distance – working-class and black women.

When WEL began, I fondly imagined that the new organization would dove-tail with W.L., both as a reformist offshoot, and a point of contact between those who had been living and breathing feminist politics for some years before WEL was born, and apolitical women who flocked to join WEL because of its simple action program. But, in Sydney at least the W.L. old guard, with some exceptions, remained aloof from the infant WEL. Overlap in membership can be counted on the fingers of one hand, and the W.L. woman attending a WEL event is more likely to be there as a critical observer than a helpful participant. Two such observers have published articles this year based on WEL events (Anne Summers in *Mejane* no.10, Helen Garner in the *Digger*, June) which have more overtones of 19th century anthropologists watching the untutored natives at play than of sisterhood. (My God! They wear make-up! They have structured meetings! They argue! etc.) Though Summers ends her piece with a call for closer links between WEL and W.L., both writers suggest darkly that WEL's reformism is on the wrong track and perhaps even a danger to all Australian women. Neither substantiates this gut feeling with actual evidence i.e. from a hard look at WEL submissions, policies and actions.

* Reprinted from *The WEL Papers*, The National Journal of the Women's Electoral Lobby 1973/4.

Summers presents WEL as an un-sisterly group 'jumping on the Labor bandwagon' to press for 'piecemeal' reforms which may not 'really get to the heart of a problem'. 'Band-aid stuff', according to Garner.

Is there really such a thing as 'the heart of a problem' which can be perfectly encompassed? And are there any reforms which are somehow immutable? Even if this were so – which it isn't – the amount of homework, the number of late-night meetings and discussions, not entirely unenlightened by feminist ideology, from which WEL policy, such as it is, has emerged, is dismissed in rather a cavalier fashion. Moreover, the basic reforms demanded by both WEL and W.L. are identical.

Probably we have to look beyond charges of reckless bourgeois reformism to find the source of W.L. hostility to WEL, where it exists; and difference in life-style is the key factor. It is facile to generalize too wildly – some W.L. women wear make-up, some WEL women don't, etc. but still it's possibly not far wrong to say that more WEL women than W.L. women are bound by suburban-home-and-family commitments, and on the whole have less political experience. They are perhaps not prepared for revolution in their own lives, but are prepared to work for a revolutionary choice of options for future generations, and tend to admire W.L. women who are living single or childless lives as a matter of principle.

However reformist activities are innocuous only insofar as the system is prepared to accommodate and placate. So far, thanks to a government which has initiated WEL-oriented reforms, and which calls for conferences with WEL delegations occasionally, most of us feel that our actions are worthwhile – it's a matter of striking while the iron is hot. A double dissolution or a fossilized government might spell the end of WEL's present opportunities. WEL may be imperfect, but there is no other mass feminist movement in a position to influence government policy right now. When this fails – or when tokenism becomes apparent – the present *joie de vivre* so conspicuous at WEL meetings in Sydney may become more broody and introspective and divine discontent may prevail.

Some women in WEL in Sydney want to study feminist

ideology more systematically; some W.L. women want more action; but instead of participating selectively in each others' programmes it looks as though the two groups will continue to operate on parallels – WEL has a new feminist study group: W.L. a new Theory and Action group. However if a recent WEL decision to approach W.L. groups about renting office space in the Women's Centre, Alberta Street, works out, physical proximity may break down some unnecessary barriers, and the two groups may work out a complementary *modus vivendi*.

WEL needs to borrow from W.L. groups a feminist vision of a possible future society. So far WEL has not produced a coherent ideal of social change to work towards. We have mostly been concerned with giving all women, as a right rather than a privilege, benefits which the middle-class woman has enjoyed for a few generations – easily available abortion, equal education, good child-minding facilities, adequate income for single mothers. WEL also plugs for women to be included in decision-making processes at all levels. These are matters of social justice, and as such, are eminently worthy goals to pursue. But they are pursued in a society in which public forms, processes and power structures have been entirely concocted by males, according to masculine needs. To liberate women from domesticity, to push them through a competitive education system just so we can participate equally in structures defined by males and previously reserved for men only, is a fairly limited and even selfish aim. Women have more to offer society than a mere adoption of masculine roles, and that is reform in its purest sense – a reformation of decision-making processes, with feminine participation acting as a counterweight to masculine aggression and competitiveness.

Of course this argument depends on a basic belief in biologically determined sex differences. Ann Oakley, in her book *Sex, Gender and Society* – a review of the latest research into sex differences – is no doubt correct when she maintains that most of us exist towards the middle of a sort of biological continuum with the All Male (hairy, aggressive, dominating) at one end and the All Female (unhairy, passive, gentle) at the other.

Nevertheless, a person whose body is programmed by a menstrual cycle – not to mention the odd pregnancy/labour/lactation cycle – is likely to be more attuned to intimations of mortality, less prone to fantasies of pomposity and absolute power than the male whose body is not subject to such obvious changes. But so far societies have been organized by and for the most dominant males – perhaps about 10 per cent of the total population. This organization has enormous implications for both foreign and domestic policy. WEL should consider the question of whether its main aim is to encourage women to emulate and compete for the roles carved out by the dominant 10 per cent, or whether we should be trying to re-define these roles and altering the very structure of decision-making processes, so that it is not only the most competitive and dominant people who run our society.

WEL in Sydney has acted along these lines in organizing itself – almost, it seems, with blind instinct, for feminist ideals are rarely articulated. Yet we have tried to abolish leadership-and-led structures, resisting minority arguments which claim that this will mean less efficiency. We are in the interesting process of re-defining efficiency. And the organization itself acts as a sanction against women who may try to use WEL as a personal power base. Any hostility expressed in WEL towards other members is reserved for those suspected of ego-tripping in the masculine manner . . .

WEL may benefit from W.L. theorists in sharpening its awareness of what it is doing, but equally W.L. has something to learn from WEL. Firstly, tolerance – WEL meetings are free from the kind of moral authoritarianism which emanates from those who are convinced they have a monopoly of truth (isn't absolutism just another masculine hang-up ?). WEL women do not have pressure on them to conform to any kind of theoretical standards of dress, behaviour or traditional political convictions. It simply doesn't matter whether they appear at meetings wearing jeans and untended hair, or bouffants and hand-bags; whether they are socialists or Liberal party members, whether they have husbands, lovers or nothing, whether they are old or young, rich or poor. All women are listened to with equal respect, for all have something to offer. Though the monthly general meetings are structured to the extent of having an agenda and a rotating chairwoman, other meetings form themselves around the business on hand rather than around individuals, and in general the atmosphere may be more liberating, because less self-conscious, than that of some W.L. meetings. WEL may need an injection of feminist vision, but I hope and believe it will reject anything so rigid and un-organic as 'a total critique of the relationship of the sexes' as prescribed for WEL by Anne Summers in *Mejane*. Total critiques of anything spring from a fantasy of intellectual omnipotence, and have no place in feminist politics. Long live WEL, if it can continue to exist as a large political grouping which refutes both the leadership principle, and the constraints of abstract theoretical framework, as opposed to vision.

Notes

1. Helen Glezer and Jan Mercer, 'Blueprint for a lobby: the birth of WEL as a social movement', Henry Mayer (ed.) *Labor to Power, Australia's 1972 election*, Angus and Robertson, Sydney, 1973.
2. B. Fausteau and B. Lobel, 'Rating the Candidates', *Ms*, 1, 1972.
3. The adoption of a constitution led to the resignation of the more radical members of WEL who were also members of the Women's Liberation Movement.
4. For details of WEL's present organizational structure see reports of WEL national conferences for 1973 and 1974.
5. Examples of articles written by women journalists: Anne Summers, *National Times*, May 1–6, 1972; Suzanne Baker, *Sydney Morning Herald*, May 17, 1972; Caroline Graham, *Australian*, June 2, 1972; Marion Macdonald, *Bulletin*, July 15, 1972; Megan Stoyles, *Australian Financial Review*, July 26, 1972; Women's issue of *Nation Review*, October 14–20, 1972; Sally White, Michelle Grattan, 'The *Age* women voters' guide' – an *Age* special feature, November 20, 1972.
6. See *Woman's Day*, July 10, 1972; *Bulletin*, July 15, August 12, and October 23, 1972, and January 13, 1973.
7. This runs counter to much research on mass communications which

claims to show that personal influence is of greater significance than direct mass media contact.

8. Distribution figures of the *Age* show that these three electorates have very high readership figures compared with other areas in Melbourne.

9. Paulo Freire, *Pedagogy of the Oppressed*, Sheed and Ward, London, 1972.

Twenty-Four
Woman's Place in the Counter Culture

Any attempt to discuss the counter culture is necessarily controversial, raising questions concerning its nature and boundaries, both of which seem to elude precise definition. To discuss the place of women in this culture is even more difficult. There are those who argue that the Women's Liberation movement is an integral part of it, and that the counter culture proposes a 'new biological person', a 'wo/man' no longer capable of tolerating 'the aggressiveness, brutality, and ugliness of the established way of life'.[1] The basic argument of this chapter, however, is that the counter culture is essentially a male creation, in which the sexual inequalities of the dominant culture are maintained – albeit in hip form. While agreeing with Dennis Altman's argument that 'a genuine counter-culture' does exist among parts of the Women's and Gay Liberation movements,[1] I would argue that we must distinguish between these groups and the various descendants of the hippie movement of the mid-1960s which have been lumped together and labelled 'the counter culture' by various observers.[2] The groups that Altman describes as 'genuinely counter' rest on a fundamental rejection of traditional definitions of sexuality; the counter culture seems to rest as firmly on these traditional definitions as the society that it rejects.

Some observers have argued that there is a shift toward sexual equality and a blurring of sex roles implicit in the adoption by counter-culture men of styles of dress and manner generally considered 'feminine' in the dominant culture, and in the rejection of traditional 'macho' definitions of what it means to be 'masculine'. Bennett Berger, for example, sees evidence of sexual equality in 'the insistence that men may be gentle' and 'the merging of sexually related symbols of adornment (long hair, colourful clothes, and so on)'.[3] While not denying the potential significance of these changes in style, it seems simplistic to take them at face value as evidence of a basic shift in relations between the sexes. An alternative hypothesis – one which I think is borne out by an examination of woman's place in the counter culture – is that while there has been a superficial redefinition of 'masculine style', there has been little change in the fundamental pattern of male-female relationships. Men might be softer around the edges, gentler and less aggressive in interaction, but the traditional character of sexual politics – male dominance and female passivity – is preserved.

Maintenance of traditional sex-role definitions is evident in patterns of male and female participation in counter-culture institutions, where there appears to be an unequal distribution of power and prestige along sex lines. There are few, if any, women owners or editors in the underground press,[4] few women creating rock music, few women operating as entrepreneurs in the drug scene. The manifestos and novels identified with the counter culture have all been written by men. Even the transcendental mystical experiences of Eastern religions, which occupy a central place in the formation of the 'new consciousness', are essentially a male preserve: these religions, and thus their definitions of women, derive from rigidly patriarchal societies.

Women in the Drug Scene

The emergence of the counter culture is linked historically to the psychedelic movement, and the 'new consciousness' is in important respects a product of psychedelic experience. The implications of this experience have been extensively analysed, both by those who advocate it as a means of 'liberation' and 'consciousness expansion', and those who oppose it on medical, psychological, or moral grounds. Common to both sides of the debate is a belief in the symbolic importance of drug use as an expression of counter-culture solidarity and rejection of the dominant culture. One might point out, however, that while there may be a cultural division between the stoned 'freak' and the beer-swilling 'straight', they share a common economic situation – consumerism. Whatever its wider social implications, drug use supports a thriving form of hip capitalism, and like his 'straight' counterpart the hip capitalist is invariably a man.

If we look beneath the ideological superstructure of the soft-drug scene, and focus on the material base, we find a classic market situation. Marijuana may, as Charles Reich says, be a 'maker of revolution' and a 'truth serum'.[5] but it is also a business, and the dealer is the archetypal entrepreneur. 'Selling dope' is a highly competitive private enterprise, where the risks are great and the stakes are high – the dealer stands to make big profits, but he can also end up in jail. The fact that dealing is a high-risk activity makes it particularly conducive to stereo-typical 'masculine' behaviour. The social dynamics of the dealer's situation make it an unusually effective vehicle for the expression of male manipulativeness and the playing out of 'macho' fantasies.

The observation that competitive private enterprises are apt to be dominated by men, especially if the risk is high and there are large profits to be made,[6] seems to apply as well to the drug scene as to the straight business world. Research on soft-drug distribution hierarchies indicates that they are essentially male, with female participation restricted to the lowest levels and initiated by men. Speck describes the drug network as 'primarily a male-oriented institution, with the girls playing subsidiary and peripheral roles'.[7] Mouledoux, in his study of drug entrepreneurship in a north American city, describes a male-dominated 'pyramid', in which the man at the top has an 'office staff' of three young women who 'make deliveries, transport drugs, answer the phone, and carry out all the routine tasks required to maintain the business'.[8] The only woman participating in the hierarchy as a dealer in her own right is on the third level – one step removed from street distribution. Even her participation, however, is ultimately dependent on her relationships with men. Mouledoux describes her as follows:

> . . . she became exposed to drugs through her husband and his friends. Subsequently she became unofficially divorced from her husband, and over a period of time, was mistress of several middle-level dealers. In this way she was able to receive LSD on consignment, and in time her sales permitted her to make cash purchases.[9]

Discussion with people in the Australian drug scene indicates that the situation described by Mouledoux is typical. Women are rarely involved in dealing, and those who participate at all appear to have gained access to the scene by virtue of relationships with male dealers. These women are usually involved in a small way, dealing only to cover the cost of their own smoking. Dealing for profit is a male activity: as in the 'straight' world, women are essentially passive consumers.

Analysing their passivity, women in the Melbourne drug scene gave reasons which were strikingly similar to those used to explain low female participation at executive level in the business world – for example problems of access in a male-dominated situation, and restrictive sex-role definitions. Direct access to higher levels of the distribution hierarchy was seen as virtually impossible. As one woman commented: 'It's a male scene. The big distributors are all men – they'd only deal with men – so it gets to be men dealing with men right down the network.' The accusation levelled at women in the business world that they are 'too emotional' to be given responsible positions finds a parallel in the statement that 'men don't like you to deal because they don't trust you – they think you'd freak out if anything happened – any hassles with the law or anything – they think you wouldn't be able to handle it'. Nor, it seems, are the gentle liberated males of the counter culture immune to ego threat when faced with female competition: 'If you deal, you're competing with them. Men don't like that. The chicks that follow the big dealers around support them.' Sex-role stereotypes are called on to justify the situation: 'Being a dealer is a real ego trip. I suppose the guys really need that – I don't think women do.' 'If you deal you really have to hustle to get the stuff, then you have to get rid of it really quickly – I couldn't do that – guys are more aggressive.'[10]

Mysticism and the Oppression of Women

The path from psychedelics to Eastern mysticism, while it might transcend ego involvement and 'macho' role playing, does not lead to the elimination of sex-role stereotyping. The traditionally subordinate role of women is maintained. According to Baba Ram Das, for example, women are of the earth, men of the spirit, and because women are on a lower plane, they cannot really hope to reach nirvana.[11] In a recent interview, Ram Das argued: 'Most women's major work is to understand why they were born a woman. It wasn't random. You take a woman's body because you have certain work to do, and it's my understanding that it's not a full incarnation if you don't honour your biological impulses – to reproduce and nurture children.'[12]

In the Hare Krishna sect, women are explicitly defined as inferior. A sociological study of the Sydney temple describes the relationship between the sexes as one of 'strictly structured inequality': 'Women are believed to be deemed by Krishna to be intellectually inferior to men. Women also suffer the disadvantage of being "covered with a layer of lust and greed seven times greater than men". This assures male superiority and gives men an easier journey back to Godhead.'[13]

The practical implications of this view are evident in Robert Houriet's description of New Vrindiban, an ashram in West Virginia, where women were assigned all cleaning, darning, sewing, cooking, and churning of butter.[14] The evening meal at New Vrindiban is described as follows: 'We sat on the floor, quiet and smiling. The two women brought bowls of rice and vegetables from the kitchen and served the men. When the meal was over, the women cleared the dishes, then sat down and ate separately.'[15]

The relegation of women to domestic roles has also been observed in the ashrams of the Divine Light Mission: each one has a 'house mother' who cooks, cleans, and washes.[16] To the devotees of these sects, concern with the question of sexual equality is no doubt an indication that one has missed the point entirely – work done in the service of Krishna, or the Perfect Master, is by definition selfless. To the cynical outsider, however, the fact that the menial work is always done by women is inescapable. That such a definition of women is built in to the belief system seems to suggest that – even in the counter culture – religion is 'a way in which the male projects a vision of the world as he would wish it to be'.[17]

Woman's Work: The Division of Labour in Communes

It might be argued that if we want to make generalizations about woman's place in the counter culture, we must look primarily at the structure of sexual relationships and sex-role definitions in communes, for it is there, rather than in the drug scene or the religious sects, that people are attempting to give concrete expression to counter-culture ideals. If the modern nuclear family institutionalizes the oppression of women, surely the communal alternative must contribute to their liberation? As the editors of *Grass Roots* point out, communal living 'relieves the boredom of domestic chores by the sharing of day-to-day tasks', and diversifies child care, 'leaving the mother free to enjoy her leisure hours and return refreshed and attentive'.[18] The central question, however, is the extent to which both men and women are involved in these tasks. Communal living may relieve the isolation and intensity of the nuclear family but, as studies of kibbutz life clearly indicate, it does not preclude the division of labour along sex lines.[19]

The maintenance of traditional sex roles in communes has been noted by numerous observers. Roberts comments that despite their 'prophecies of freedom for the individual', hip communes often fall into the same division of labour as that of the larger society – 'the women cook, wash, or do other "womanly" things, while the men plant, work in the fields or gardens, and generally do "manly" things'.[20] Houriet argues that out in the country there is a 'natural impetus to revert to traditional roles', so that women tend to 'stay inside, cook, and look after the children, while men plough, chop, and build roads'.[21] As Westhues notes, the role of women is that of 'frontier housewife', and the males behave 'in what is variously called the paternalistic or chauvinistic pattern'.[22] This pattern is clearly evident in scenes such as these, described by Houriet:

Back at the house, Jean was baking bread with handgrown whole wheat. Laura was pulverizing eggshells to be mixed with the chicken feed. Jack and Bill sat over their third cup of breakfast tea discussing techniques of identifying Amanita muscaria, hallucinogenic mushrooms, from spores. Bluegrass music twanged on the phonograph.

* * *

It was the evening hour. Each day at this time, the men gathered outside the greenhouse to watch the last minutes of the sun's slow descent. The talk and laughter were subdued. From the open kitchen door wafted the smell of frying vegetables and the clatter of women preparing dinner.[23]

Within the counter culture, the emphasis is on 'natural living', and modern household technology is rejected as a 'false need' created by the consumer society. While this has obvious nutritional and ecological advantages, it also adds to what has traditionally been defined as 'woman's work'. Unless a more equitable division of labour is worked out, the women in these communes are likely to spend more time doing 'housework' than the average suburban housewife!

Child care in communes

Child care, too, appears to remain the primary responsibility of women, and even where children are defined as 'belonging to the commune', the pattern of sharing their care is largely limited to the group of mothers-with-children. To some extent, this can be explained in terms of the women's reluctance to trust their children to others. One woman is reported as saying: 'It's hard at first for women to trust other people with kids, no matter how much you want to. Men who haven't got kids often don't know their habits, needs, things like warm clothes ... Women have got to stop acting as if it's *their* responsibility to look after kids.'[24]

A more fundamental explanation, however, seems to be that the belief in the 'autonomy' of children, combined with the rejection of long-term commitment to monogamous relationships, creates a situation in which there are no norms requiring paternal responsibility.

Bennett Berger, in his study of child-rearing practices in communes, argues that communal ideologies tend to be elaborated by men, who use the view that children are autonomous to legitimate their own freedom from parental responsibility which, if acknowledged, would hamper their mobility.[25] While the view that children are autonomous people whose experiences need not implicate their parents might lead to a more equitable distribution of responsibility for their care in a stable communal situation, in the context of fragile relationships where people are free to 'split' whenever things become tense or unsatisfying, the burden of child care seems to fall even more heavily on women. Berger analyses the situation as follows:

> We mentioned previously that children (especially very young ones) 'belong' to their mothers, and that norms requiring paternal solicitude are largely absent. What this means is that fathers are 'free' – at the very least free to split whenever they are so moved. Since they are not 'legally' fathers (even if they biologically are) they have no claims on the child, and since there is generally a strong communal norm against invoking the legal sanctions of straight society . . . fathers have no obligation to the child that anyone is willing to enforce. Moreover, no norm takes priority over the individual's (particularly the male's) search for himself, or meaning or transcendence, and if this search requires father's wandering elsewhere 'for a while', there is nothing to prevent it.[26]

The Cultural Mirror: Reflecting a Masculine Version of Reality

In the counter culture, as in the wider society, women see themselves in a 'cultural mirror' created by men. Not surprisingly, the image they see there is a reflection of male experience: woman's place is defined not in terms of a range of interests and abilities, but in terms of sex, and women's issues are simply ignored.

With the notable exception of Philip Slater's work, none of the popular commentaries on the counter culture deals with the question of sexual inequality.[27] Theodore Roszak's analysis of the 'new consciousness' concentrates on the rejection of technology and rationality, and on the liberating power of Eastern mysticism and psychedelics. Sexual oppression and liberation are not mentioned. They are similarly ignored in Charles Reich's over-rated eulogy of 'Consciousness III', in which he devotes a great deal of discussion to the oppression inherent in homogenized peanut butter, but none to the oppression inherent in traditional sex-role socialization. Both *The Making of a Counter Culture* and *The Greening of America* are peculiarly male documents, Roszak focusing on 'weening men away from the technocracy',[28] Reich complaining that 'there are no longer any man-sized jobs, no challenges, no occasions that will cause an individual to extend himself, to grow to his utmost powers'.[29] Women are not mentioned in either book, except under the rubric of 'man' and 'makind'.

While Richard Neville discusses the 'sexual revolution' in *Play Power* he appears to be completely unaware of the contradiction inherent in equating liberation with availability. For Neville, the essential feature of the 'new sexual consciousness' appears to be the belief that 'it's groovy to be carnal',[30] which relieves men of the hassle of seduction and guarantees them unlimited sexual gratification 'without feigned love or hollow promises'.[31] Neville notes that the 'libertarian sex ethic' serves to boost recruitment to the Underground, and approvingly quotes Paul Krassner's comment: 'I'm only in the Movement to meet chicks and get laid anyway'.[32] Other self-styled 'manifestos' of the counter-culture ethos such as Jerry Rubin's *Do It* and Abbie Hoffman's *Revolution for the Hell of It* contain similarly 'macho' celebrations of the increased availability of casual sexual gratification.[33] These writers provide only one role model for women – the 'groovy chick', whose sole function is to enhance the lives of men.

The literature identified with the counter culture provides further indication of 'woman's place' – the hero symbols are all men, and women are presented only in the context of a 'masculine' version of reality. In the much-read novels of Herman Hesse, for example, the search for 'enlightenment' is presented as an exclusively male activity, and women appear only as shadowy background figures.[34] The novels of cult-hero Ken Kesey focus on the struggles of larger-than-life exponents of the lusty, brawling, masculine ethos. The action and vitality in

Kesey's world is all male. The women watch from the sidelines, pale and long-suffering like the wife in *Sometimes a Great Notion*, or vindictive and castrating like Big Nurse in *One Flew Over the Cuckoo's Nest.*[35] As portrayed in Tom Wolfe's *Elektrik Kool-Aid Acid Test*, Kesey's 'real' world seems to operate in terms of similar sex-role definitions:

Faye, the eternal beatific pioneer wife, in the house, at the stove, at the sewing machine, at the washing machine, with the children, Shannon and Zane, gathered around her skirts. Out in a wooden shack near the creek, Kesey has his desk and typewriter, where he has just finished the revisions on *Sometimes a Great Notion* . . .[36]

This pattern of creative male, supportive female is also apparent in *Divine Right's Trip*, which first appeared in the *Whole Earth Catalogue* – the ultimate expression of simple down-home back-to-the-land counter culturism. The dedication of the book is reminiscent of the prefatory cliches used by male academics: 'First I want to send greetings to some men who in the last ten years have been good friends, teachers, and brothers to me . . . And then I want to dedicate this book to Chloe, my friend, wife, and lover.'[37]

Thus, like their 'straight' sisters, women in the counter culture play a supportive role while their men get on with the 'heavy' business of creativity, and like their 'straight' brothers, counter-culture men acknowledge the intellectual contributions of their male 'colleagues' and offer the sop of 'dedication' to their wives. Whatever else may have changed, the relationship of women to culture has clearly been maintained.

The *Rolling Stone* review of *Divine Right's Trip* is perhaps the most telling comment of all. The book is described in these terms:

A folk-tale; our folk tale. Us land-grabbing long-haired broken-chromosomed aquarian anarcho-syndicalist Whole Earth Catalog readers; this is our epic . . . Divine Right Davenport is *our* hero, our Odysseus, our Jason, our Beowulf, our Boone; and his quest for his identity, his Wholeness, is our quest, his struggle our struggle, his triumph ours, too.[38]

'We', of course, are counter culture *men*. If we consider this 'folk-tale' from the perspective of Divine Right's 'old lady' Estelle, it changes from an epic quest for 'wholeness' to a masochistic exercise in self-destruction. Undaunted by the generous helpings of emotional pain that Divine Right – in the best 'alienated wanderer' tradition – inflicts on her, Estelle waits patiently until he 'gets his head together', then flies to his side for a 'hip' wedding. Thus, the woman in the counter culture is in the same situation vis-a-vis 'our hero' as women have always been in relation to the male 'heroic' tradition – identification is only possible through a distortion of sexual identity, an acceptance of male values, and a denial of experience. As Shulamith Firestone argues:

> ... women have no means of coming to an understanding of what their experience *is*, or even that it is different from male experience. The tool for representing, for objectifying one's experience in order to deal with it, culture, is so saturated with male bias that women almost never have a chance to see themselves culturally through their own eyes.[39]

Nowhere is this male bias more evident, or more important, than in the rock music that is so central to the counter culture experience. Rock has been perhaps the major vehicle for the articulation of the 'new consciousness', in that it is a more immediate form of communication, and reaches a wider audience than the novels and manifestos. As Charles Reich puts it: 'The dominant means of communication in our society – words – has been so abused, distorted, and pre-empted that at present it does not seem adequate for people of the new consciousness. Music, on the other hand, says all the things they want to say or feel.'[40]

It is impossible to separate rock music from its lyrics, however, and if *they* represent the 'new consciousness', one can only conclude that it offers very little for women. The tone may be contemptuous, as in songs like the Rolling Stones' 'Stupid Girl' and 'Yesterday's Papers', or Dylan's 'Don't Look Back' and 'Like a Rolling Stone', or painfully nostalgic and romantic as in Jesse Winchester's 'Yankee Lady' or Neil Young's 'A Man Needs a Maid', but the message never varies. As Marion Meade argues: 'For those who have taken the trouble to listen carefully, rock's message couldn't be clearer. It's a man's world, baby, and women have only one place in it. Between the sheets or, if they're talented like Arlo Guthrie's Alice, in the kitchen.'[41]

Summary: Prospects for Change

Clearly, traditional sex-role definitions are alive and well in the counter culture. Men continue to be 'active' and 'creative', while women remain 'passive' and 'supportive'. Ironically, the emphasis on 'gentleness' which has helped to change masculine style, and created a semblance of equality between the sexes, is also a most effective weapon for keeping women down. If the assertiveness and aggressiveness which tend to accompany women's consciousness of their oppression are considered 'strident' in the straight world, they are even less acceptable in the context of strong norms against 'heavy' or 'uncool' behaviour.

The situation is, of course, less clear cut than it has been presented here. There are doubtless many groups within the counter culture who are attempting to break away from the pattern of male dominance, and there may even be some who have succeeded. The situation is also flexible, and one can predict that as the impact of the Women's Liberation Movement brings changes to sex-role definitions in the wider society, parallel changes will occur in the counter culture. One thing is clear, however. Rejection of the dominant culture does not in itself guarantee any change in 'woman's place'.

Notes

1. Dennis Altman, 'Revolution by Consciousness', in H. Mayer and H. Nelson, *Australian Politics: A Third Reader*, Cheshire, Melbourne, 1973, p.723.

2. See particularly Theodore Roszak, *The Making of a Counter Culture*, Charles Reich, *The Greening of America*, and Philip Slater, *The Pursuit of Loneliness*.

3. Bennett Berger, 'Hippie Morality – More Old Than New', *TransAction*, vol.5, no.2, 1967, p.20.

4. I would consider that papers produced by women's collectives belong to the Women's Movement rather than the Underground.

5. Charles Reich, *The Greening of America*, Bantam Books, New York, 1971, p.281.

6. Caroline Bird, *Born Female*, Pocket Book, Richmond Hill, Ontario, 1969, p.73.

7. Ross V. Speck, *The New Families*, Basic Books, New York, 1972, p.109.

8. Joseph Mouledoux, 'Ideological Aspects of a Drug Dealership', in K. Westhues, (ed.) *Society's Shadow: Studies in the Sociology of Counter-cultures*, McGraw-Hill Ryerson, Toronto, 1972, p.112.

9. Mouledoux, ibid. p.114.

10. Quotations from interviews with women in the Melbourne drug scene conducted in June and July, 1973.

11. Author's notes taken at a lecture given by Baba Ram Das in Toronto, April 1970.

12. Sara Davidson, 'Baba Ram Das: The Metamorphic Journey of Richard Alpert', *Ramparts*, February 1973, p.68.

13. Roland Breckwoldt, 'The Hare Krishna Movement in Australia: A Sociological Perspective', Unpublished paper, June 1972.

14. Robert Houriet, *Getting Back Together*, Abacus, London, 1971, p.316.

15. Houriet, ibid. p.312.

16. Alistair Jones, 'Who's This Little Bastard Trying to Ban Sex', The *Digger*, August 11-August 25, 1973.

17. Eva Figes, *Patriarchal Attitudes*, Panther Books, London, 1972, p.53.

18. *Grass Roots*, no. 1. April-June 1973, p.16.

19. See particularly Shulamith Firestone's discussion of the kibbutz in *The Dialectic of Sex*, pp.199–201.

20. Ron E. Roberts, *The New Communes: Coming Together in America*, Prentice Hall, Englewood Cliffs, N.J., 1971, p.89.

21. Houriet, op.cit., p.77.

22. Westhues, op.cit., p.200.

23. Houriet, op.cit., pp.54 and 170.

24. The *Digger*, July 28–August 11, 1973.

25. Bennett Berger, et al, 'Child-Rearing Practices in the Communal Family', in H. P. Dreitzel, *Family, Marriage, and the Struggle of the Sexes*, Macmillan, New York, 1972, p.289.

26. Berger, ibid. pp.291–2.

27. Philip Slater, *The Pursuit of Loneliness*, Beacon Press, Boston, 1970.

28. Theodore Roszak, *The Making of a Counter Culture*, Doubleday, New York, 1969, p.267.

29. Reich, op.cit., p.407.

30. Richard Neville, *Play Power*, Paladin, London, 1971, p.59.

31. Neville, ibid. p.60.

32. Neville, ibid. p.61.

33. Perhaps the fact that Neville, Krassner, Rubin, and Hoffman were reared in the sexually repressive forties and reached adolescence in the early fifties is significant in explaining their obsession with the orgiastic. Subsequent generations of counter-culture men, less dizzied by the sudden plunge from scarcity to abundance, might be expected to adopt a more critical approach to traditional definitions of sexuality.

34. See *Siddhartha* and *Journey to the East*, which are particularly popular. There are no women mentioned *at all* in *Journey to the East* and in *Siddhartha* the only woman is Kamala, the beautiful courtesan who temporarily distracts Siddhartha from his quest for 'knowledge'.

35. Ken Kesey, *One Flew Over the Cuckoo's Nest*, Methuen, London, 1962; *Sometimes a Great Notion*, Bantam Books, New York, 1965.

36. Tom Wolfe, *The Electik Kool-Aid Acid Test*, Bantam Books, New York, 1968, p.50.

37. Norman Gurney, *Divine Right's Trip*, Bantam Books, New York, 1972.

38. Ed. McClanahan, *Rolling Stone*, quoted in the Bantam edition of *Divine Right's Trip*.

39. Shulamith Firestone, *The Dialectic of Sex*, Paladin, London, 1971, p.149.

40. Reich, op.cit. p.261.

41. Marion Meade, 'The Degradation of Women', in R.S. Denisoff, and R.A. Peterson, *The Sounds of Social Change*, Rand McNally, Chicago, 1972, p.174.

Twenty-Five
The Melbourne Gay Women's Group

The Melbourne Gay Women's Group (which is also known as the Melbourne Radicalesbians) grew out of the Gay Liberation Front (GLF). Women were involved in Melbourne GLF from the beginning and in January 1973 about a quarter of the members were women. Several attempts to form a women's group had failed. Many people believed that lesbians would always be in a minority in GLF. Despite the fact that a third of the activists were women it was thought that lesbians were more conservative and more apathetic than male homosexuals. Since the establishment of the Gay Women's Group we have shown that this is not so. In fact Melbourne GLF was caught in a vicious circle – there were few women members and so the women felt ill at ease and there was no check on male chauvinism; hence the movement could not attract new women members. It is worth noting that Gay Liberation and similar organizations in other places have also suffered from male domination, and this has usually led to the women forming separate groups. This has happened in Sydney Gay Liberation and Sydney Campaign Against Moral Persecution, in London Gay Liberation and the Gay Activists' Alliance in New York.

In January 1973 six women met to write an article for the *Gay Ray*, the GLF newspaper. Suddenly we found that we all felt the same anger and frustration. It seemed obvious that we needed to organize together as women and so we decided to hold regular women's meetings. The very fact that we had held a meeting excluding men provoked considerable reaction in GLF. At the next general meeting of GLF (general meetings were held weekly), the issue of sexism arose spontaneously and was discussed at length. The discussion continued for several weeks with the Gay Women's Group preparing papers on *Sexism in Gay Liberation* and *Role-Playing* which were discussed in general meetings. As soon as the issue of sexism was brought into the open more women began to appear at general meetings. The Gay Women's Group itself was attracting new members every week. Rapport between the members of the group was growing and consequently our analysis of our situation was becoming sharper.

Along with considering our relationship to Gay Liberation, we began to want closer links with the rest of the Women's Movement. We had a discussion at the Women's Centre on lesbianism/feminism – the first time that a broad spectrum of women had talked openly about this. A lot of barriers on both sides were broken down, heterosexual women beginning to change their preconceived notions of lesbians, gay women beginning to see that other women were not their oppressors. When the GLF centre closed temporarily, we began to meet at the Women's Centre.

The Gay Women's Group now has a membership of about sixty. It contains a number of small consciousness-raising groups, where we learn to trust each other and extend our analysis of a society based on division of sex roles. We also meet in a large action group where we write leaflets and articles and plan protest action, for example demonstrations against pornography, beauty contests and sexist advertising. We have put together a collection of local feminist writings, organized the first national Radicalesbian conference and spoken to many groups including other women's groups, high school and university students.

As a starting point for discussions among ourselves and with other groups we drew up the following Manifesto.

Lesbian. We do not accept the word in the sense that it is traditionally used – to describe, explain and limit us. Through our experience we have come to see its political significance. Lesbian is the label which holds every woman in line. It's the fear word that says a woman has stepped outside her sex role. When that's what we want to do, the label loses its bite.

Conditioning as a woman begins early. Women are deluded into thinking that they are getting as good a deal as a man, just different. Lesbians are not allowed to accept their situation but are taught that lesbianism is a product of penis envy, arrested development, personality inadequacies, hormones, etc. Society expects concealment of us. To the oppression of being a women is added the oppression of concealment. This is why 'coming out' – declaring ourselves publicly – is important. While we continue to hide from society we are accepting our own oppression. To become visible is the indication that we no longer accept their terms. We widen the range of honesty with ourselves and everyone we meet. We break down our isolation. We recognize our oppression and refuse to internalize it. To say that Gay is Good may seem divisive but is necessary in reaction to our sexist conditioning. We will not let society rest. Anyone who wishes to disapprove will be obliged to do this to our faces.

We want to overcome the division between women – to touch, relate, to give strength and validity to each other. We want women to be able to relate to women on all levels. We want to relate as individuals, not as elements in a correct ideology. Relating sexually to another woman just removes one more barrier in our minds – enables us to learn to love our womenselves in another woman. It is another eradication of oppression. But every women who no longer identifies herself in male terms, who is a woman identified woman, is 'gay' by society's standards. For us, gay consciousness is feminist consciousness.

We want a genderless society, that is a society that doesn't differentiate on the basis of sex, where people relate to each other irrespective of gender. But we recognize that at this time and in this place women are just more likely to be able to form relationships with other women than with men, if our criterion is warmth and honesty between *people* not roles. We know our relationships are natural. The only sexual perversion is a relationship based on exploitation and dishonesty.

We understand that our oppression stems from a sexist society. We recognize our oppression as women. We understand the specific threat that our living without men poses to the institutions of monogamy and the nuclear family, institutions which are the basis and the training schools of the patriarchy. This is why we organize as gay woman apart from our gay brothers. Gay men, though oppressed, do still receive the automatic benefits of being male in a patriarchal society. Lesbians can only receive the automatic oppression of being female in a patriarchal society. There are professions traditionally allotted to gay men, but there's not even a paternalistic handout to women. Gay men have figures in history and literature to identify with (Oscar Wilde for instance), while ours are suppressed. How often do we hear about Florence Nightingale and Joan of Arc relating to women? Homosexual men have always had the option of compromising, of receiving approval by being worthwhile citizens. Women aren't supposed to act for themselves, they are the power behind the man. So a lesbian, logically, has no place at all in the patriarchal society. At the same time this makes us freer to act against it.

We are going to fight our oppression on all levels. We refuse to regard ourselves as free while women are oppressed. We recognize the institutions which oppress us, and will not set up copies of marriage, of role-playing, of power dominance. We are fighting our oppression with honesty, in ourselves and towards others. We will destroy the nuclear family in ourselves. We do not want equality, but liberation. We do not believe in individual solutions.

Our immediate aims and tactics are not fixed. Preconceptions affect tactics: we think that the whole society must change, and work at what comes, fixing at no one level. It is part of our oppression that we do not know how much we do not know. We cannot say what freedom will be like. We do not have a programme. A new society of aware people is very much a vision still. But we can say certain things. We believe that leadership is destructive, power is sexist, and as we aim for a leaderless society so we work in a leaderless group. And we attack the power basis of sexism in existing institutions. We work through consciousness-raising to free our own heads. We work through actions and demonstrations to raise the consciousness of others, always bearing in mind that though confrontation may open people's eyes, it may also alienate them. We do not groove on militancy but adapt tactics to situations. But we do not shirk confrontations, knowing that our silence oppresses our silent sisters. Our existence is an argument in itself.

We want more than equality. We want total change. Male power, embodied in the male institutions of our present culture, is aggression. To ask for equality is only to get into *that* – into ruthlessness and non-caring. So forget about that concept of power and talk about collective feminist consciousness, about development as people in strength and love. 'Lying in the arms of the individual solution', we won't get anywhere. So we want to establish our own feminist culture. We want a distinct feminist community where we can learn to be/act out ourselves as people. We are not going to be seen through the eyes of male culture. And there's no point in conquering male culture when we can create our own.

In militant, enduring sisterhood,
Melbourne Radicalesbians

Twenty-Six
Liberation – Reform or Revolution?

It is not enough to struggle for particular reforms, important as these are. Unless we understand the relationship of the various elements within the structure of male-dominated capitalism, we will find the improvements are twisted against us, or serve one group at the expense of the rest.

Sheila Rowbotham, *Wôman's Consciousness, Man's World**

It is more than seventy years since Australian women were given the vote. The early suffragettes who fought for this right, saw 'the vote' as political equality and assumed that a new system of social relations based on real equality would follow. They were wrong. Today inequality of the sexes is as rampant as ever. Indeed, at the turn of the century Lily Gair Wilkinson had written in Britain:

'Votes for women!' There is a cracked and treble sound about that.

The call for 'votes' can never be a call to freedom. For what is to vote? To vote is to register assent to being ruled by one legislator or another. Such and such a man (or woman perhaps) is to make laws and to administer the law *with the assent of the person who votes*. That is all. How, then, can a demand for votes be a call to freedom?[1]

She wanted a call for real freedom for a real change in the relations between people, not a call for the right to make a pencil mark. Yet today, the Women's Electoral Lobby, still believing in the power of the vote, calls on women to change society by exercising their right to vote in their own interest. They have fast become yet another organization in society to be used by politicians who wish to appear 'liberal'.†

* Penguin Books, 1973, p.122.

† See Chapter 23.

Thus the suffragettes of the 1900s aimed, and the Women's Electoral Lobby still aims, for a goal which is not concerned with relations between people. If one wants freedom it is a freedom manifested in the quality of interpersonal relationships and backed up by institutions organized around true equality. 'Getting the vote', 'abolishing the nuclear family', '24 hour child care' or 'equal pay', mean nothing on their own and cannot be catalysts to widespread social change unless they are part of much wider demands for qualitative changes in social relations. Therefore if women are to alter society we must understand how society changes. For Marx, an understanding of the constant flux of social life, of the mechanisms behind the processes of history, would enable *man*, through praxis, to manipulate the social process and so steer history in particular directions. Marx saw revolution as resulting from the increasing misery of the working classes, but he saw revolution also as a far more immediate possibility once philosophy was oriented towards understanding social processes, leading to the possible manipulation of change through the promotion of class consciousness.* Similarly, women's liberation movements can only hope to achieve results if first they understand the nature of the social processes they are trying to manipulate.

The first part of this chapter is therefore a discussion in general terms of the nature of social reality; it will be possible then to discuss the manipulation of social change in perspective, through the examination of the nature of such organizing principles as equality, reciprocity, exploitation and sexism – principles which motivate people to orient their behaviour in particular ways towards particular ends. These principles structure social reality, encompassing and directing the flux of history.

* This chapter searches for a theoretical understanding of the forces which motivate behaviour, an understanding which can then be applied to any social situation. For a discussion of the particularities of reform and revolution in the Australian political context see Chapter 23 'The Women's Electoral Lobby and the Women's Liberation Movement' in particular Part Two.

The Nature of Social Reality

Social reality is dynamic. It is by definition *interaction* between people. Values, roles and norms are the ideals against which people measure their behaviour towards others. Every piece of interaction involves some calculation about the reactions of the person or persons being interacted with, however habitual. Social interaction is based on a range of expected behaviour which is calculated on the basis of learnt norms and values. This is most apparent in secondary relationships, in relationships based not on knowledge of personalities but on knowledge of how people in particular positions ought to behave. The friend Jane may be seen as a complex personality with idiosyncracies which influence one's interaction with her; but Jane the policewoman, is expected to behave and interact as policewomen ought.

The dialectical nature of social interaction becomes most apparent when the actor has a specific end or range of ends to achieve through her interaction with others. She must become conscious of how to manipulate the values and interests of those with whom she is interacting in order to achieve her ends, often asking far more than she really wants in order to achieve that truly dialectical compromise which she is prepared to accept. But the dialectic is not only between the actors it is within the individual actor as well.

Values and norms are consciously social. As the 'ought' of our behaviour they are beyond the individual. But interests are much more immediate and personal, and when a person sets out to achieve an end, that end or interest must be gained by the manipulation of or accommodation to values. The dialectical interaction between values and interests constantly, though often imperceptibly, redefines values to suit ends, at the same time redefining ends to fit values. The resultant social activity is born of both the initial value and the initial interest within the individual.

But these dialectics are not free interaction between people. They are constantly constrained by their subordination to the demands of the organizations which regulate institutional behaviour. These organizations are essentially apart from and more resilient than their inhabitants. This is necessary to allow for changes of personnel without disturbing the functioning of the organization and to prevent the people occupying the roles from 'rocking the boat' as individual personalities. They are the tools of the powerful, and in line with the needs of the 'establishment' to promote stability they are defined as permanent – 'they were there before you were born and they will be there after you are dead'. There is nothing inevitable about organizing education through schools. The schools exist because they are effective mechanisms for maintaining some sort of *status quo* and so serve the vested interests of the establishment. People are cajoled into believing the organizations of society to be inevitable. Thus the rules and bundles of clear expectations associated with the performance of roles all make up another force with which people must interact when striving to achieve desired ends.

Social Reality and Social Change

So social change is a constant process, be it slow or rapid. It just happens as people cope with balancing the values they feel imposed on themselves by others, by themselves and by institutions, with the particular interests they have in achieving particular ends. Compromises are sometimes reached and then new values, new expectations, develop. There is therefore no need to look to the past or to other cultures for alternative models of behaviour since we don't live models, we live processes; and most importantly because we are all quite capable of developing new modes of behaviour through dialectical confrontation with others and with institutions. Whether such confrontation will be engaged in and the extent of that confrontation, depends on how much the change is desired, for confrontation may be traumatic, even deadly.

Therefore, solutions to sexual discrimination cannot be defined in terms of total situations. To map out the ideal society is to ignore the inevitable dynamics of social interaction within that society.[2] Such a Utopian vision has value only in so much as it serves to inject new ideas into the dialectics of social life thus affecting the directions of social change. Social change becomes truly dramatic and challenging of apparent social 'order' when the dialectical interactions between ideas and between the people associated with them become antagonistic, and it is only by the injection of basically antagonistic ideas into society that radical solutions can be found. It should also be noted that although through the dialectical process of social interaction consciousness of oppression may build up without the purposeful injection into the situation of antagonistic values, consciousness of unhappiness does not necessarily lead to a consciousness of the possibility for change.*

The importance of such a conception of social reality for Womens' Liberation becomes even more apparent when it is understood that notions of static ideologies and social orders are not only unreal but are held and propagated by those who would mould others to their own image. Such ideologies and social orders are the agents of oppression. To quote Stokely Carmichael, 'Those who can define are masters. And white Western society has been able to define, and that's why she has been the master'.[3] Stokely Carmichael quotes Camus, '. . . when a slave stops accepting definitions imposed on him by his master, then and only then does he begin to move and create a life for himself'.[4] So too have men done the defining for society, so too have they been the masters and so too must women begin to create life for themselves by rejecting the definitions imposed by men.[5]

Women's Liberation is a movement of an oppressed political and economic minority which aims to heighten the consciousness of women to an awareness of their oppression and to a need for change.[6] This change is seen as being possible only through confrontation with the oppressors – men, and will hopefully lead, through confrontation, to a new social situation in which women are no longer oppressed. They point to the fact that the

* A good example of this is the number of middle-aged women who unaware of possible alternatives but dissatisfied with their life resort to pill-taking in an attempt to find a 'cure' or 'solution' to their meaningless existence.

oppression they particularly oppose is that which results from role ascriptions purely along sex lines – an oppression which, like racism, uses physical characteristics, in this case sex, as a role sign. The male society defines how women should behave and so men maintain their position of mastery. What women aim to achieve is their individuality, their right to take part in the defining of their reality, but unlike men they do not wish their freedom to be at the expense of others.

What are 'individuality' and 'wholeness' – for their realization is liberation? Marx mapped out the liberation process for *man*. He wrote about the oppression of man by man and the way in which *mankind* would achieve freedom. Like so many radicals today he virtually ignored the oppression of women, implicitly assuming that they would subjugate themselves to their men on the road to revolution. His vision of a free truly communistic society was false in that it did not consider the process by which women too would achieve wholeness. Whole men relating to whole men at the continuing expense of women is far from a truly free and equal society. Despite his chauvinistic analysis Marx has contributed more than anyone to the understanding of the nature of social relationships under capitalism, and so we propose to critically develop aspects of his analysis which provide an understanding of how women can hope to achieve liberation.

From Exploitation to Liberation

For Marx, the continuing history of *man*, the evolution of *man*, is the slow development of his wholeness, of his consciousness of himself, of his individuality.[8] In the first stage of his development, that of primitive communism, man is one with nature, dependent on nature, he knows little of himself. In the many variations of agricultural society man is freed from domination by nature but lives under systems of marked social inequality, be they forms of slavery or serfdom, in which direct control over natural resources gives rise to mastery by a minority, to a mastery which exploits people as whole persons, a direct exploitation of the individual. From these social forms there was progression to capitalism only when the internal contradictions of a particular system gave rise through industrialization to a form of social interaction in which the buying and selling of abstract capital dominated economic activity, in which a new class of merchants, the bourgeoisie, channelled the whole productive capacity of society to their ends, to their enrichment through the accumulation of capital. In doing so they also gave birth to a class for whom there was no profit, the proletariat, whom the bourgeoisie regarded not as people but as labour power for the production of a surplus.

It is in capitalist society where man, though liberated from nature and personal servitude, is according to Marx, most alienated. He becomes an abstraction as he is split up into those aspects of his activity which have use value for the capitalist, for the priest and, when he is a capitalist, for his competitors. Man is thereby, and most of all, alienated from his fellow man and from himself. He lives for his work which is exploited for the gain it gives to others. The individual is not valued as a whole but only for the labour and satisfaction that his abstract activities provide. Even religion, which at one level provides false security and meaning as the 'opiate of the masses', completely devalues man to himself and his fellows. And so in Christianity:

> Men are asked to love each other because they are made in God's image, or because God loves them. Rather than affection based on an appreciation of the other's real personality, Christian love is the ethereal love of God in which individuals can partake. It rests on man's love of God, itself the denial of his humanity.[9]

While man suffers from 'false consciousness' he accepts alienation as his lot in life, he accepts the definitions of reality handed to him by his masters, but he is, because of the depth of his alienation, only one step from full self-realization.

Man, as he becomes increasingly conscious of the oppressive nature of his relations with his employers, enters into conflict with them. This dialectical conflict leads to revolution and the eventual liberation of man from oppression into a state of communistic relations where, in contrast to the subjugation to tribe and nature of primitive communism, he is whole in his relations with others. He is unexploited, no longer alienated by his actions from himself. But this state of communistic relations is not achieved immediately:

Between capitalist and communist society lies the period of the revolutionary transformation of the one into the other. Corresponding to this is also a political transition period in which the state can be nothing but *the revolutionary dictatorship of the proletariat.*[10]

The dictatorship of the proletariat is a period during which the formerly oppressed establish a society based on true communism. Once this period of adjustment is achieved, subsequent social relations will be based on relations between whole and individual human beings.

But, warns Marx, man's consciousness of his oppression might not come easily, for the capitalist subtly maintains the false consciousness of the workers by setting up a whole range of created needs in the workers which are satisfied by the capitalist at little expense to himself. These created needs today range through muzak in the factories and a company car for the junior executive. So successful are these sops to employees in diverting their attention from real problems concerning employer-employee relations that strikes are often over problems associated with these created needs – the length of a tea break, for example. Thus, says Marx, it is the task of philosophy, through its understanding of society, to reveal man's false consciousness to him and to show him the way in which he can, through the injection of antagonistic values and interests into the social system, channel social change towards revolution.

But a system of social relations can become so containing of antagonistic relations that there is virtual stagnation. In this case too it is only by the injection of new antagonisms that the system can change enough to advance towards the conflict which will free man from oppression by himself and others. Therefore women must inject antagonistic values into social systems which through space and time continuously oppress women by subjugating us to static ideologies which stress man as master.

Women too are alienated. We do what we do and are allowed what we are allowed as members of a sex, not as individuals independent of our sex. We are justified as incubators for the sons of men, as free household labour and as cheap industrial labour providing even greater surplus value for the employer than do his male employees.[11] Men too are alienated but the alienation of women is even more oppressive. For Marx man is the subject of history, not ideas as Hegel had held, and so man has the power to change ideas, to manipulate the process of history. So too have women.

If women are to achieve liberation from oppression, to be whole human beings, to seek freedom from exploitation in general and from exploitation as women in particular, they must propagate those principles of social organization which are antagonistic to exploitation and promote equality. They must understand the nature of exploitation and the nature of equality as organizing principles behind forms of social interaction. The following discussion of the nature of modern capitalist exploitation will lead on to a discussion of reciprocity as the underlying principle to the practice of social equality. In particular two aspects of Marxian analysis outlined above are highlighted as being critical. Just as Marx discussed the manipulation of workers within the capitalist system, so too are women manipulated through a bevy of created needs to believe that they are equal but different, and in this way their continued exploitation is ensured. Also the management or containment of antagonisms in advanced capitalism results in the control and manipulation of reforms for the benefit of the power elite.

Exploitation and Manipulation

It is not easy for many people to acknowledge that social life is constant flux. They prefer the false security of 'stability', of 'the establishment'. This security is false not only because it is based on a static ideology but because it is in the interests of those in power to maintain the apparent *status quo* of social relations which satisfies their needs at the expense of others. People are subtly manipulated into believing that security lies in social behaviour which is governed by clear-cut role allocation, where people act according to well-defined expected patterns of behaviour. Living a life of 'false-consciousness' they fear anomie, a normless existence which conjures up pictures of chaos and mental disturbance caused by uncertainty and evidenced by increased suicide rates. Such fears promote and support structured social systems in which social behaviour is governed by clearly delineated norms governing role performance, such that in all social situations a person knows clearly what to expect from those with whom she is interacting. Promotion of 'the establishment' by those in power is often explicit and is born of the fear of confrontation by people and ideas antagonistic to it'. Those in power promote criticism in the name of 'liberalism' but are fearful of truly antagonistic criticism. So the then Treasurer, the Rt Hon. B.M. Snedden, began a speech to the Young Liberals and Graduates Club of the University of NSW in Sydney on 5th September 1972 by saying,

There are four sets of people who we could class as permanent opposition to the establishment in our society. They are all regarded to a greater or lesser extent as damn nuisances. They all provide continuing challenge to establishments. They all deserve to be fostered and encouraged. Those groups are young people, academics, the Press and that more amorphous group of people to which we all, to a greater or lesser extent, belong – the 'Aortas' and the people who are always saying 'Aorta do this and Aorta do that'!

We could be excused for adding to the list women, but I have enough faith in our society to suggest that while establishments will always have opposition from youth, academics, the Press and 'Aortas', the objectives of the movement forming and reforming around the role of women will be achieved in our society, *and that proper opposition which we now observe to much of what we can call the establishment, will be temporary*. (our italics)

'Proper opposition' is encouraged as challenging and creative of an even more securely entrenched establishment. So the Rt Hon. B.M. Snedden concluded his speech as follows:

> We the Liberal Party must regard the sources of creative opposition to established social order and inherited values, not in terms of their nuisance value, but *harness* their creativity. Political power with this adjudication between competing claims and values will limit the immediacy of their response to these opposition groups, but we must accept what is valuable from them and continue to encourage them, because they thrive in and contribute to that great spirit of freedom and individual endeavour which is the characteristic of our social and political philosophy.

The establishment thus pays lip service to freedom and individuality to create and maintain a false-consciousness of freedom among those who question the social order. The questioning is explicitly 'harnessed' to keep the powerful in power. It must not 'rock the boat' for the ultimate value is social stability, the security of order. So the Women's Electoral Lobby was quickly harnessed and thus effectively silenced as 'creative criticism'. WEL was asked to make formal submissions on child care, women in the workforce, equal pay, the budget and a minimum wage, and so, eased quietly into the bureaucracy of government, it was no longer a threat. So too, the Prime Minister's adviser on women was made a public servant and thus, bound by the rules of the public service, was emasculated of any effective exercise of power, bound by the rules, the definitions, of an establishment oriented towards the continuing oppression of women. Were the Government serious about pursuing an anti-sexist policy it would have to be prepared to invest the women's representative with real power, but it is not.

Ideologies which stress order and stability, be they explicit or camouflaged by 'liberal' philosophies, are the antithesis of liberation for they attempt to channel the behaviour of all to the service of and in the interests of a few. Capitalist ideologies devalue people by dissecting them into bundles of abstract roles, regardless of the needs, capabilities and aspirations of individual, whole persons. Clear-cut role allocation and the delineation of stable patterns of behaviour are integral to such ideologies, and it is the imposition on the individual of predetermined role patterns that is restrictive and therefore exploitative of individuality. Liberation lies in the promotion of the maximum flexibility in roles such that relations between *people* are based not on inflexible expected patterns of behaviour but on the conscious operation of the principle of reciprocity, for where there is not reciprocity there is exploitation. Barrington Moore states:

> ... we can say that exploitation forms part of an exchange of goods and services when 1) the goods and services exchanged are quite obviously not of equal value, and 2) one party to the exchange uses a substantial degree of coercion ... It goes without saying that there are wide grey areas between fair exchange and exploitation.[12]

True, reciprocity is a relative concept. What is 'fair' will vary with personal interpretation, based on a whole range of values and interests. Thus those who are living in fear of chaos, who are manipulated by the ideologies of capitalism into valuing the *status quo* as the safest, if not necessarily the happiest and best way of life, in other words those who suffer exploitation through false consciousness, will not realize how unfair are the social exchanges they take part in. But they must be given the chance, by the injection of antagonistic values into their lives, to decide for themselves. Most importantly, it is only by the injection of a consciousness of the need for reciprocity in social situations that exploitation is constantly challenged and as often as possible overcome. The individual personality is given freer reign as each social situation is treated not as a predetermined pattern but as a unique situation for the symbiotic satisfaction of needs. What these needs are – and even the most basic needs are culturally conditioned – will be decided by much more open dialectics of social interaction.

True reciprocity is the symbiotic satisfaction of *uncoerced* needs and, as will be discussed below, it is in the overcoming of both direct and masked coercion that the need for antagonistic confrontation with the supporters of the 'established order' becomes necessary. True reciprocity, as represented here, is a guiding principle for behaviour, an aim, an orientation for behaviour, not a state of being. The constant asking of the question, 'is this situation reciprocal?', results in the dialectics of each social situation becoming more conscious, more active, since people question relationships and do not, because of socially induced fears, see obviously inferior and unequal rewards as their lot.

Such constant questioning, where possible prompted by the injection of provocative antagonistic ideas, becomes particularly necessary because exploitation in modern capitalist societies has become more subtle than ever before. And likewise the exploitation of women in modern capitalist society has become more and more subtle and devious.[13] People are constantly, subtly, coerced into accepting as proper, or at least as inevitable, situations which are blatantly exploitative. The young are encouraged to be 'creatively critical', workers are subtly coerced into purchasing their tiny blocks of land, building their brick veneers and furnishing them with 'the latest', and women are warned of the effect of the advancing years on their attractiveness for their ageless husbands and advised to follow 'the Ford diet chart' and then purchase 'at least one new outfit'. These all inhibit the awareness of, and blind people to the real exploitative nature of the relationships they are engaged in. More importantly it shows up the dubious efficacy of reforms which result only in individuals seeing the system as democratic or liberal.

Women's Liberation and Revolution – Aims and Tactics

Integral to the development of the need for reciprocity is a consciousness of the need for equality, for true reciprocity in social relations *is* equality. But, like reciprocity, equality can only be a guiding principle for behaviour, not a static state of existence. It involves 'the removal of those obstacles and impediments which stand in the way of the development of human capacities',[14] through a moral commitment to the equal worth of all human beings. The removal of obstacles to the development of the capacities of each individual woman is the task of Women's Liberation.

What of the form that Women's Liberation must take? Must it be revolution and if so what sort of revolution? And if we take the stance that we have taken here that Women's Liberation is only part of a more general liberation of all human beings, where do men fit in? Must all women be antagonistic to all men or must those conscious of the need for liberation seek together, whatever their sex to achieve the liberation of people regardless of sex or race?

What sort of social change will be necessary? Since liberation can only be achieved through the destruction of exploitation and oppression, it cannot be achieved within a capitalist system. It must be highly antagonistic to existing patterns of social relations and therefore must involve conflict. Whether this conflict is violent will in large part depend on the reactions of those who are threatened by change. If the threatened are violent the conflict will be violent and since capitalist society is based on an intricate system of cut-throat, self-centred game-playing which becomes the whole rationale for living, violence seems inevitable. As mentioned earlier, attempts at change within the system get so bound up within the 'rational' world of bureaucracies that they become part of the oppressive system. These small rebellions are subtly manipulated by 'liberal' governments backed by 'liberal' philosophies into becoming 'creative criticism', firmly 'harnessed' to the oppressive, exploitative cause of capitalism.

The attitudes of 'liberals' such as those that have ruled Australia for so long, to oppression and possible violence are beautifully epitomized in an analogy by Stokely Carmichael. He says:

It's obvious to me that if I were walking down the street, and a man had a gun on another man, and I was going to help, I'd help the man who didn't have the gun, if the man who had the gun was just pulling the gun on the other man for no apparent reason – if he was just going to rob him or shoot him because he didn't like him. The only way I could help is either to get a gun and shoot the man with the gun, or join the fellow who doesn't have a gun and both of us gang up on the man with the gun. But white liberals never do that. When the man has the gun, they walk around him and they come to the victim, and they say 'can I help you?'. And what they mean is 'help you to adjust to the situation with the man who has the gun on you'.[15]

So our liberal politicians are not about to join up with women against their oppressors. They gratuitously offer to help us to adjust to the oppression. They expect women to be grateful for small mercies.[16] But if those small mercies are accompanied by antagonistic ideas injected by Womens Liberation, resulting in antagonistic demands, they can become the genesis of a consciousness of oppression which can lead to a myriad of antagonistic eruptions within and between people which will make the road to liberation very much shorter. And the oppressors can expect little gratitude. When amazed by the ungratefulness of the women towards whom they were so liberal, they should heed Sartre's admonition of the white man's attitude towards the African:

What then did you expect when you unbound the gag that had muted those black mouths? That they would chant your praises? Did you think that when those heads that our fathers had forcefully bowed down to the ground were raised again, you would find adoration in their eyes?[17]

Women's Liberation demands radical change, fundamental change and as such demands revolution – a revolution which is part of the drive towards the liberation of humanity. Krishnan Kumar quotes Robert Tucker as saying that 'history for Marx is the "process of man's revolutionary evolution . . . the growth process of humanity from the primitive beginnings to complete maturity and self-realization in future communism" '[18]. Kumar concludes:

But if history itself is the Revolution, then the particular revolutions within history have to be seen as stages or 'moments' in the making of that Revolution. They could not be studied in isolation as self-sufficient phenomena; their pretentions to be final and consummating acts of liberation had to be inspected critically.[19]

Is Women's Liberation one of those 'particular revolutions' within the history of the evolution of human kind towards liberation?

First we must decide what we are going to mean by 'revolution'. It is a highly emotive term which refers to social change of a particular kind. Revolutionary social change is change which is both *fundamental* and *sudden*, which results in the establishment of social relationships based on new guiding principles and resulting in the transfer of power from one governing class to a new class of people. Thus, according to Marx, a transfer of power from bourgeoisie to proletariat would result, through the dictatorship of the proletariat, in an eventual transfer to all people equally – true communism. Although for many a theoretician a revolution may be a change in any direction – from radical to conservative as much as the reverse – for most revolutionaries the word has distinct moral connotations. And so Condorcet states, 'the word *revolutionary* can be applied only to revolutions which have liberty as their object'.[20] The Oxford English Dictionary quotes an anonymous writer of 1796 who states that 'Rebellion is the subversion of the laws, Revolution that of tyrants'.[21] Women's Liberation must certainly involve the subversion of tyrants, does have liberty as its object and requires very fundamental change. Whether a dictatorship of the 'proletariat' of women will be necessary is a problem which must be faced, but Women's Liberation does not wish to change the balance of power but rather exclude it as a factor in *all* social relationships.

Kumar concludes that revolution is 'a change of style, of the "generative principle" governing the norms of an activity'.[22] The 'generative principles' governing the norms of capitalism are exchange for profit, competition and a concern for self-advancement at the expense of others. A constantly propagated ideology of equality leads to a completely unwarranted justification by such competitors for their selfish exploitation of others, namely that there is equal opportunity for all and if people are poor it is their own fault. The continuous oppression of the majority of the population through inadequate education, nutrition and most importantly, inadequate rewards for their labour, is conveniently forgotten. If modern capitalist society is individualistic it is a brutal aggressive individualism constantly at the expense of others, through the exploitation of completely de-personalized labour. It is the source of alienation, not liberation from it. 'Equality' is defined by capitalism as the right to climb to the top over others, at the expense of others. The capitalists claim that all have an equal right to do so but conveniently fail to consider whether all have an equal chance. 'Equality' thus becomes a very relative term defined to the advantage of the definers, the masters.

The 'generative principles' which must be established if there is to be liberation for women in particular and eventually for human kind are completely antagonistic to those of capitalism: truly reciprocal exchange in social relations which involves a concern for the symbiotic satisfaction of the uncoerced needs of *people*. There can be no ideology of equality but rather a consciousness that the pursuit of truly reciprocal social relations requires that people continuously evaluate their behaviour in terms of the 'generative principles' of liberation, rather than acquiesce into any sort of self-satisfaction which is likely to allow the dialectics of social life to proceed unchecked towards the possible re-establishment of social forms which do not allow for a liberated existence.

Where then does Women's Liberation fit into the more general drive for the liberation of people? It is clear that Women's Liberation involves revolutionary action, action oriented towards a change of style, of the 'generative principles' governing behaviour, in the cause of liberty. But can Women's Liberation be a revolution of and for itself? Can Women's Liberation, as an autonomous movement, precipitate a conflict which will lead to a situation in which women's aims are realized, in which there has been a change of style such that behaviour is now governed by new generative principles? Unless the aim is either a lesbian nation or a society ruled by women for the oppression of men, the answer must be 'no'. If the aim of Women's Liberation were simply release from the oppression of men then both solutions would be in accordance with stated aims, but apart from some radical feminist sections of the movement, expressed by writers such as Jill Johnston[23] and in Manifestos such as that of SCUM (Society for Cutting Up Men)[24], most of the movement, though still amorphous, stresses the final goal to be a society in which interaction is non-exploitative, based on that symbiotic satisfacion of un-coerced needs. So the Redstockings Manifesto of July 7, 1969, states: 'We call on all men to give up their male privileges and support Women's Liberation in the interest of our humanity and their own'.[25] Such aims refer to a revolution which cannot be complete until women and men coexist in a non-exploitative, liberated social environment.

Robin Morgan ends 'Goodbye to All That' with '*Power to all the people or to none.* All the way down, this time.'[26] She also clearly shows where Women's Liberation fits into the more general drive for the liberation of humanity, especially in relation to socialist revolution:

Goodbye, goodbye. The hell with the simplistic notion that automatic freedom for women – or non-white peoples – will come about ZAP! with the advent of a socialist revolution. Bullshit. Two evils pre-date capitalism and have been clearly able to survive and post-date socialism: sexism and racism.[27]

Sheila Rowbotham puts it another way: 'The paralysis of a male-defined revolutionary movement is as evident as the paralysis of a consciousness which can comprehend only the liberation of women. Both are caught in their own particularity.[28]

Capitalism is exploitative, self-oriented and firmly male-dominated. It must be destroyed if there is to be liberation, true reciprocity in social relations, but its destruction, though a necessary condition for the liberation of woman and finally humanity, is not sufficient in itself. *Women's Liberation must come first*, for otherwise revolutionary movements will, in their organization and their conceptualization, perpetuate male dominance and act as a block to liberation. Male chauvinism will not be faced with a truly antagonistic situation productive of real dialectical change until it meets and is forced to experience its opposite, *female chauvinism*.

Those dialectics of social life which will be productive of truly liberating change must be antagonistic and must be forced. They won't just happen. Setting an example by practising liberation is unfortunately not good enough. It may be productive of consciousness in some but it will not be productive of radical change. People will be made to face up to the need to change, to reach new value positions through dialectical confrontation between antagonistic values, if they are faced with realities which are antagonistic to those they practise and value. In this regard it is interesting to note that in Sweden, it was found that children only started to positively question traditional sex role stereotypes when their textbooks systematically *reversed* the role structures or *never* pictured people as behaving according to conventional sex roles. When, at an earlier stage, books had merely mixed up the roles so that there was no constant sex bias but where, in a random distribution of roles, some people continued to be pictured performing roles according to conventional allocation along sex lines, traditional sexist attitudes continued to be expressed by the children. The establishment had not been challenged nearly firmly enough. Role reversal is not the aim of Women's Liberation since it would be oppressively sexist like the present one and far from liberating for humankind; but some role reversal will be a necessary tactic and a necessary *stage* in that liberation. Those male radicals who yearn for the dictatorship of the proletariat must see an equal logic in the need for them to suffer a dictatorship of women.

What are the stages in the course of Women's Liberation? Can we map out the road to revolution? Sick societies generate contradictory relations which are the seeds of their destruction. Radical movements which aim to raise the consciousnesses of people to the meaningless alienation of their lives are expressions of those contradictions, mechanisms for co-ordinated revolutionary action. Radical movements must, on the basis of their understanding of the forces which generate and order the flux of history, co-ordinate revolutionary action, and employ tactics which will generate a continuously growing consciousness of the need for liberation. They must map out a flexible road to revolution, one based on an understanding of the principles which guide social behaviour and therefore capable of adjusting to changing situations, not advancing blindly towards a Utopian goal according to a set of inflexible tactics. They must promote a new set of 'generative principles', fully aware of what the implementation of those principles involves. And this is where nearly all 'socialist' revolutions have gone wrong, very wrong. They have been, as Robin Morgan and Sheila Rowbotham made so clear, male-defined movements, formulated by men, run by men, *for* men, constantly at the continuing expense of women. To quote Robin Morgan again:

Women are Something Else. This time, we're going to kick out all the jams, and the boys will just have to hustle to keep up, or else drop out and openly join the power structure of which they are already the illegitimate sons. Any man who claims he is serious about wanting to divest himself of cock privileges should trip on this: all male leadership out of the Left is the only way; and it's going to happen, whether through men stepping down or through women seizing the helm. It's up to the 'brothers' – after all, sexism is their concern, not ours; we're too busy getting ourselves together to have to deal with their bigotry. So they'll have to make up their own minds as to whether they will be divested of just cock privilege or – what the hell, why not say it, *say* it? – divested of cocks. How deep the fear of that loss must be, that it can be suppressed only by the building of empires and the waging of genocidal wars![29]

So these radical movements, which are supposed to bring about the destruction of capitalism in the interests of liberation, bear within themselves the seeds for their own destruction. They generate a basic contradiction – a manifesto for liberation which depends on the continuing oppression of women. There must be revolution *within* these movements before they can sow seeds of revolution elsewhere. That is why Women's Liberation must come first. The energies of all revolutionaries must be oriented towards Women's Liberation, whatever the oppression they are fighting against, be it capitalism, racism, imperialism, slavery or serfdom. So now back to the tactics of Women's Liberation, for the first tactic for the liberation of people is recognition of the need for Women's Liberation as a first step.

If women could peacefully occupy positions of power and influence in society, the aim would have to be to infiltrate 'the world of men', encourage reforms* which would give women 'time to think' – child-care facilities etc. – and once the Women's Movement had enough mass support, systematically start to subvert the institutions of capitalism in the interests of women in order to change the underlying principles which motivate behaviour under capitalism. Such revolutionary action could not be peaceful however, for men are sure to react with violence; but if there were enough mass support the conflict could be traumatic enough to be productive of radically different sets of social relations which bring liberation much closer. But why a mass movement? And how is it achieved?

To quote Sheila Rowbotham:

> No woman can stand alone and demand liberation *for* others because by doing so she takes away from other women the capacity to organize and speak for themselves. Also she presents no threat. An individual 'emancipated' woman is an amusing incongruity, a titillating commodity, easily consumed. It is only when women start to organize in large numbers that we become a political force, and begin to move towards the possibility of a truly democratic society in which every human being can be brave, responsible, thinking and diligent in the struggle to live at once freely and unselfishly.[30]

And it is here, in the achieving of mass support, in raising the

* The only tactically possible reforms are those which raise consciousness rather than those which subtly manipulate women into believing they are gaining equality, e.g. child care reforms are of little use if they operate on the basic expectation that child care is the primary responsibility of women. To alleviate child care problems for the working woman will not on its own raise her awareness of her oppression.

awareness of women to their oppression, that the consciousness-raising group (CR), fits into the tactics for liberation. But it is only a stage, only a step towards mass consciousness and one that often must precede other liberation tactics such as role reversal. The CR group is destructive of liberation if it becomes the be-all and end-all of Women's Liberation. CR groups must be constantly conscious of the world outside their cosy, ego-moulding coveys, of the images they must present to others, of the consciousness they must encourage in others. Inward-looking CR groups which are no more than institutions for ego-tripping and floods of reinforced self-pity by their closed circle of members, simply help people to adjust to capitalism and to feel superior and self-important through the company of their little closed band of fellow sufferers. They are far from productive of revolution. The CR group has an essential place in the progress towards liberation but it must not become an end in itself.

A sick system contains contradictions which lead to consciousness of antagonisms which in turn leads some to ponder the way to change the sick system. Since human beings are the subjects of history they have the power to put theory into practice (*praxis*) and so an understanding of the dialectical nature of social interaction can set out to manipulate social change by influencing the content of those dialectics. Since antagonistic relations are most productive of radical change, antagonistic values, interests and demands must be constantly promoted. This process has been outlined earlier in this chapter but it is reiterated here because now, when talking about tactics, we must realize that this manipulative action becomes only really effective when it goes beyond the individual consciousness to a mass movement organized around a deeply-felt and motivated collective consciousness. This will be deep because of the depth of women's oppression and it must be organized for the alleviation of that oppression.

Male chauvinism is so deeply-rooted that it must be very firmly jolted, but most effectively when by a mass movement, which challenges every individual's daily life. The individual jolts of everyday individual interaction by liberationists with others are sources of change too but the spirit of capitalism is so firmly entrenched in and expressed through a mass of firmly-established institutions above and beyond the individual that only an organized and deeply-felt antagonistic mass consciousness can shake them. Men too can be part of this developed, liberating collective consciousness but only by conscious subjugation of themselves to the needs of Women's Liberation, for women must be liberated before people as a whole.

Men cannot be part of Women's Liberation CR groups because those are the early stages of consciousness-raising when women must reinforce each other in nurturing a firm consciousness of their rights as human beings. In later stages men must, as Robin Morgan makes patently clear, be prepared to subordinate themselves to women. And when mass action by Women's Liberation comes about men must take orders, not give them. They must wait for equality, for true reciprocity, because they must liberate themselves from sexism. It is only by taking such subordinate positions, by being prepared to suffer female chauvinism, that they can be liberated from their own ingrained sexism.

No radical movements can be successful until first sexism has been abolished. Other radical movements must continue but must put women in command, men taking secondary roles. Liberation movements of all kinds must complement each other, first by realizing that within their movements Women's Liberation is a necessary first step, and secondly by realizing that sexism, racism, imperialism and capitalism, indeed any forms of mass oppression, are based on the sublimation of the individual to predetermined patterns of behaviour. And therefore in the abolition of sexism lie the seeds for the liberation of humankind. Sexism is racism, it is imperialism, it is tyranny, serfdom, slavery and capitalism. Abolish sexism and the world will never be the same again.*

* Since this chapter was written Sheila Rowbotham's *Woman's Consciousness, Man's World*, has been published by Penguin. It provides a similar perspective but stated in a different way and therefore although it is not referred to here it should also be consulted.

Conclusion

If social behaviour is motivated by true reciprocity then sexist behaviour becomes deviant since it is motivated by principles contradictory to a liberated existence. But obviously, if behaviour is motivated by such truly humanistic values the capitalist mode of production and its associated institutions such as the church, the family, the law and the schools must go, since capitalism, like racism and imperialism, is generated by forces which are directly contradictory to the values which generate liberation. We must not be blinded by the apparent liberalism of modern capitalism but must look deep for the ultimate motives for all behaviour, for capitalism has reached a stage where its exploitation is so subtly disguised beneath a veneer of false equality and created needs that it has succeeded in institutionalizing reform in such a way that it is harnessed to serve exploitative ends even when apparently generated by a spirit of equality. Where motivations for behaviour are seen to be contradictory to reciprocity they must be opposed by the injection of behaviour and values antagonistic to them in the hope that the dialectics so generated will result in real change towards liberation.

The majority of the chapters in this book have been concerned with unveiling the sexist discrimination which characterizes our behaviour, with showing how particular institutions and norms current in society result in clearly prescribed yet different expectations for the behaviour of men and women, differences which are defined as 'natural'. If we are to change society to reject these definitions of what is feminine and what is masculine, if we are to stop playing at being 'woman' and 'man' and instead be ourselves, we need to look more closely at how society generates such restrictions on behaviour. This chapter has attempted to abstract theoretically from the particularities of everyday life an understanding of the underlying forces which shape our needs, our values, our decisions and our individuality to demonstrate that our social reality is a potentially flexible, constantly changing reality which contains within it the possibility for widespread social change through the day-to-day behaviour of individuals. We must not be inhibited by the apparent changeless permanence of our institutional life for it is only defined as such by and in the interests of the establishment. Ultimately all our behaviour is generated by very basic principles which operate in our relationships with each other. If we consciously relate to each other in terms of truly humanistic values and forcefully oppose rules, regulations and people that attempt to generate relationships which are contradictory to such values then the institutional structures must change or crumble and their apparent solidity will be seen to be a sham.

Thus one cannot simply let sexist attitudes, jokes, behaviour and regulations go unchallenged for they are the manifestations of the principles which generate the quality of our relationships, but rather we must continually query every aspect of behaviour for it is only by so doing that we can engage in a revolutionary action which is constant and which has any hope of success. Past revolutions which aimed at liberation have failed because they have been conceptualized and organized in terms of male ideals, seeking simply a reallocation of power, itself a male concept. We have to reject all such male-defined concepts and goals and start from scratch with the forces which are the source of all our behaviour, as free as possible from the maze of male-defined symbols which cloud our perceptivity.

Thus it is not possible for any individual, female or male, to be liberated. We all live in society and cannot escape its restrictions. It is not possible to opt out – to form a counter culture or a lesbian nation. To do so is merely to shelve responsibility. Although it may mean gaining slightly more individual freedom it in fact results in greater loss of freedom for others as it results in a failure to challenge the system by presenting antagonisms and confrontations for people to face. Nor is it possible to have a truly liberated relationship with a male. It is impossible to have a relationshop completely untainted by the evaluations imposed by the wider sexist society. All that is possible is to aim for liberation by constant revolutionary action which is the continual challenging of every aspect of oppression.

Notes

1. L. G. Wilkinson, 'Women's Freedom' in *Women in Rebellion – 1900: Two Views on Class, Socialism and Liberation*, Square One Pamphlet no.6, I.L.P. Square One Publications, Leeds, pp.21–22.
2. This is one of the problems not faced by the counter-culture – see Chapter 24.
3. S. Carmichael, 'Black Power' in D. Cooper, (ed.), *The Dialectics of Liberation*, Penguin Books, 1968, p.153.
4. Ibid.
5. The myth of the vaginal orgasm is an example of how men have defined their penises as indispensible for female sexual enjoyment. See A. Koedt, 'The Myth of the Vaginal Orgasm' in A. Koedt, E. Levine, and A. Rapone, (eds), *Radical Feminism*, Quadrangle Books, New York, 1973.
6. In 1967, as Minister for the Army, P. Lynch stated in a speech given to the Australian/American Association's Women's Group, that only 2.36 per cent of Australia's female workforce earned over $5,000.
7. Though some men may not be actively oppressive, while they are prepared to occupy institutionalized male roles they are acquiescing in the advantages to be gained from participating in institutional activity designed by actively oppressive men for the continuing oppression of women. Therefore they too are oppressors.
8. For discussions of Marx's philosophy and particularly of his view of the evolution of man the following are particularly good:

A. Giddens, *Capitalism and Modern Social Theory: An Analysis of the writings of Marx, Durkheim and Weber*, Cambridge University Press, Cambridge, 1971.

E. Hobsbawm, 'Introduction' to K. Marx, *Pre-Capitalist Economic Formations*, New World Paperbacks, New York, 1965.

D. McLellan, *Marx's Grundisse*, Paladin Books, St Albans, 1973.

E. Mandel, *The Formation of the Economic Thought of Karl Marx*, Monthly Review Press, New York & London, 1971.

H. Marcuse, *Reason and Revolution*, Routledge and Kegan Paul, London, 1967.

B. Ollman, *Alienation: Marx's Conception of Man in Capitalist Society*, Cambridge University Press, Cambridge, 1971.

9. Ollman, op.cit., p.226.
10. K. Marx, 'Critique of the Gotha Programme', in K. Marx and

F. Engels, *Selected Works* (one volume), Progress Publishers, Moscow, 1970, p.327.

11. For further discussion see the Introduction to this book and Chapter 4.

12. B. Moore, *Reflections on the Causes of Human Misery*, Allen Lane, London, 1972, p.53.

13. See the quotation from Reimut Reiche's *Sexuality and Class Struggle* in the Introduction to this book.

14. J. Rees, *Equality*, Pall Mall, London, 1971, p.123.

15. S. Carmichael, 'Black Power' in D. Cooper (ed.), *The Dialectics of Liberation*, Penguin Books, 1968, p.173.

16. At a public election meeting held in Frankston, Victoria, in 1973, the Hon. B. M. Snedden snapped back at some queries about the $8 million being spent on child care by the Liberal Government, 'you women should be grateful for the $8 million the Government is spending'.

17. Quoted in S. Carmichael, op.cit., p.167.

18. K. Kumar, (ed.), *Revolution, The Theory and Practice of a European Idea*, Weidenfeld and Nicholson, London, 1971, p.36.

19. Ibid.

20. Ibid., p.20.

21. Ibid., p.1.

22. Ibid., p.14.

23. J. Johnston, *Lesbian Nation*, Simon and Schuster, New York, 1973.

24. For excerpts from the SCUM manifesto see R. Morgan, (ed.), *Sisterhood is Powerful: An Anthology of Writings from the Women's Liberation Movement*, Vintage Books, New York, 1970, pp.514–519.

25. L. B. Tanner, (ed.), *Voices from Women's Liberation*, Signet Book, New York, 1971, p.111.

26. W. Martin, (ed.), *The American Sisterhood: Writings of the Feminist Movement from Colonial Times to the Present*, Harper and Row, New York, 1972, p.367.

27. Ibid., p.365.

28. S. Rowbotham, *Women, Resistance and Revolution*, Allen Lane, London, 1972, p.12.

29. W. Martin, op.cit., pp.366–367.

30. S. Rowbotham, op.cit., pp.12–13.

Twenty-Seven
A Beginning

Women are not the same as other oppressed groups. Unlike the working class, who have no need for the capitalist under socialism, the liberation of women does not mean that men will be eliminated. Sex and class are not the same. Similarly people from oppressed races have a memory of a cultural alternative somewhere in the past. Women have only myths made by men.

Sheila Rowbotham, *Woman's Consciousness, Man's World**

Clearly, we cannot have a reconstructed society without a critical revamping of our established ways of thinking about society.

Alvin W. Gouldner, *For Sociology*†

Despite the paucity of research by social scientists into the position of women in Australia there is ample evidence, as the first three sections of this book have shown, to establish beyond doubt that women have always been and continue to be exploited and oppressed in a society run by and for men. Male ethologists have manipulated available biological evidence to justify male dominance and aggression. Historians have evolved a historiography which ensures that men remain centre-stage. The administrators of the early years of white settlement in Australia ensured that the roles white women would perform in the colonization process would be constantly subservient to those of men. Working women in Australia today are channelled into a narrow range of occupations where few receive any job security and almost all receive wages far below those of men. Most are treated as a pool of expendable labour power to be hired and fired at the whim of male employers. The law formalizes the subordinate position of women, treating them as

* Penguin Books, 1973, p.117.

† Allen Lane, 1973, p.82.

'rapacious succubi or virginal and dependent waifs, rather than treating them as sensate individuals'.[1] Even though the woman may be paternalistically protected by the law as written, most laws can be interpreted in practice in favour of the male. In the schools girls are channelled into activities which militate against their eventual incorporation into public life in any role other than that of wife. Even the wealthy female is 'cultivated' to serve as a cultured foil for her husband's glory, not to shine in her own right. Because we are regarded as incompetents to be given charity when in need rather than as autonomous individuals with a potentially productive role to play in the economy, women form a large majority of the people who must seek welfare handouts to remain alive. Aboriginal women are branded by the oppressive white male society as doubley incompetent since they fail to conform even to the stereotypes assigned to white women. Migrant women have apparently remained invisible to social scientists but there is little doubt that many have been rapidly channelled into the manipulated pool of cheap labour power on which the capitalist economy depends for much of its profits.

But if we are to hope to change the motivating forces behind such oppressive social behaviour it is not enough to say that such discrimination exists. The question must be answered as to how more than half the population of Australia, let alone the women of the rest of the world, have been made to accept such an inferior position without physical coercion. What are the processes, the myths, the created needs associated with the acceptance by women of such a situation as 'normal', 'natural', or 'their lot'? The constant and many facetted socialization process consistently assigns women from birth to an inferior and secondary position devoid of power. In some cases this is accomplished simply by exclusion from social privileges and opportunities for advancement, particularly through schools and then through the discriminatory nature of the workforce; but there are other processes which much more subtly operate to engender in women beliefs which lead us to accept and aspire to our male defined role. These are the myths, the attitudes, the norms and the superstitions which through the family, the law, the schools, the church and the media are instilled into women to ensure that they accept as 'natural' that reality which ensures the perpetuation of male dominance. It is here too that the academic plays an active role by showing the prejudices of society to be 'reasonable' or 'scientific'. The fallacious claim to 'objectivity' by a male-dominated academia, as full of prejudices as the rest of society, is taken up by the powerful to help them claim legitimacy for their oppressive position.

What has been the place assigned to women in sociological theory and method? A revealing example is provided by a particularly pertinent area of sociological enquiry, that of social stratification, which seeks to understand the nature of social inequality. In studies of social status, of the esteem accorded by society to the positions people occupy, the role of housewife is not scored but is rather regarded as a non-status occupation. The housewife earns no money for her labours because they are regarded as her 'natural lot' and so she is not seen as instrumental in the running of the capitalist economy. The sociologist then reaffirms this status, not only recording social reality but passing it back into society as *legitimate* fact. The norm receives the accolade of academic reason. The role of housewife is performed in the service of others in isolation from public life, ensuring the continued subjugation of the majority of women to the needs of men, but sociologists have been instrumental not only in the perpetuation of the low esteem accorded women in society but in robbing the role of housewife of what little esteem and creativity it ever had.

In modern capitalist society, gone even are the notions of the 'good wife' with her jam-making, bread-making, cake-making skills, who cooked and even washed with skill. Modern technology is fast ruling out these skills. Packet soups, cake mixes, bottled jams, frozen dinners, pickles, sauces and chutneys are available at the supermarket and the housewife anguishes over which brand is best; and so too with washing machines. The housewife has been made expendable, subservient not only to the males of her household but to a male technology which she is not taught to understand – she must call in male assistance when it all goes wrong. This is all characterized by sociologists as 'the declining role of the housewife' or 'the declining functions of the family'. There is no concern with the oppressive, exploitative social system which is robbing women of the last vestiges of identity as they are driven into feeling more and more useless and incompetent. The role of housewife as defined in our society must be damned, not accorded legitimacy, and the continuing loss of identity appalled at, not depersonalized into unconcern as a 'declining role'.

Even the sociology of deviance, while recognizing that notions of deviance are creations of society, reinforces the idea that such behaviour is outside the norm, legitimatizing 'deviance' rather than seeking to eradicate notions of 'normality' which result in types of behaviour being discriminated against as 'abnormal' or 'unnatural'. Women who, like those described in Part 4 of this book, do not feel that they can be or want to be conventional, 'normal', 'natural' women, continue to be treated as exceptional, as the special objects of study for the sociology of deviance. So, through the active involvement of sociologists, mediators to society of its norms, attempts by women to be people in their own right, to fight against the oppression of a male-defined system, continue to be defined and studied as 'abnormal' and therefore as 'unnatural'. They were included as a separate group in this book to indicate the double nature of their oppression. They are penalized not only for being female but also because they do not behave according to conventional female stereotypes, thus posing a threat to male dominance.

But is change possible? If it is, how can it be accomplished? Even when we seek to alleviate our oppressed and exploited position in society we are well socialized to seek change according to terms and rules laid down by men. As we work for change through established channels we are quickly incorporated into the existing system as yet more 'creative criticism' to be harnessed in the service of a male establishment. The fate of the Women's Electoral Lobby showed clearly how entrenched and pervasive are the myths and processes which support male dominance. So effective are the mechanisms which support the present system that to quibble about which political party is best in our 'liberal democracy' is meaningless.

If there is to be change it must be revolutionary. The very bases on which society proceeds must change so that all behaviour is oriented in terms of reciprocity and not in terms of coersive oppression and exploitation as at present. But the revolution sought is not a revolution in the conventional sense. It is not a transfer of power but rather a whittling away of all power. It is men who are concerned with power, with the aggressive domination of many by a few. As it stands, 'revolution' with its connotations of violence, guns and war as rival groups fight for absolute power, is a concept which supports the male ego and the perpetuation of male dominance. Women seek not 'the revolution' but the pursuit of constant revolutionary action as exploitative behaviour is challenged and opposed, both in interpersonal behaviour and in the organizations which constantly reinforce institutional behaviour. If there is violence it will be because those who have had their exploitative behaviour laid bare of its mythical masks have had to resort to overt oppression to stay in power. Men must not be allowed to acquiesce in oppressive behaviour towards willing wives who accept their role, but must be made to actively face up to the fact that their behaviour is exploitative and oppressive. It is in this regard that the role of the sociologist in revolutionary action becomes vital, for sociologists must be instrumental in destroying the myths originally legitimatized by them.

Sociology can never be value-free. 'Objective', 'true', 'value-free' and 'scientific' are labels attached to statements to place them beyond question. To ensure that such statements are not challenged a myth of academic neutrality from involvement in the wider society has grown up bearing the label 'science'. Science is no more value-free than any other sort of social activity. What are treated or labelled as 'rational', 'objective' and 'factual' are those pieces of information which serve to reinforce white male superiority. Information to the contrary is labelled 'propaganda', 'irrational', 'subjective' and therefore 'untrue'. Sociology has a lot to answer for in its preservation of the *status quo* and its acquiescence in it. This book starts off with the assumption that the division of people into social categories and the discriminatory treatment of people on the basis of these categories so that some benefit at the expense of others, is wrong. In the past, social science has acquiesced in these divisions. It has seen them as its subject matter, described them, toyed with them but rarely condemned them because it claimed an objective, value-free position above the 'vulgar' actions and ideas of the multitudes. Today, sociology includes what is labelled 'radical sociology', a sociology committed to involvement in society, in the active profession of a value position and a dedication to social change.

Is 'radical sociology' truly radical and concerned with the sort of direct involvement which the revolutionary action demanded by women's liberation requires? The answer is 'no!' for the radical sociologists bear all the marks of male chauvinism born of radical political movements throughout the world. Like the male-defined socialist movements criticized for their inbuilt hypocrisy by Robin Morgan and Sheila Rowbotham,[2] radical sociology suffers the paralysis of all male-defined revolutionary movements. It contains within it a basic contradiction: liberation of society at the continuing expense of women. Male-defined 'radical sociology' continues to acquiesce in the oppression of women. Gouldner says that all sociologists must be 'reflexive', to use their sociological knowledge, their sociological imaginations, to reflect on their own behaviour as sociologists and individuals in order to actively involve themselves in social change. 'A Reflexive Sociology is distinguished by its refusal to segregate the intimate or personal from the public and collective, or the everyday life from the occasional "political" act'.[3] But Gouldner writes consistently about men and for men, with no mention of the need for the liberation of women from male bondage. How many 'radical sociologists' are reflexive about their own behaviour in their own homes or about their behaviour towards their secretaries and research assistants? The answer must be 'very few if any at all', for such concerns are absent from their writings. Their reflexiveness apparently only applies to what they see as 'problems' for the wider male society and as such their reflexiveness is a sham. To be a truly radical sociologist intimately involved with the liberation of people from oppression one must put the liberation of women first, for to fail to do so makes nonsense of any radical posture.

It is hoped that male academia will not get bogged down in academic criticism of this book but that they will use it as a source for truly reflexive sociology which recognizes the oppression of women and seeks to destroy it. Its aim is to initiate a dialogue which involves not only words but action. In this sense it is nothing more than a beginning.

Notes

1. See the conclusion to Chapter 5, 'Women and the Law'.
2. See references to Sheila Rowbotham and Robin Morgan in Chapter 26 'Liberation – Reform or Revolution ?'
3. Alvin W. Gouldner, *The Coming Crisis in Western Sociology*, Avon Books, New York, 1971, p.504.

Name Index

Subject Index

Woman's Consciousness, Man's World

Sheila Rowbotham

'It seems to me that the cultural and economic liberation of women is inseparable from the creation of a society in which all people no longer have their lives stolen from them, and in which the conditions of their production and reproduction will no longer be distorted or held back by the subordination of sex, race or class.'

Here Sheila Rowbotham adds her voice to the cause of women's liberation.

In Part One she examines the development of the new Feminist consciousness and describes the social changes that have triggered off its growth. In Part Two she focusses her attention on women within the capitalist state and discusses the part they play in maintaining commodity production – showing how the family and sexuality at once reflect and influence other aspects of social and economic life.

Hidden From History

300 Years of Women's Oppression and the Fight Against It

Sheila Rowbotham

Hidden from History is a study of the changing position of women in England over the three hundred years between the Puritan Revolution and the 1930s.

This book comes directly from a political movement: women's liberation – a movement which has already made many of us ask different questions of our past. Sheila Rowbotham shows that while the development of capitalism brought new relationships of property and domination, men continued to own women long after they themselves ceased to be the property of other men. She explores the complex relationship between women's oppression and class exploitation, and chronicles the attempts to merge the struggles against both.

Ultimately the revolutionary re-awakening of women's liberation challenges capitalism with the prospect of 'a society in which all human beings can control every aspect of their lives'.